P9-DCI-924

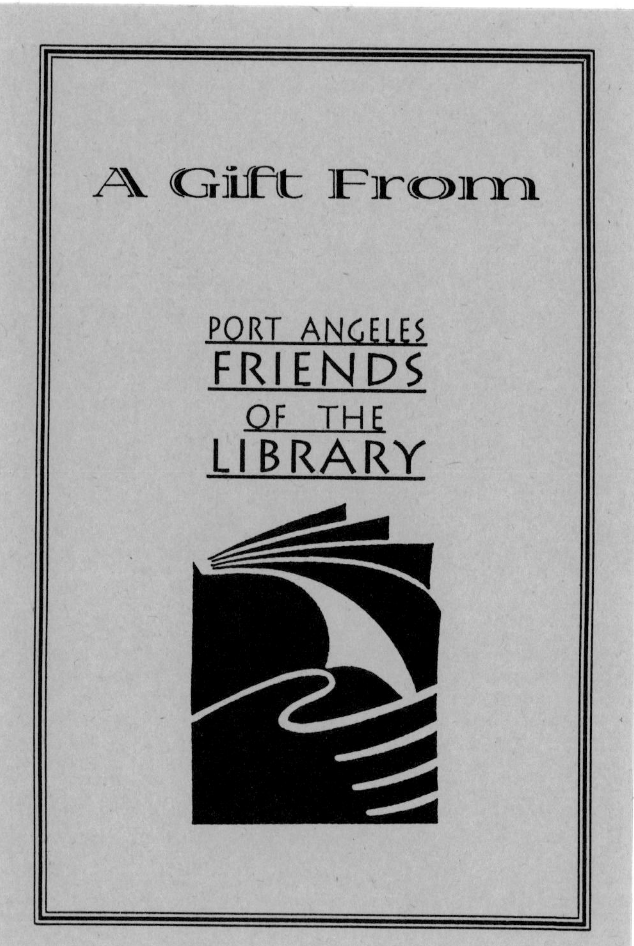
A Gift From
PORT ANGELES
FRIENDS
OF THE
LIBRARY

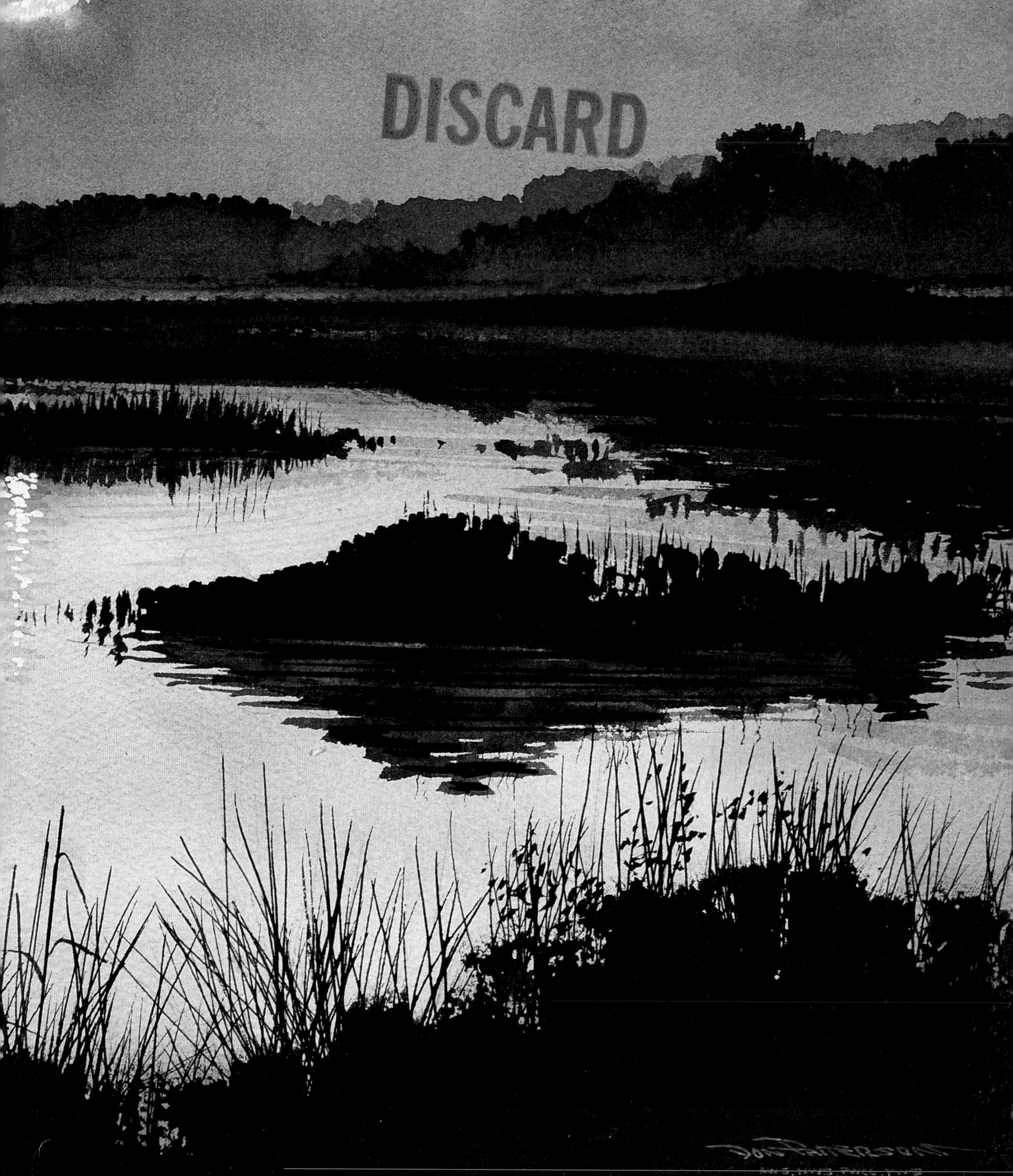

About the Author

Rachel Rubin Wolf is a freelance editor and writer. She acquires fine art books for North Light Books, working with many fine artist-authors. She is the project editor for the *Splash* watercolor series, *The Best of Wildlife Art*, *The Best of Portrait Painting* and *The Best of Flower Painting 2*, as well as a number of paperback compilations. She is the author and editor of two other instructional art books, *The Acrylic Painter's Book of Styles and Techniques* and *Painting Ships, Shores and the Sea*. Wolf studied painting and drawing at the Philadelphia College of Art (now University of the Arts), Kansas City Art Institute and Temple University. She resides in Cincinnati, Ohio.

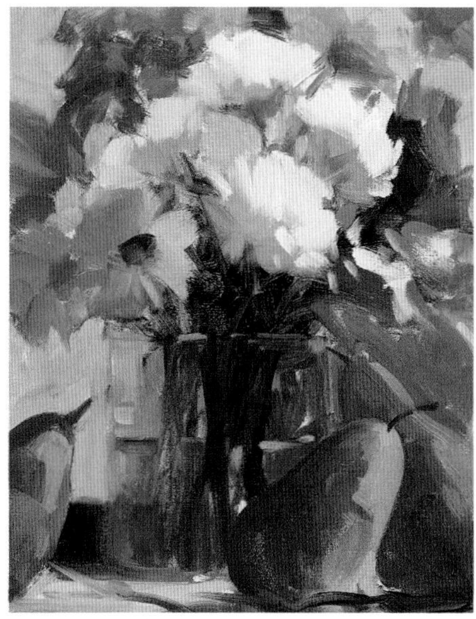

THREE PEARS
Howard Carr, oil, 16″×20″ (40.6cm×50.8cm)

 Published by North Light Books, an imprint of F&W Publications, Inc., 1507 Dana Avenue, Cincinnati, Ohio 45207. (800) 289-0963. First edition.

Other fine North Light Books are available from your local bookstore, art supply store or direct from the publisher.

03 02 01 00 99 5 4 3 2 1

Library of Congress Cataloging-in-Publication Data

Wolf, Rachel Rubin.
Painting the many moods of light / Rachel Rubin Wolf.
p. cm.
Includes index.
ISBN 0-89134-879-4 (hardcover : alk. paper)
1. Light in art. 2. Painting—Technique. I. Title.
ND1484.R83 1999
751.4—dc21 98-37194
CIP

Editor: Jennifer Lepore
Production editor: Amy Jeynes
Designer: Angela Lennert Wilcox

Contributor art used by permission.
Pages 2-3: *Assateague Sunset*, Donald W. Patterson, watercolor, 12″×20″ (30.5cm×50.8cm)

Acknowledgments

Thanks to Barb for inputting the first draft. Thanks to the editors at North Light who worked on this book, Jennifer Lepore and Amy Jeynes, and to the designer, Angela Lennert Wilcox. Most of all, thanks to the nine wonderful artists in the book. I have abundantly enjoyed and benefited from the numerous conversations I have had with each one of you. I hope the friendships and associations made in the process will indeed continue.

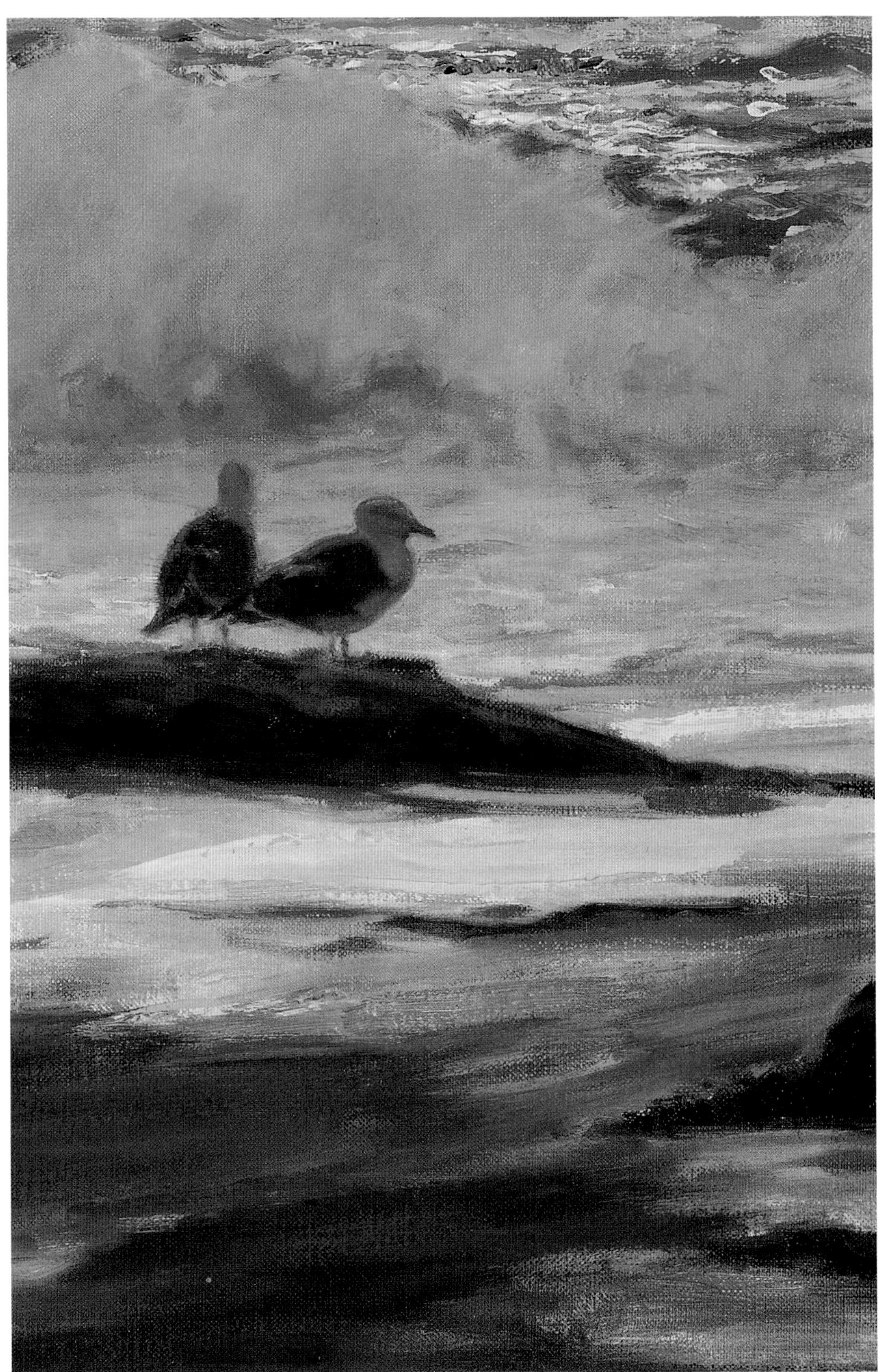

DAY'S END

Randal M. Dutra, oil on Belgian linen, 14" × 18" (35.6cm × 45.7cm)

Table of Contents

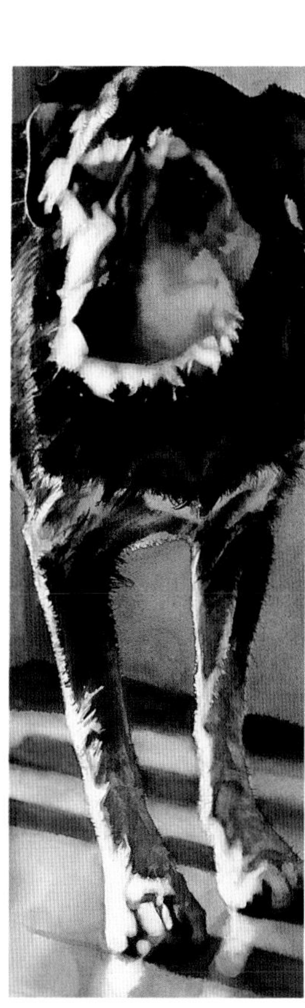

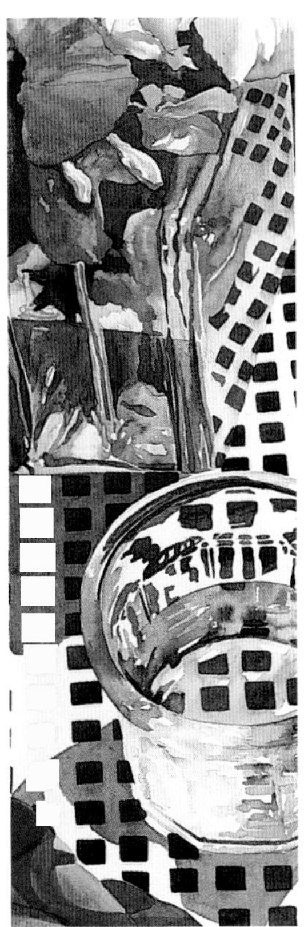

3 CREATE SPARKLING WINDOW-LIT STILL LIFES IN WATERCOLOR

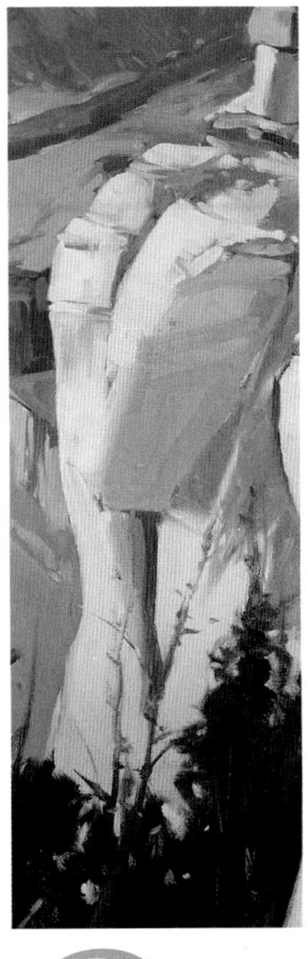

4 BOLDLY EXPRESS THE MOOD OF THE MOMENT IN OILS

7 DARE TO DRAMATIZE DOMESTIC SCENES IN WATERCOLOR

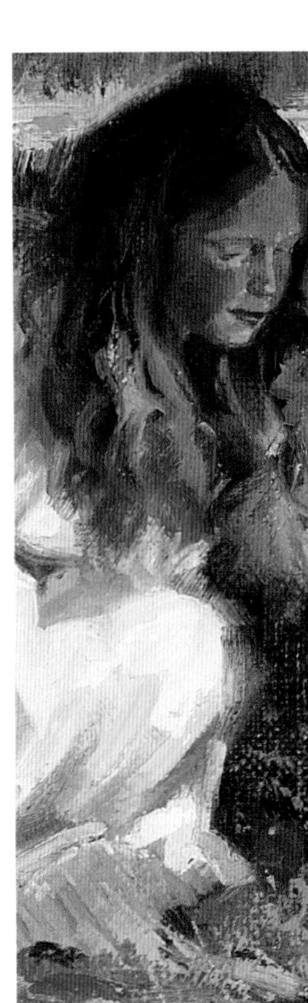

8 EXPLORE THE ENERGY OF NATURAL LIGHT IN OILS

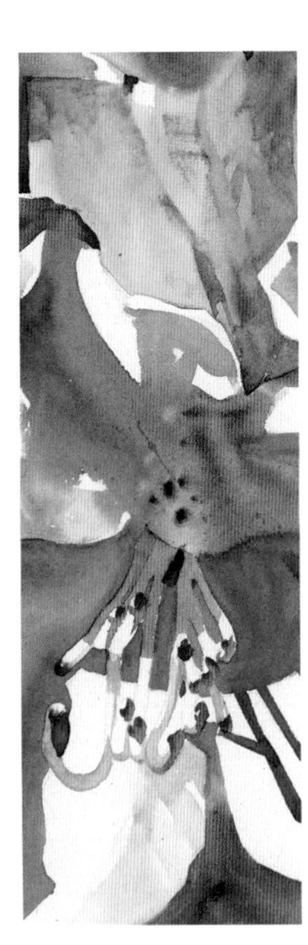

9 FLOWER POWER WITH DRAMATIC LIGHT IN WATERCOLOR

Ann Pember

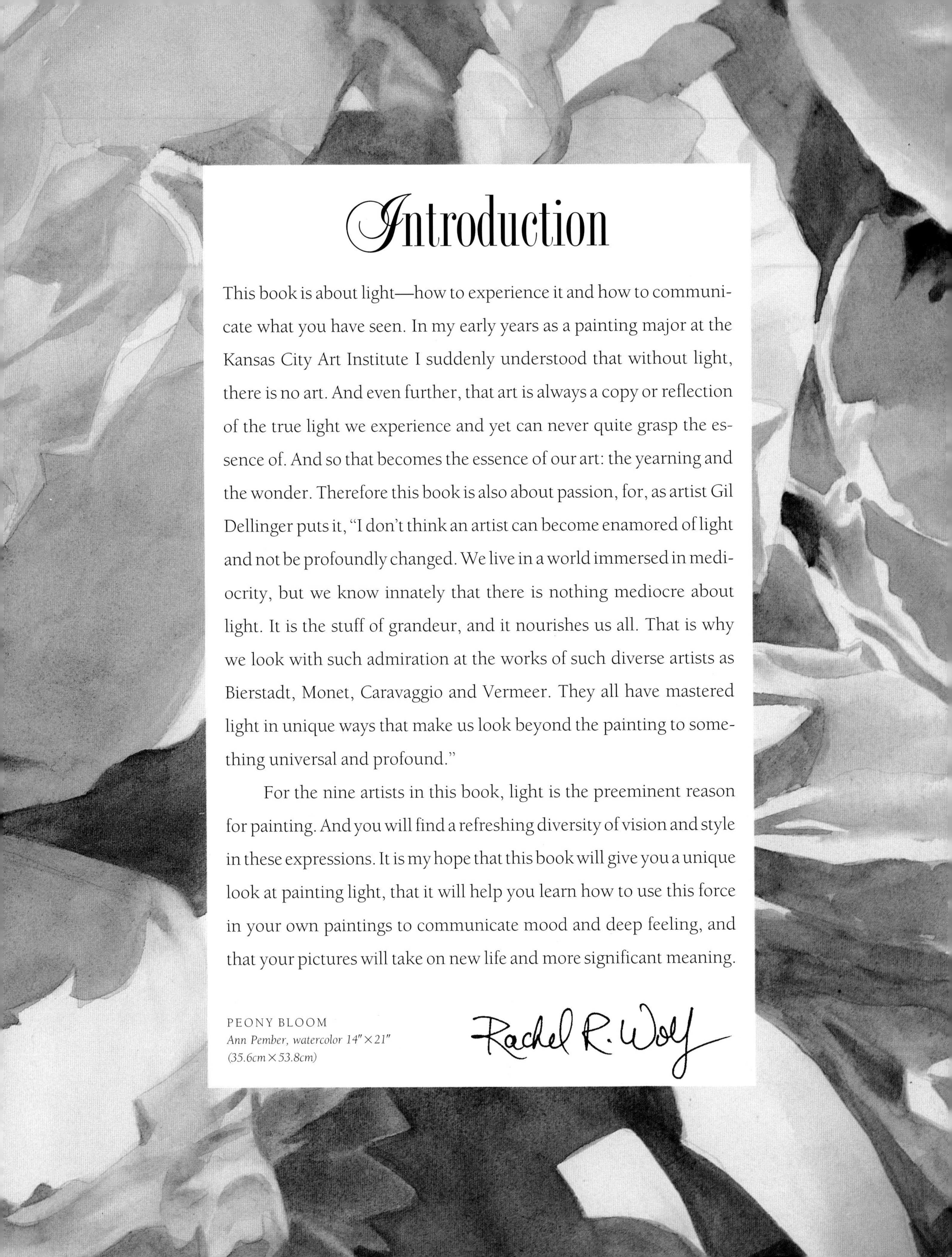

Introduction

This book is about light—how to experience it and how to communicate what you have seen. In my early years as a painting major at the Kansas City Art Institute I suddenly understood that without light, there is no art. And even further, that art is always a copy or reflection of the true light we experience and yet can never quite grasp the essence of. And so that becomes the essence of our art: the yearning and the wonder. Therefore this book is also about passion, for, as artist Gil Dellinger puts it, "I don't think an artist can become enamored of light and not be profoundly changed. We live in a world immersed in mediocrity, but we know innately that there is nothing mediocre about light. It is the stuff of grandeur, and it nourishes us all. That is why we look with such admiration at the works of such diverse artists as Bierstadt, Monet, Caravaggio and Vermeer. They all have mastered light in unique ways that make us look beyond the painting to something universal and profound."

For the nine artists in this book, light is the preeminent reason for painting. And you will find a refreshing diversity of vision and style in these expressions. It is my hope that this book will give you a unique look at painting light, that it will help you learn how to use this force in your own paintings to communicate mood and deep feeling, and that your pictures will take on new life and more significant meaning.

Rachel R. Wolf

PEONY BLOOM
Ann Pember, watercolor 14″ × 21″ (35.6cm × 53.8cm)

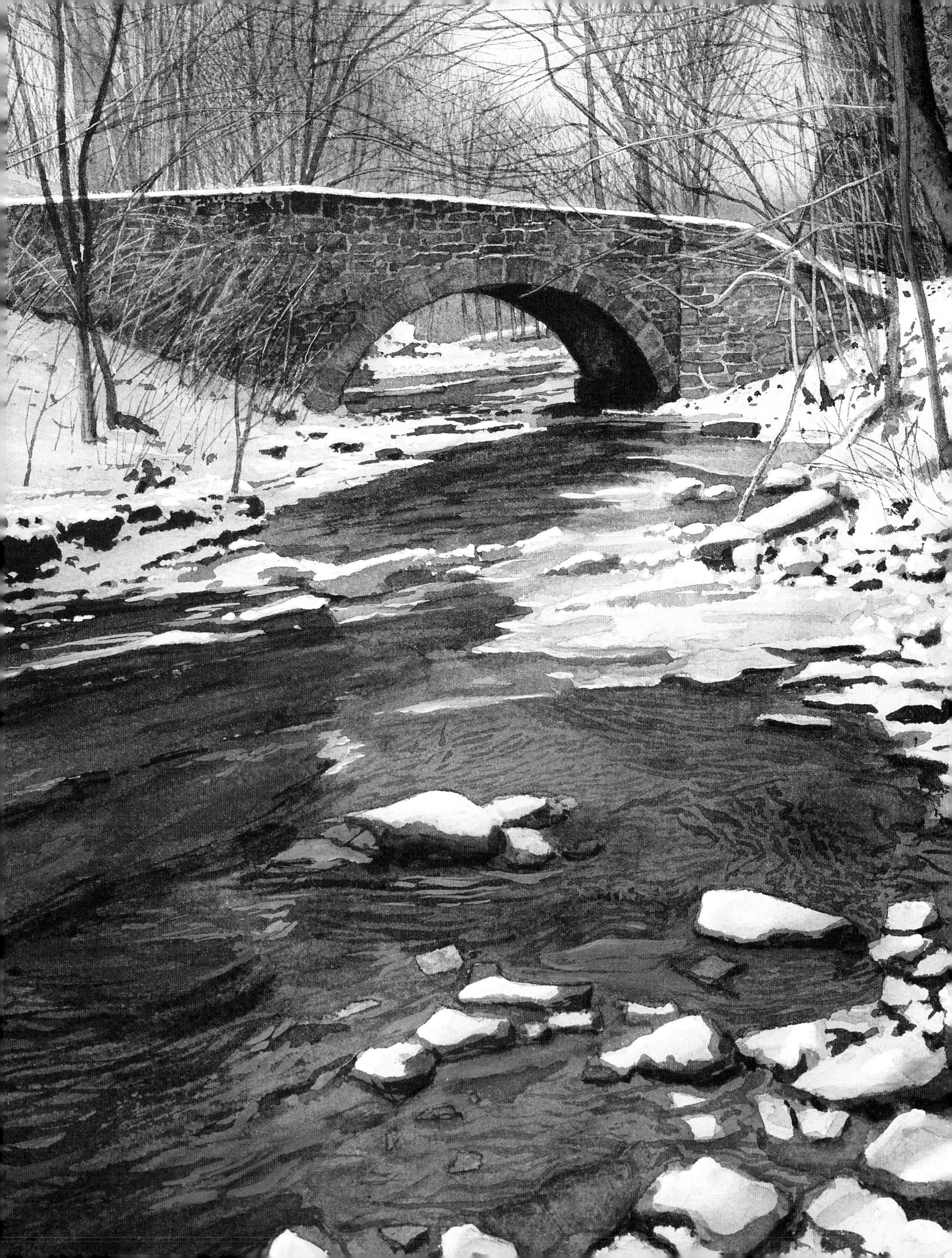

PAINT PEACEFUL, LUMINOUS LANDSCAPES IN WATERCOLOR

DONALD W. PATTERSON

CHAPTER 1

"No wonder artists paint light," says Don Patterson. "Light is everything to the subject; it defines the subject." Each type of light that Patterson chooses to paint has a specific color to him. This color, usually painted over the paper as underpainting, influences the overall color effect of the whole painting. In so doing, he sets the mood: the excitement of a colorful sunset, the warm glow and long shadows of a late afternoon, or quiet hazy images on a misty morning. Each has its own appeal for his brush. Demonstrations on the following pages will help you set the mood of your paintings. Patterson suggests colors and brushes to use along the way but focuses on his techniques for capturing the mood of light.

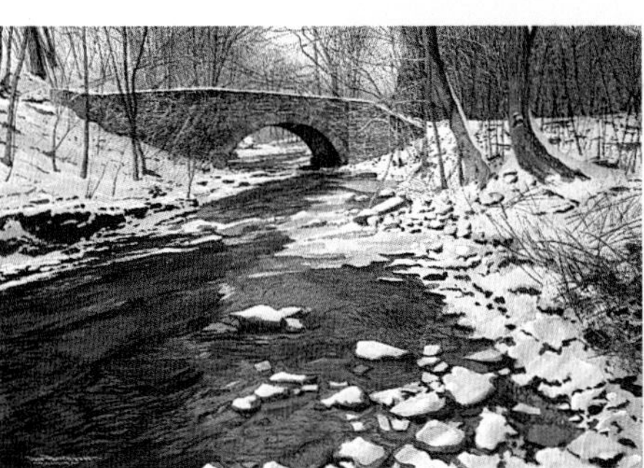

SNOWY COPPER CREEK
Donald W. Patterson, watercolor, 14" × 20" (35.6cm × 50.8cm)

Just as in *Winding Stream* on page 21, except for some highlights, there is no "white" snow here. The shady side of the creek valley on the left serves as a contrast to the sunny bank on the right.

Patterson's painting process begins when he ventures out with his camera to record reference material. He is not a plein air painter. The way he works and what he is trying to say in his work are not compatible with outdoor conditions. Therefore he considers his camera an indispensable art tool: It is part of his painting equipment in the same manner his brushes are. He prefers to work from slides because of their lifelike quality, but recently Kodak introduced a new technology called Image Magic, a way of computer-generating a large print from a slide, which in his view is truly amazing in quality. It is easier on the eyes than viewing a slide. Either way, the results seen in his paintings are infinitely varied and beautiful—all because of this thing called light.

PAINT WARM, MOIST LIGHT AFTER A SHOWER Watercolor

The strong overhead light after a shower makes colors more intense and makes details stand out distinctly. This is especially true when these saturated colors are set against a backdrop of lingering dark clouds.

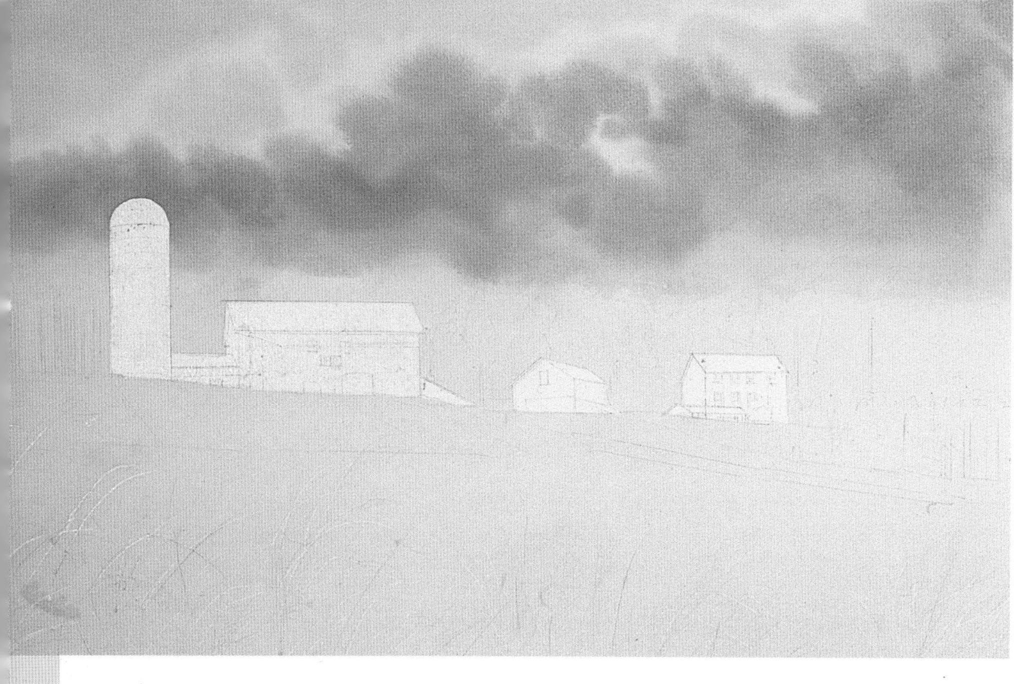

STEP 1

Paint the Light

After you have prepared your paper (see instructions on page 15) and have completed your basic drawing, apply masking fluid to the buildings, cornfield and foreground grasses. Use a ruling pen (a traditional graphic design tool) to outline buildings with masking fluid, and then fill them in with a brush. (I prefer colorless Winsor and Newton Liquid Masking Fluid because it flows well from a ruling pen.) To "paint the light," apply four glazes of about 5 percent color intensity over the entire surface, using, in sequence, Yellow Ochre, Prussian Blue, Alizarin Crimson and Cadmium Lemon. Make sure glazes are dry between applications. Mix three light washes for the sky: Prussian Blue; Prussian Blue and Payne's Gray; and a denser wash of Prussian Blue and Payne's Gray. Wet the entire sky area until your paper is very damp but not dripping. With your board slightly tilted toward you, use a no. 12 round sable to brush on sky colors in the order the washes appear above. Have fun—wet-into-wet is not a precise science.

STEP 2

The Trees

Using brushes and natural sponges, dab on the fall foliage. Use the following palette: Hooker's Green Dark, Olive Green, Sap Green, Alizarin Crimson, Raw Sienna, Yellow Ochre and Payne's Gray.

STEP 3

Leaves and Middle Ground

To paint leaves highlighted by the sun, use Winsor and Newton gouache colors: Cadmium Yellow Pale, Flame Red, Cadmium Orange, Yellow Ochre, Permanent Green Light and Zinc White. For this kind of highlighting I prefer older no. 3 and no. 4 round sables that no longer come to a fine point, because they help produce an uneven, textured effect. When the trees are complete, remove the masking fluid from the buildings with a rubber cement pickup. Paint the field over the masked foreground grasses using a wash of Sap Green, Hooker's Green Dark and Yellow Ochre. Paint the driveway with Payne's Gray and Yellow Ochre; paint the cornfield with Yellow Ochre.

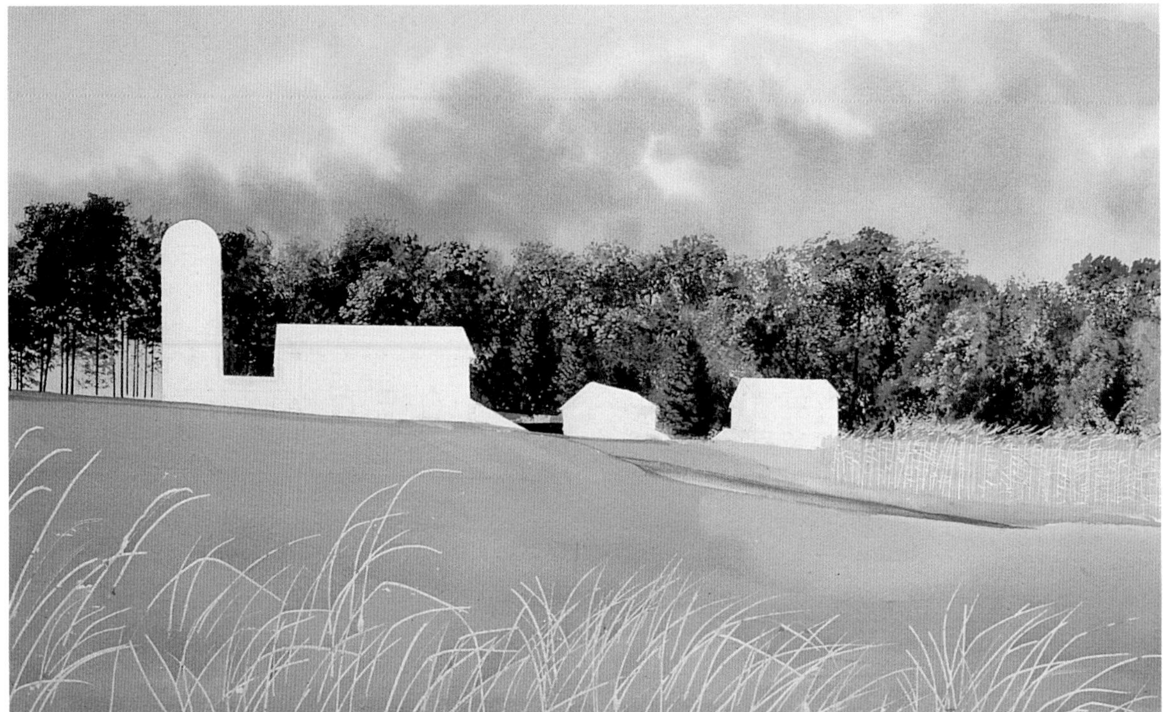

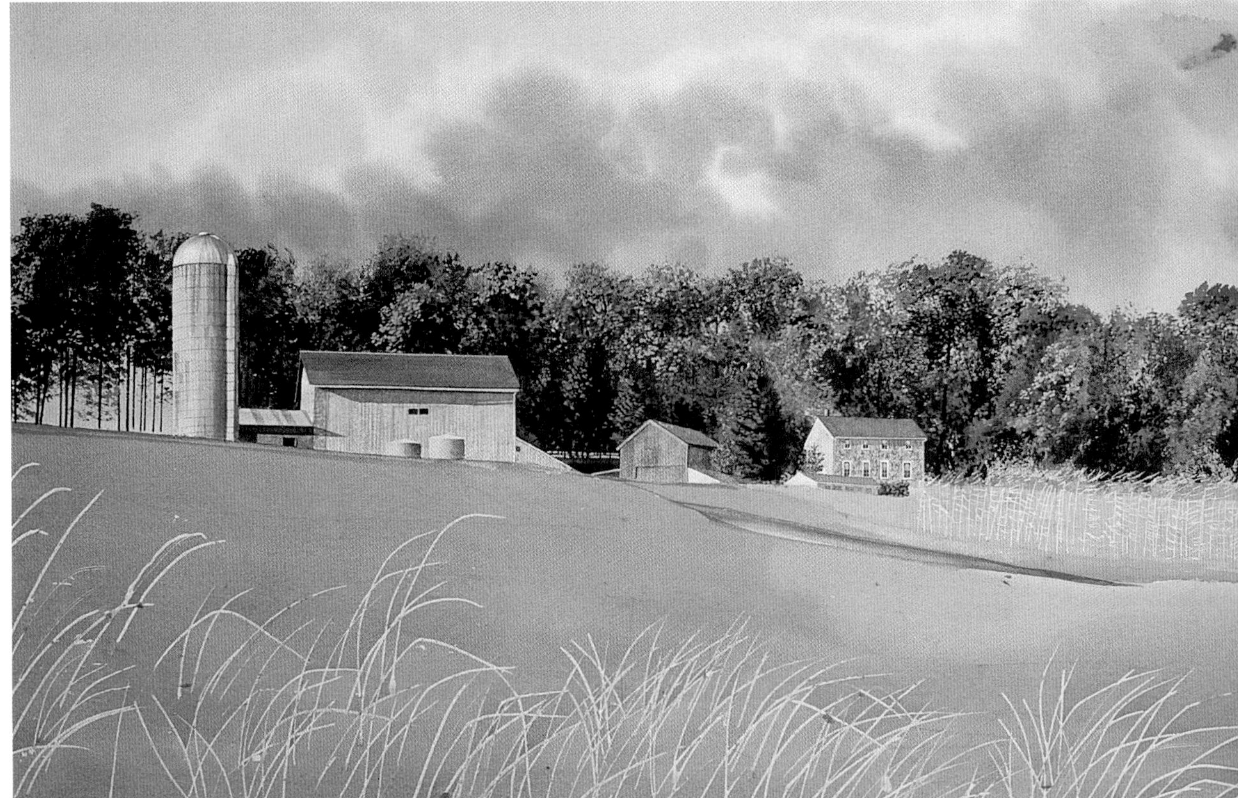

STEP 4

Paint the Buildings

Lay color on the buildings in stages, starting with transparent colors: Yellow Ochre, Burnt Sienna, Payne's Gray, Prussian Blue and Winsor Green. Continue to fill in the buildings, and begin to add details (window mullions, etc.) with gouache. Add masking fluid to the foreground grasses and corn for additional texture.

Correct a Masking Fluid Error

If you have incorrectly masked an area of your painting, remove the mask and paint over the area, matching the colors in your painting and adding textural detail at the same time. Then go back in and repaint the area correctly.

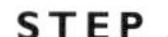

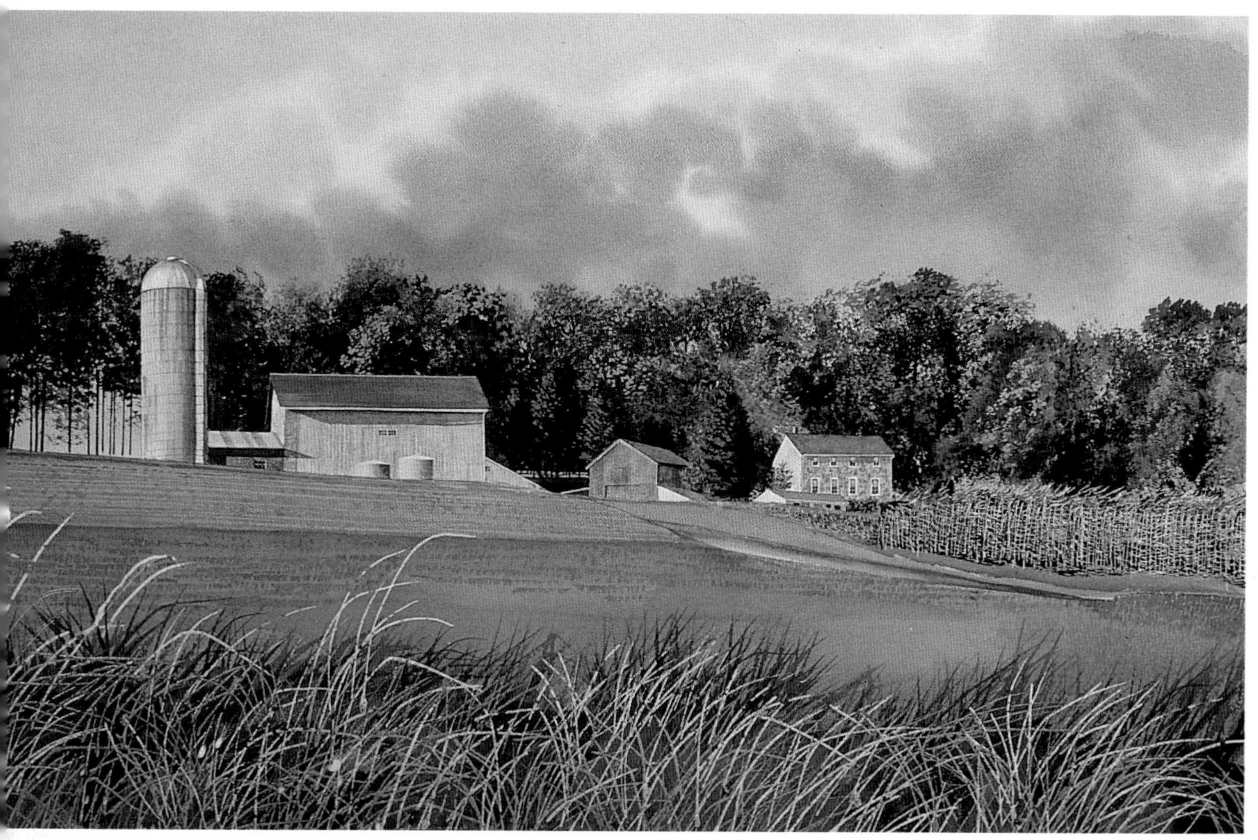

STEP 5

Darken the Negative Areas in the Grasses

Deepen the colors on the field and cornfield. Using the dry-brush technique, add texture to the field. Make a final application of masking fluid to the grasses and corn (see the demonstration on grasses on page 16). Brush a very dark wash of Sepia and Payne's Gray over the corn. Brush darker greens over the grasses.

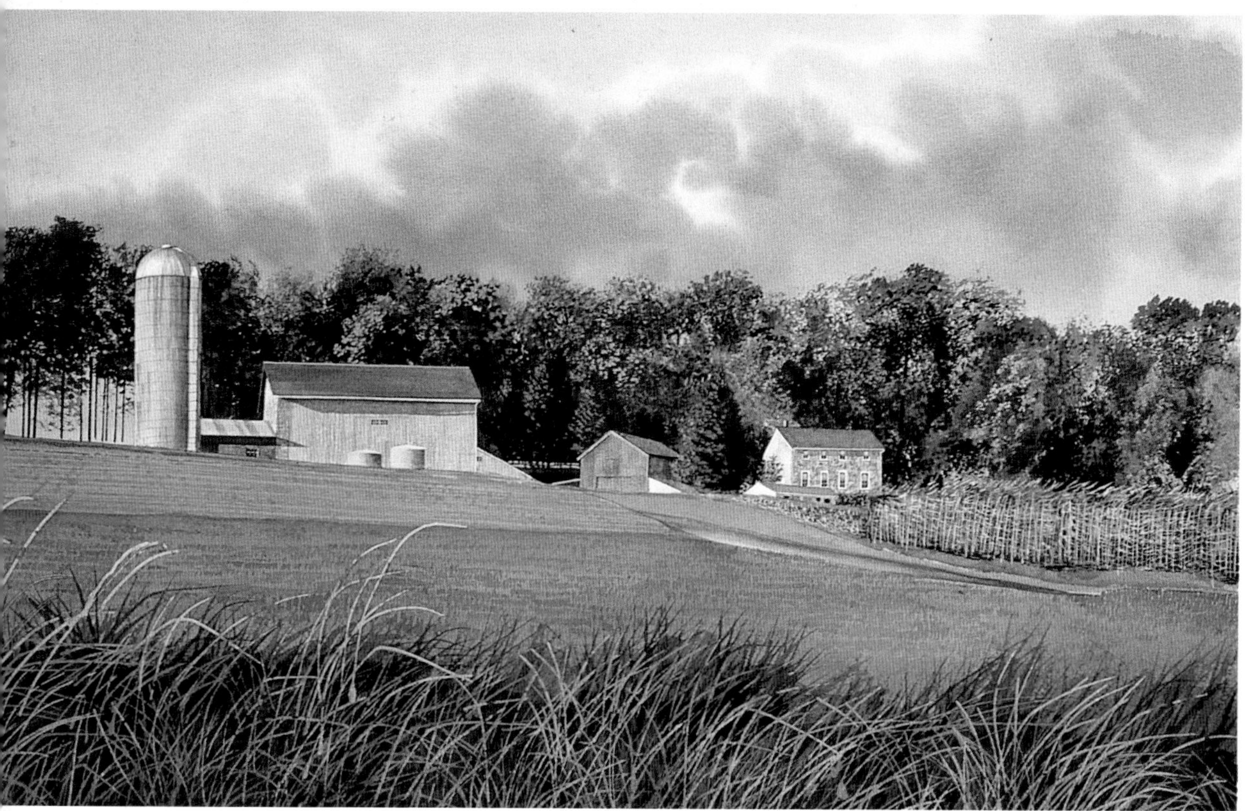

STEP 6

Remove the Masking Fluid

Remove all of the masking fluid and wash a light color all over the areas of grass and corn. Use a soft no. 12 sable or equivalent to avoid disturbing the dark colors in the negative areas.

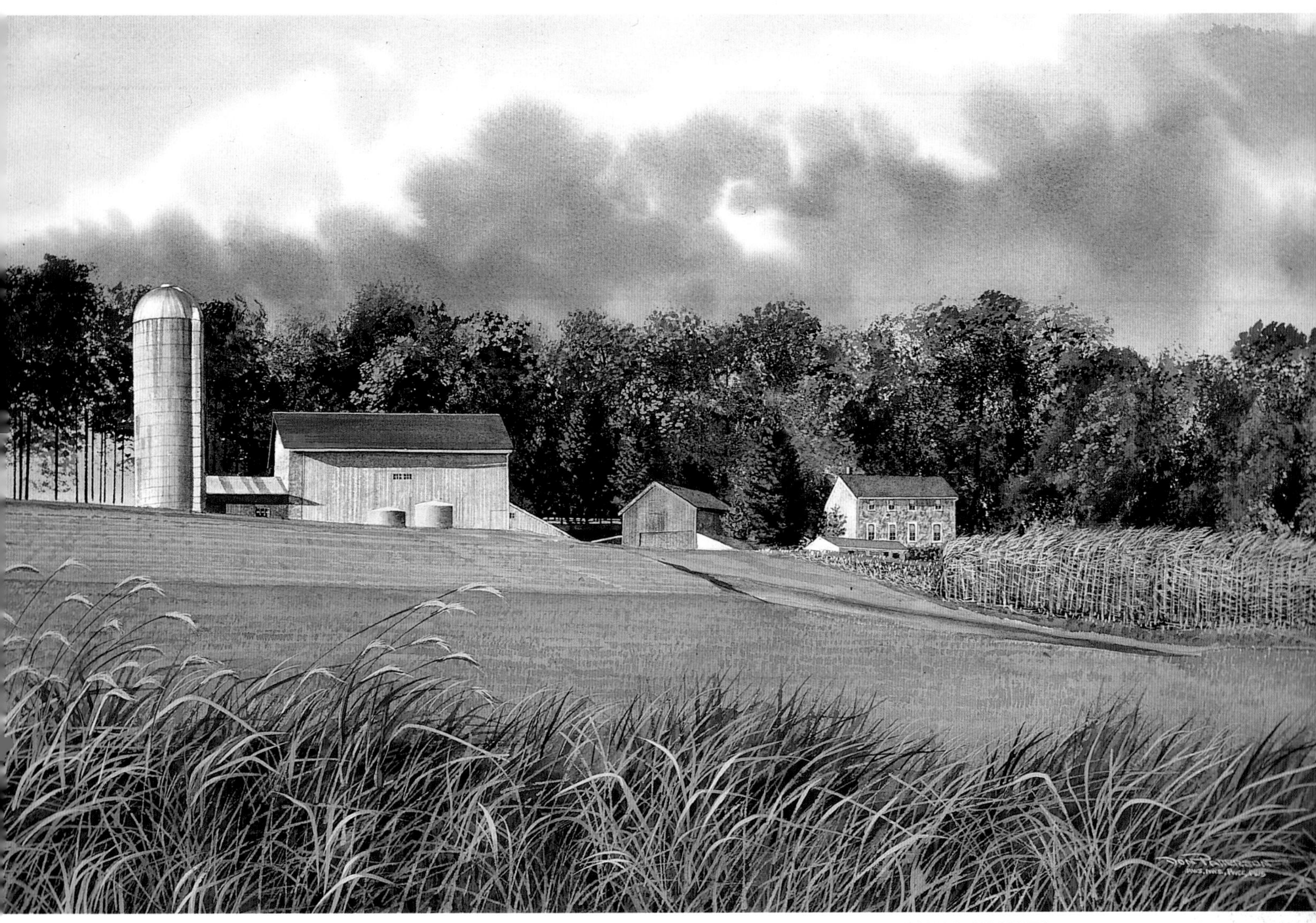

PASSING SHOWER
Donald W. Patterson, watercolor, 17" × 27" (43.2cm × 68.6cm)

STEP 7

Final Touches

Using gouache, paint in the blades of grass highlighted by the sun, and then highlight some leaves and stalks of corn. Notice the unified lighting of the finished work. "Paint the Light" (step one) helps hold the sky and the ground together to create this distinct mood.

Paper Preparation, Patterson Style

Staple a full sheet of 300-lb. (640g/m²) Arches cold-press paper to a piece of Homosote board using a staple gun and ¼" (6mm) staples approximately 3" (7.6cm) apart. The paper will be very easy to lift off upon completion of the painting. Next, make a careful graphite drawing of the painting with a moderately hard pencil. Use a T square and a 30°/60° triangle to draw the four sides of the painting centered on the paper (in other words, draw borders). Tape these four sides with 1" (2.5cm) drafting tape. I prefer drafting tape for its low-tack property: It will not damage the paper's surface when removed. Taping provides a clean white border after removal—an "instant mat."

PAINT LIGHT-STRUCK GRASSES AND REEDS Watercolor

Reeds and grasses interact exquisitely with sunlight. The intricate pattern of fine lines, some glowing with light, some in shadow, is an important element in a composition, especially in the foreground, as seen in *Passing Shower* on page 15. I struggled with how to paint this pattern in transparent watercolor. Painting thousands of negative areas created by the many layers of crisscrossing stalks is a daunting task. By experimenting with liquid masking fluid I developed a technique that has served me well over the years. I alternate layers of fine-lined masking fluid with layers of increasingly dark washes. If you are interested in trying this technique, purchase the finest ruling pen you can afford. A student-quality pen does not work very well. The pen should lay down a controlled, heavy coating of fluid with an easily adjustable line weight.

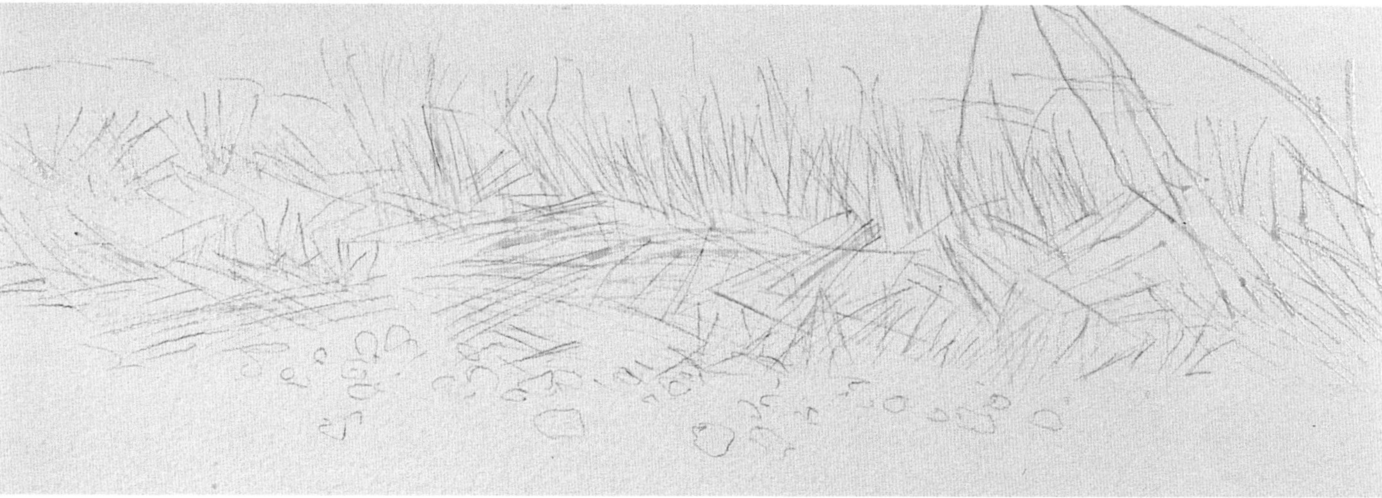

STEP 1

The Drawing

With a graphite pencil, very quickly draw the directional patterns of the stalks. Do not attempt to pencil in every stalk. Use a ruling pen to apply masking fluid to the stalks you want to remain the lightest.

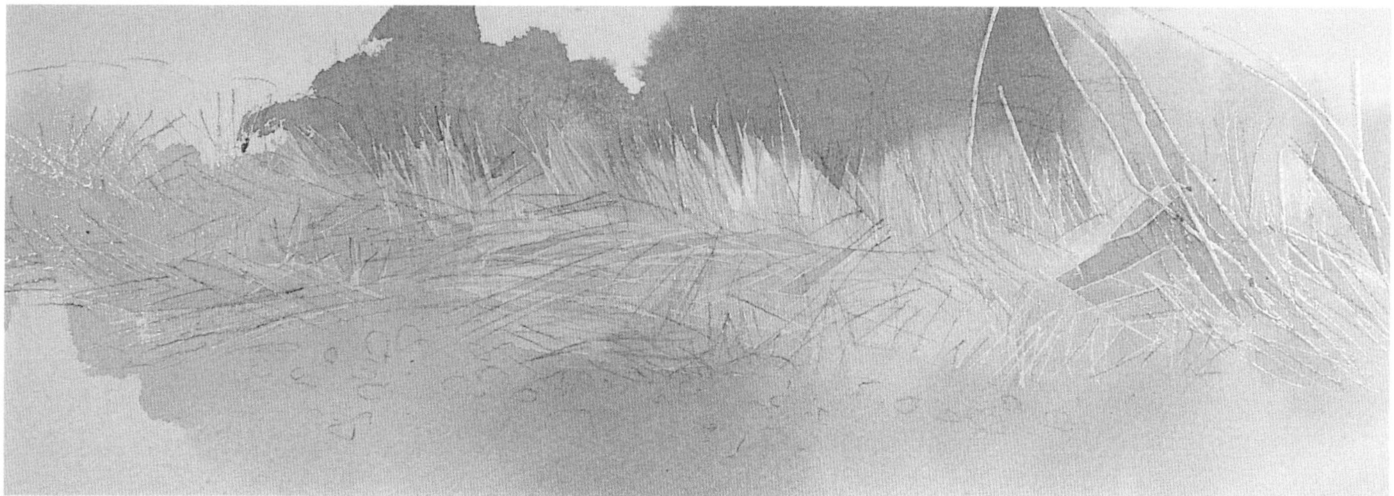

STEP 2

Alternate Color and Masking Fluid

When the masking fluid is dry, apply a wash of light colors over the entire area. Use a soft brush large enough to do this quickly. When the wash is completely dry, stroke on masking fluid for the second layer of darker stalks.

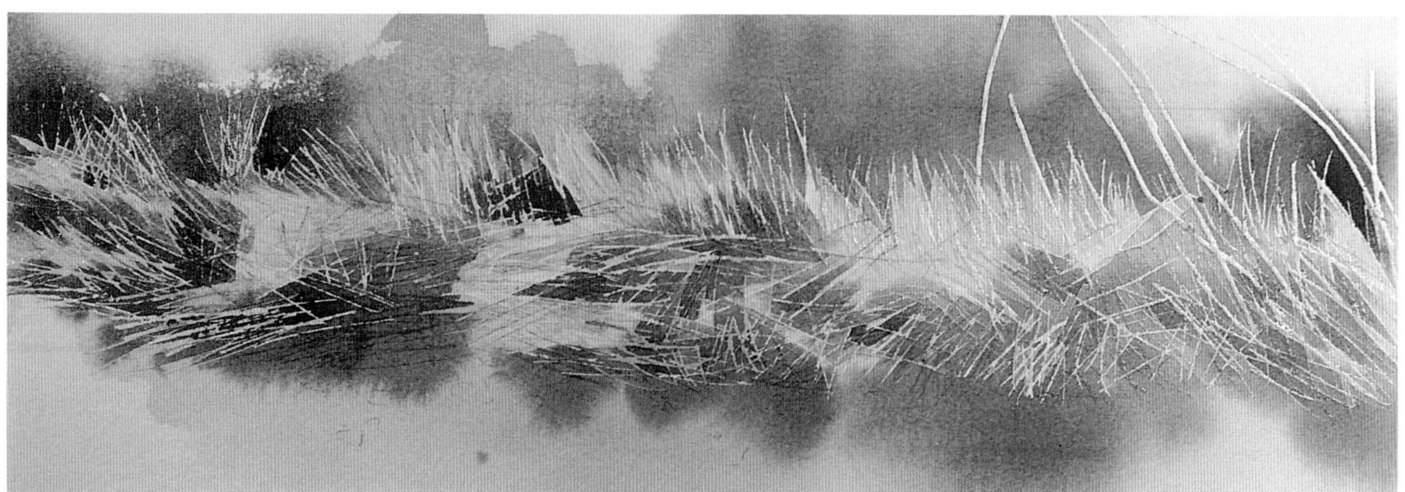

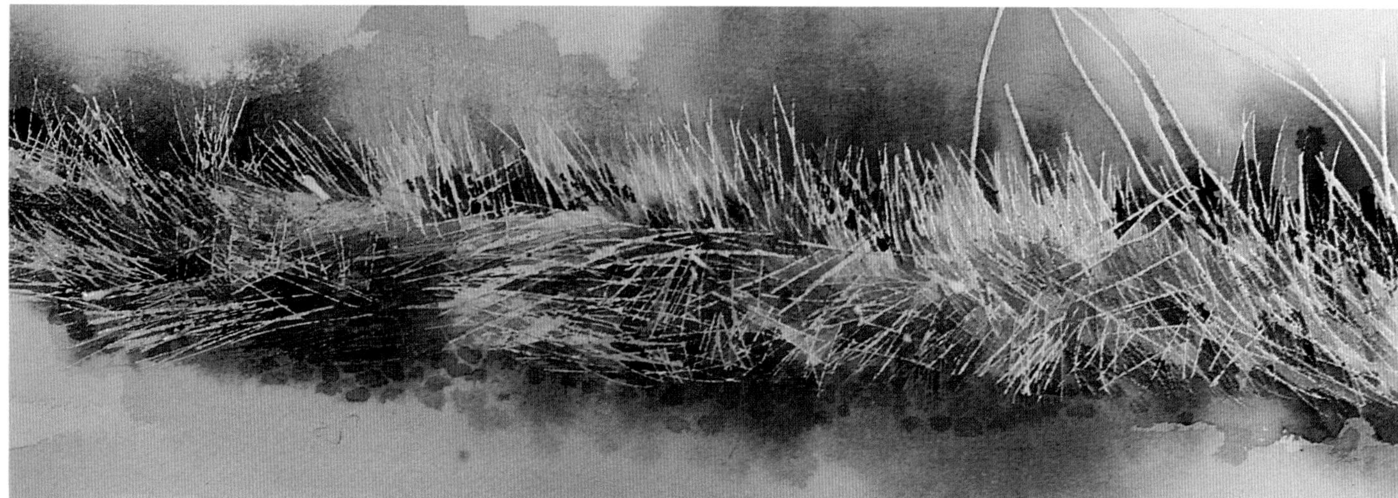

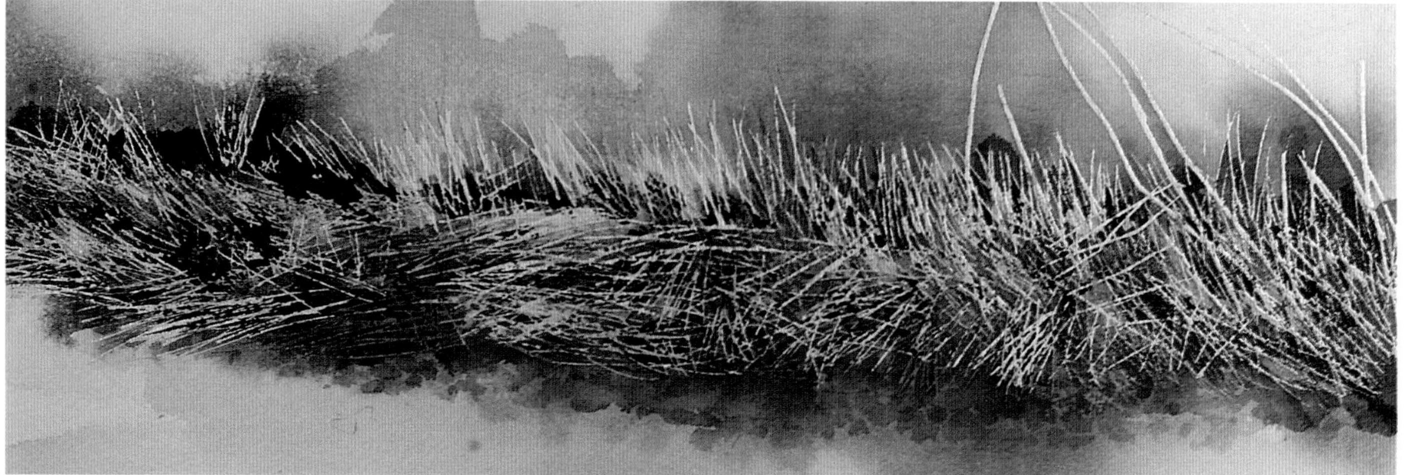

STEP 3

Continue Layering

Repeat the process, using darker washes each time, until only the darkest negative areas are not coated with masking fluid (top and middle). Wash over these negative areas with your darkest color (bottom).

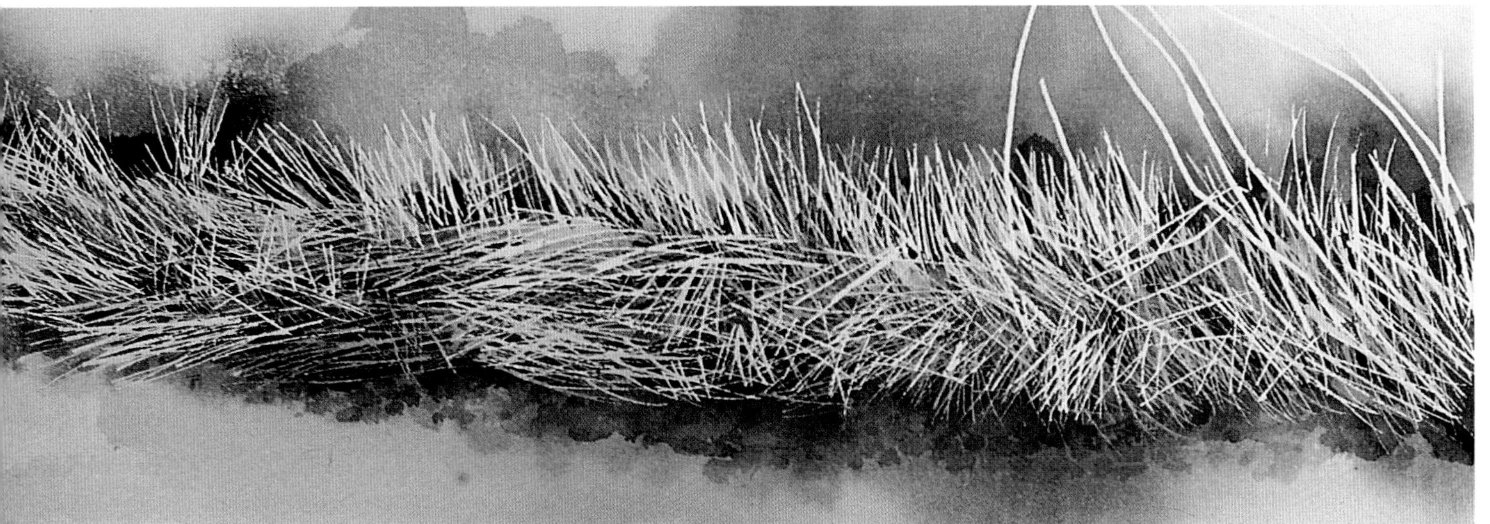

STEP 4

Remove the Masking Fluid

When the masking fluid is completely dry, remove all of it with a rubber cement pickup. To make sure you removed it completely, gently rub across the painting surface with clean, dry hands. You will easily feel any mask remaining.

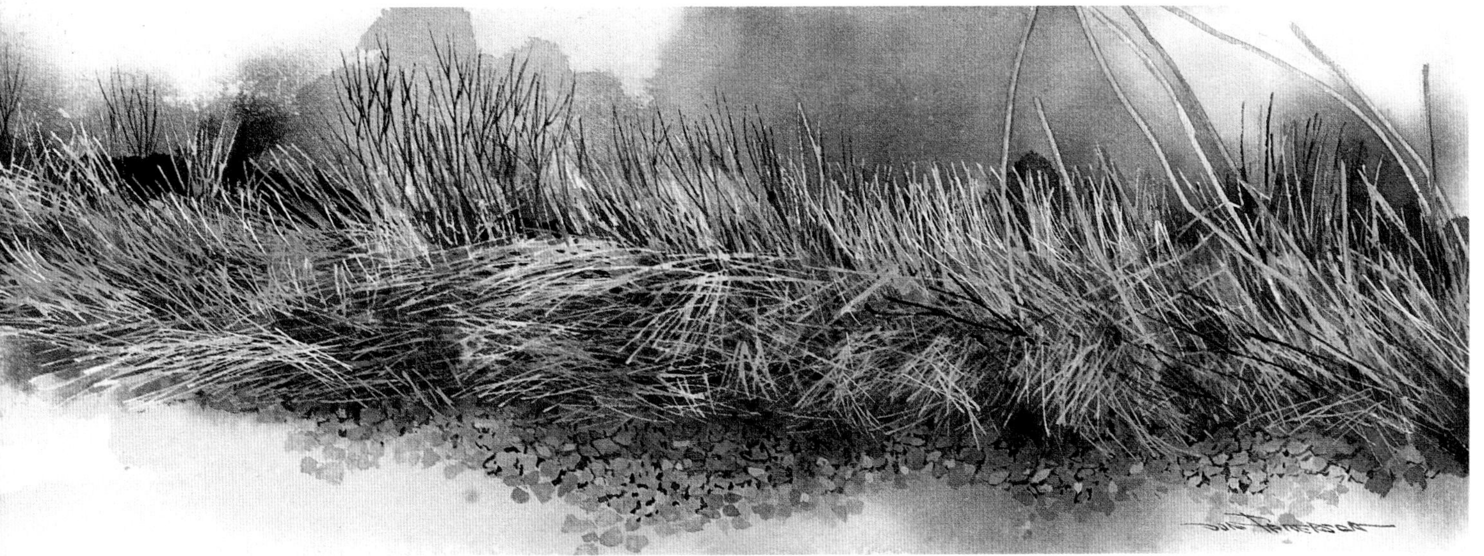

STEP 5

Final Touches

You can now wash a light color (or colors) over the white stalks left by your first application of masking fluid (step one). I usually paint on a darker value and then blot it with a paper towel to get the correct, lighter value. The blotting blends in any overlapped color on the previously painted areas. Create form and depth within the masses of stalks by brushing in shadow areas with either a dry or wet surface, depending on the effect you desire. Finally, use gouache to highlight certain stalks where necessary. Sometimes I darken selected negative areas for extra punch. Here I added dark reeds across the back and on the right side.

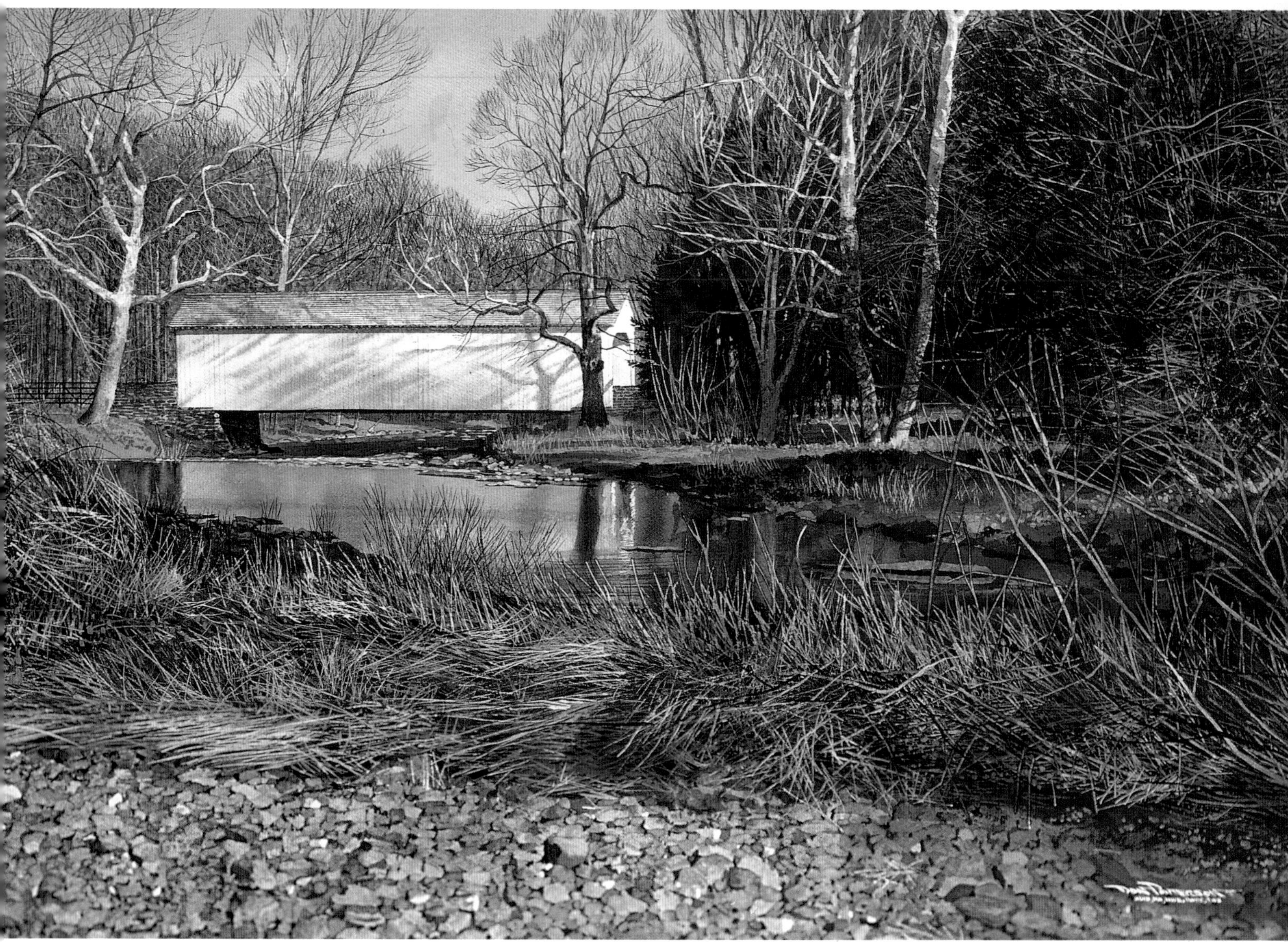

CABIN RUN
Donald W. Patterson, watercolor, 18" × 26" (45.7cm × 66cm)

Another Example of Layering

The most prevalent technique used in *Cabin Run* is the one demonstrated in "Paint Light-Struck Grasses and Reeds" on pages 16-18. The texture created by the countless branches and reeds makes this scene compelling. It seems paradoxical that the small rocks in the foreground required a technique more painstaking than the technique used for the branches. The rocks were painted carefully, one at a time; the darker negative areas were filled in last.

PAINT WARM LIGHT IN A COOL SCENE Watercolor

Forget "white snow." There are no absolute whites in this subject; the entire scene is bathed in a warm late-afternoon sun.

STEP 1

Paint the Light

After completing your drawing and lining it with tape, use a large, flat brush to paint over the entire surface with two separate thin glazes: one of Yellow Ochre followed by one of Cadmium Lemon. Make sure the glazes are dry between applications. Now you have established the color of the light. You have a background that will permeate every transparent color used to complete this painting, which gives you a color saturation like that of nature.

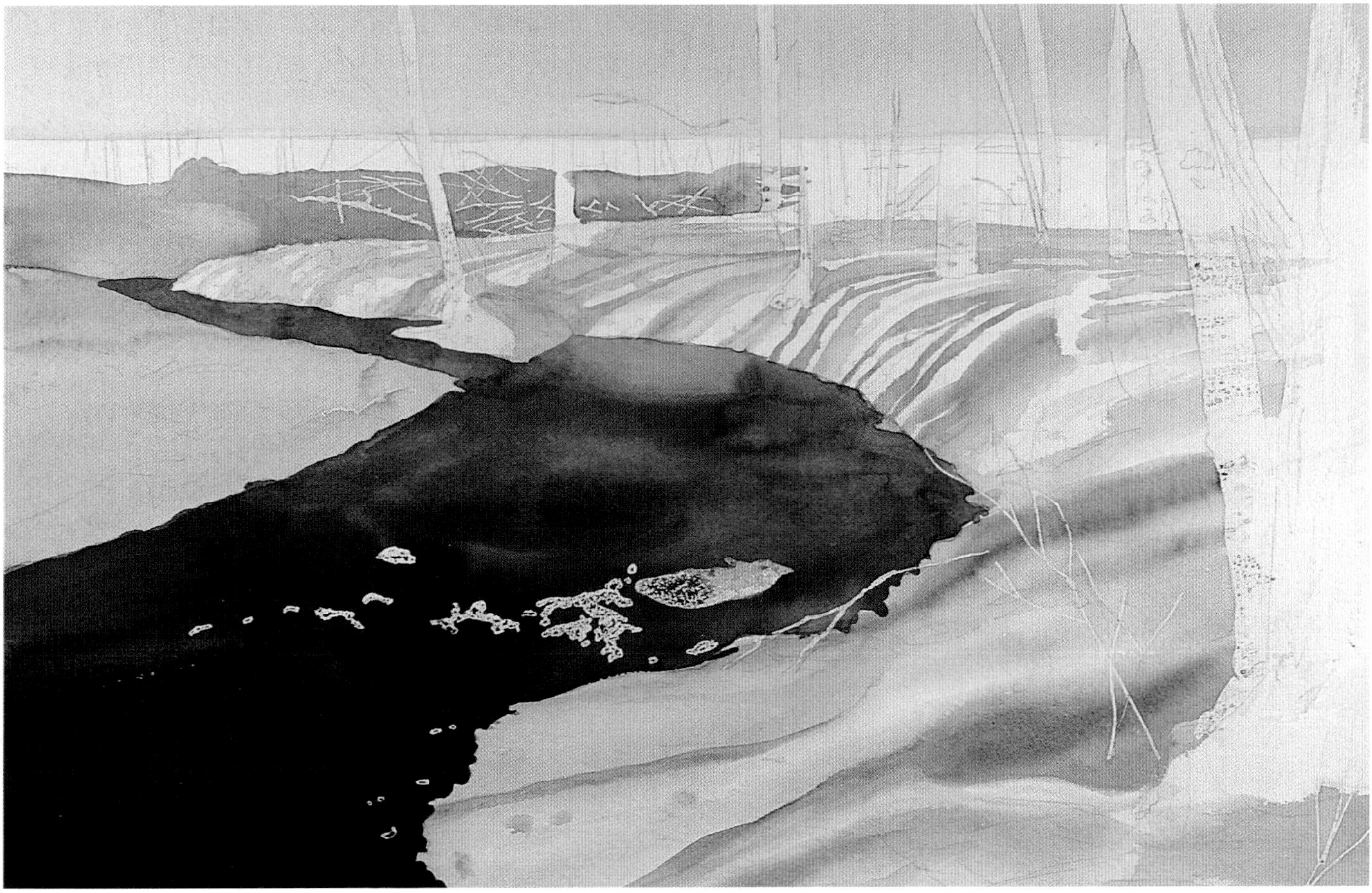

STEP 2

Masking Fluid, Sky and Shadows

Using masking fluid, cover all the sunstruck tree trunks, small branches and small islands of snow in the water area. Next, paint in the sky area with two consecutive washes: first Yellow Ochre and then Prussian Blue, letting the washes dry between applications. Next, using Prussian Blue and a touch of Payne's Gray, paint in the shadows on the snow, softening the edges where necessary as you work. Using a wet-into-wet technique to allow colors to mingle, paint in the stream with progressively darker washes of a mixture of Prussian Blue, a little Alizarin Crimson and Payne's Gray. I dropped in a warm note of Raw Sienna next to the upper right snowbank to use later in a reflection.

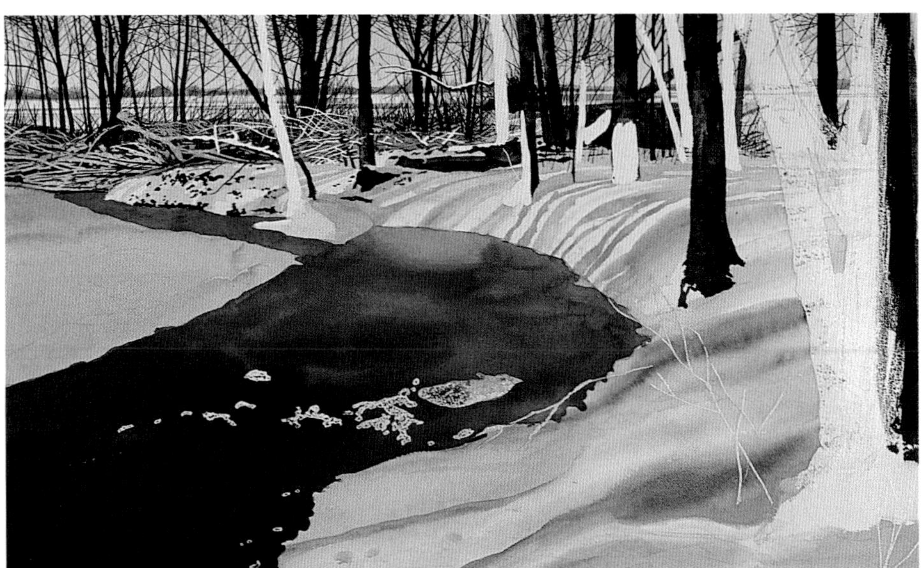

STEP 3

Paint the Trees

Apply masking fluid to the small branches lying in the shadow area under the row of middle ground trees. Paint in all the unmasked trees as well as the background field. For the fine branches and thicket in the middle ground, I prefer to use a ruling pen rather than a brush. Using a rubber cement pickup, remove all the masking fluid except for what is on the large tree in the right foreground and the small areas of snow in the stream. Paint all of the trunks and branches that were covered with masking fluid with varying warm washes of Yellow Ochre mixed with Payne's Gray and Burnt Sienna.

WINDING STREAM
Donald W. Patterson, watercolor, 18" × 27" (45.7cm × 68.6cm)

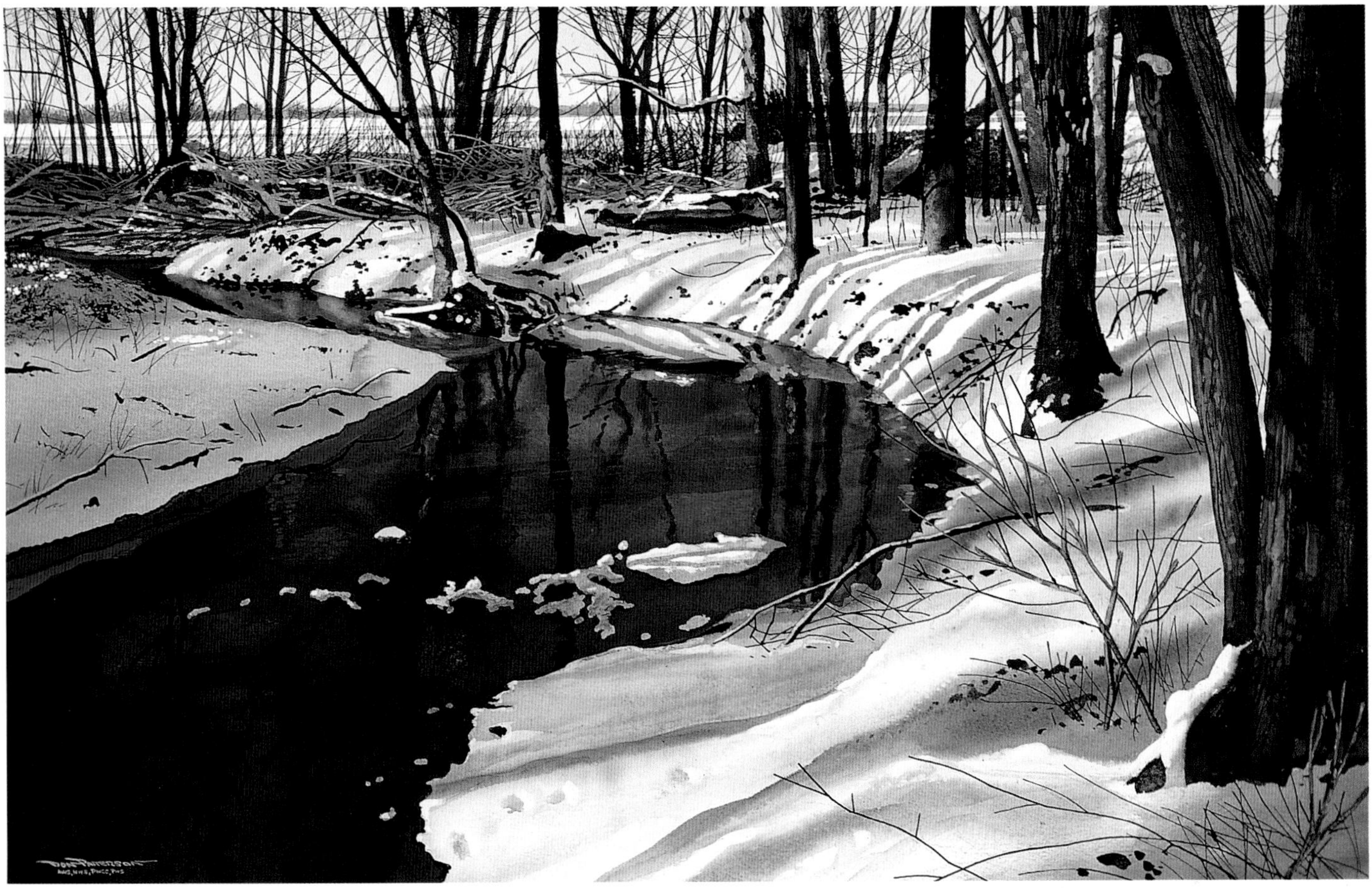

STEP 4

Final Touches

Paint in the ground area details—rocks, twigs, sticks and shadow details. Next, with a round brush, use Payne's Gray and Sepia to paint reflections in the stream, making sure the reflections line up with actual objects. Using thin, watery Zinc White, Yellow Ochre or Prussian Blue, add details such as lighter reflections and warm sun streaks across the stream to the water, and add light accents on the tree trunks. Next, remove the masking fluid from the small areas of snow in the stream and add shadows to these areas. Remove the masking fluid from the large tree trunk in the foreground and paint in the sun's highlights using the colors used for previous trees (step three). Finally, use Zinc White with a touch of Yellow Ochre to make a smooth, creamy off-white color for subtle highlights on the snow. Soften and blend the edges of these highlights with a wet bristle brush.

CAPTURE A SUNSET ON STILL WATER Watercolor

Water is one of my favorite subjects to paint because of its endless variety and challenge. Two main factors create this variety: movement and light. Movement causes the surface "texture," and light brings to life the reflections on the water's surface.

In *Assateague Sunset* on page 24 the water is calm, so the light of the setting sun is reflected undisturbed, making the water in this scene colorful and contrasted against the landmasses. In order to capture the "feel" of water, I wash glazes of reflected color over the entire painting surface, guaranteeing that the sky colors underlie and read through the water's surface. In this way, the water and sky are tied together, allowing the water to become a convincing part of the whole painting. A painting like this is relatively simple, having only three basic steps: Paint the light; paint the clouds in midtones; paint the landmasses in darks.

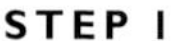

STEP 1

Paint the Light

After completing your drawing, the first step is to paint the color and tone of the pervading light. This is done in three steps: First, cover the entire surface with four separate glazes of approximately 5 percent color intensity using Yellow Ochre, Alizarin Crimson, Prussian Blue and Cadmium Orange. Use a hair dryer to dry each glaze before applying the next one. Second, wet the entire surface. While the surface is damp, brush light values of Cadmium Lemon and Cadmium Yellow into the sky and Prussian Blue into the water. Dry this layer with a hair dryer. Third, wet the entire surface again and brush light values of Cadmium Orange and Flame Red into the sky and water. Dry this layer with a hair dryer.

STEP 2

Cloud Formations

Wet the sky area and indicate clouds in midtones using a mix of Prussian Blue and a touch of Payne's Gray. Dry the surface with a hair dryer. Using an airbrush (so you don't disturb the clouds), spray the sky lightly with Flame Red. Also spray Cadmium Yellow in the area of the setting sun. Wet the water area and add more Flame Red with a brush.

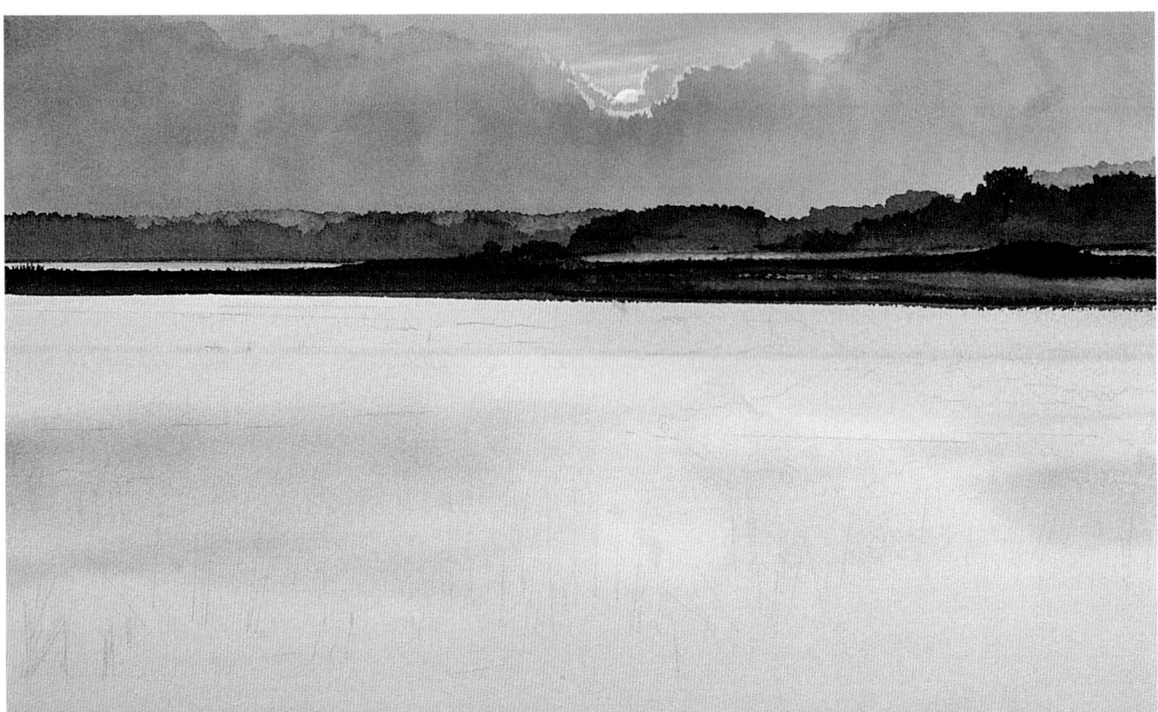

STEP 3

Paint the Background Land Areas

Use the wet-into-wet technique to paint in the land areas with Prussian Blue, Sepia, Burnt Sienna and Payne's Gray. Create texture and atmosphere by blotting the surface gently with paper towels and then, while it is still damp, go back in with darker colors. With gouache Zinc White, Cadmium Yellow and Flame Red, add color accents to the clouds near the setting sun.

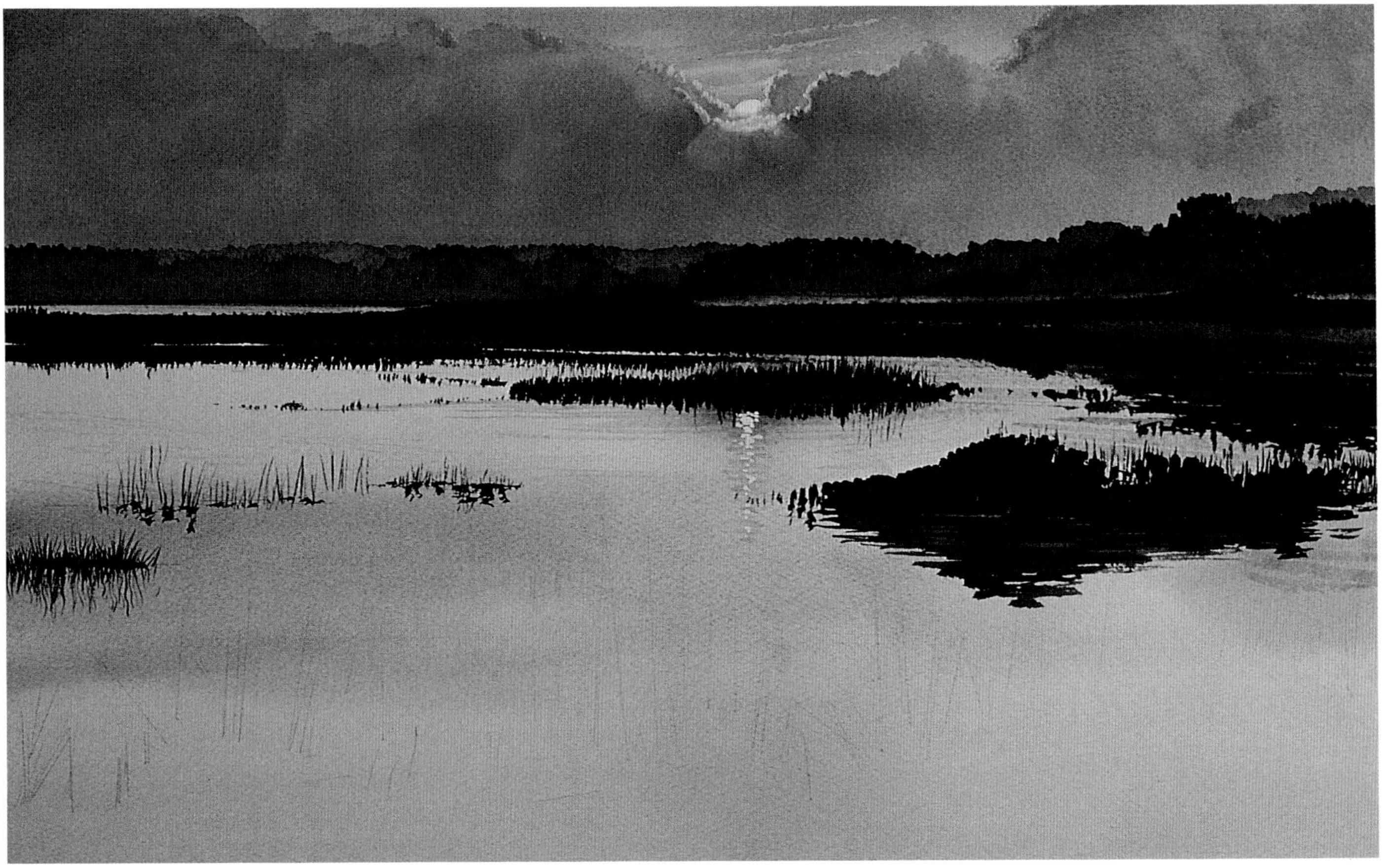

STEP 4

Refine the Clouds

Continue refining color accents on the clouds with gouache. Strengthen the colors in the water, adding the sun's reflection, and continue to add reeds and details with either delicate brushwork or an airbrush.

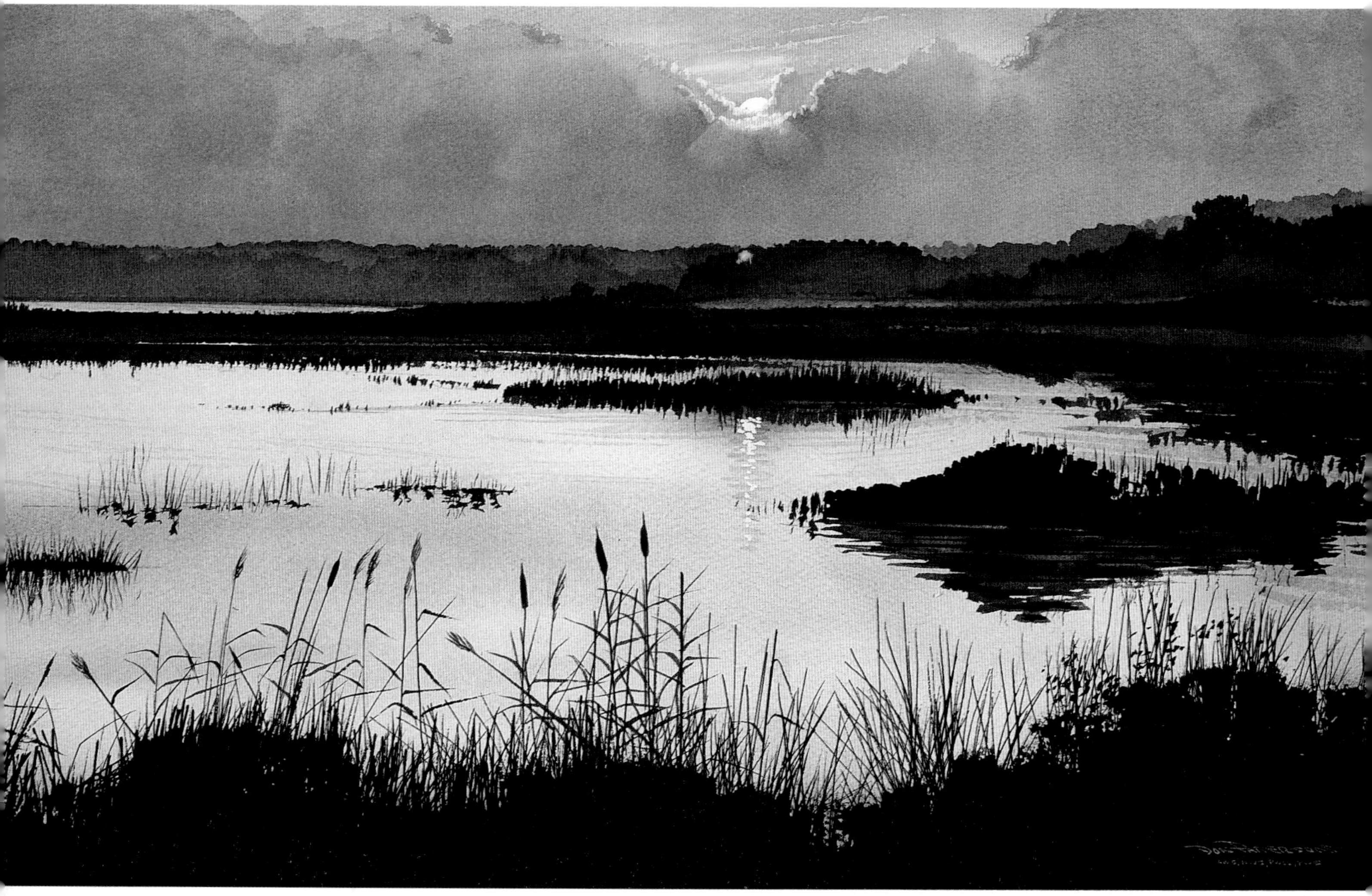

STEP 5

Final Touches

Airbrush in sun rays using Zinc White and a touch of Cadmium Yellow. Hold a piece of stiff paper slightly away from the painting surface to help direct the airbrushing into a triangular "ray" shape while keeping the edges of the sun rays somewhat soft. Add a dark foreground silhouette of reeds and grasses, and airbrush some blue along the top edge of the foreground and the right side of the middle ground. Strengthen the horizon land area.

ASSATEAGUE SUNSET
Donald W. Patterson, watercolor, 12″ × 20″ (30.5cm × 50.8cm)

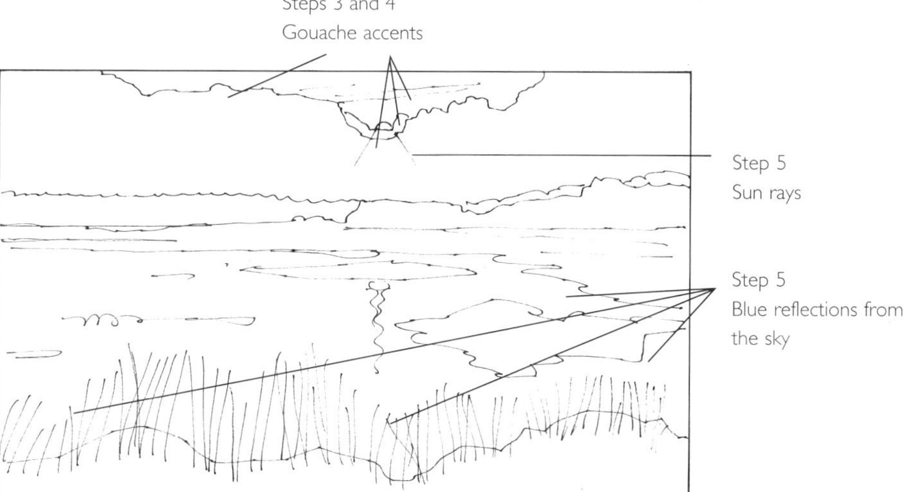

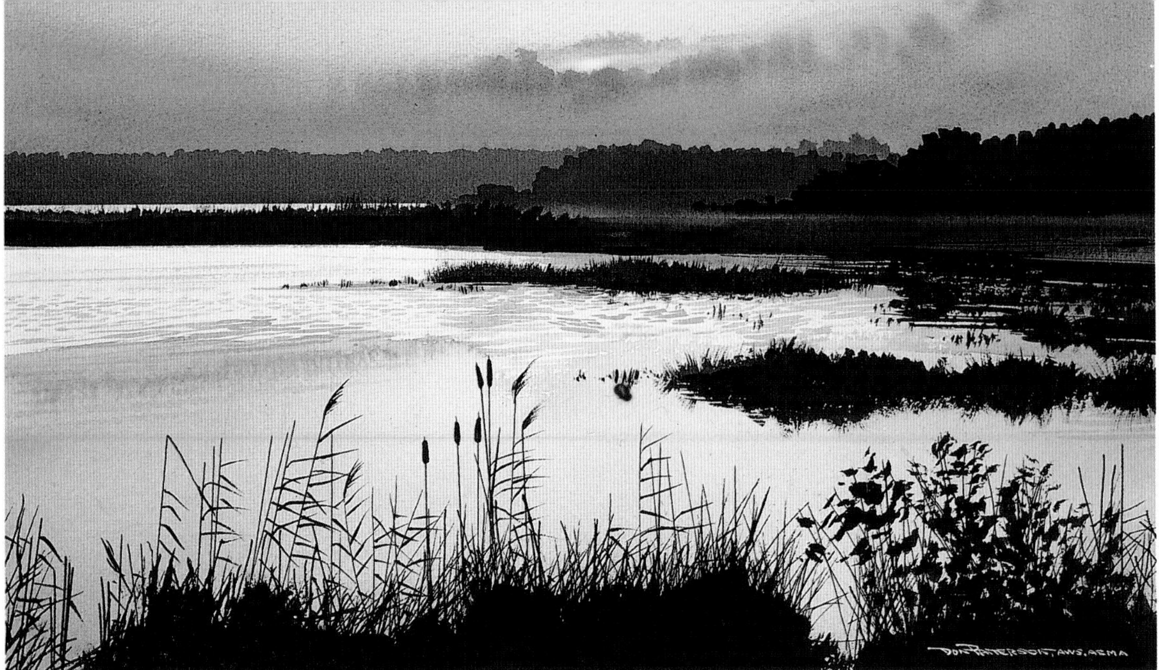

The sun has sunk completely beneath the clouds in this version of the same scene.

ASSATEAGUE SUNSET 2
Donald W. Patterson, watercolor, 11″ × 18″ (27.9cm × 45.7cm)

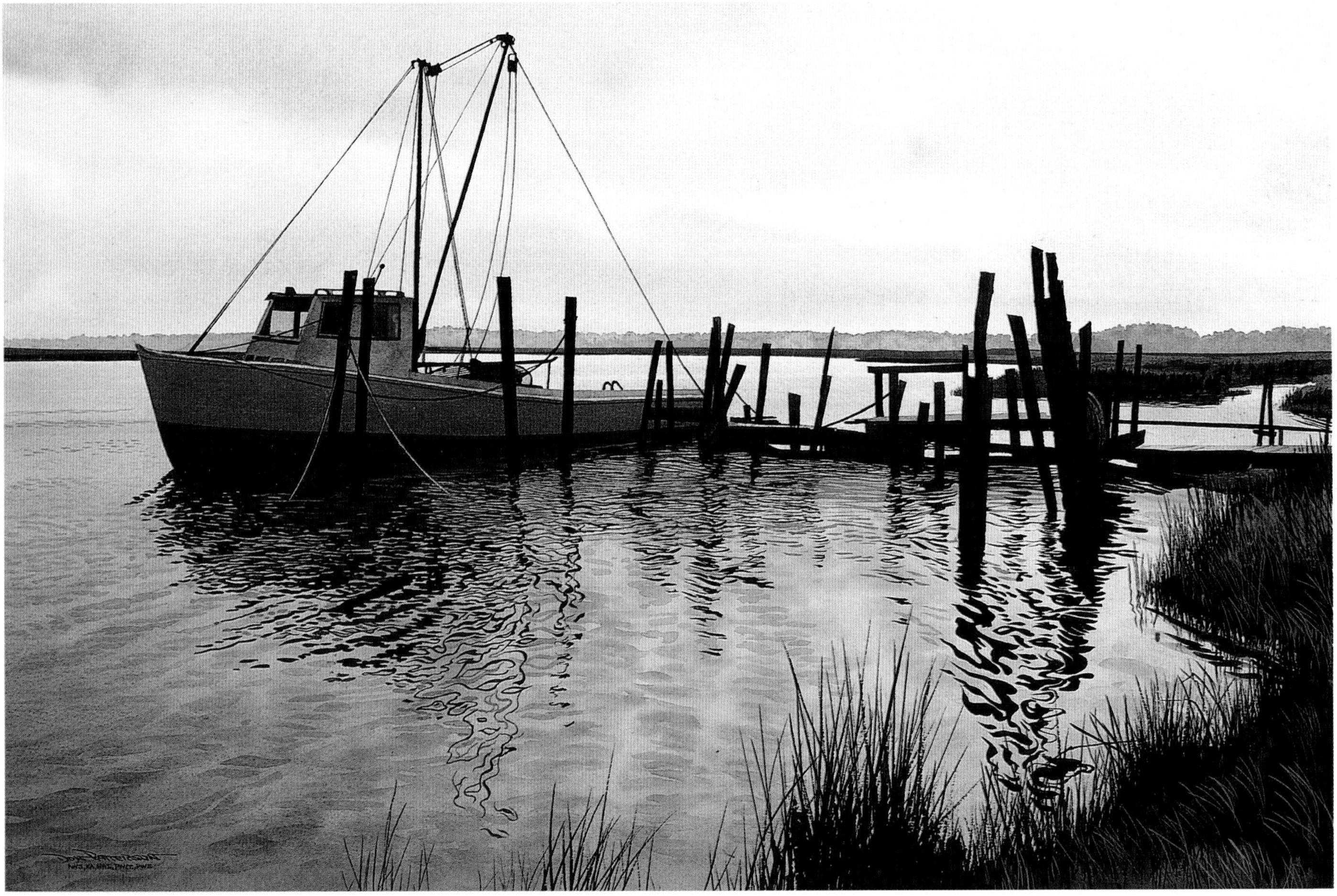

CLOUDY CHINCOTEAGUE
Donald W. Patterson, watercolor, 16″ × 24″ (40.6cm × 61cm)

A Gray, Moody Day

This is a good example of a different mood resulting from the technique of glazing unified light over the entire painting surface. Glazes of Yellow Ochre, Payne's Gray and Alizarin Crimson are the basis for both the sky and water, ensuring the perfect marriage of these elements on this gray, moody day. Notice there are no "whites" in this painting—only a full value scale of mostly grays. The jutting pilings and grasses combined with the intricate reflections contribute to the visual impact.

GALLERY

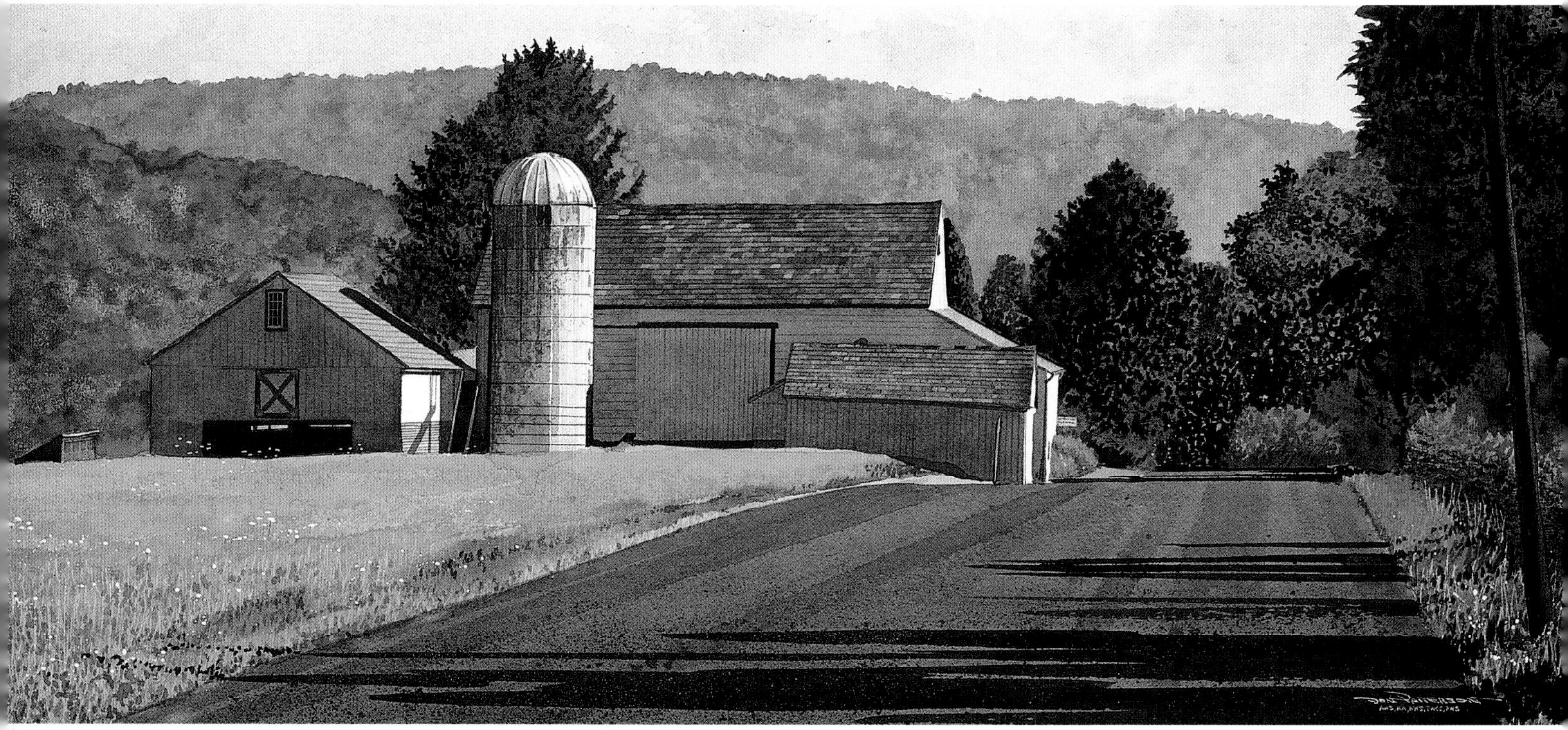

Slifer Valley Road is bathed in an October morning sunlight that brings life and excitement to every inch of this scene. The lower angle of an October sun creates long, dramatic shadows, and at the same time its intensity makes the whole landscape sparkle.

SLIFER VALLEY ROAD
Donald W. Patterson, watercolor, 11″ × 26″ (27.9cm × 66cm)

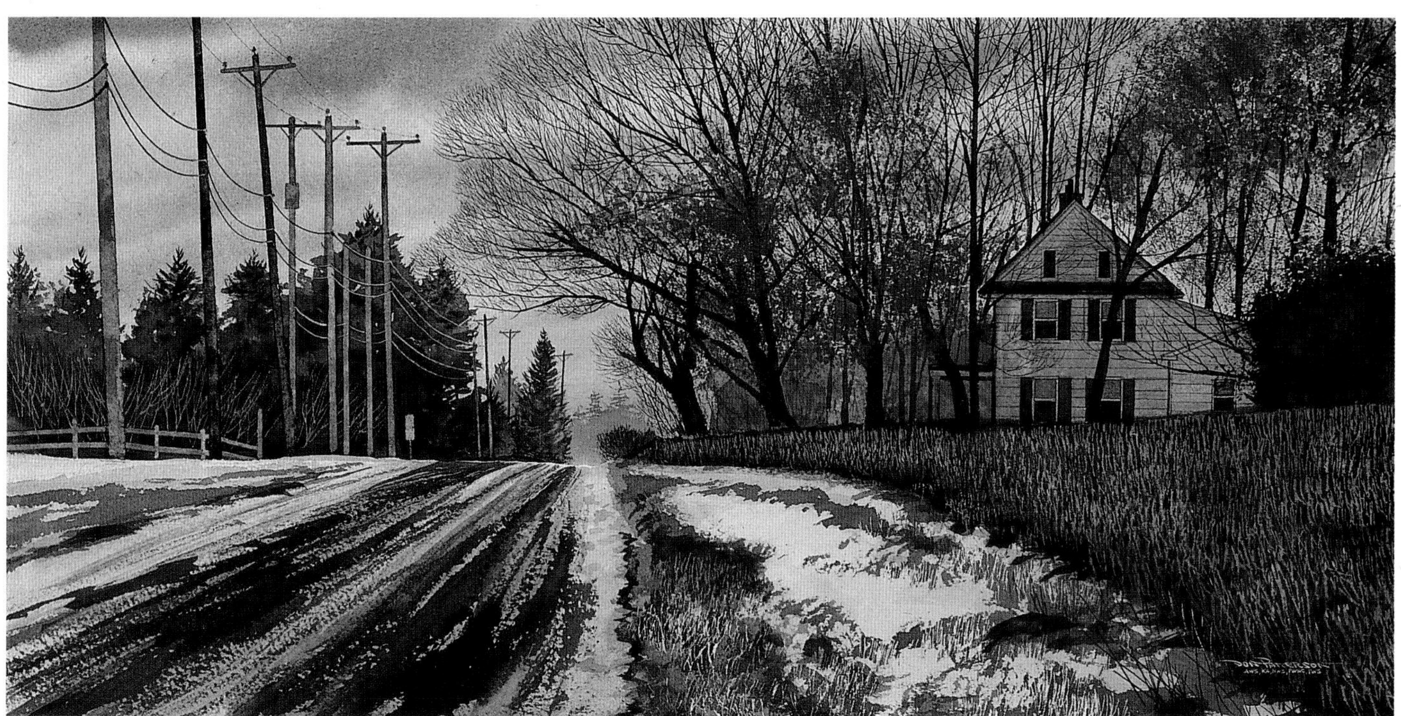

This painting captures the rapidly fading light of dusk. This fleeting transition from day to night provides some of the most exciting light. I actually photographed this scene in the morning without the snow on the road. By adding snow and changing the time of day, I gave this scene a mood that touches memories in the viewer.

RIDGE ROAD
Donald W. Patterson, watercolor, 12″ × 24″ (30.5cm × 61cm)

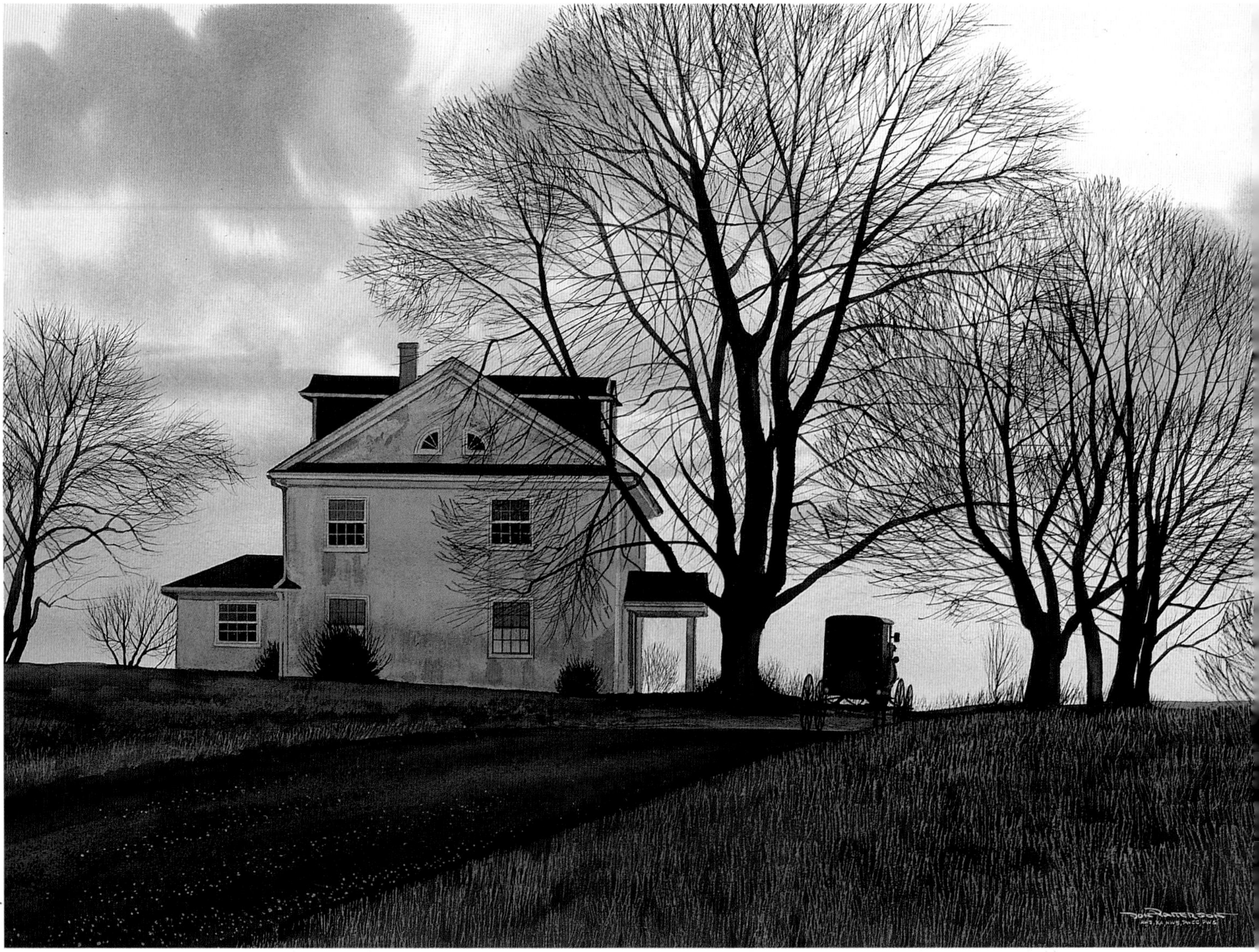

One of my favorite times of day is twilight. There is still a lot of light and color in the sky, but because the sun has just dipped below the horizon, the color and values of the landscape become low-key. Add this feeling to a well-designed composition and an interesting subject, and you have all the ingredients for a successful painting.

TWILIGHT
Donald W. Patterson, watercolor, 20″ × 27″ (50.8cm × 68.6cm)

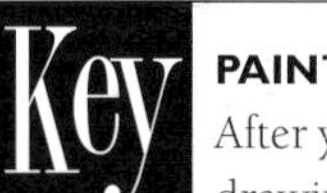

PAINT THE LIGHT FIRST
After you lightly sketch in your drawing and before you start painting your subject, brush a wash over the entire surface to indicate the color of the light. This gives the light and color in your painting a unity similar to that which occurs in nature.

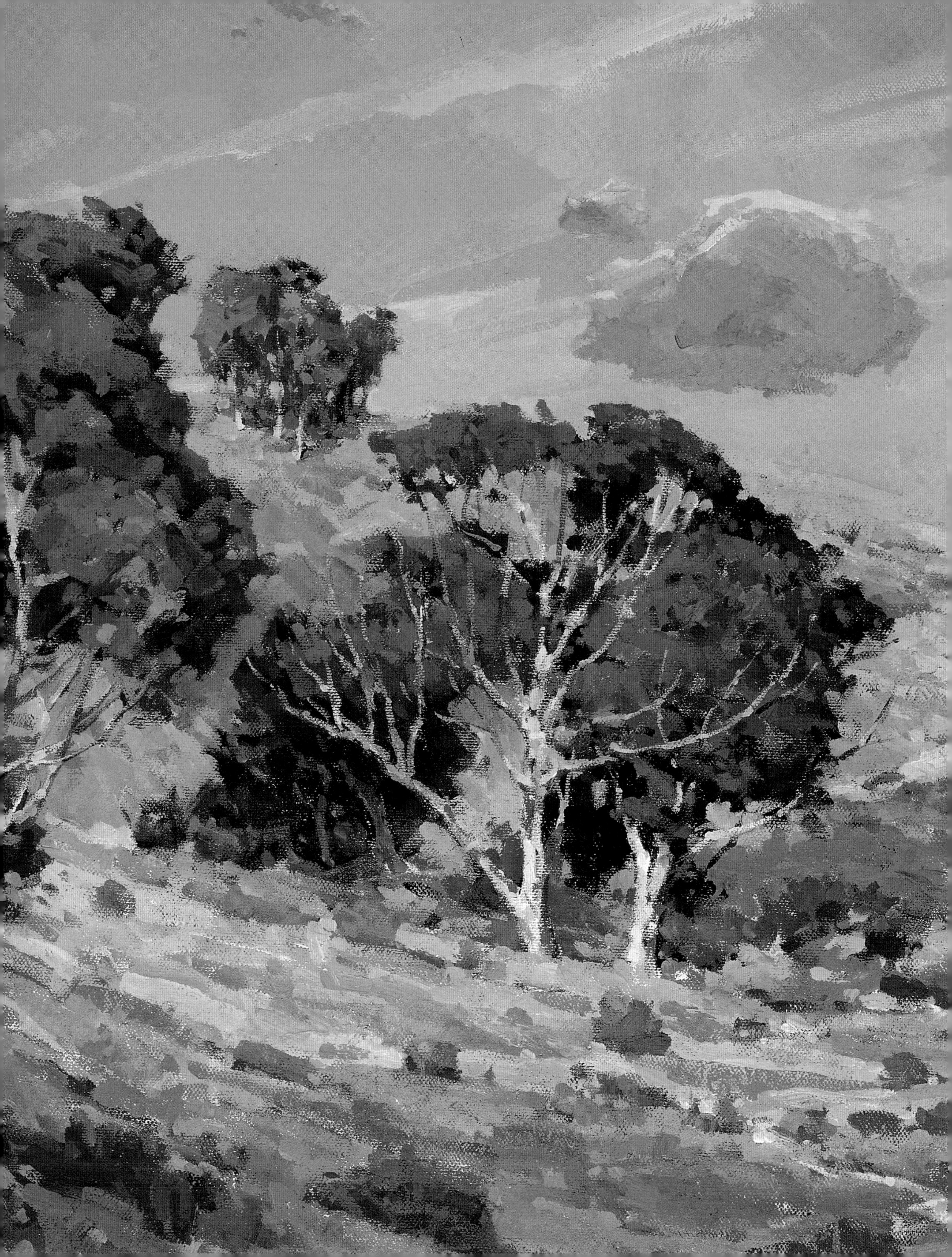

CHAPTER 2

SHAPE MOODY AND STRIKING SKIES WITH ACRYLICS

BRAD FAEGRE

Believing in the adage, "Strike while the iron is hot," Brad Faegre tries, when possible, to complete a work in one or two sessions. He almost always does small painting studies on site, and then uses these studies to provide information and inspiration for his studio paintings. Faegre particularly enjoys painting his studies outside in the early morning or late afternoon: Painting outside helps him get in touch with nature in a fundamental way that hearkens back to childhood feelings. Back inside, away from the hot sun and blowing winds, acrylic paint stays wet longer, encouraging greater freedom on the surface of the canvas. Still, the medium does dry quickly, so in order to manipulate it effectively, Faegre divides his paintings into regions and tackles them individually: sky, background, middle ground and foreground. Before he approaches the challenge of the actual painting, Faegre has an idea and a plan for implementing it. Working with a clear purpose in mind brings unity to the elements in the painting. Faegre is moved by various weather or lighting conditions; he especially takes note of the effects of these conditions on the sky. In his paintings, the sky is usually a main feature, although it may be absent altogether, its presence implied by cloud shadows or the color of light. The following landscape demonstrations show the techniques Faegre uses to set the mood of his paintings as determined by the light of his skies.

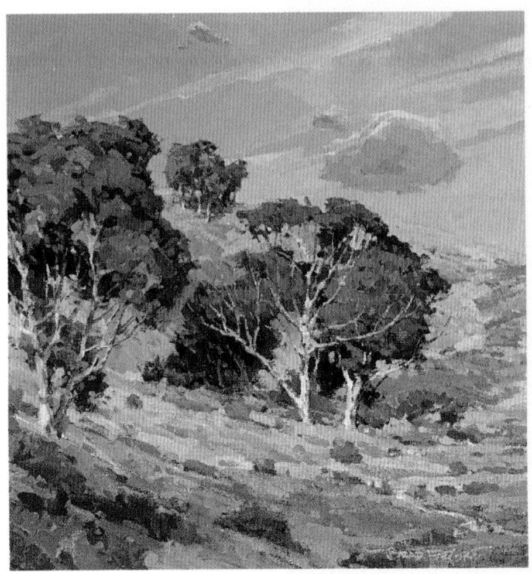

HIGH SKY
Brad Faegre, 18" × 18" (46cm × 46cm)

I may have experienced an afternoon like the one depicted in *High Sky*; it feels as though I did. Most of the landscapes I create are worlds that I would like to visit—if they existed. I enjoy finding adult expressions for childhood enthusiasms.

A DRAMATIC SKY AFTER A RAIN Acrylic

I did this small painting study (below, top) of Laguna Beach on site to record the dramatic contrast of color and value that takes place at the close of the day as the light is fading. It provided a springboard for the finished painting on page 34. As you will see, the light and mood of the sky changed from the initial study to the finished painting.

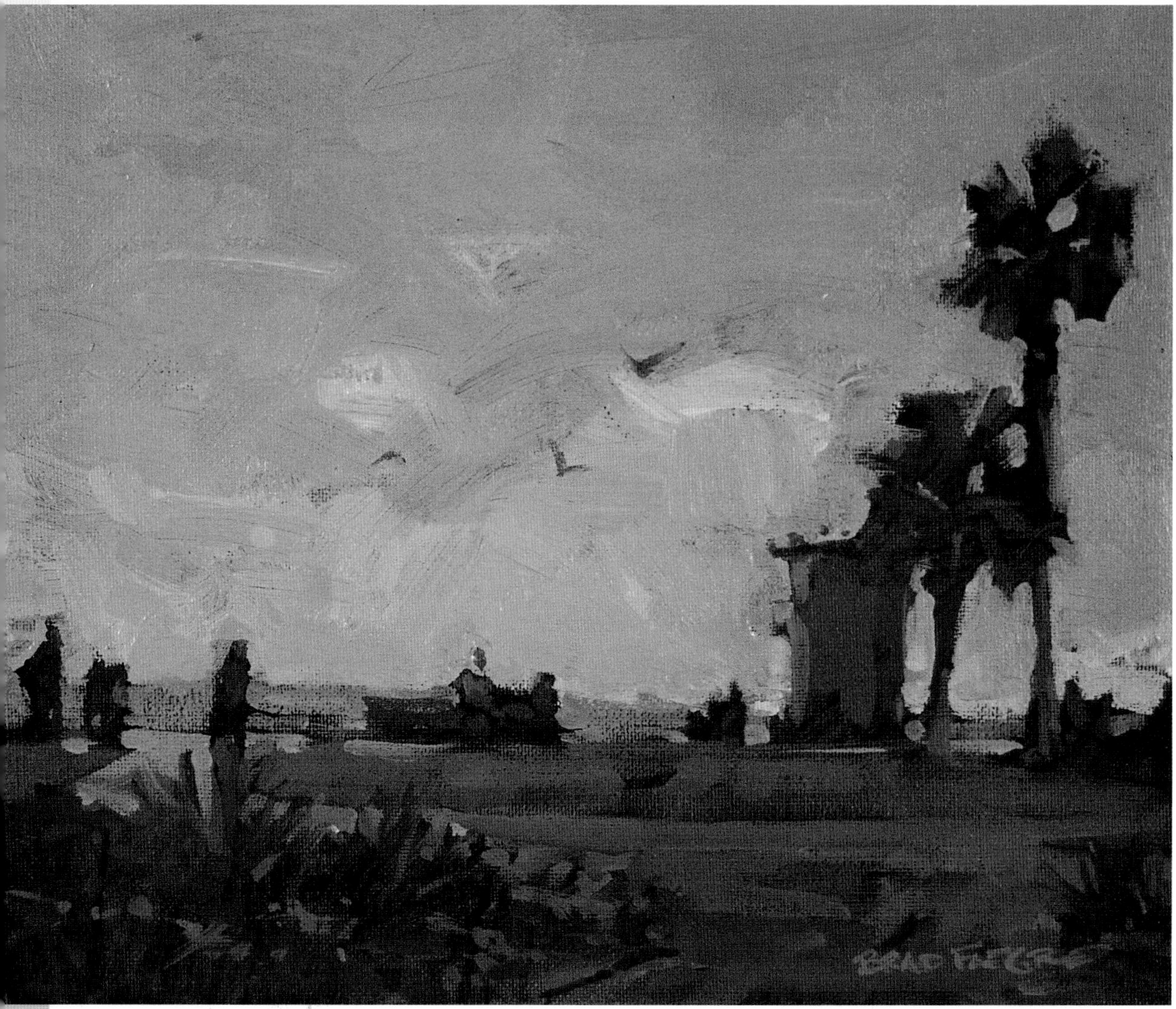

Preliminary study for *Pacific Winds*, 8″ × 10″ (20.3cm × 25.4cm).

STEP 1

Prepare the Surface and Define the Shapes

Prepare the surface of a primed canvas by loosely applying a wash of Dioxide Purple, Thalo Green, Ultramarine Blue and Lamp Black diluted with water, using a 2″ (51mm) flat nylon bristle brush. Mix these colors on the surface of the canvas to create a variegated effect that will peek through subsequent layers of paint. Against this dark background, compose the painting by defining the shapes that break above the horizon using a negative painting technique—carving out the shapes of objects from the space surrounding them.

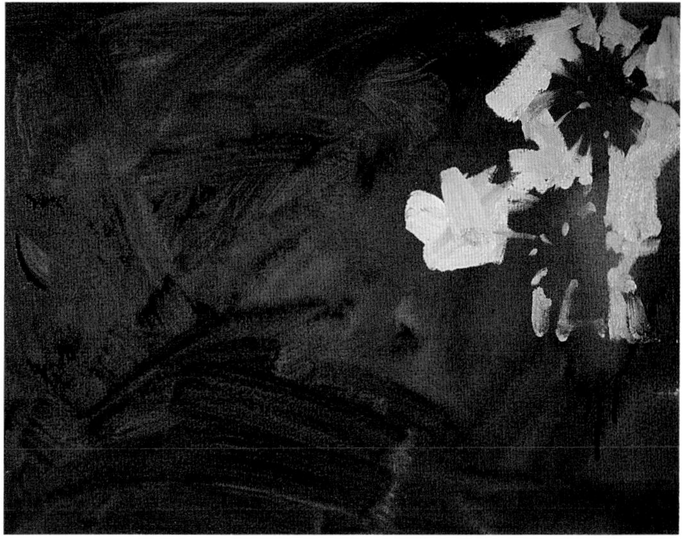

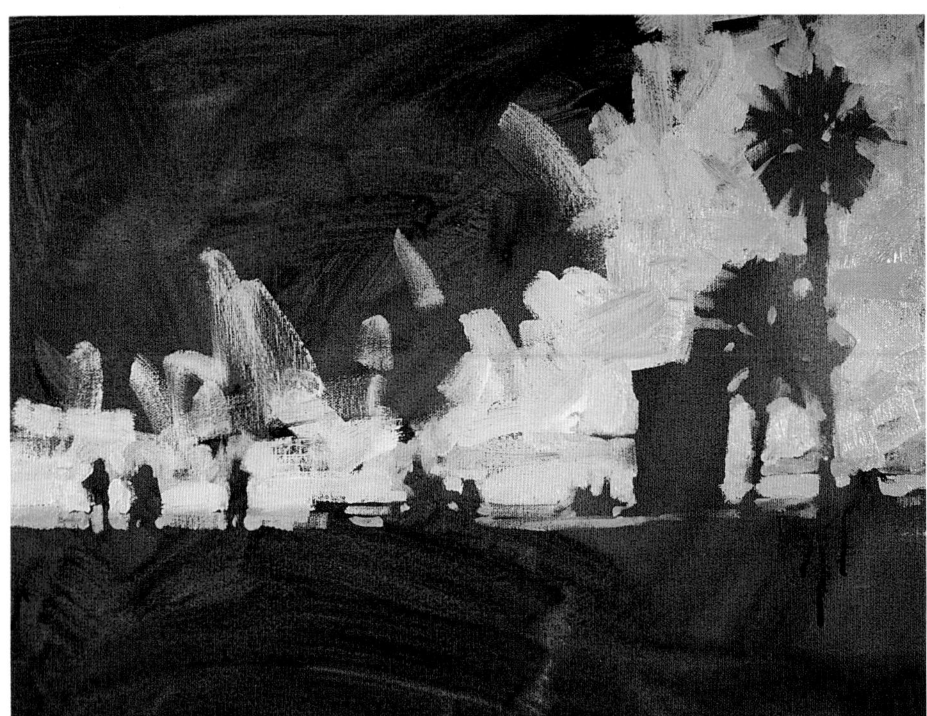

STEP 2

Carve Out More Shapes

For small- to medium-size canvases I use an assortment of brushes—anywhere from a no. 6 to a no. 10. It's handy to have a variety of sizes to choose from based on the type of work you are doing and what size you feel comfortable working with. Using negative painting, continue to rough out shapes: palm trees, a lifeguard station and figures along the boardwalk. Use a Lemon Yellow, Cadmium Orange and Thalo Green tint, subdued slightly with the addition of its close complement, Dioxide Purple. Indicate the suggestion of the beach and distant coastal rocks.

STEP 3

Describe the Middle Ground

Use cool grays and muted red-browns to describe the figures and lifeguard tower in more detail. Use the same muted colors to connect these middle-distance shapes with the foreground by indicating a concrete walkway.

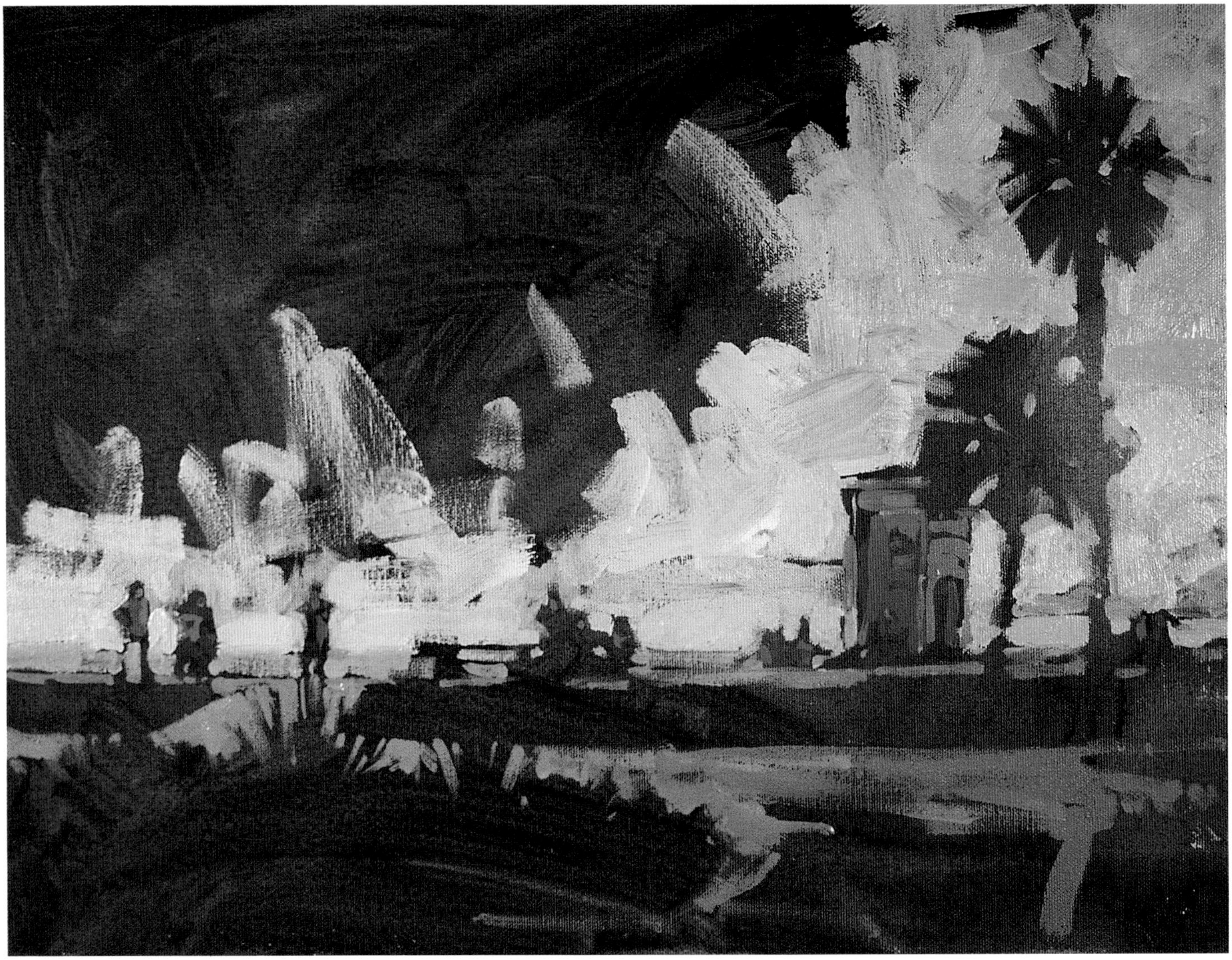

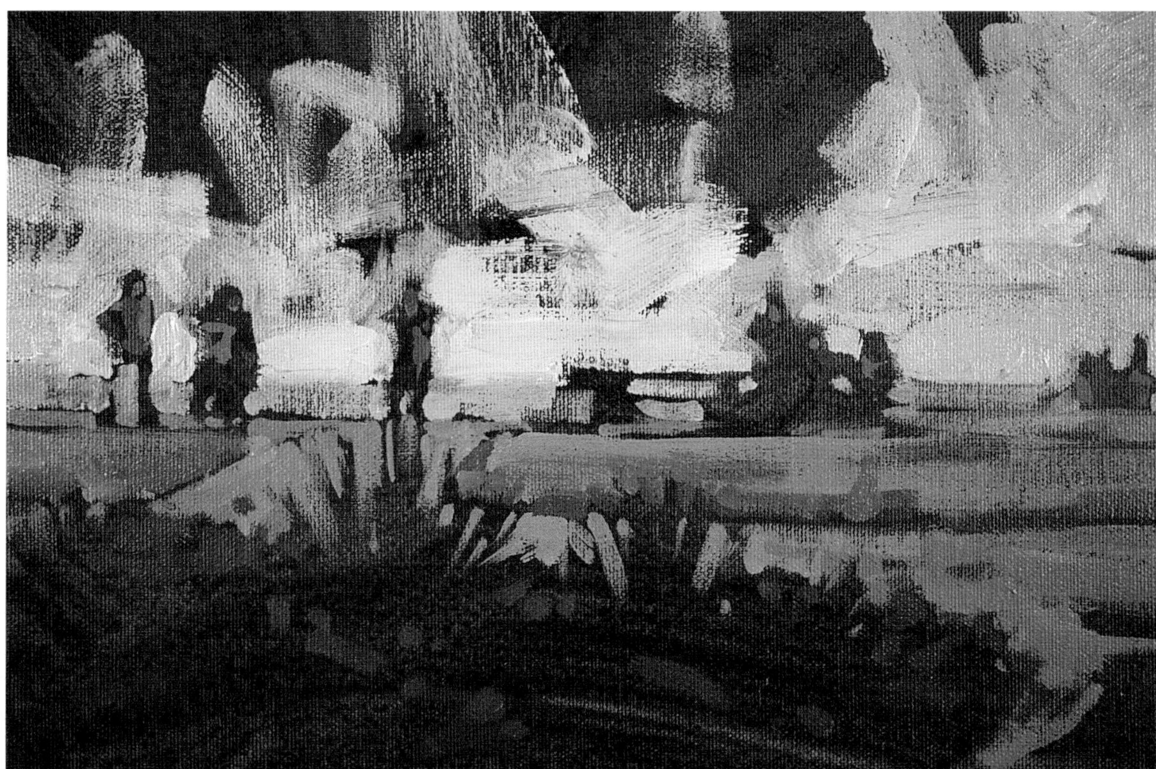

STEP 4

Define the Center of Interest

Add lawns and vegetation to further refine and connect the foreground to the painting's center of interest: the shapes that dominate the middle distance.

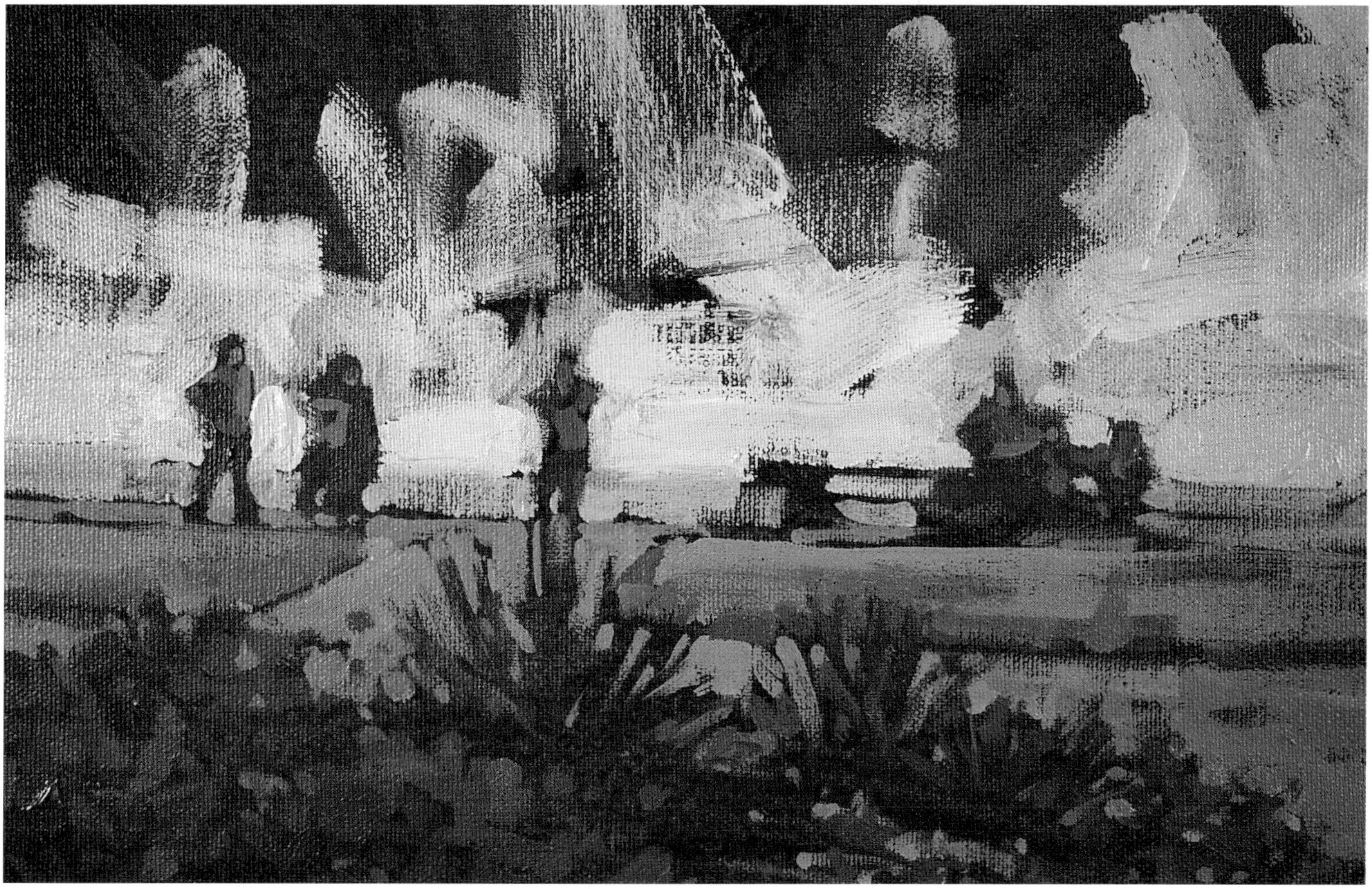

STEP 5

Foreground Vegetation

Use muted, contrasting warm and cool color mixes to build up the foreground vegetation.

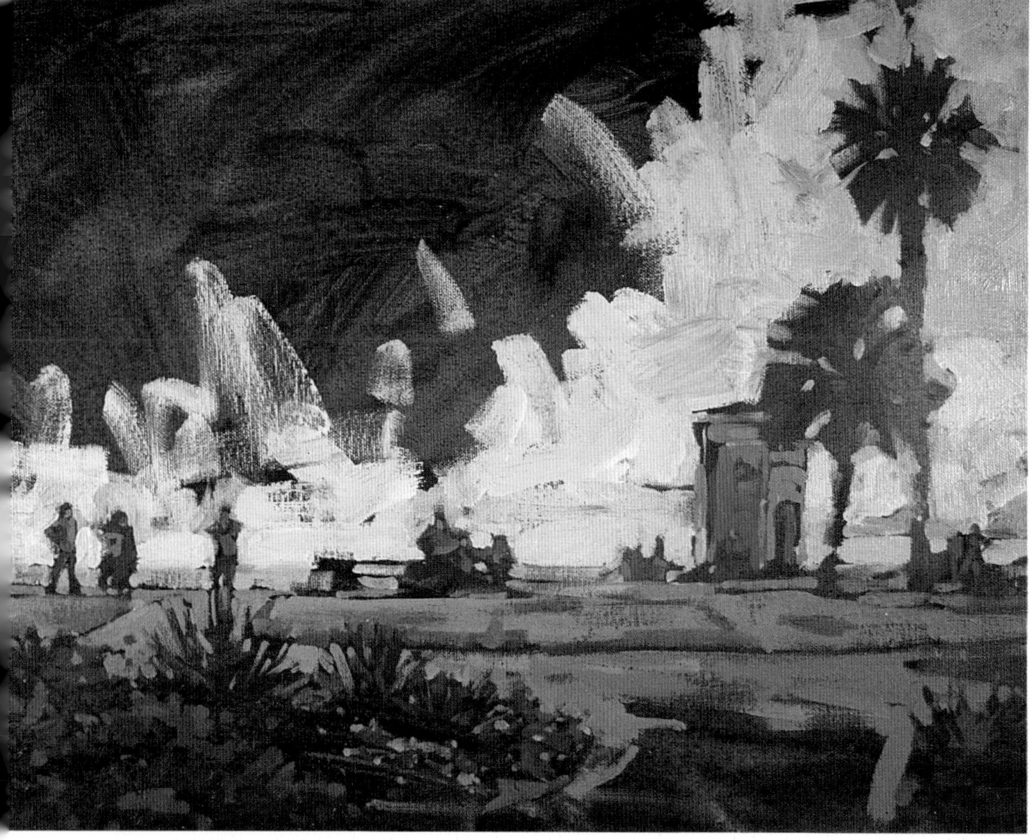

STEP 6

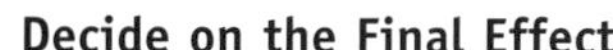

Decide on the Final Effect

Step back and look at the painting as a whole. At this stage I pause to consider which direction I want to go in. Although the preliminary study describes a moody scene of failing light, I decide to brighten this painting to create a different dramatic effect.

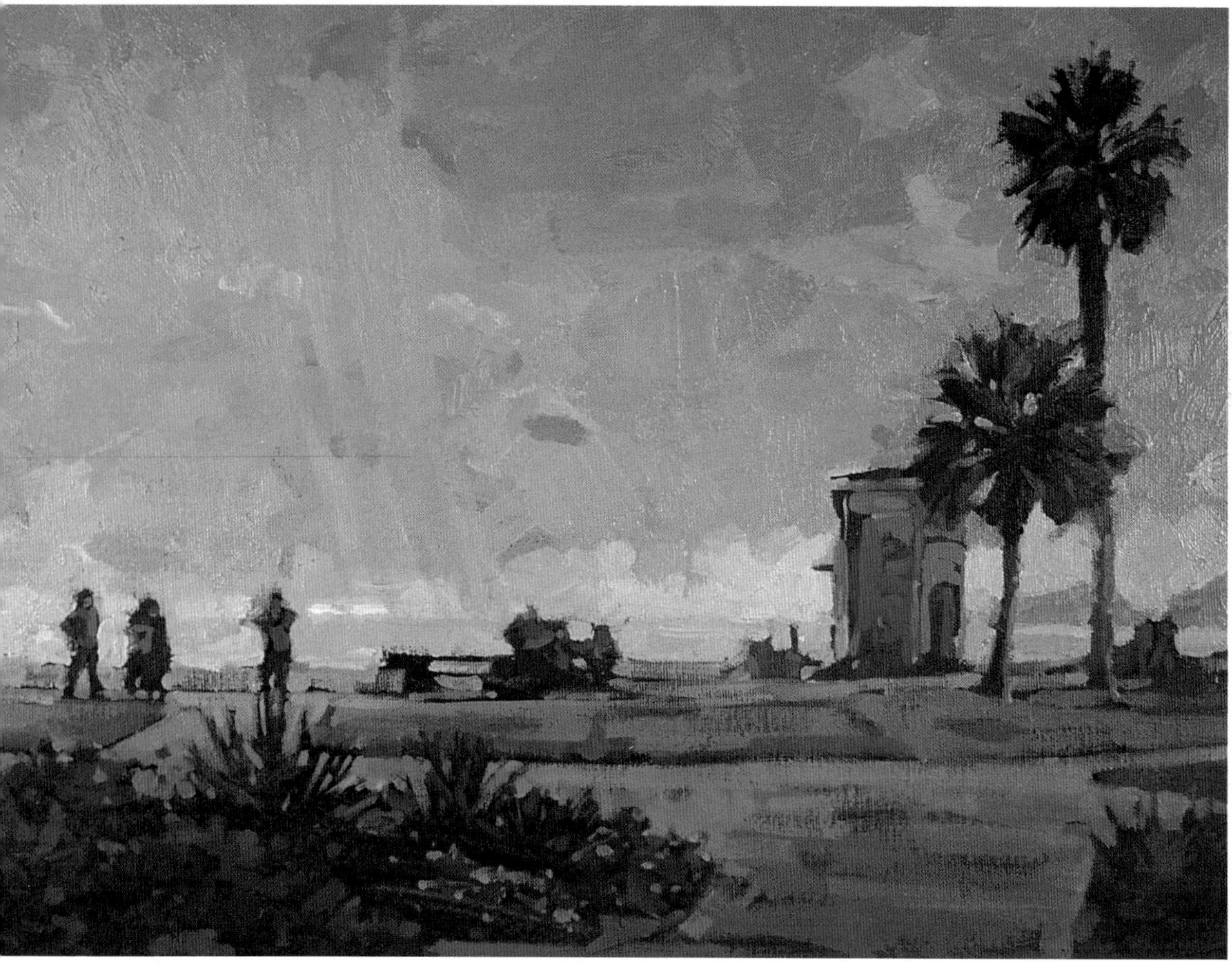

STEP 7

Develop Sky for Specific Mood

Apply a generous supply of paint to the entire sky. The heavy application offers time to explore and to discover, through trial and error, the best way to express yourself. I settle on a sun-drenched afternoon sky under a parade of clouds and occasional rain showers.

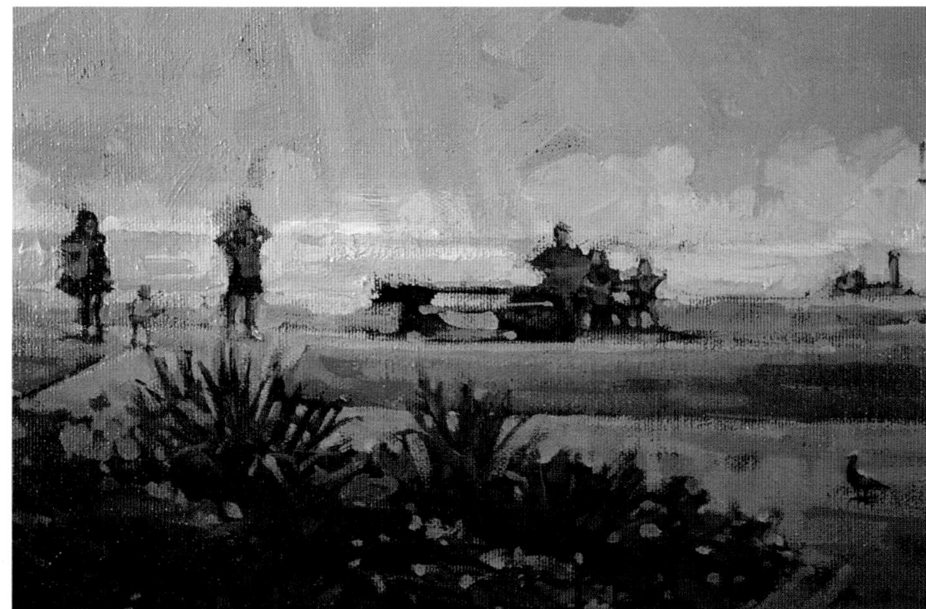

STEP 8

Complete the Figures

Continue to work on the figures to make them look natural within their environment. I decide to eliminate the figure on the far left by painting the background over this area. Once it dries I add a small child to suggest a family grouping. I complete much of this work with a no. 4 round nylon brush.

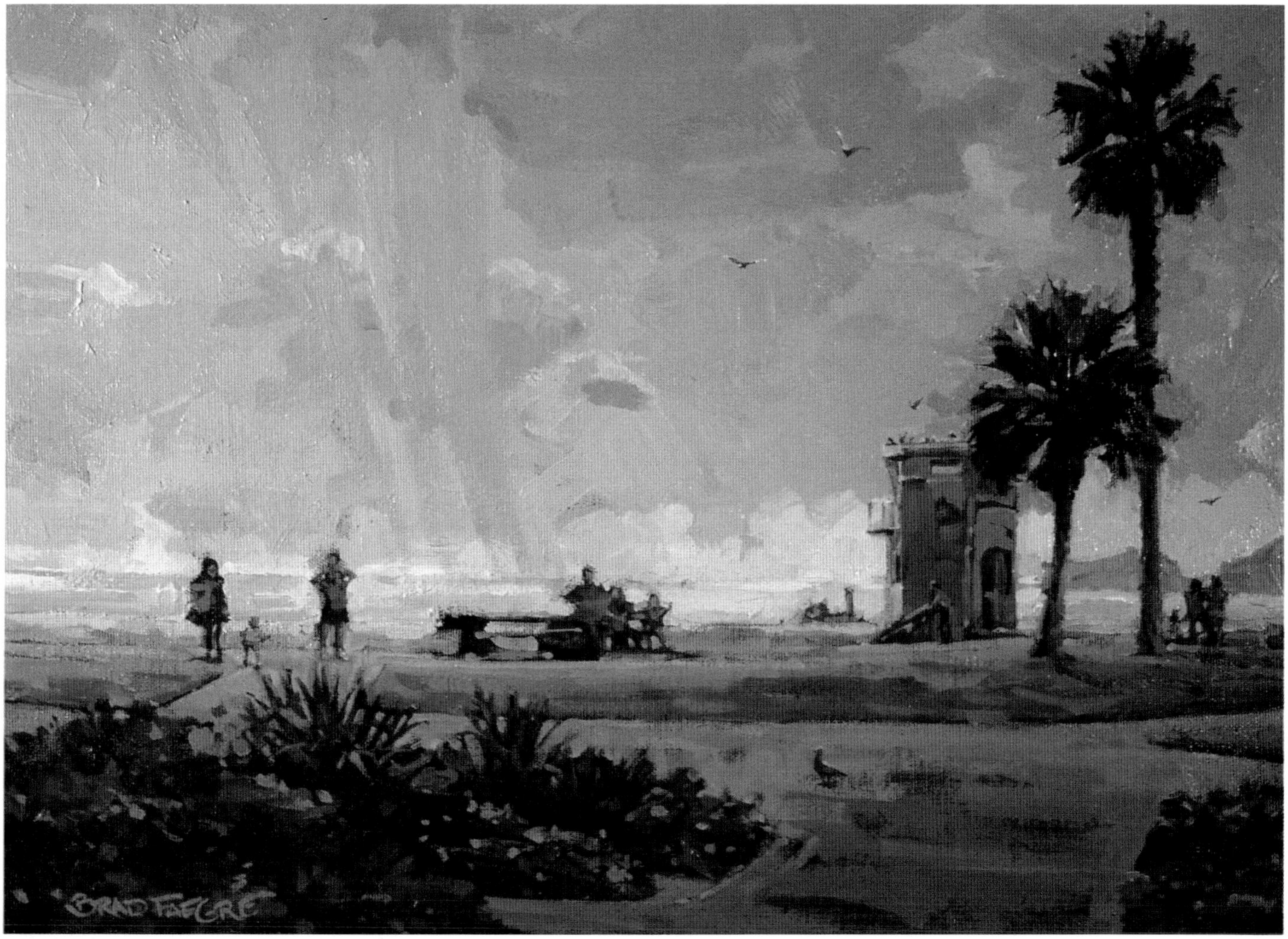

STEP 9

Final Touches

I added a pigeon to the foreground; carefully placed touches of saturated color heighten visual interest and help unify the painting's elements. Apply a final coat of diluted gloss medium with a clean no. 3 nylon bristle brush to serve as a varnish that accentuates the colors and protects the finished painting.

PACIFIC WINDS
Brad Faegre, acrylic, 14" × 18" (35.6cm × 45.7cm)

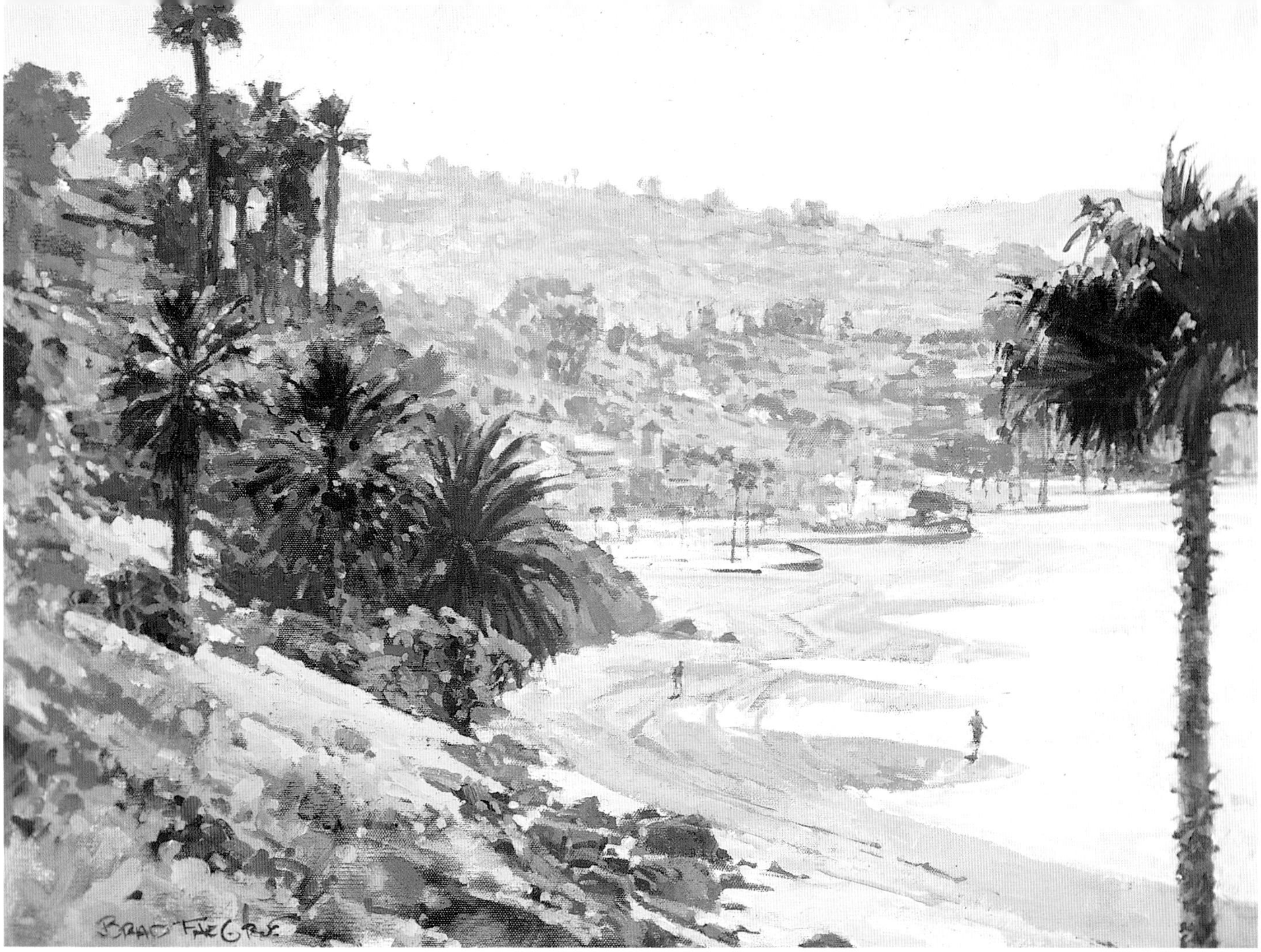

Another Coastal Scene

Without working from a preliminary study, I laid out my idea for a city coastline in soft early morning light on a white primed canvas. Using combinations of Dioxide Purple, Burnt Sienna and Hooker's Green, I sketched in my idea with a no. 6 filbert ox-hair bristle brush. The plan was to "frame" a stretch of beach and coastal hills between palm trees and sea cliffs. I applied light, warm colors on the distant coastal hills to describe the effects of atmospheric moisture. Large shrubs and small tree shapes in the middle distance vary in appearance to make way for an open slope of low vegetation. This leads the viewer's eye down to the rocks and the beach. I built up the painting's surface with opaque colors over transparent washes. Effectively tied together, the foreground, middle and background express the renewal and optimism I feel after spending a morning at the beach.

BEACH CITY VIEW
Brad Faegre, acrylic, 20" × 24" (50.8cm × 61cm)

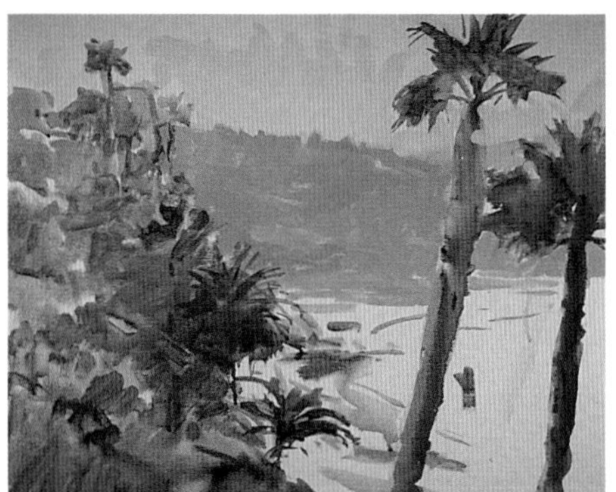

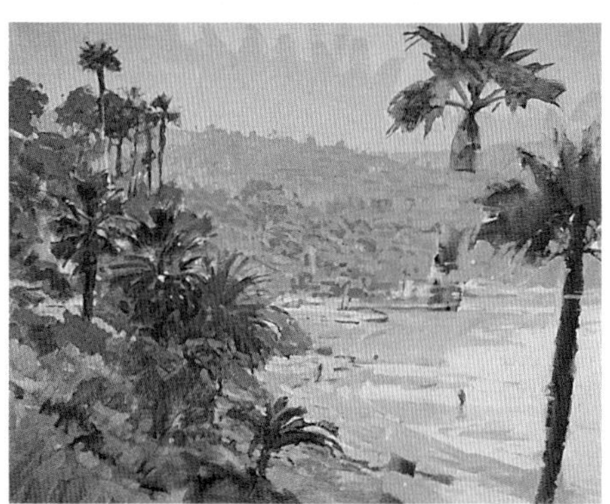

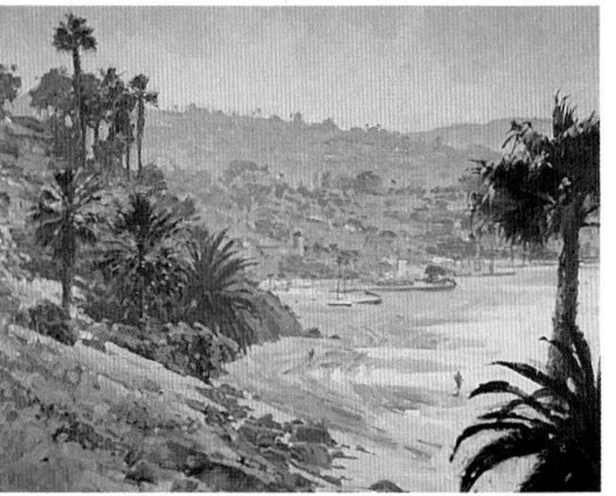

Beach City View went through several changes in composition before arriving at its final version. My first efforts had two main palm trees in the painting. Not pleased with this design, I painted out the one in the middle. That was better, but I didn't like the look of the remaining trunk and attempted to cover it up with a low, leafy palm. Not liking that either, I went back to the lone palm, but modified the angle of the trunk as seen at the top of this page.

MOOD CHANGES FROM THE OUTDOORS TO THE STUDIO Acrylic

Autumn Stand began with an idea painted on a small canvas on location. As is often the case with my paintings, the mood expressed in the finished painting differs significantly from the original idea of my preliminary study.

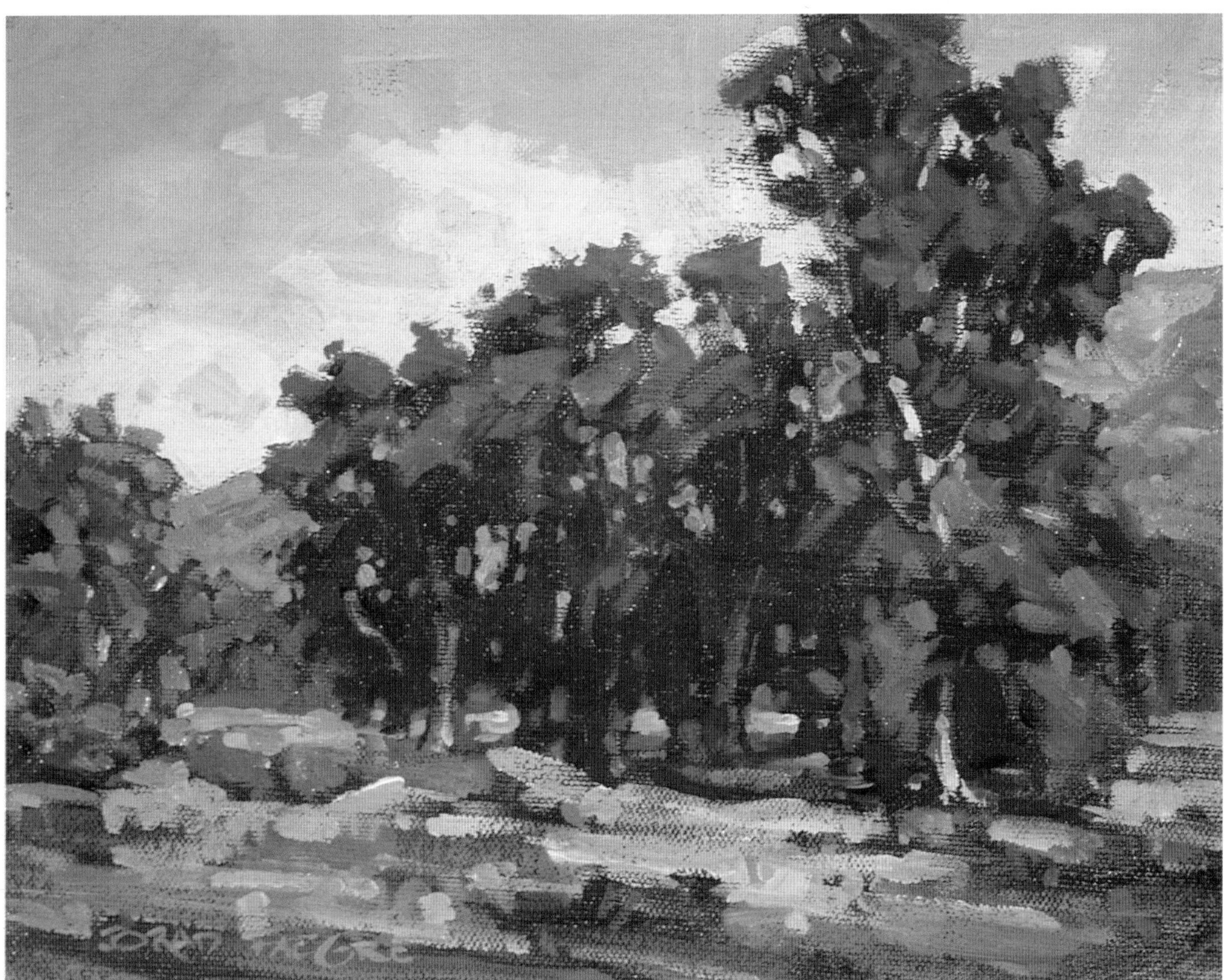

On-Site Study: A Warm, Peaceful Mood

For this study I was greatly affected by what I was seeing. Surrounded by warm colors and noting the subtle atmospheric changes that occur in late afternoon, this small painting has the peaceful, almost lazy, quality that the warm, glowing light produces late in the day as the sun dips to its resting place. It is easy to sense the original feeling of the place from this study: There is a subtle peacefulness as warm light reflects from every surface.

Key BE BOLD AND DON'T FEAR MISTAKES

Go with the mood of the painting. Be inspired by nature, but go with your instincts. The great thing about acrylics is that change is relatively easy.

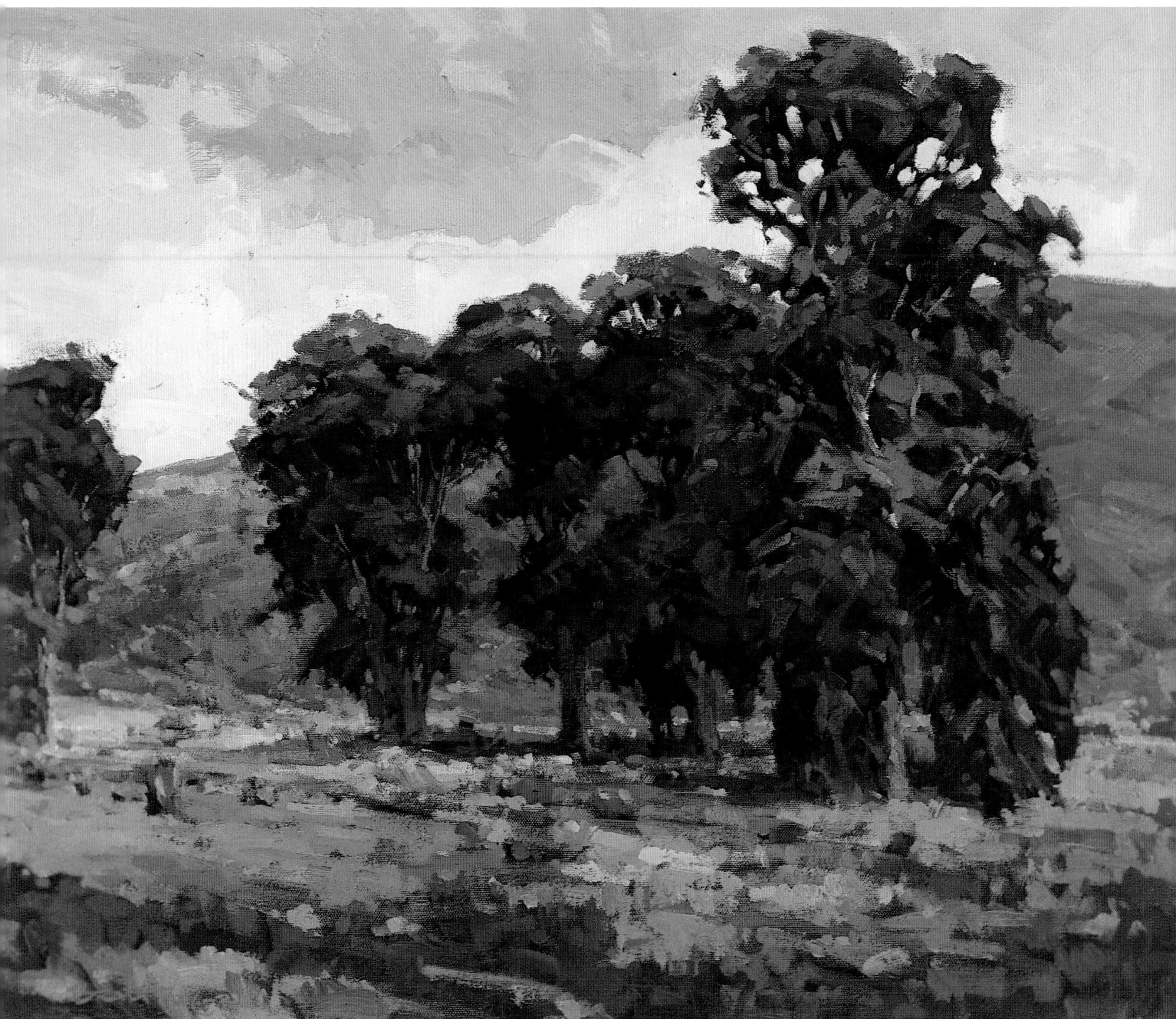

AUTUMN STAND
Brad Faegre, acrylic, 20" × 24" (50.8cm × 61cm)

Studio Finish: A Mood of Alert Anticipation

Curiously, the finished painting took on its own (different) mood as soon as I started mixing the colors, first on the palette and then on the canvas. By painting the sky first, it quickly became the most interesting part of the painting. In fact, it is the primary interest. It seemed to call for bright colors and more intense value contrasts. The movement in the brushstrokes in the sky, coupled with the darker values and brighter colors, implies that something is about to happen, in contrast to the peaceful feeling of the study. The glow of unified light that appears in the study is not there. The light seems to be undergoing a change before our eyes. Is a storm brewing? Or is the wind clearing the clouds away?

GALLERY

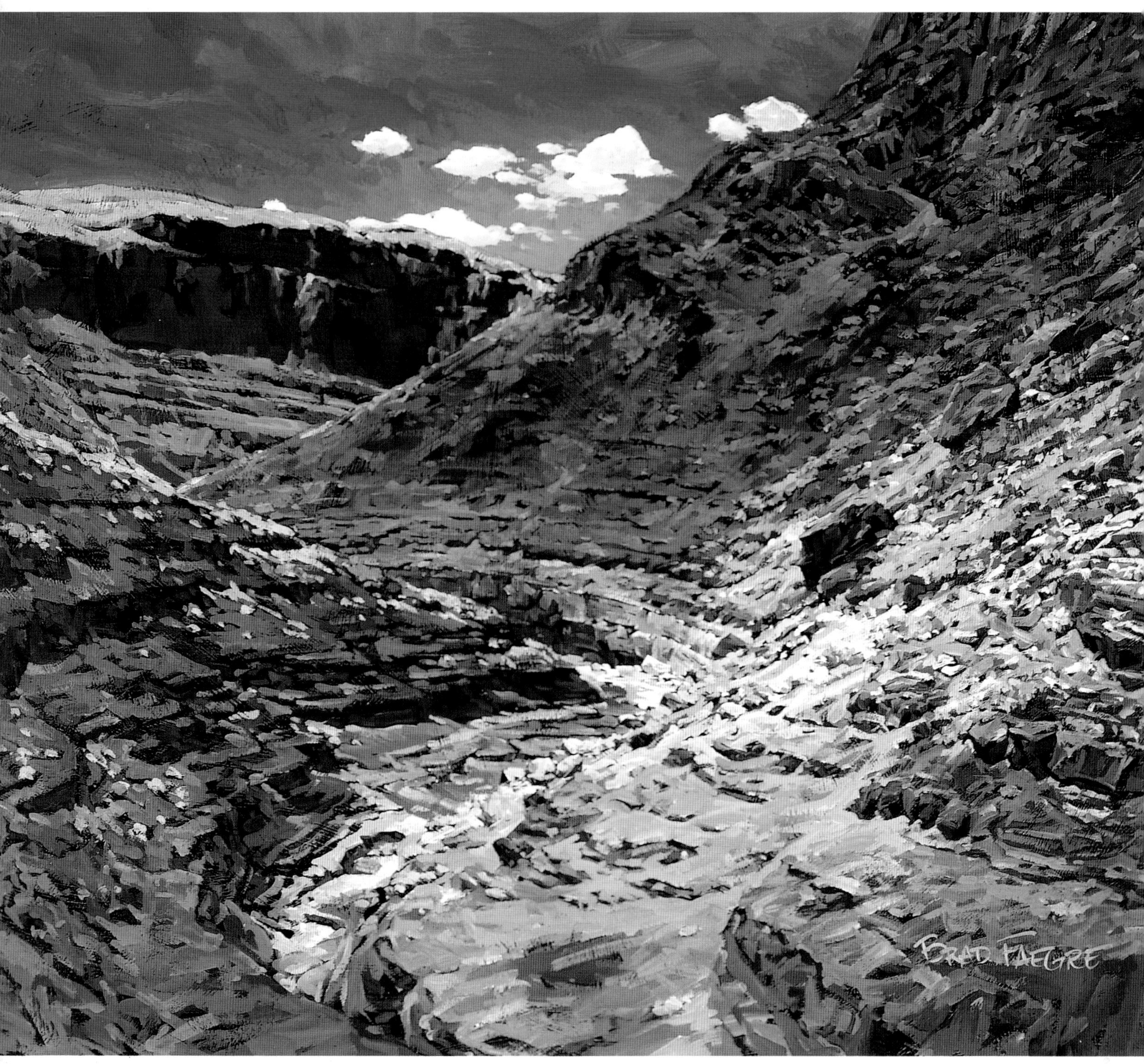

Hiking down to the floor of the Grand Canyon, my wife and I came upon this scene one hot August morning as temperatures exceeded 100°F (38°C). Rather than record the side canyon as it appeared, I exaggerated the swirling roller coaster effect of the erosion's pathway. By intensifying the contrasting colors of the blue sky, red earth and golden vegetation, I was able to express the surreal beauty of this ancient landscape.

SNAKING DOWN HANCE CREEK, GRAND CANYON
Brad Faegre, acrylic, 22" × 26" (55.9cm × 66cm)

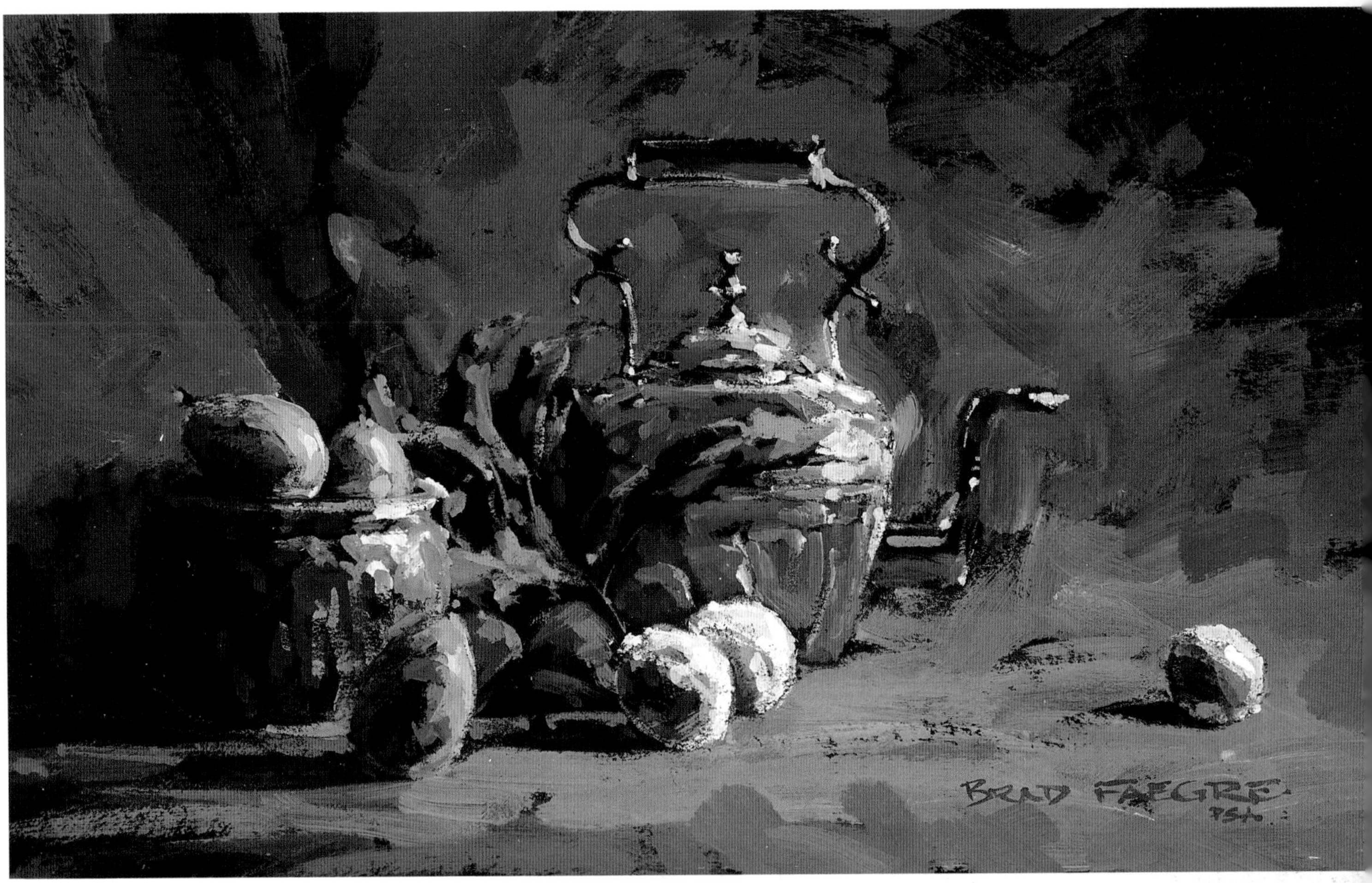

Mediterranean Light began with the loan of a lovely brass pitcher my friend and fellow painter Dr. George Riday bought in Casablanca. I searched for objects to contrast and complement its unique shape. While arranging the still life, I recalled a story George shared with me about his experience as an army chaplain in Casablanca on Christmas Eve, 1942. The warmth of his recollection affected my feeling for the piece and found its way into the light that bathes the final painting.

MEDITERRANEAN LIGHT
Brad Faegre, acrylic, 8″ × 12″ (20.3cm × 30.5cm)

I received a commission from the Los Angeles Area Chamber of Commerce to create a painting that would express my impressions of life in the city. To create the feeling behind this painting, I visited various Metrolink locations in predawn darkness, studying the subtle psychology of commuters, expressed in their gestural contours, and the bigger shapes of the station crowds. I decided to only imply the subject of trains, choreographing a scene that made human industry, isolation and community its focus.

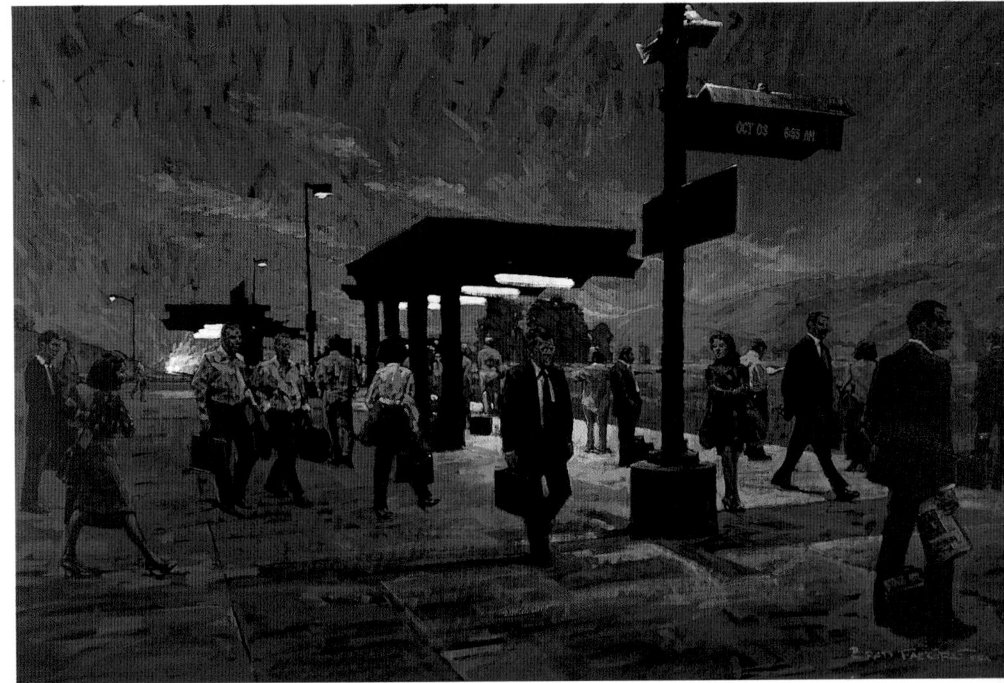

DAYBREAK AT A METROLINK STATION
Brad Faegre, acrylic, 40″ × 60″ (101.6cm × 152.4cm)
Collection of the Los Angeles Area Chamber of Commerce

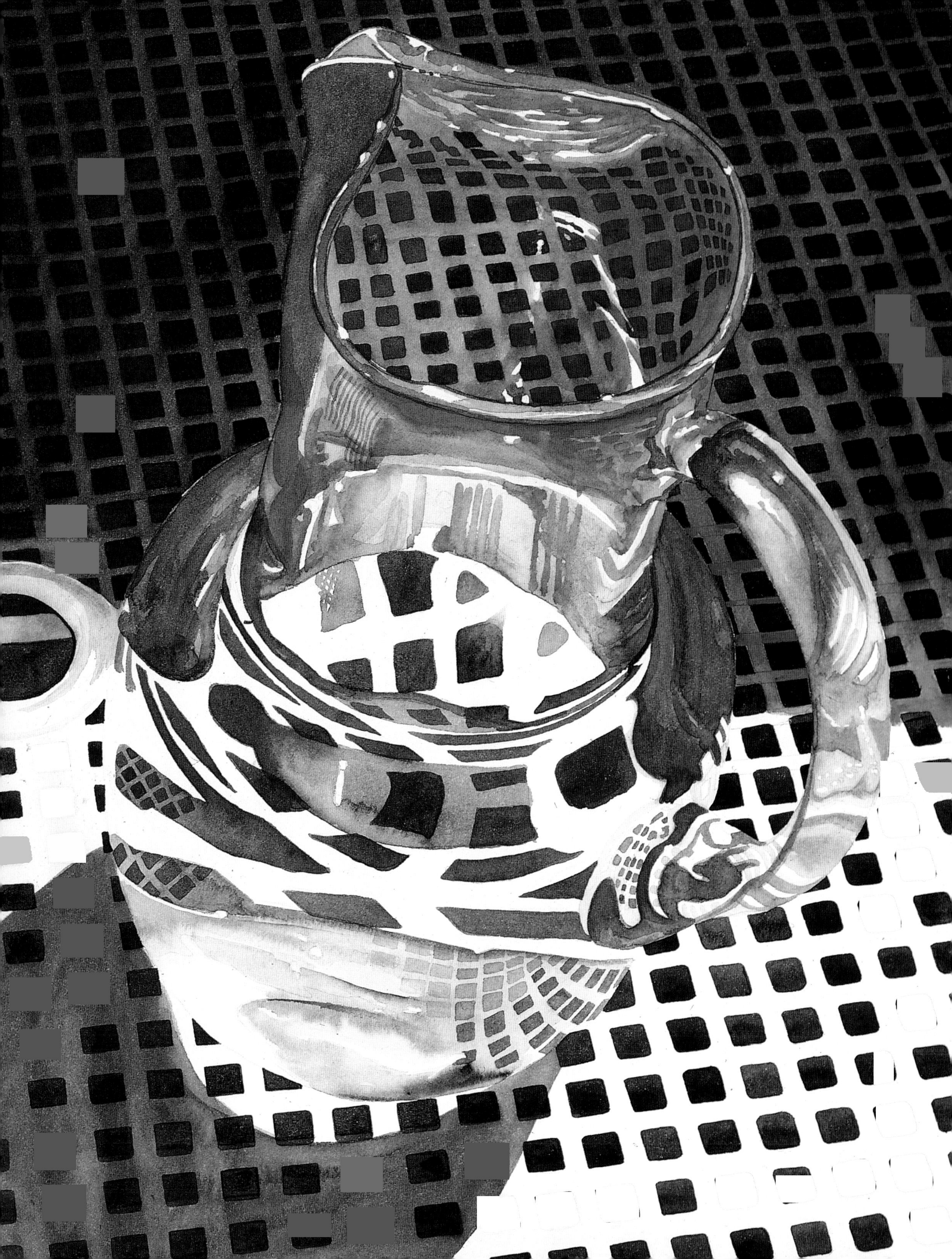

CREATE SPARKLING WINDOW-LIT STILL LIFES IN WATERCOLOR

TERI STARKWEATHER

CHAPTER 3

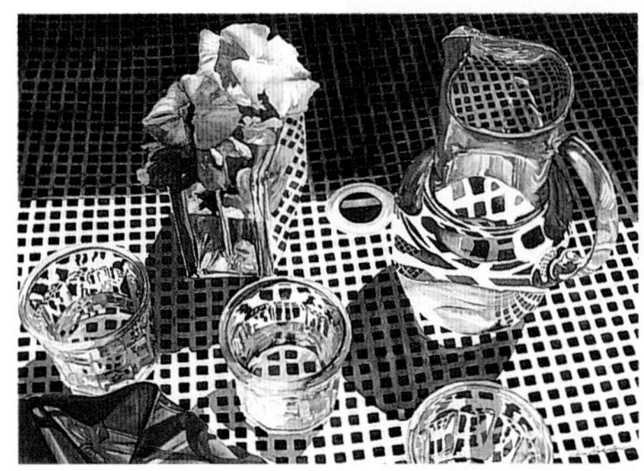

WATER PITCHER
Teri Starkweather, watercolor, 30″ × 40″ (76.2cm × 101.6cm)

I arranged this setup on the patio in the hot midday summer sun. As I played around with the position of the objects, I discovered the wonderful distortion of the grid pattern on the tabletop as seen through the glass objects. I found this exciting, and it gave some complexity to the relaxed and casual mood of the painting.

Teri Starkweather's paintings are based on still life themes she composes and photographs. One of her main objectives is to create dramatic lighting for interest and to set the mood of each painting. Her paintings usually have a mood of celebration or curious whimsy, but they *always* have a fascination with light. She has traditionally painted floral arrangements set up in front of a window, where the flowers and objects were bathed in light, and glass vases and petals were backlit by the sunlight pouring in from the outside. Her most recent work, however, is void of flowers, and consists mainly of transparent objects such as glass bottles and plastic triangles set up where the sunlight shines brightly on them, producing long dramatic shadows and many reflections. She likes to pair the positive life force of light with the fragility and transparency of glass, producing an almost spiritual luminosity as seen on the following pages in the demonstrations of her techniques.

PAINTING GLOWING OBJECTS IN WINDOW LIGHT Watercolor

There are many ways to be creative with art, and specifically with putting light into your paintings. Starkweather plays and experiments with her art the most in her photo sessions. She does her paintings from a reference photo (usually an 8×10), but that reference photo represents several hours of creative camera work.

Starkweather brings together a large number of objects, most of them transparent, and sets up a variety of arrangements in front of a window. She uses only sunlight, and prefers low morning and afternoon light because it streams more directly through the window. This gives her only an hour or two per photo session. During that session, she continually rearranges the setup, adding and subtracting objects and photographing from different angles. She works almost exclusively with backlighting, because it shows off the transparency or translucency of the objects. However, sometimes this backlighting causes foreground detail to be lost in the photograph—an occupational hazard. Reviewing her slides is another creative activity: She selects only one picture per roll of thirty-six to be used for a painting. She projects the slide onto her watercolor paper to do a basic drawing, and then has an 8×10 print made to use for reference.

She uses no masking, preferring to save whites as highlights. Painting methodically and usually completing one object at a time, she studies her photo carefully, making sure to place the lights and shadows correctly to produce the dramatic results she wants.

Starkweather never uses black or white, but keeps the paint as transparent as her still life objects. She uses gradations of colors in the shadows to keep them interesting.

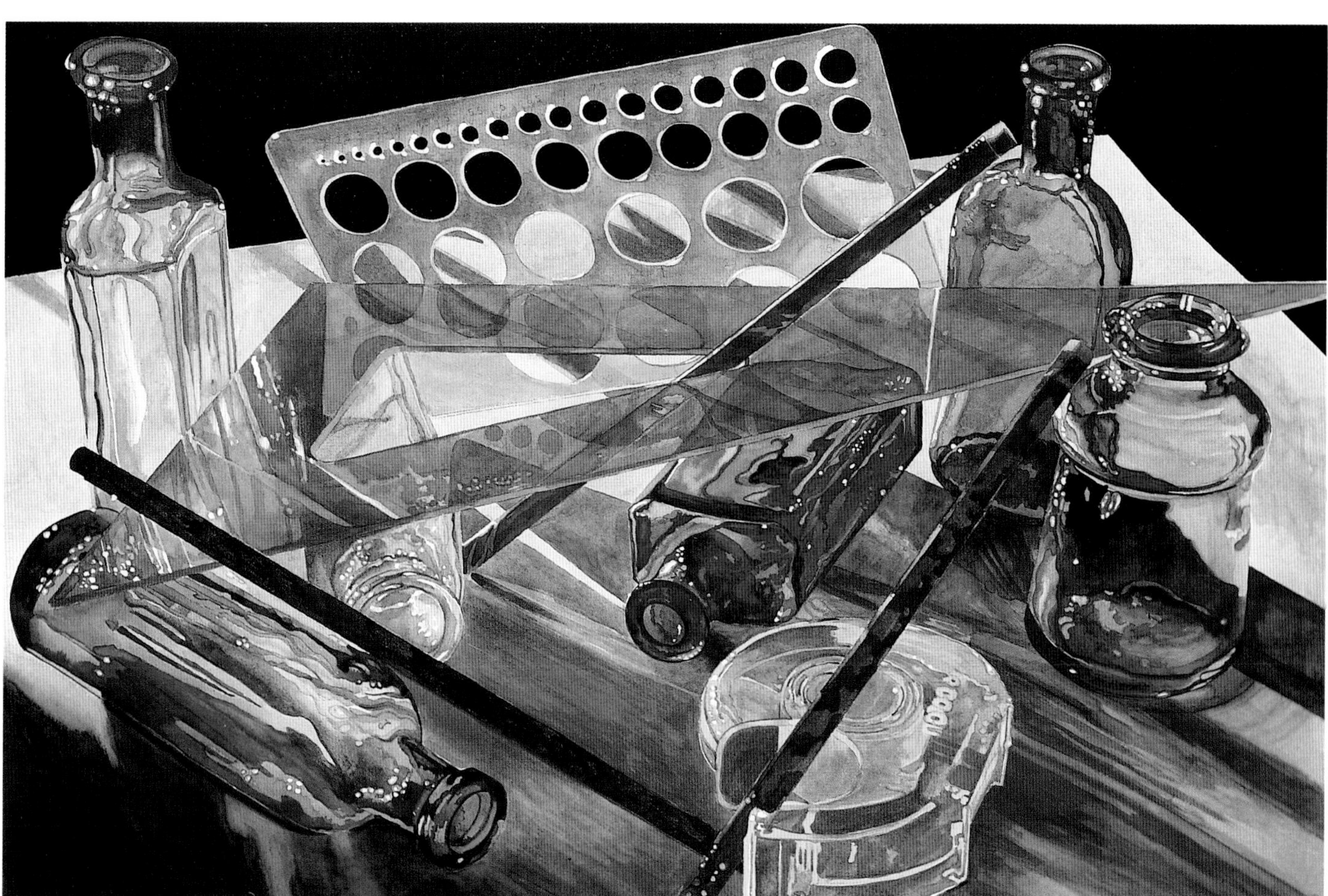

Low Light

I set up this still life in front of a window in the late afternoon sun. The low sun created long, dramatic shadows and colorful reflections. I was looking for a hint of mystery with the dark background, long shadows and fallen objects.

GEOMETRIC ROMANCE
Teri Starkweather, watercolor, 20″ × 30″ (50.8cm × 76.2cm)

opposite

Warm, Glowing Light

The mood in this painting is pure happiness with the midmorning sun pouring in the window, bathing the still life with a warm, glowing light. I portrayed the intensity of the light by painting strong white areas of light in the candy jar and rose petals.

CANDY AND ROSES
Teri Starkweather, acrylic, 40″ × 30″ (101.6cm × 76.2cm)

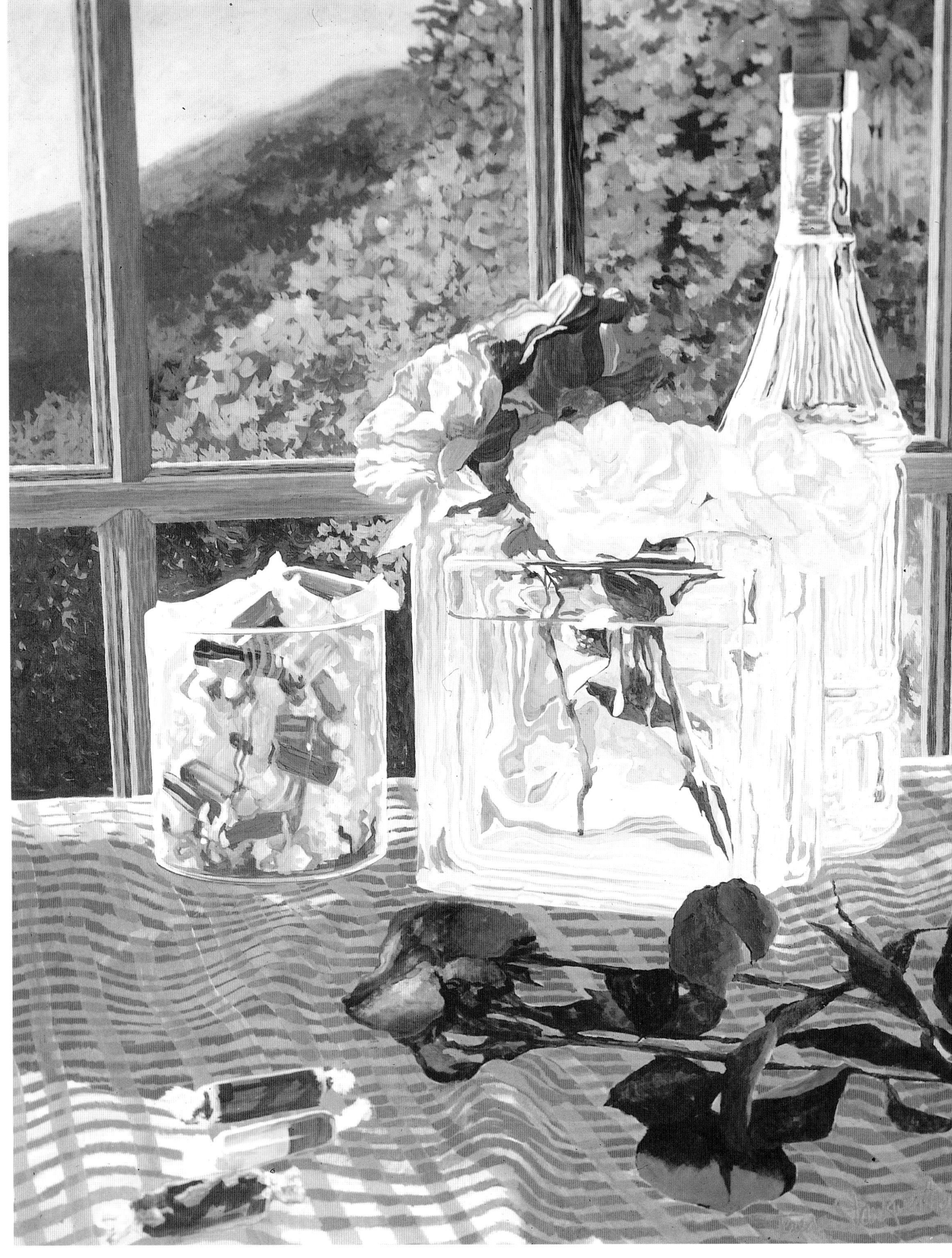

DEMONSTRATION

WINDOW FLORAL WITH DRAMATIC LIGHTS AND DARKS Watercolor

I break my paintings down into small sections, bringing each to completion before going on to the next section. I observe the reference photo carefully, using a large variety of colors in each flower or object. When adding new colors I am sensitive to cool/warm contrasts, and will often drop a new color into a wet wash to achieve variations in color.

Before painting, spray water on all the paints in your palette so they become liquid and are ready to use. Then take the colors for the first object (here, rose petals) and make a wash in the center of that section with these colors separated but running together in places. Because this technique is much the same in each section of my paintings, what follows are highlights of the development of *Sunshine and Roses*. You can paint most of the details in the painting with a no. 4 watercolor brush.

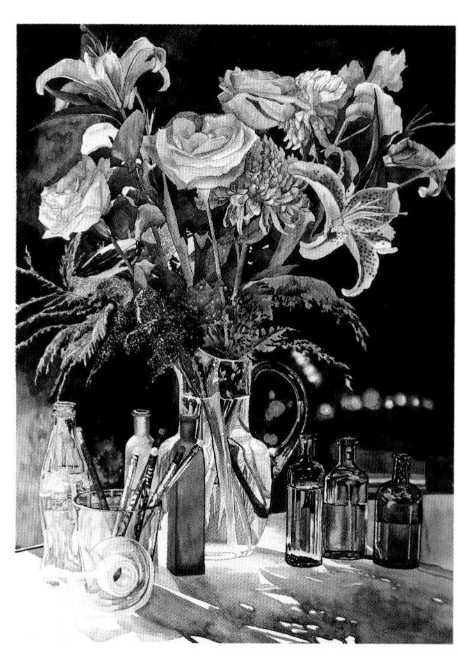

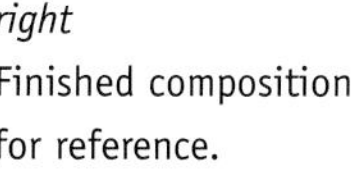

right
Finished composition for reference.

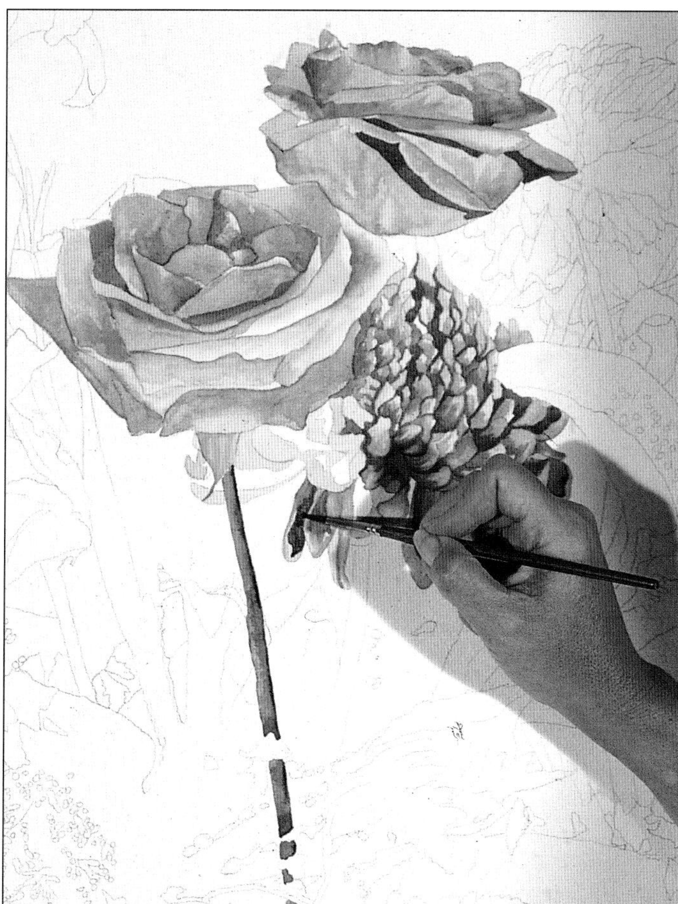

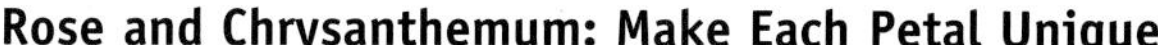

Rose and Chrysanthemum: Make Each Petal Unique
After completing a basic drawing, use Permanent Rose, Rose Madder, Cobalt Blue, Aureolin, Burnt Sienna, Cadmium Red and Sepia to paint the rose petals. Fill in each petal with a light wash first; go back later and add darks. Try to make each petal a distinct value and hue so it stands out from the neighboring petals. Paint the mum with the first four colors listed above plus Cobalt Violet.

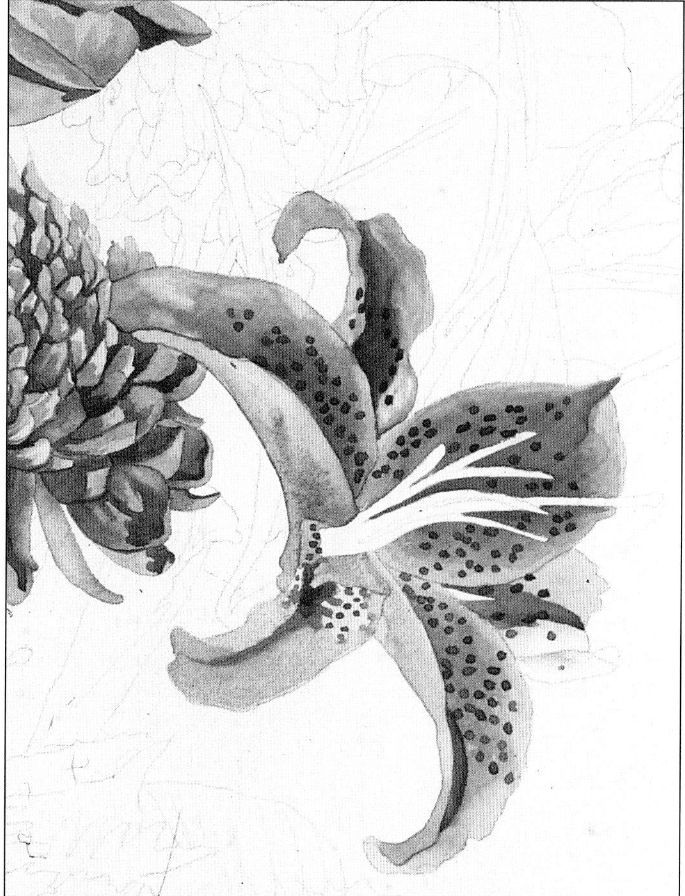

The Stargazer: Let Washes Dry for Hard Edges
After painting all the petals of the stargazer, leave the stamens paper white so their edges remain crisp and separate. Once the petals dry, paint the center stamens with Sap Green, Aureolin and Cadmium Yellow.

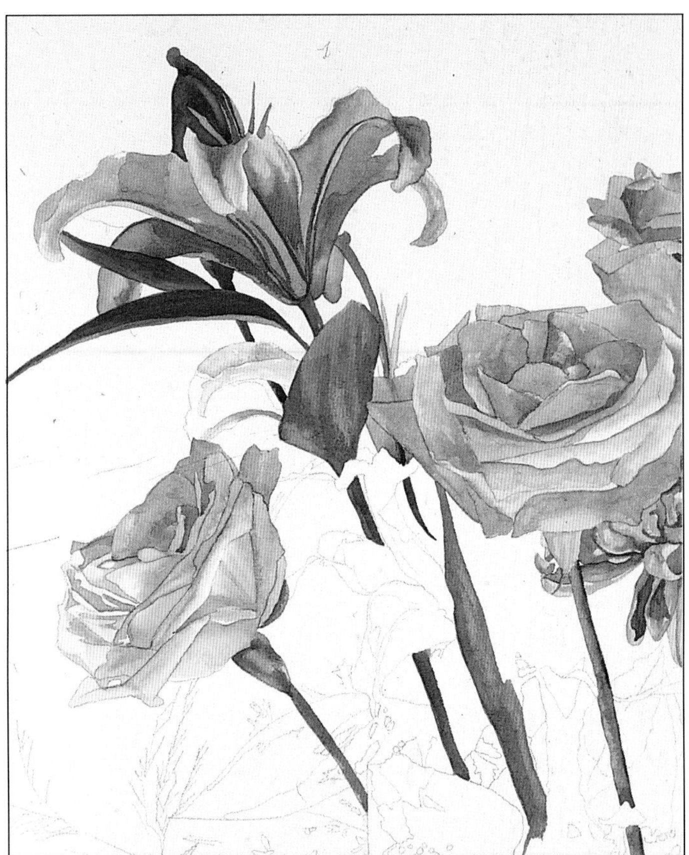

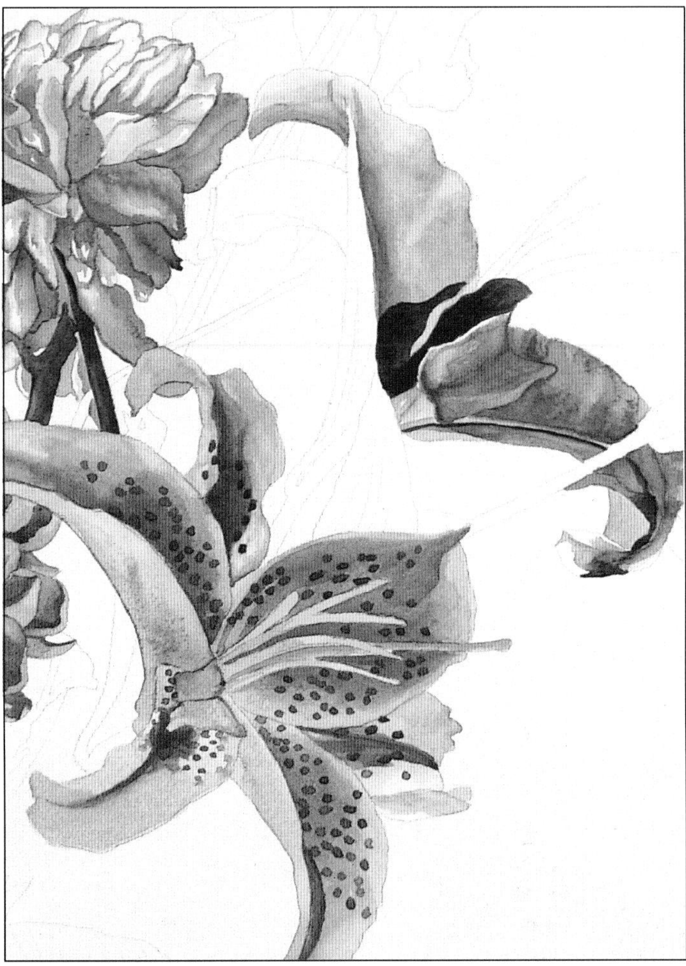

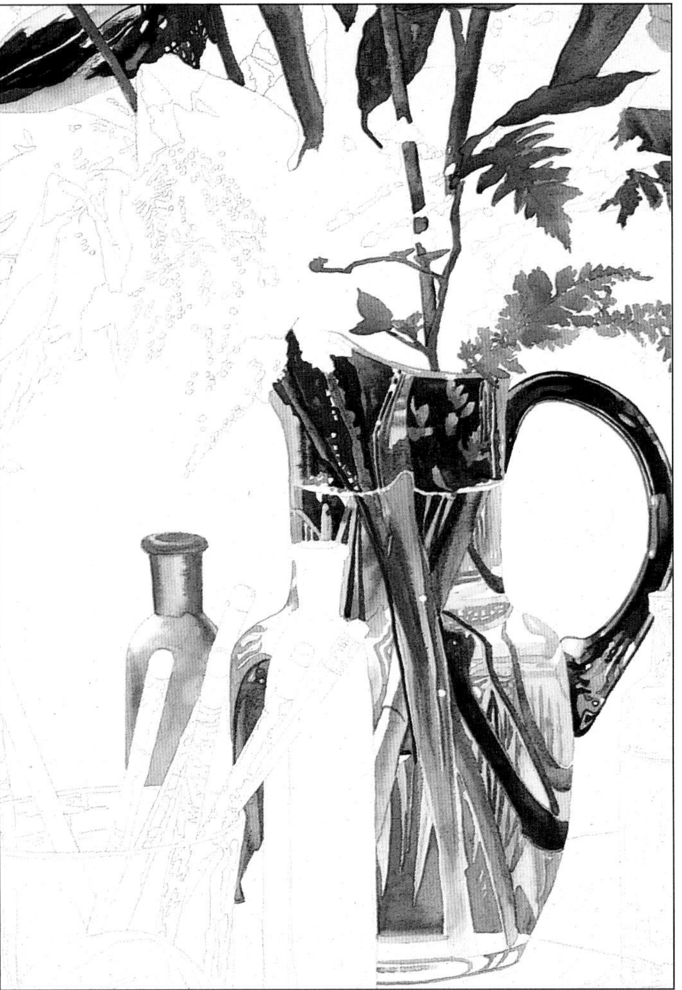

above, left

Left Stargazer and Rose: Contrast Warms and Cools

The underside of this stargazer should look cool in comparison to the top side of the other flowers. The rose on the left has a warmer glow than the others because the sun's reflection bounces on it from the objects below. To achieve this effect use Cadmium Orange and Cadmium Yellow along with some of the other rose colors. Use Cobalt Blue for shading.

above, right

Background Flowers: Use Cool Complements

The chrysanthemum in the back of the bouquet looked gray in the original photo, but a cool blue-green (Cobalt Blue and Viridian) would work better to liven up the pinks of the main flowers, because red and green are complements. Give the petals of this turned-away stargazer dramatic shading by glazing the same blue-green mixture used in the chrysanthemum over the Permanent Rose petals.

left

Leaves and Stems: Use Lots of Colors and Glaze for Darks

Paint in the leaves and stems using Sap Green, Viridian, Aureolin, Yellow Ochre, Cobalt Green, Cadmium Yellow and Payne's Gray. Vary the greens so that each has a slightly different hue. Use the wet-into-wet technique to add darks so colors mingle. Glaze the main stem with Sepia and Antwerp Blue for a rich, dark brown.

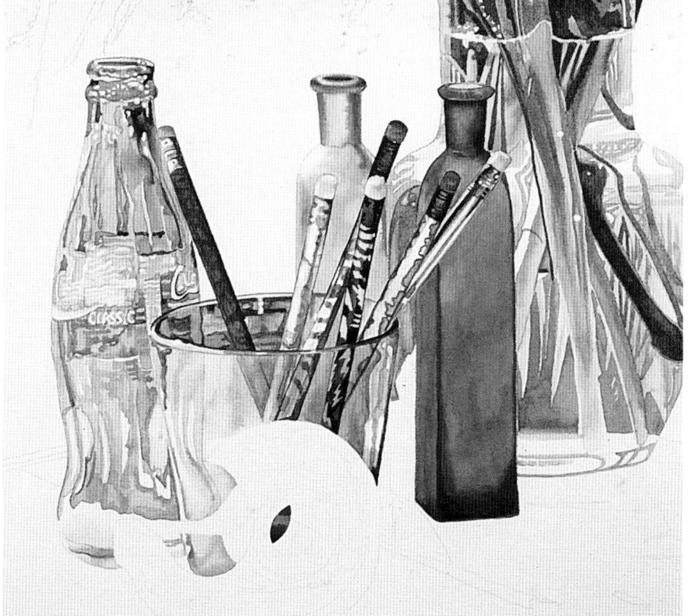

Bottles and Pencils: Observe Your Reference Carefully

Complete the glass objects and pencils, working slowly and carefully and studying your reference (whether live or in a photo) for all the intricate light and dark shapes that, when rendered faithfully, create the illusion of glass or other textures. Use a lot of colors (I used at least eighteen) in a careful wet-into-wet blending technique.

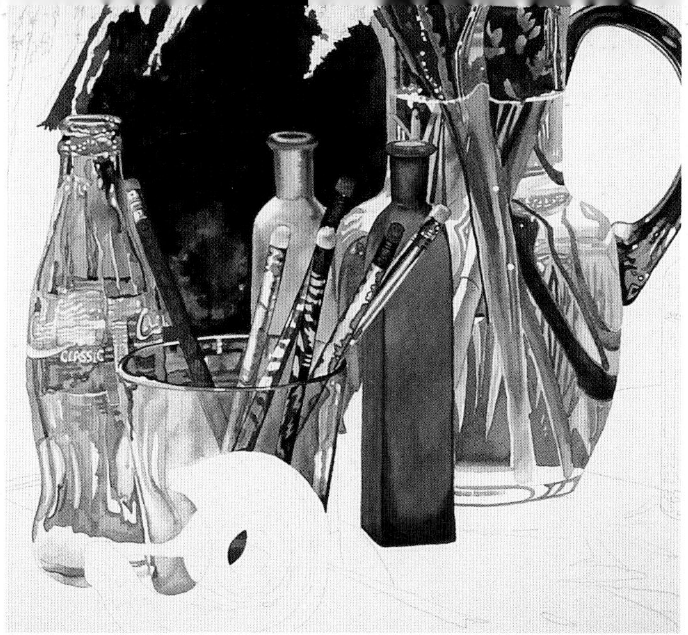

Begin the Background: Paint Colorful Blacks

Wet the background paper with a clean brush. Fill in the background with several coats of darks, using Sepia, Mauve, Prussian Blue, Sap Green and Payne's Gray.

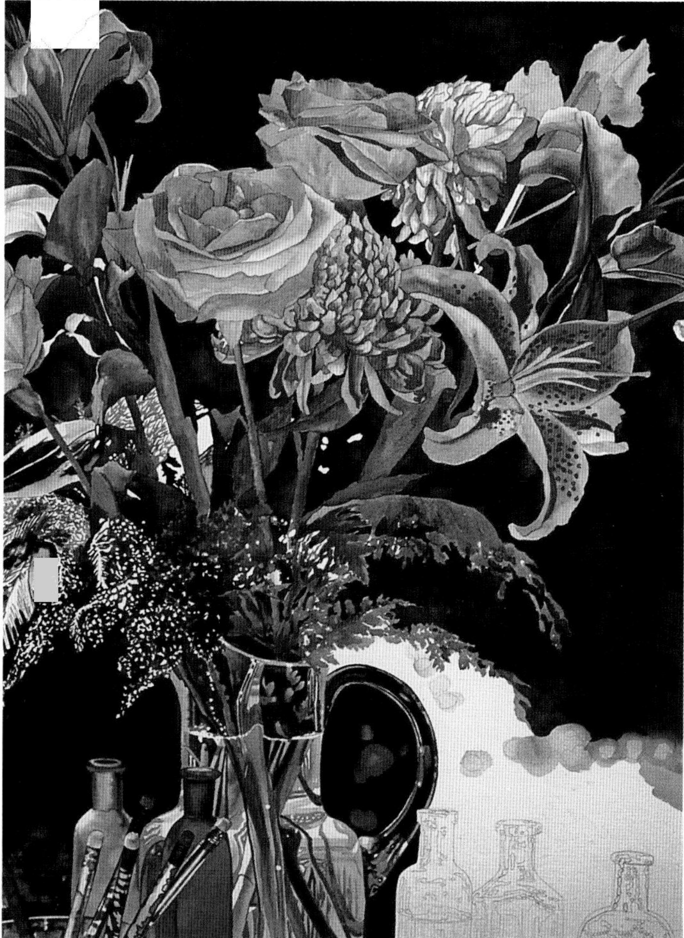

Continue the Background: Work Fast and Wet

Use a no. 10 brush in the large areas and work fast over the background so the colors blend. Stop when you get to the circular highlights. Paint these with a light wash of Payne's Gray, letting the edges feather out with the wet-into-wet technique.

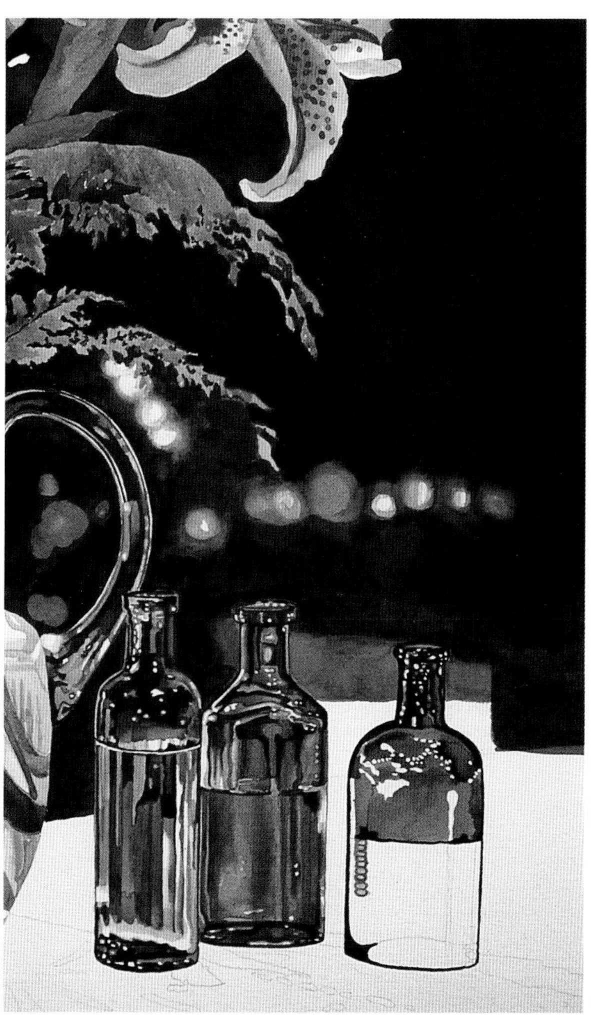

Bottles on the Right: Leave Reflective Stripe

When finishing the bottles, leave one or more white vertical stripes along the sides to show the light reflecting off the glass. Observe the lights and darks carefully and add darks on the bottoms of the bottles.

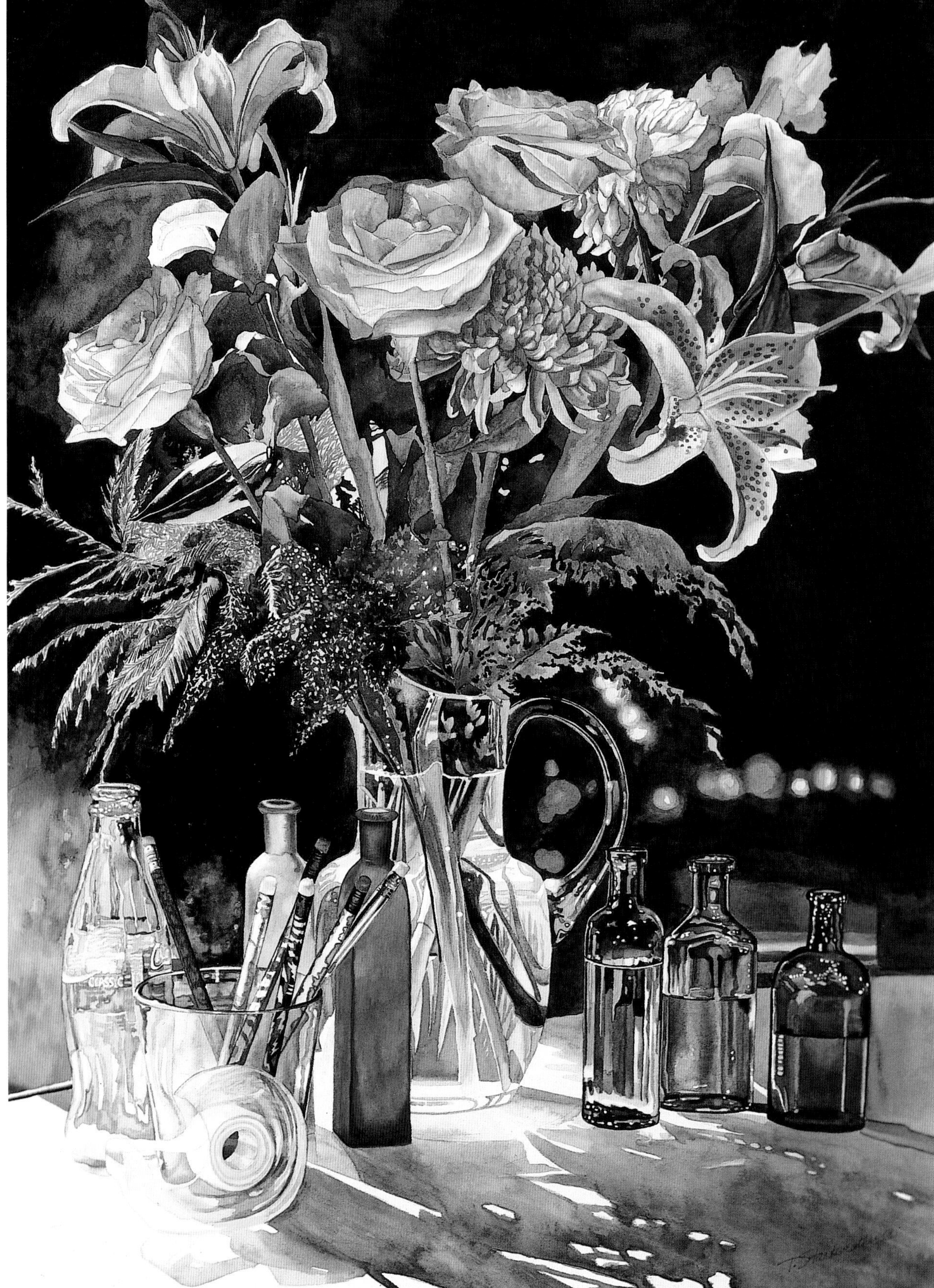

Final Touches

To mix the grays for the foreground shadow, use Cobalt Blue and Cadmium Orange. Add some Payne's Gray in areas, add Aureolin in others, and in some spots just paint pure Cobalt Blue. Paint the whole shadow with a wet-into-wet technique to blend the various hues. Be sure to leave the bright white of the paper directly underneath the pitcher to indicate the light passing through the glass. Then glaze the area with a light Aureolin wash for a warm glow. Add the tape dispenser, using Cadmium Yellow and Yellow Ochre for the bright yellows, and greens for the interior.

SUNSHINE AND ROSES
Teri Starkweather, watercolor, 40" × 30" (101.6cm × 76.2cm)

GALLERY

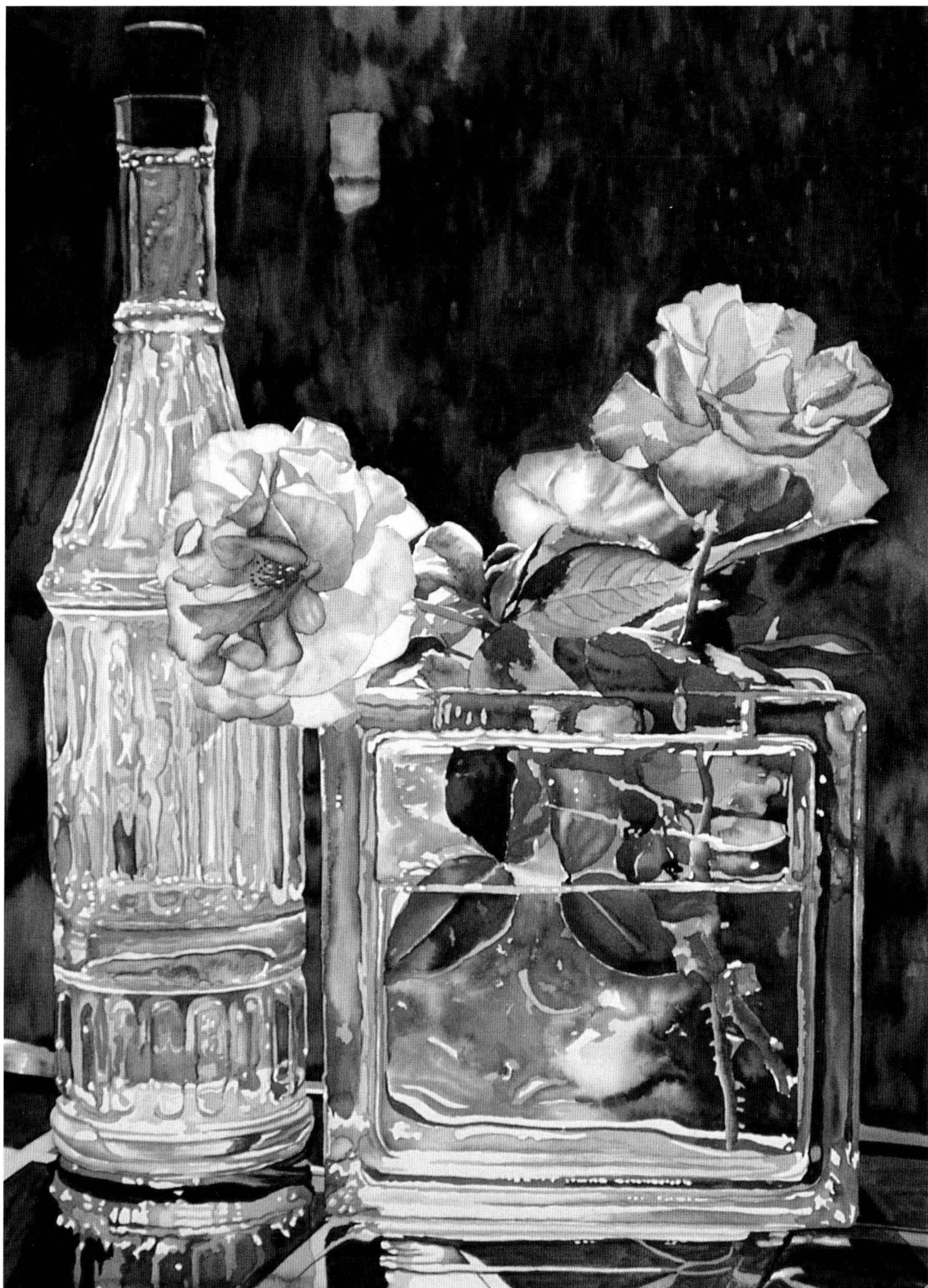

WINDOW ARRANGEMENT
Teri Starkweather, watercolor, 40″ × 30″ (101.6cm × 76.2cm)

These glass objects were sitting on the kitchen window ledge in the morning sun. I was struck by the way the rose petals were merrily backlit by the sunlight. The light pastel washes in the bottle contrast pleasantly with the dark green background. The light pink rose is the center of interest, so I accentuated the light values in the rose and played up the sensuous curves of the pink center petals.

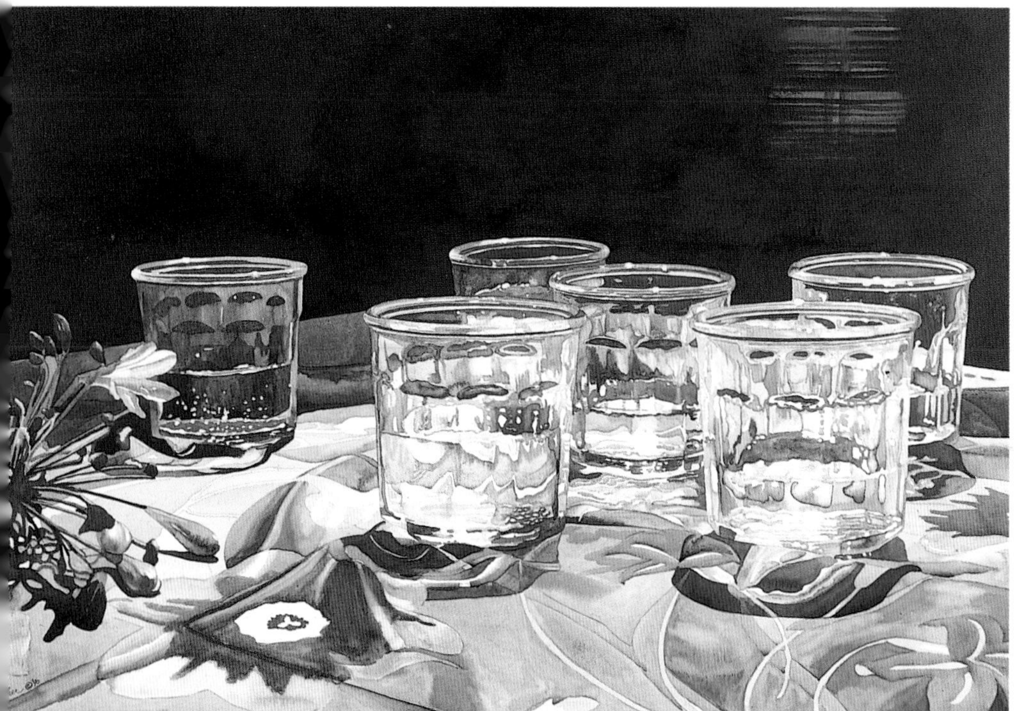

Key

OBSERVE LIGHT'S INTERACTION WITH OBJECTS

Light cannot truly be seen unless it reacts with objects, whether the surface of the moon or transparent and translucent objects closer at hand. To make objects look "real" in a painting, study the light and dark shapes and patterns and the bright highlights created by light passing through and bouncing off these surfaces.

The mood of this painting is casual and fun, with energy created by the strong contrasts of light. I set up the water glasses outside in the summer sun with a colorful silk scarf underneath. The interplay of the glistening light within the water and the reflections of the color from the scarf were compelling against the almost opaque dark of the background.

FULL OF LIGHT
Teri Starkweather, watercolor, 30" × 40" (76.2cm × 101.6cm)

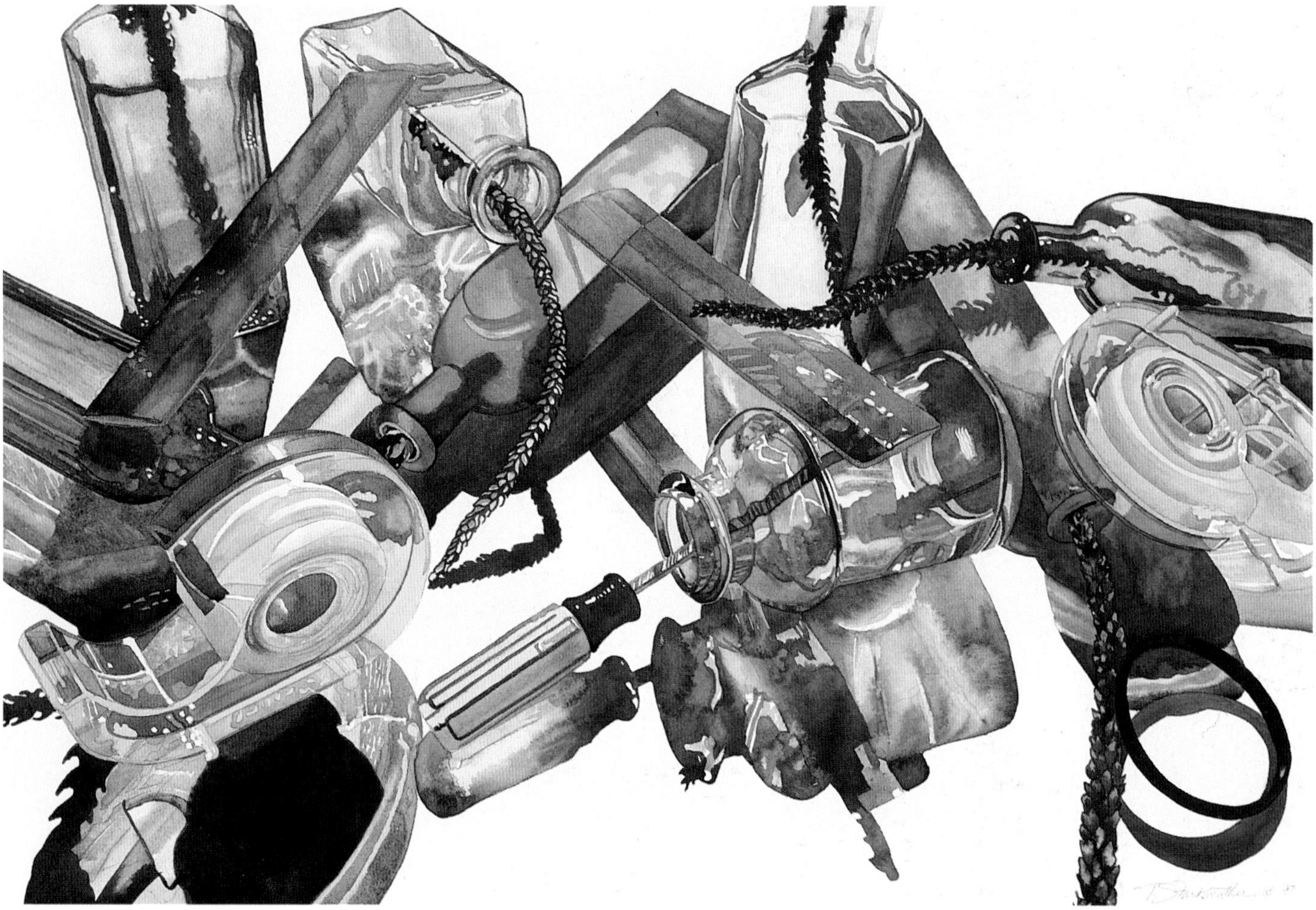

This playful painting is full of surprises from the color, transparency, shadows and organic plant forms. I was looking for an abstract quality with a strong, direct light source. I set up the objects outside on white paper. The bright sun cast long, colorful shadows, which are really half shadow and half filtered light. I have found the sun to be the greatest source of light for playing with color and transparency.

ACCIDENTAL LOVE
Teri Starkweather, watercolor, 18" × 26" (45.7cm × 66cm)

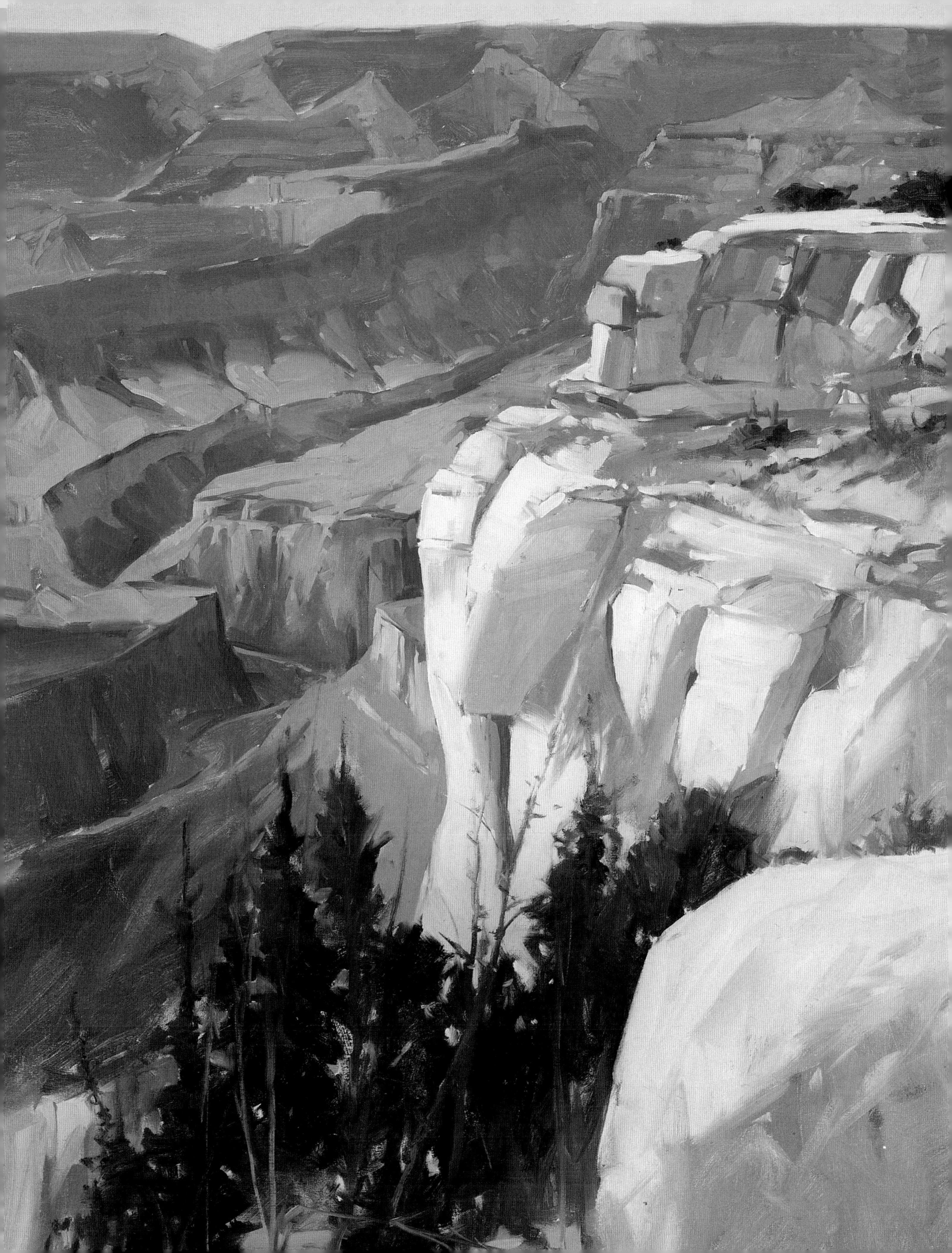

BOLDLY EXPRESS THE MOOD OF THE MOMENT IN

OILS

HOWARD CARR

CHAPTER

4

"Nothing inspires me more than light," says Howard Carr. That could mean any kind of light on any object or scene; Carr doesn't specialize. Capturing the effect of light is what it's all about—thus creating a mood people can relate to. In his paintings this does not always mean dramatic, bright contrast; it could just as well mean a dull fog across a valley. Carr tries to study the hidden colors and values present in nature (and may add a few from his own imagination), but rather than doing that in a complex way, he tries to present the color and mood simply by focusing on the important parts of the painting: the essence of the light and color. One of his favorite sayings (and one borne out by his paintings) is, "The main thing is to make the main thing the main thing." Light!

His colors may not be *copied* from nature, but they are almost always *inspired* by nature. Carr often softens a harsh lighting situation or adds some intensity of color. These decisions are based on the mood Carr wants to elicit in his painting. His subjects range from vast Western landscapes to suburban scenes to flower still lifes in natural light. In the following demonstrations, Carr guides you through the techniques he uses to express mood. His thick, confident brushstrokes (with large brushes) make for passionate and spontaneous paintings.

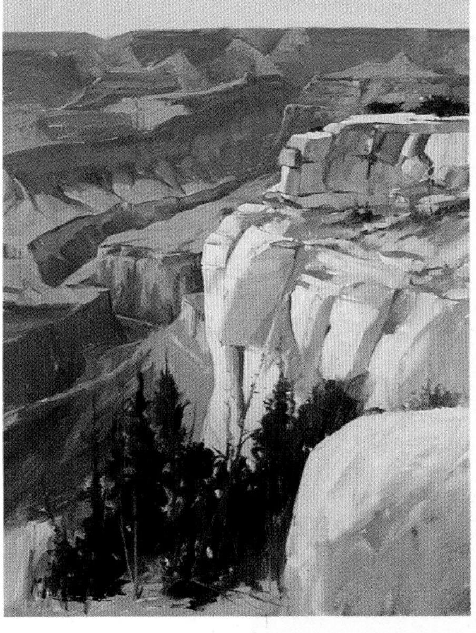

VALLEY BELOW
Howard Carr, oil,
36" × 24"
(91.4cm × 61cm)

This was painted from a forty-five-minute oil sketch done on location and a couple of photos shot at the scene. Photos alone would not have given me the essence and mood my small oil sketch provided, treating the foreground cliffs with hard-edged warm tones and the distant canyon with cooler colors and softer edges. I went through a tube of Viridian on this one.

IMPORTANT STEPS BEFORE YOU PICK UP YOUR BRUSH

1 Get Excited
You need to be fired up about what you paint. It's hard to do a nice painting if you're only doing it to pass the time. If you're excited, the person viewing your work should think, "It looks like you had fun painting this."

2 Develop a Plan
Once you're excited about a subject, develop a plan. Ask yourself:

- What mood do I want to convey?
- How will I treat the light to express that mood?
- Are there any areas in this subject I want to exclude or be sure to include?
- Will my center of interest be subtle, punchy, obvious or not?
- Do I want a looser, impressionistic style, or would this subject look better with a tighter, more realistic approach?

3 Visualize
Visualize the subject you are about to paint as a completed piece of art. At different stages of the project, visualize how that portion might look completed the way you would like to see it.

4 Set the Mood
What is the mood? Your lighting and color scheme have everything to do with the painting's mood. Lots of intense colors throughout may set the painting in a joyful, alive, even frenzied mood; a painting with subtle lighting and a dominant darker, grayer color scheme may provoke a somber or introspective mood.

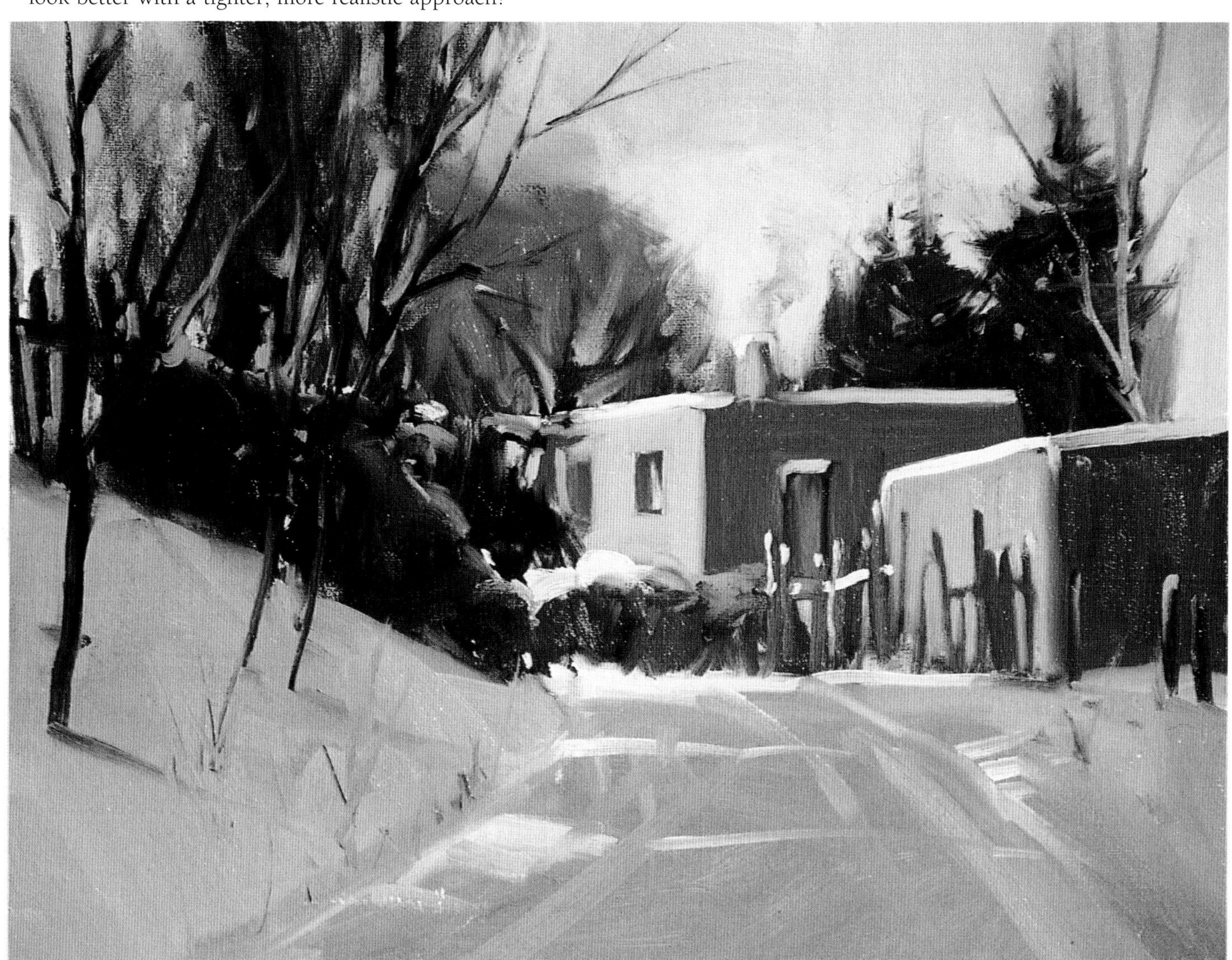

Warming Up a Cool Scene
You want to set the mood for a cold winter scene. Do you want it to look icy and foreboding, or bracing and fun? I prefer to warm up a winter painting by adding just enough warm color to my palette of mostly cool colors to give an inviting sense of warmth, yet not hot enough to melt the snow.

AROUND THE CORNER
Howard Carr, oil, 30" × 24" (76.2cm × 61cm)

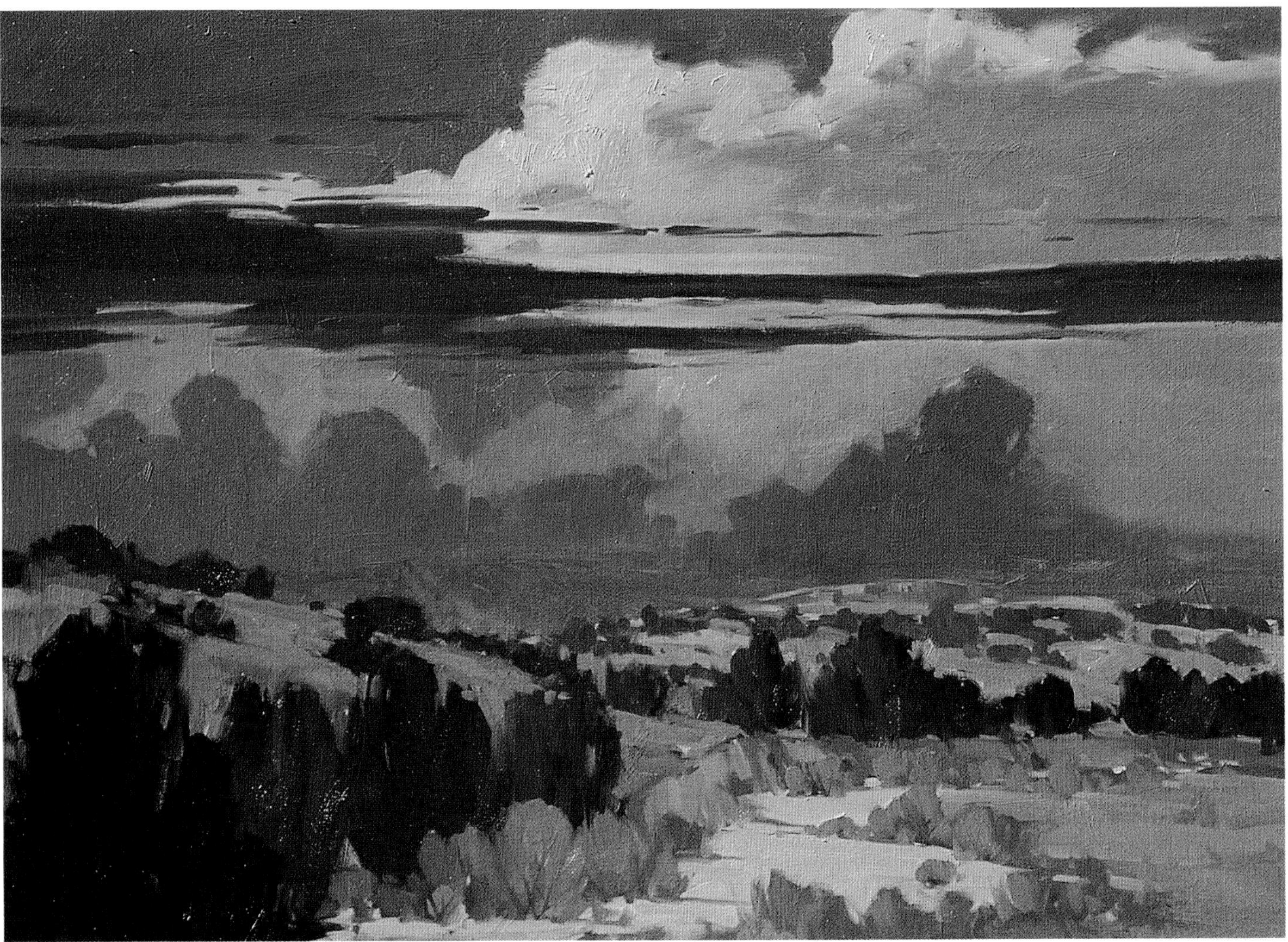

Use Hard and Soft Brushstrokes to Set the Mood

In *Storm's Over* I wanted to give the feeling of moving shadows and changing light. For this I used soft, wispy brushwork, substituting my fingers for brushes in the upper clouds to convey movement. Hard, more deliberate brushstrokes were used for the lower and closer cloud formations.

STORM'S OVER
Howard Carr, oil, 30"×24" (76.2cm×61cm)

HOWARD CARR'S BASIC PAINTING TECHNIQUE

1 Use a paper towel to wet your canvas with mineral spirits.

2 While the canvas is wet, wipe on some of the colors you will be using later in the areas where those colors will be painted. This will knock out the pure white surface and help with the block-in stage.

3 While the surface is still damp, use a no. 2 or no. 3 filbert bristle brush to line in the subject. Don't worry about exactness, just create a good general outline and compositional placement.

4 Select the dark areas and lay them in first. When painting florals, start with the darker greenery. Try a combination of Sap Green and Ultramarine Blue with a touch of Alizarin Crimson.

5 If you are painting a brightly colored subject, paint in the brightest colors now, painting in big general shapes.

6 Use a fairly large brush for your canvas size. For example, for a 16"×20" (40.6cm×50.8cm) canvas, a no. 6 or no. 7 filbert bristle brush is a good choice for the beginning stages of the painting.

CREATE A WARM, "KITCHENY" MOOD Oil

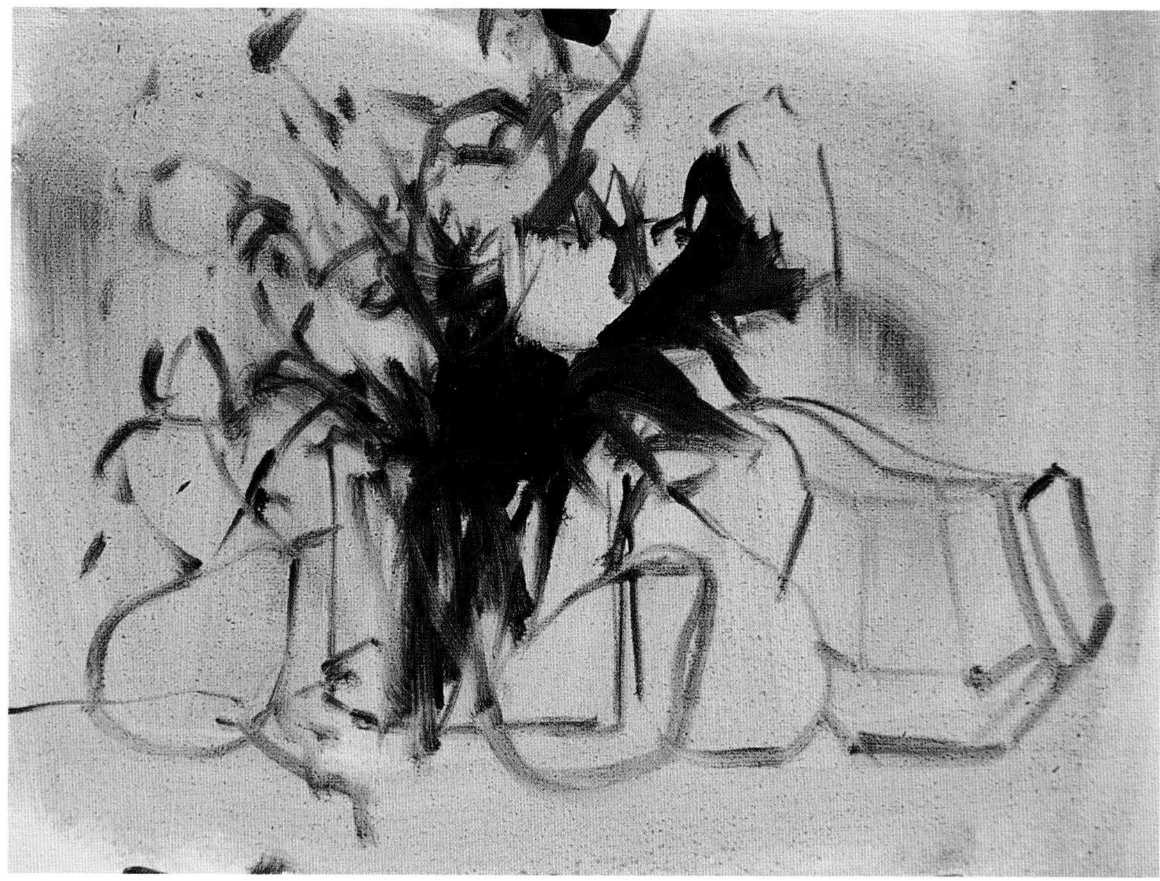

STEP 1

Block-In and Darks

Line in your basic composition on toned canvas. Add the darks in the center.

below

STEP 2

Shadows First

Flower shapes are next, and that's what they are at this stage—shapes only. Starting with the shadow of a white flower, use Light Blue and Medium Magenta, with a touch of orange to mute the violet a bit.

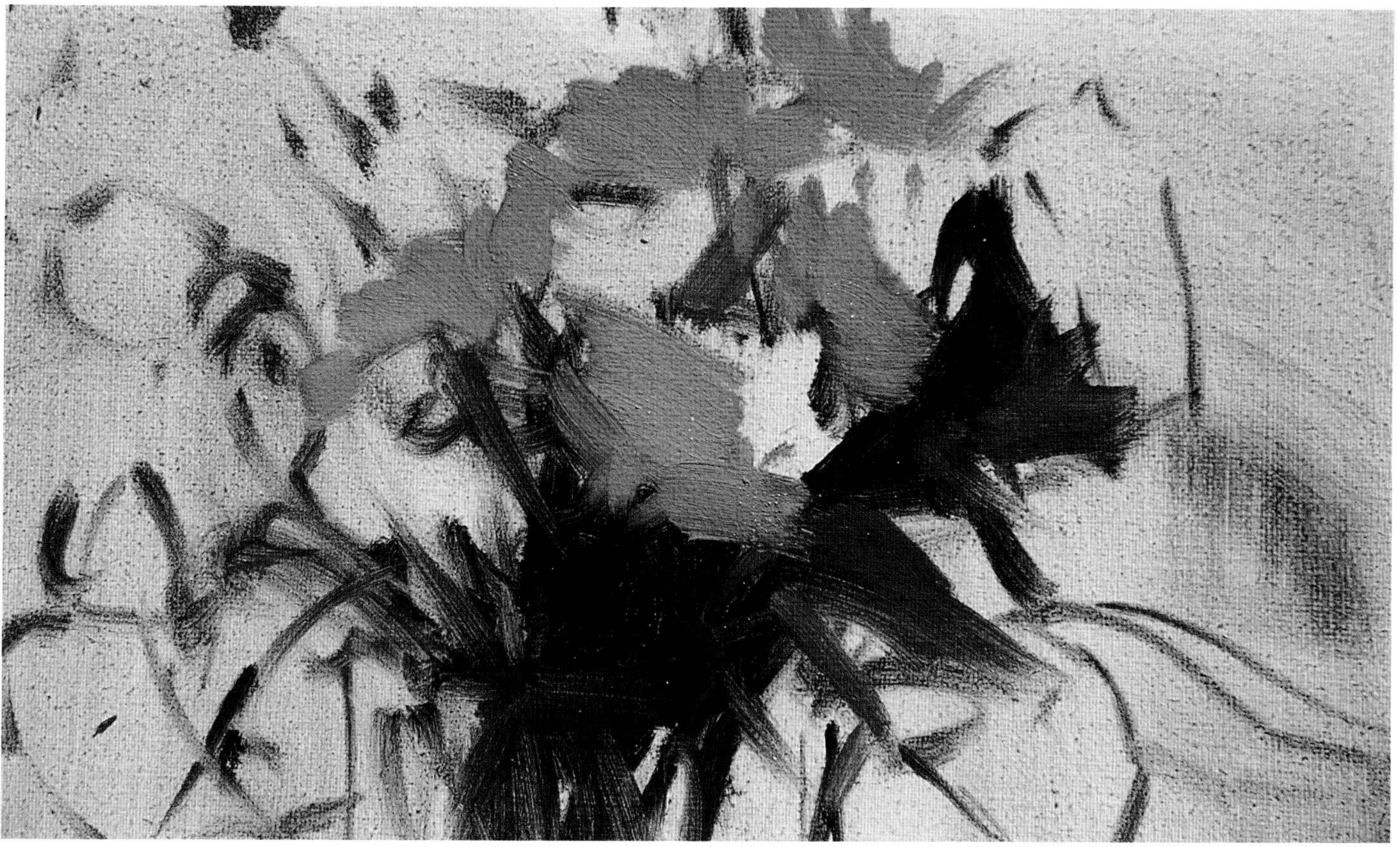

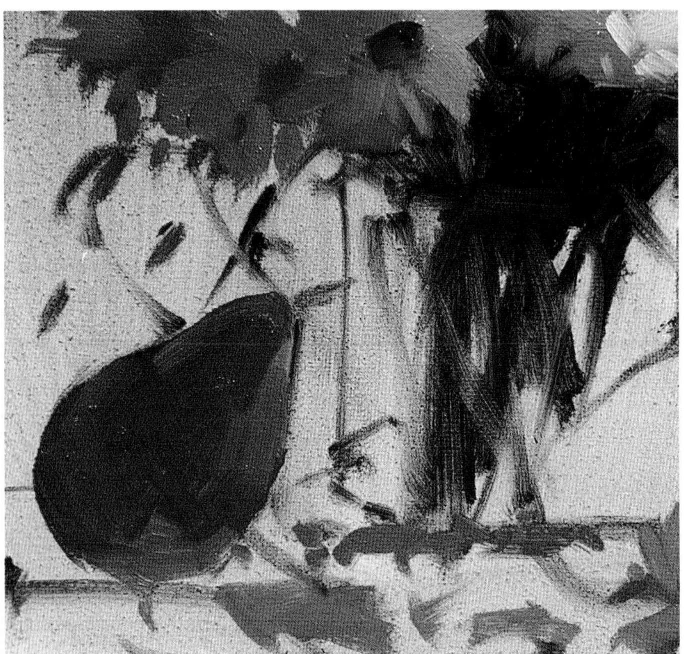

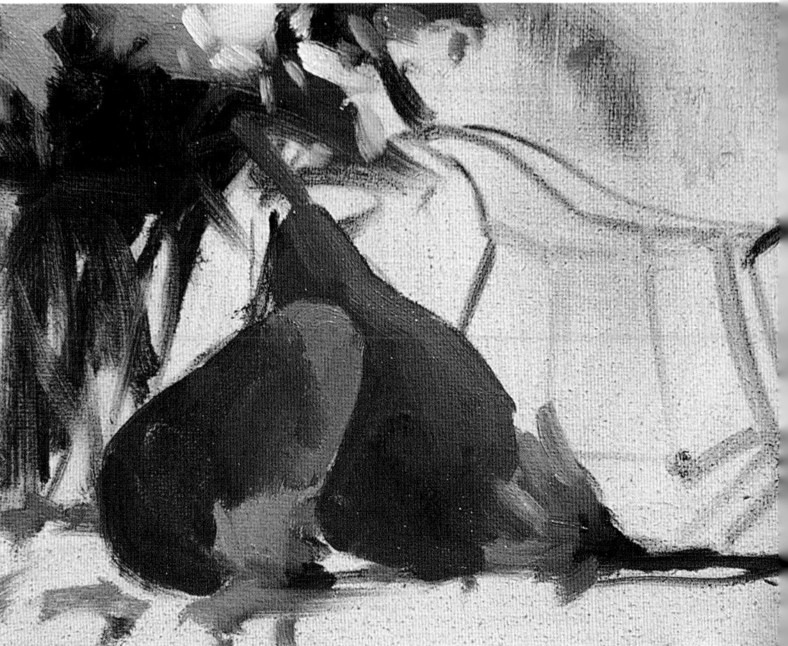

STEP 3

Orange Flowers and the Pear

Mix orange with Alizarin Crimson and a touch of Viridian for a good orange shadow color. Paint the shadow area only first, not the entire flower shape. Then, with a clean brush of Yellow Orange, paint the lighter flower area, blending shadow and light areas together carefully to create a smooth transition between the two. Use some of the orange flower shadow color, plus Ultramarine Blue, to block in the pear's shadow color.

STEP 4

Harmonize the Colors

To model the pears, use the previous color mixtures along with any new colors you have in mind to help blend and harmonize the painting. Finish off the pear shapes with yellow, red-orange, and a touch of Sap Green.

STEP 5

Reflected Light

Block in the white cream pitcher using colors from the pears to show reflected light. This gives great unity to the piece. Amazingly, the finished pitcher will still read as white.

STEP 6

Cast Shadows and Water

Fill in the water in the glass vase using various Viridian mixtures. Keep the color of the water darker near the objects that would block the light, and lighter where the vase is clear of objects, allowing the light to shine through its transparent sides. Put in the cast shadows with minimal brushstrokes. These shadows help anchor the still life objects, keeping them from floating. They also show the direction the light is coming from. Make them darker where the shadow meets the object, and lighter as they extend out.

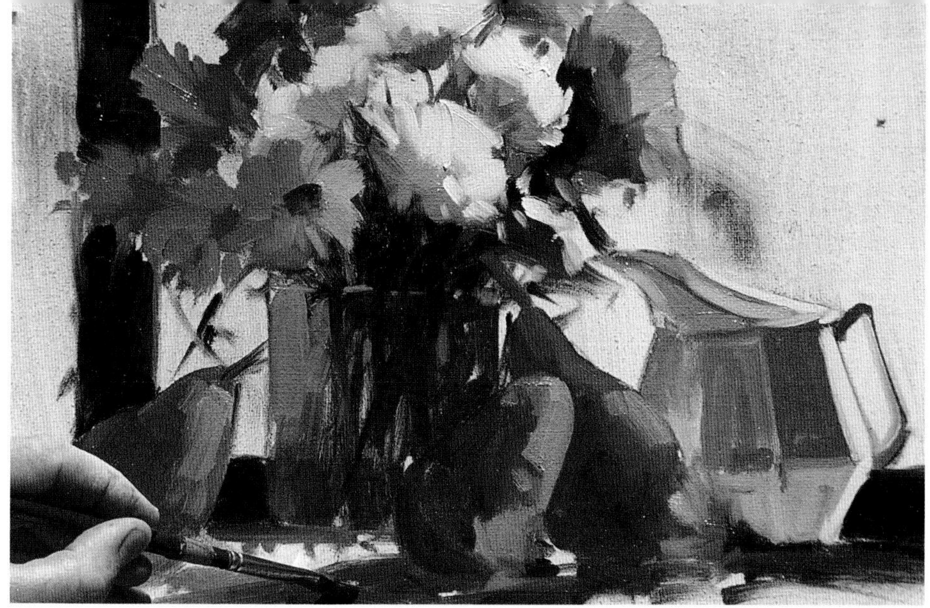

STEP 7

Background

I've chosen a cool gray as my background, keeping the brushwork and colors simple. This helps highlight the colorful flowers on which the light falls. Paint the background right up to the main objects. This gives you an opportunity to refine those shapes (such as the flowers or pitcher) by cutting into them.

STEP 8

Reflections

After the background is painted, add flower reflections to the background. This helps fill in some of the bigger negative areas that may need balance, and it adds warmth.

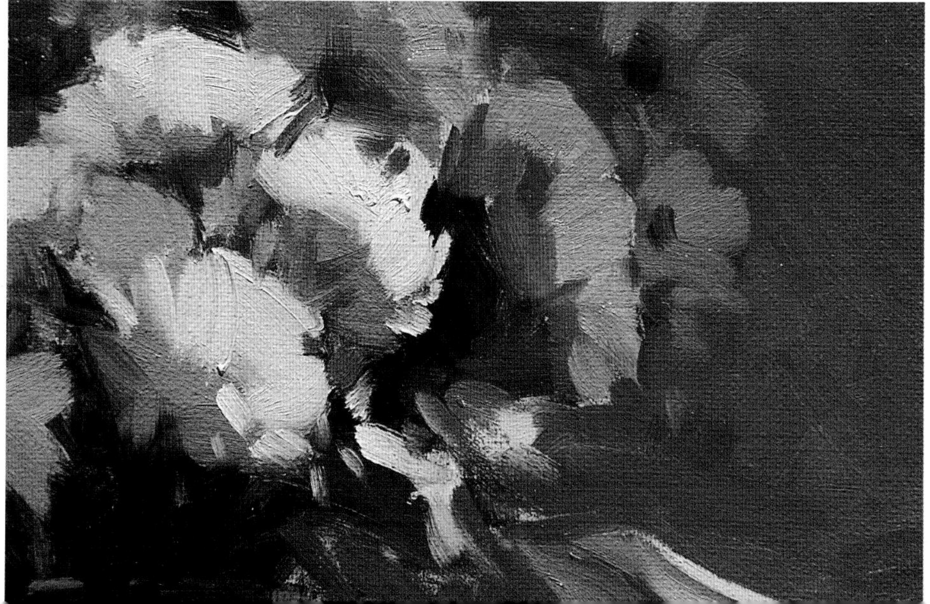

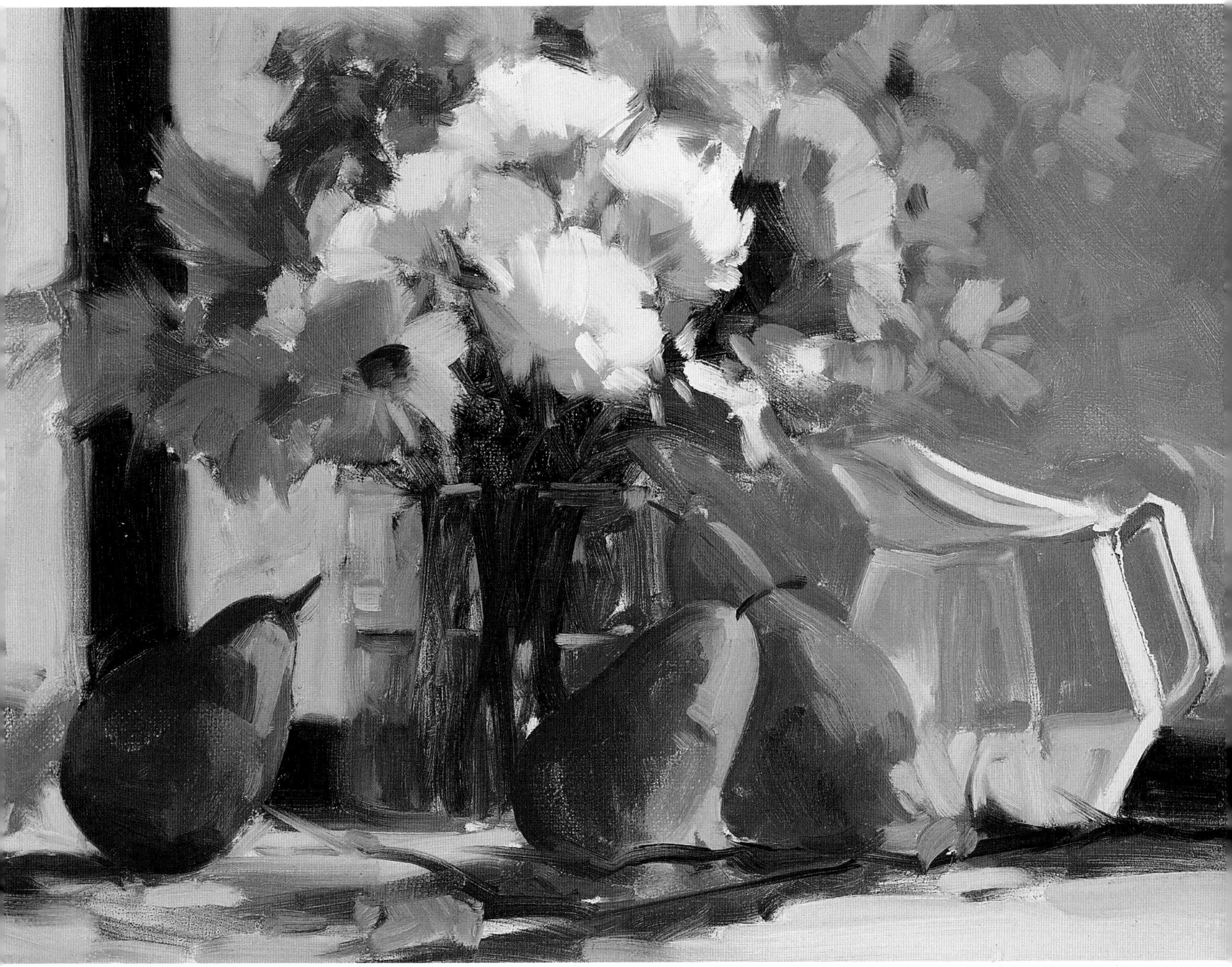

STEP 9

Final Touches

Touch up those areas that are catching more light and need to be brought forward, thus waking the painting up in that area. Don't highlight areas that should remain subordinate.

THREE PEARS
Howard Carr, oil, 16″ × 20″ (40.6cm × 50.8cm)

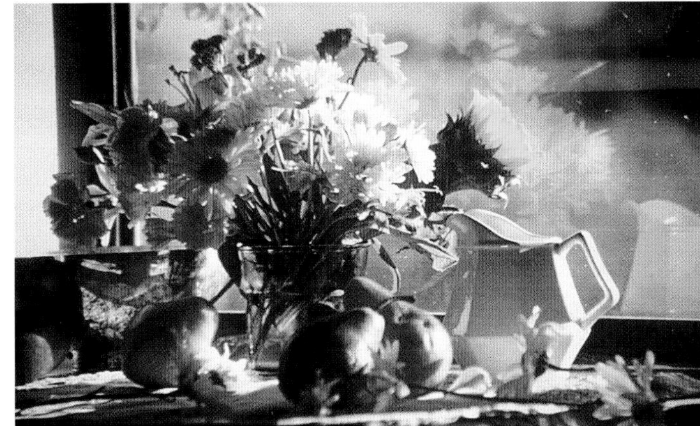

Reference Photo

When you compare this photo to the finished painting you can see that I have warmed up the light considerably. I softened the harsh white light for a cozier mood.

REVEALING TOP LIGHT Oil

It was a late summer morning, with a cool, fast-moving stream coming through a warm, comforting bank. At midday, most of the light comes from above. I decided to equalize the weight of cool and warm colors throughout the piece, relying on the revealing white top light to show those colors clearly.

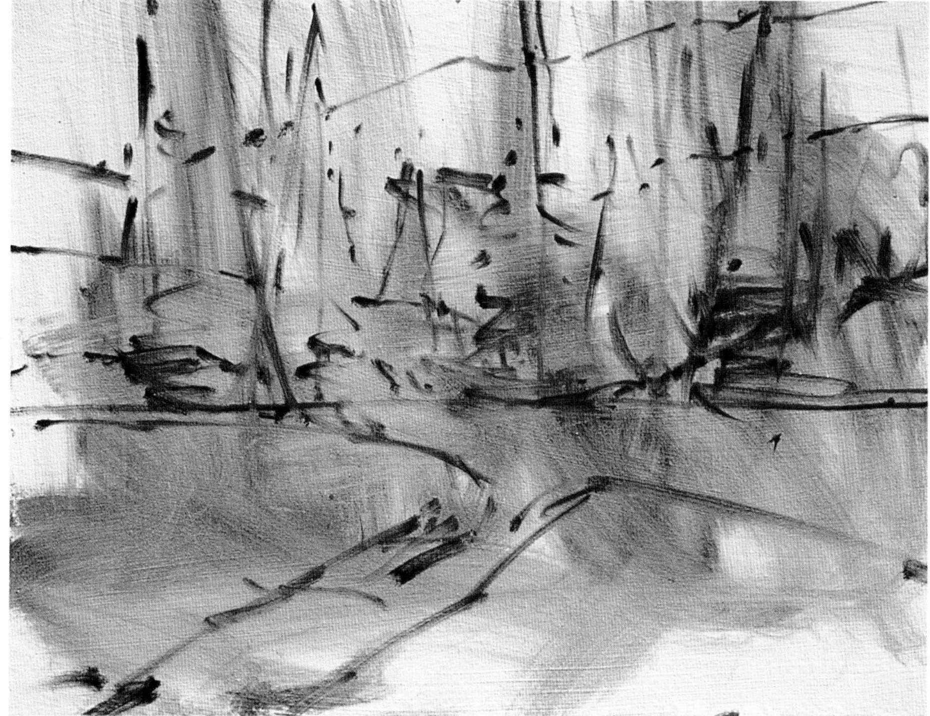

STEP 1

Tone and Sketch

Tone the canvas with a warm tone of Alizarin Crimson and Sap Green. Then, with no. 2 filbert, sketch in the basic big shapes and composition with rough lines.

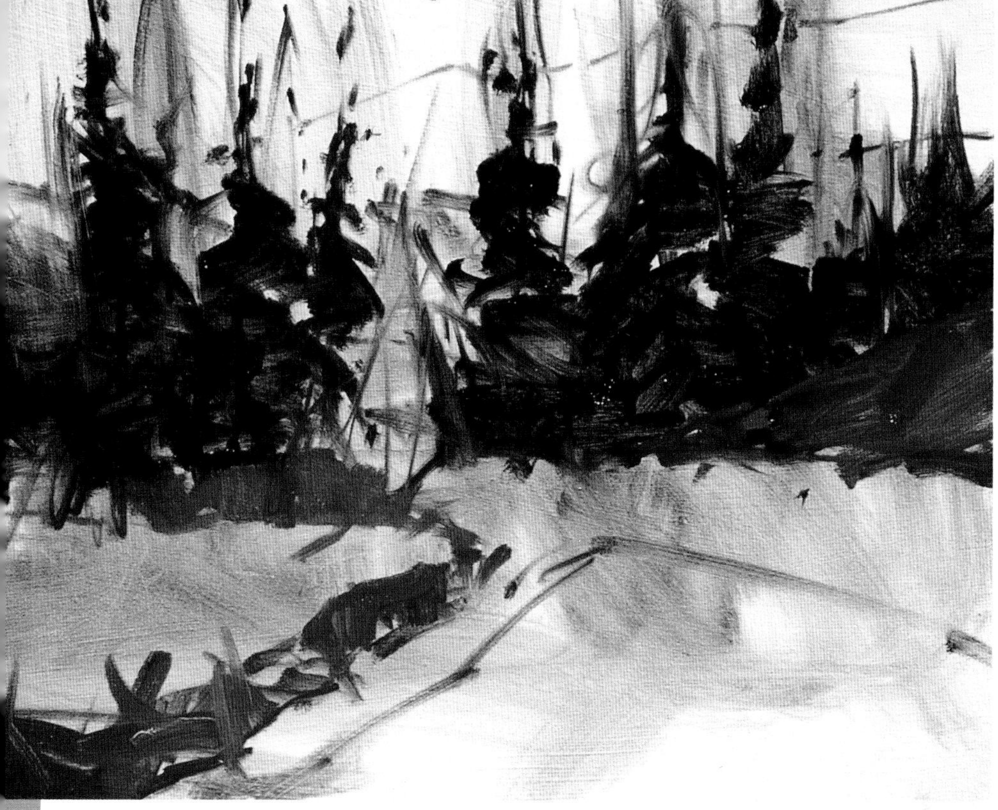

STEP 2

Block in the Darks

Block in the big, simple dark tree areas with Sap Green, Ultramarine Blue and a touch of Alizarin Crimson. Be sure to use a good-size brush for this part: It forces you to keep the block-in areas more silhouetted and simple.

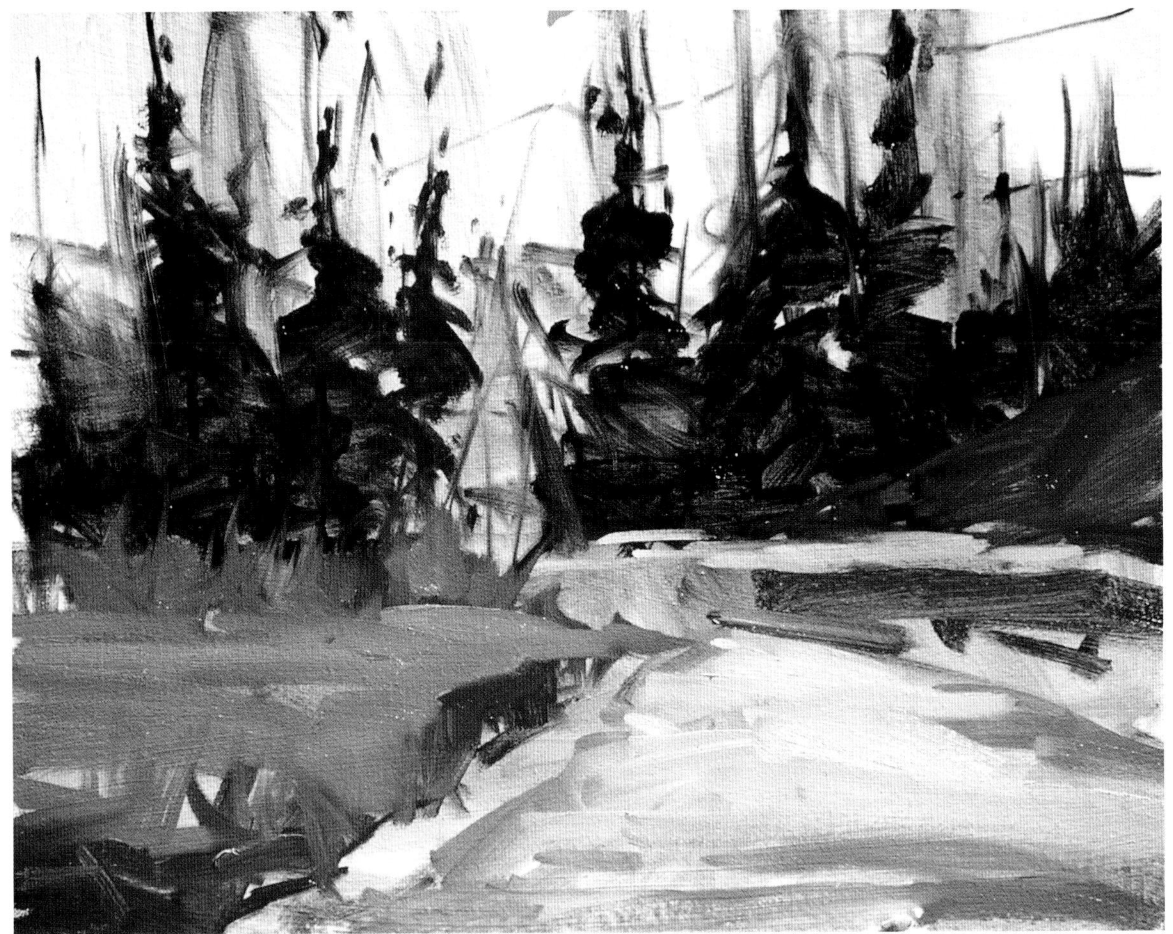

STEP 3

Scrub in the River Bank

Decide on a middle-value, warm-temperature neutral color for the riverbank. I used Yellow Ochre, Cadmium Orange and Alizarin Crimson. Block in this area with loose, fun brushstrokes.

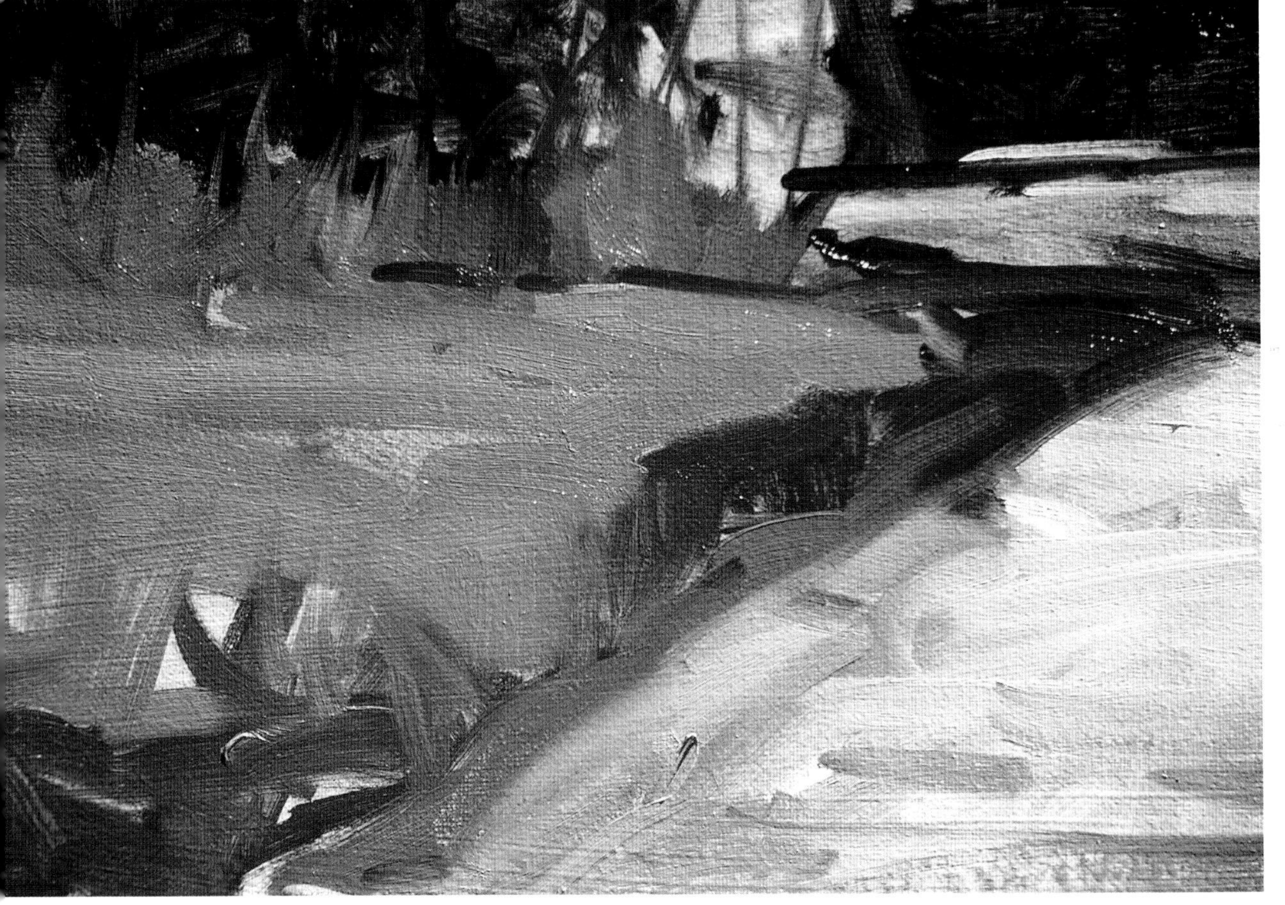

STEP 4

Bright Water

Add a strip of Cerulean Blue to indicate water. Keep the colors bright but relatively light, as the sun shines directly on these areas.

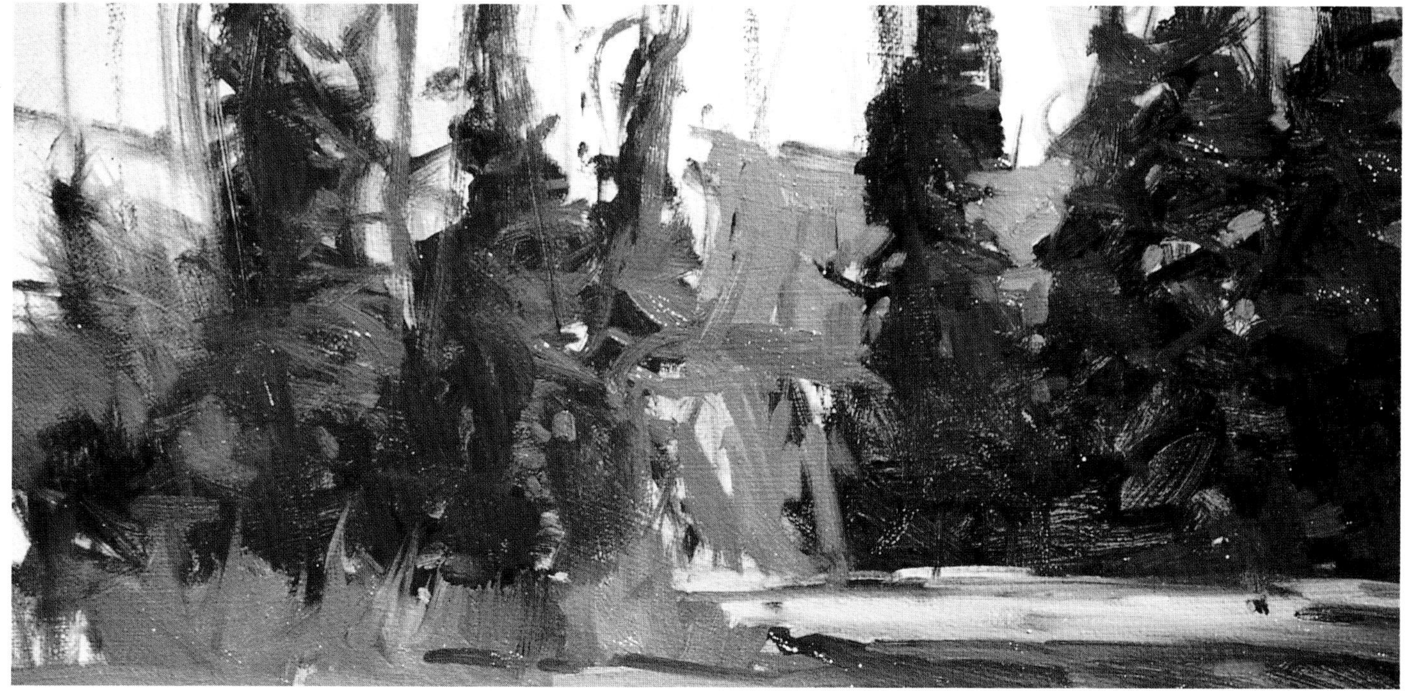

A

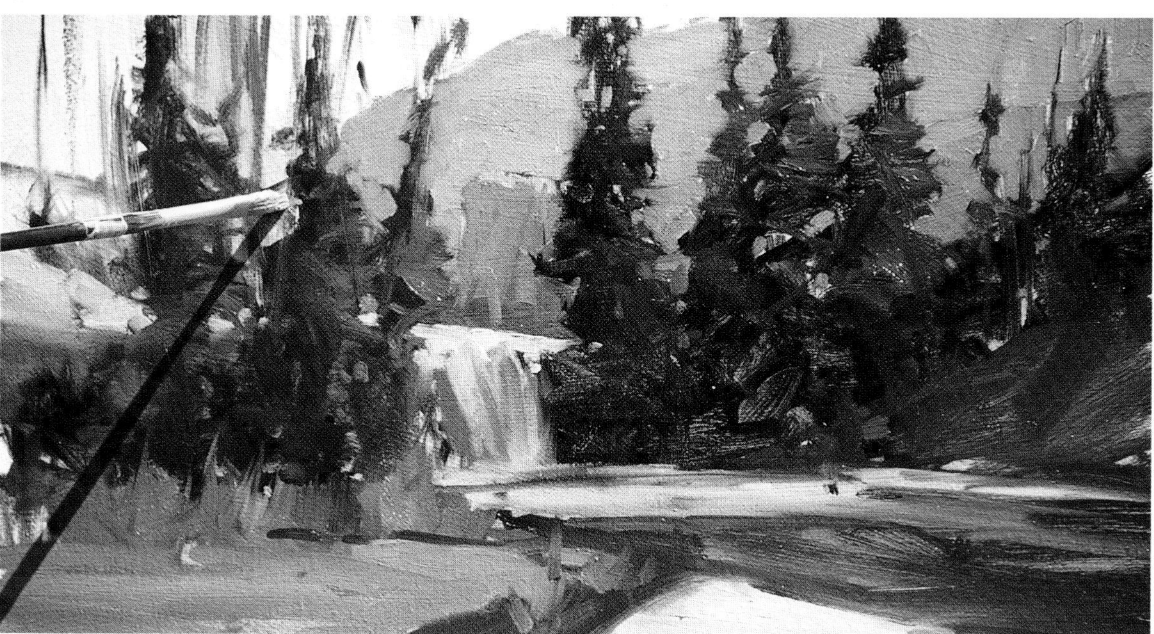

B

C

STEP 5

Fitting in the Background

There are three background areas:

A. The first is directly behind the trees, is warmer and lighter and has the hardest edges.

B. The middle hill is cooler, made up of rose violets with Viridian and softer edges.

C. The distant sky is carefully laid in with toned whites, including touches of warm yellow pinks and Cerulean.

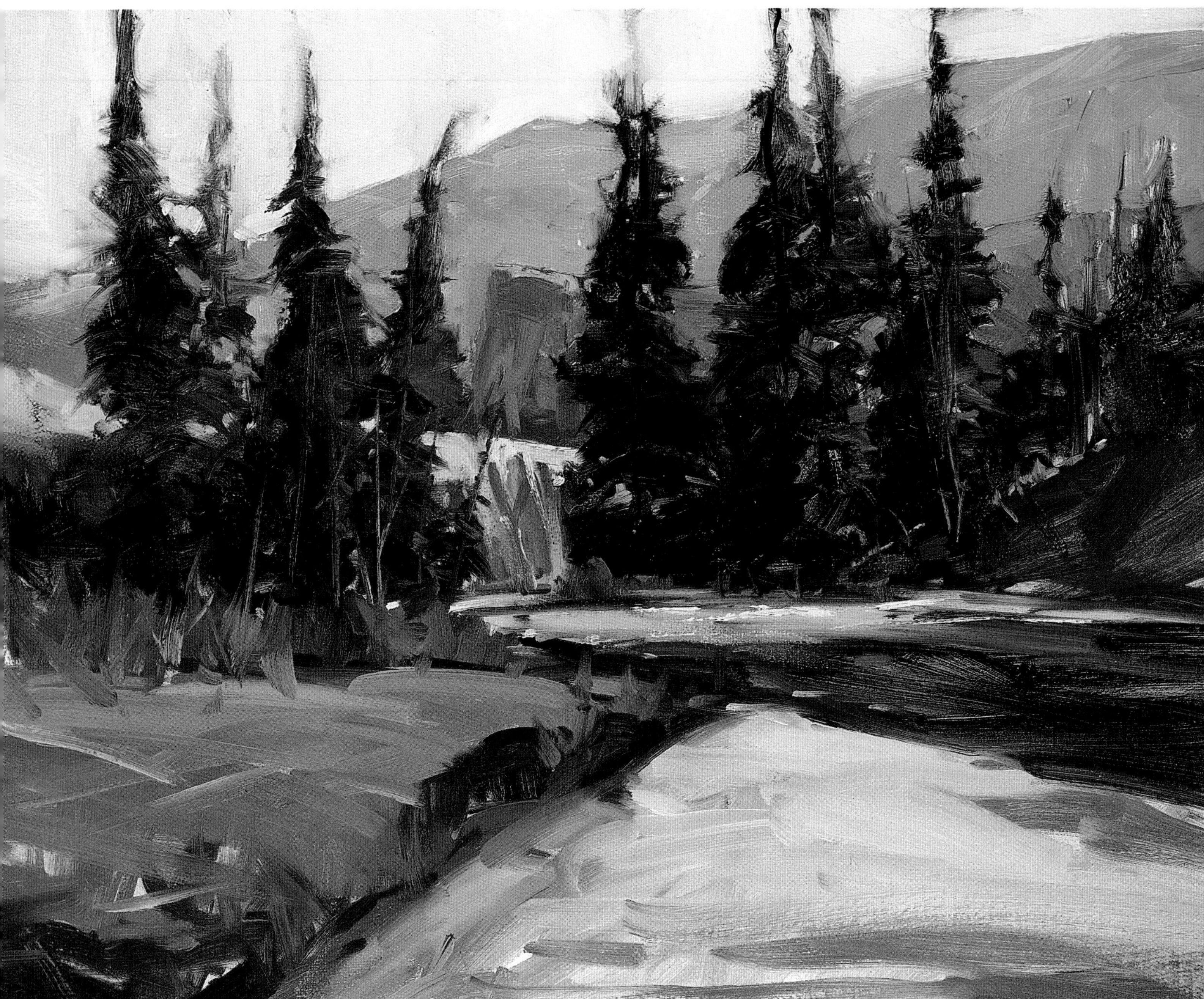

LANDSCAPE WITH PINES AND RIVER
Howard Carr, oil, 20″ × 16″ (50.8cm × 40.6cm)

STEP 6

Final Touches

Tie the painting together by softening some edges and adding highlights. Get in there with your fingers as well as with the brush to soften edges and blend, but don't overdo it: You don't want mud. Grab a clean brush, pick up a fair amount of a cream color you have already mixed and, with the side of the brush, pull in delicate strokes throughout the landscape. This helps tie the painting together and gives a nice balance of creative brushwork to those big, simple shapes you put in earlier.

Key SET THE MOOD AND SIMPLIFY

I can't say it enough: Get excited about your subject! Simplifying your subject to broad areas of light and color helps you stay excited and involved, and therefore helps you get the mood across.

AN OUTDOOR FLORAL IN BRIGHT SUNLIGHT Oil

These freshly picked cosmos from the garden were haphazardly placed in an antique ceramic pot. I wanted to convey the feeling of spontaneity. The lighting is bright but not too harsh. This clear sparkling light shows off the brilliant pinks of the flowers while creating vibrant shadows filled with colorful "bounce," or reflected light. Compare the photo (below) to the final painting (page 66) to see how I softened and warmed the white light in the photo. Softening the light gives more color to the flowers and reflections and allows for more value changes in the background. Softening the light also produces the cheerful mood I was looking for.

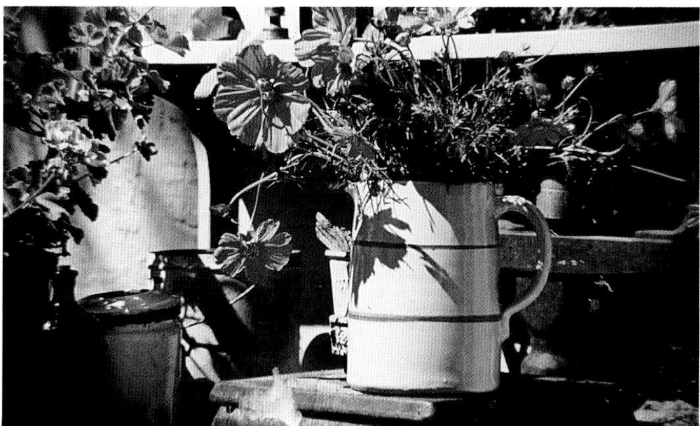

Reference Photo

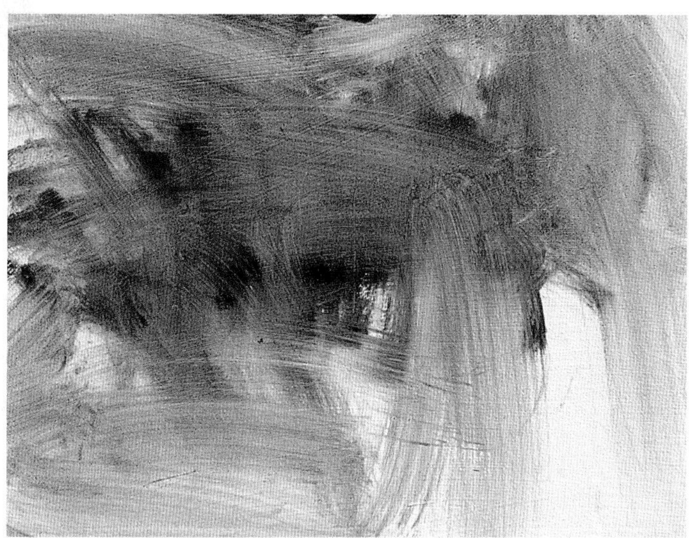

STEP 1

Tone the Canvas

Tone the canvas with some of the general colors you want to use in the painting. A towel dampened with mineral spirits helps move the paint around.

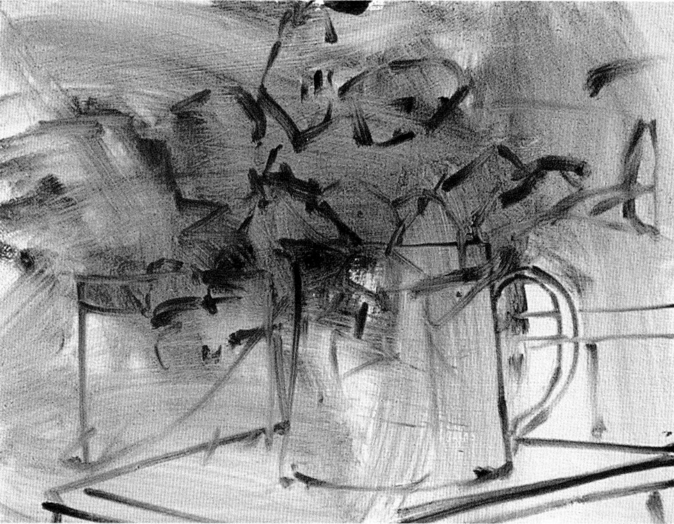

A

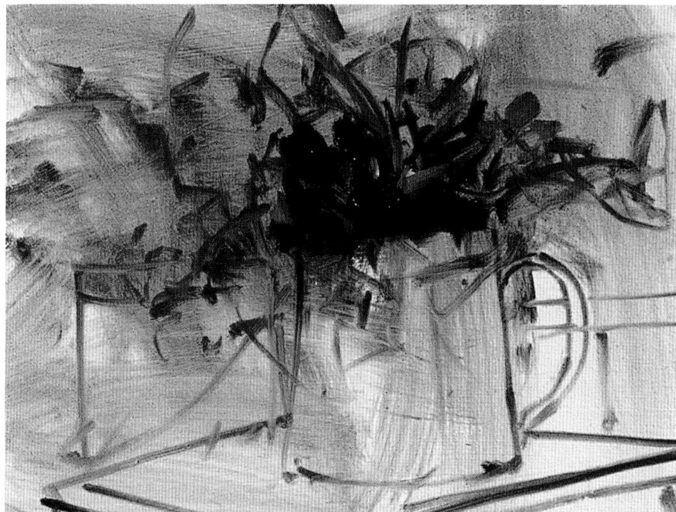

B

STEP 2

Brush Drawing

With a no. 3 filbert, line in the objects to be painted (A) and begin blocking in the dark foliage area with Sap Green and Ultramarine Blue (B).

STEP 3

Flower Shapes

Block in the basic flower shapes and paint the shadow forms on the pot. Keep the block-in loose by using a bigger brush (no. 8) and a wispy, flowing movement. You want to convey a mood of just-put-there flowers, not a stiff, designed arrangement.

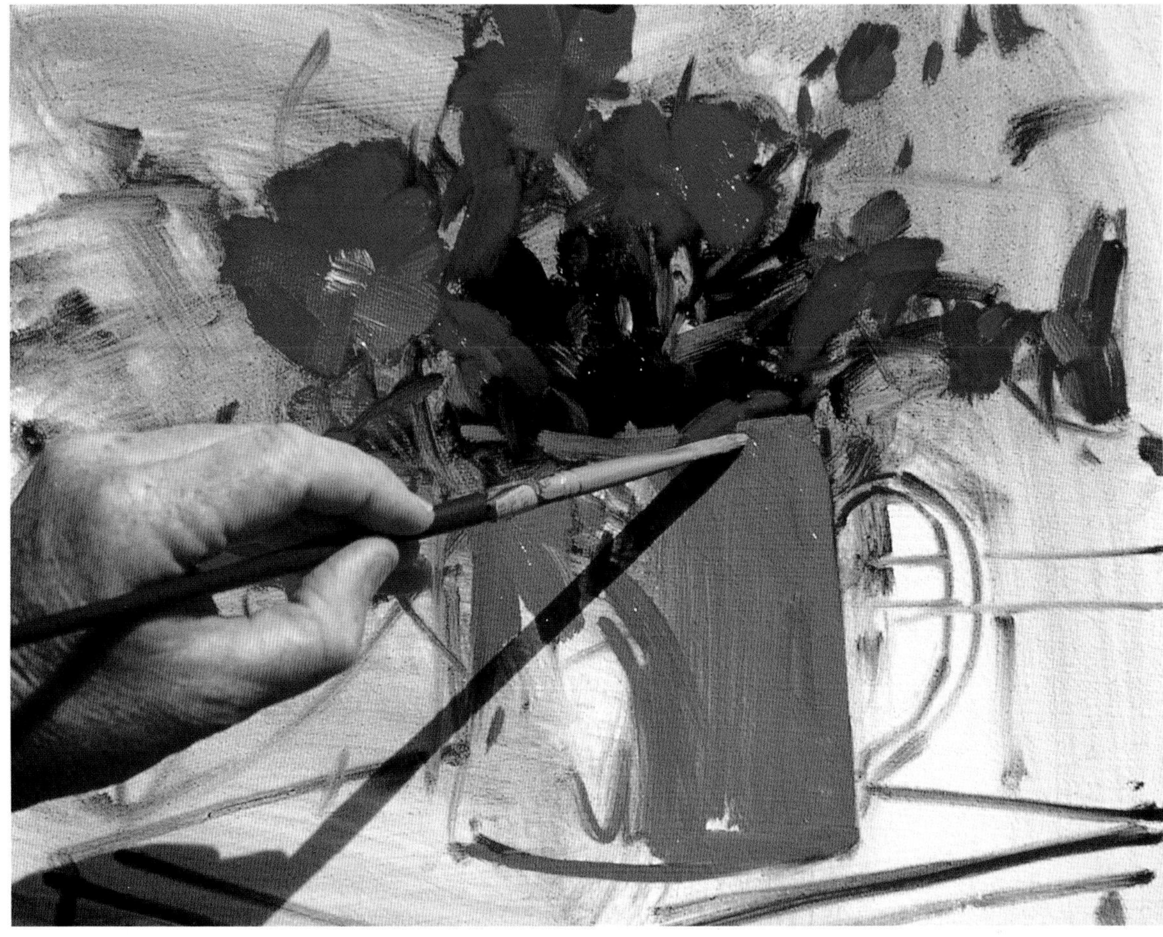

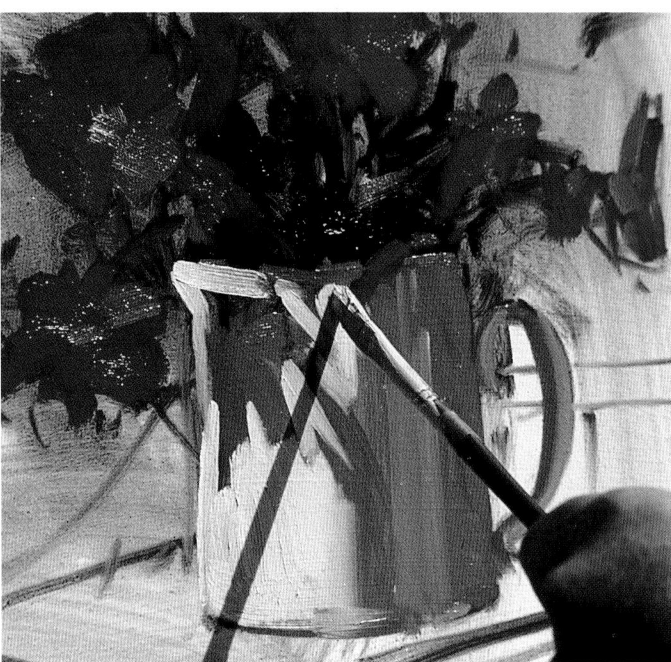

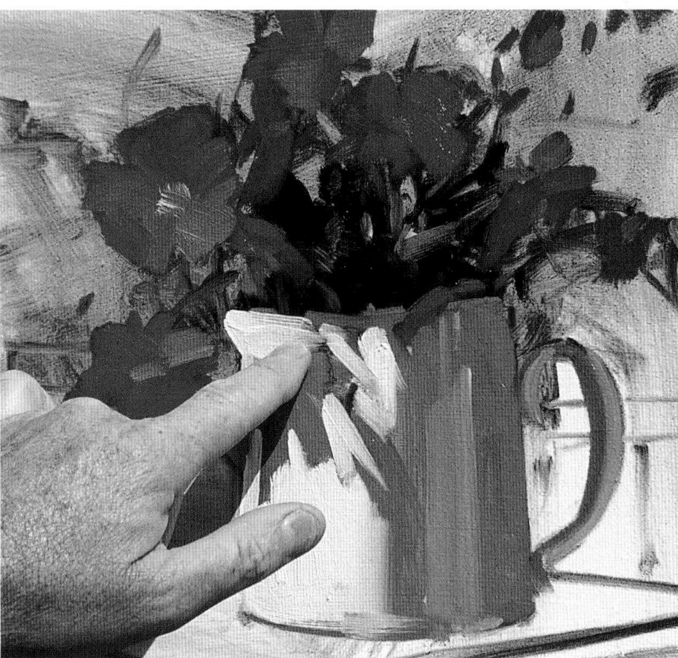

STEP 4

Shape the Shadows

Use white with a touch of Cadmium Orange and work it into the flower shadows on the pot. I've changed the original pot color to give a warmer and more comfortable mood to the painting. Define the lip of the pot and give the shadows contour to describe the rounded shape of the pot. Your finger makes a great blending tool.

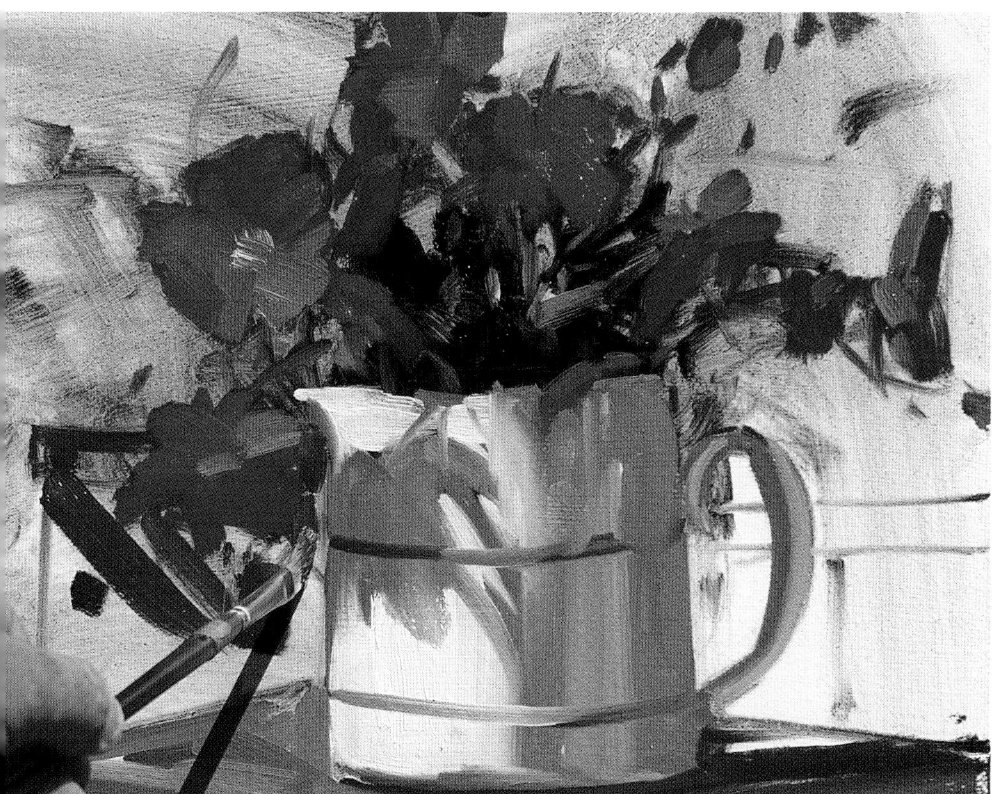

STEP 5

Finish the Pot

Adding the blue striping on the pot helps show its contour. In this picture I'm starting to block in some of the background.

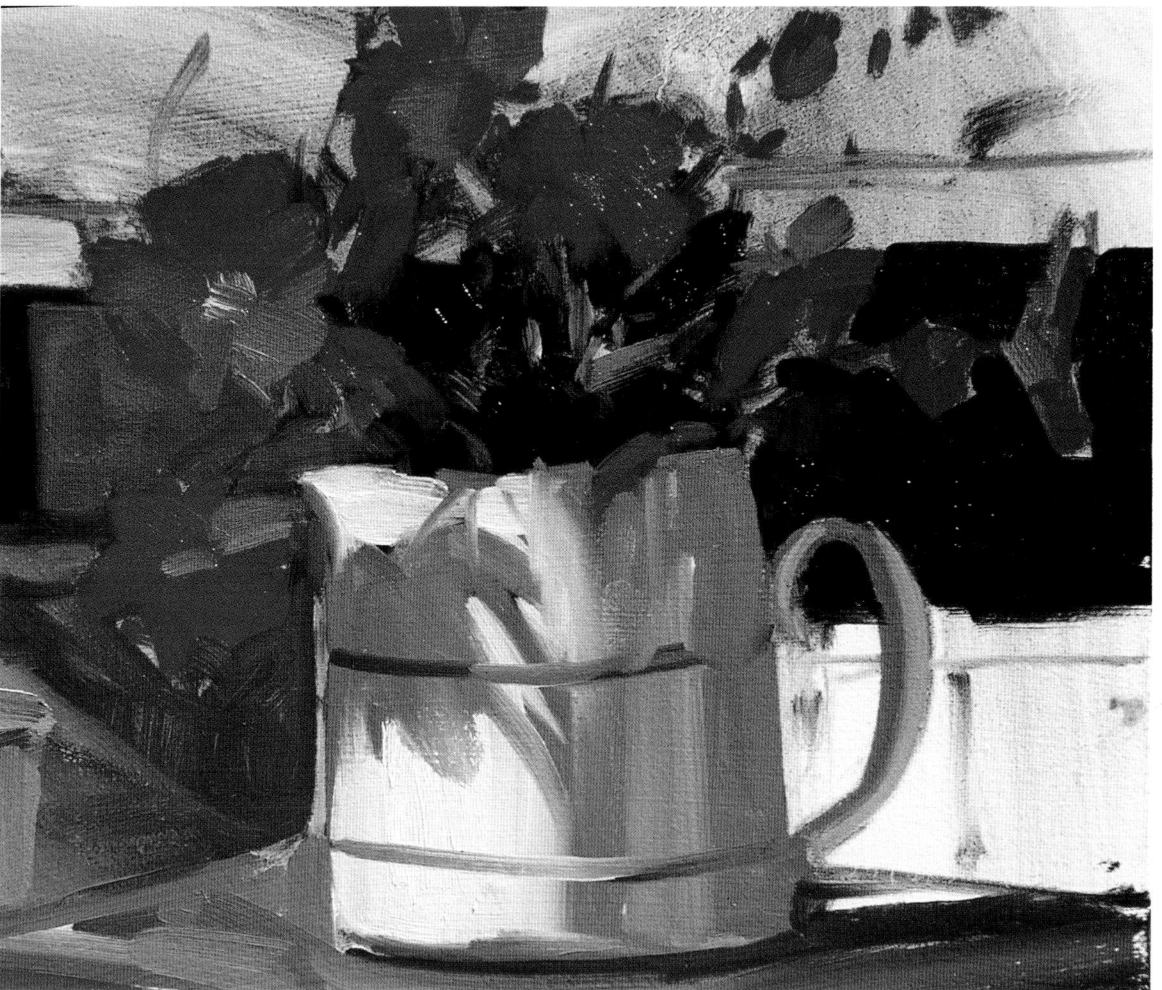

STEP 6

Get Negative

To carve out the negative background areas use a nice variety of darks and lights to balance the piece. Be careful not to upstage your main subject: the pot and flowers. Using subtle complements, go from midtones on the left to darks on the right, and to complementary (greenish) lights on the top. These colors push the flowers forward while also giving them an environment to hold onto.

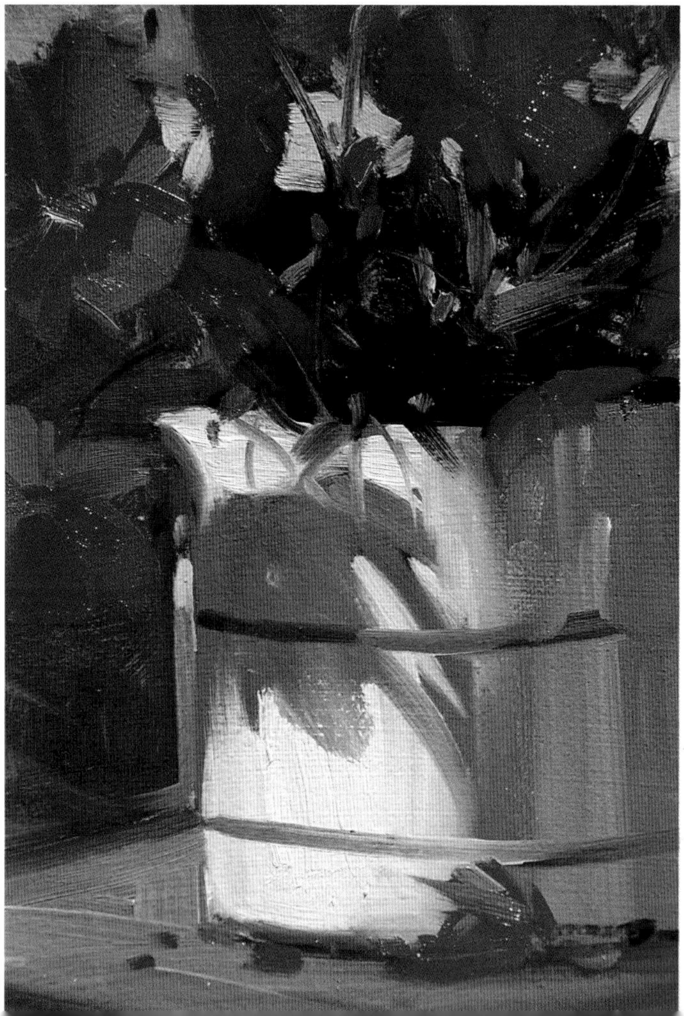

above

STEP 7

Highlights

Put some light values on the flowers and foliage to give them a more recognizable shape. The flower color is Permanent Rose, Alizarin Crimson and Cadmium Red Light. To highlight I use this same mixture, adding white and a touch of Cadmium Yellow Light.

left

STEP 8

Pass the Color Around

Add some fallen petals to the foreground, bringing the flower color to another area of the painting for more harmony and balance.

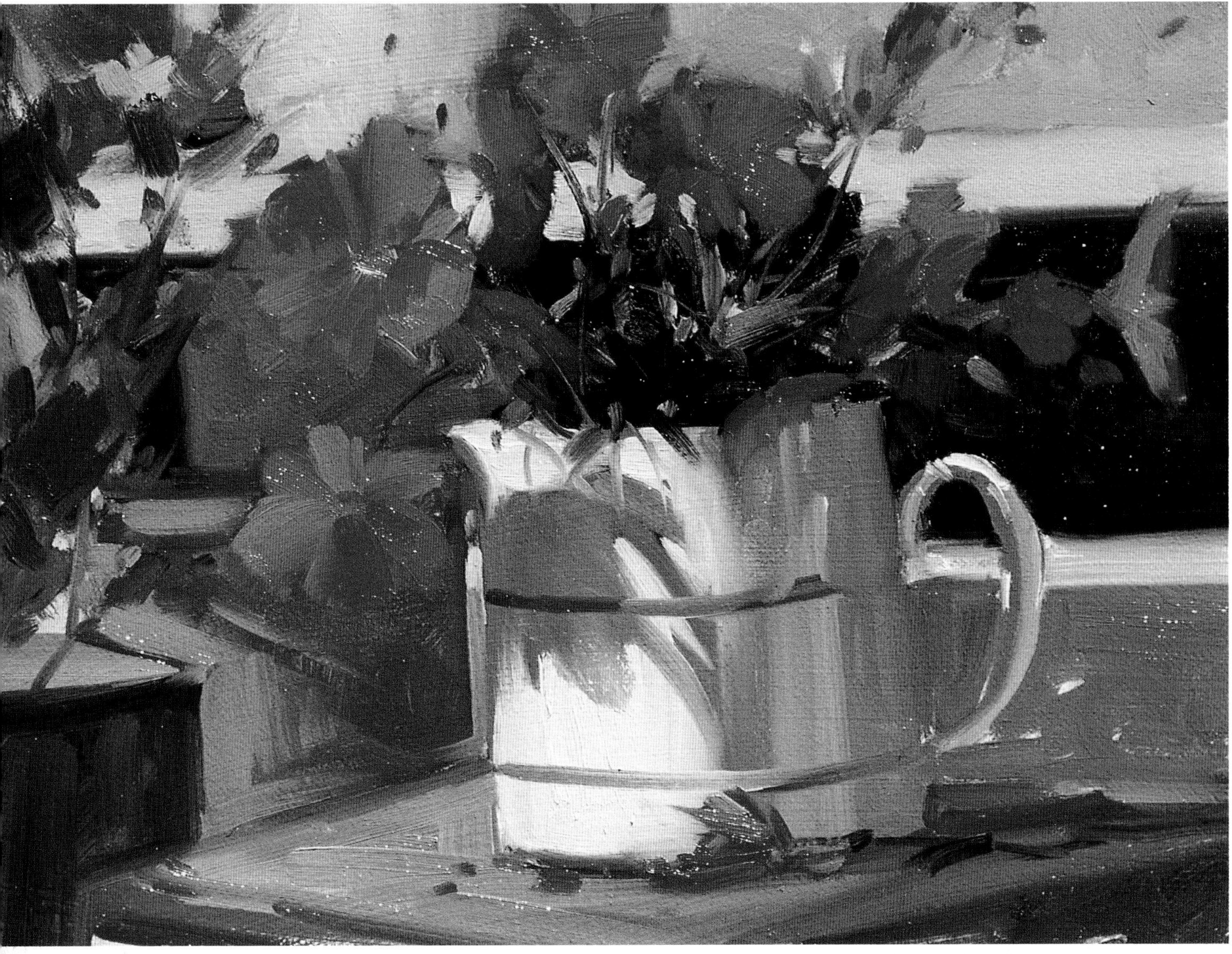

FLORAL AND POT
Howard Carr, oil, 20" × 16" (50.8cm × 40.6cm)

STEP 9

Final Touches

Add some foliage on the left to bring the viewer's eye back into the picture. The painting needed more warm notes, so I added small orange accents indicating the light hitting some small wildflowers with stems invisible in the shadow.

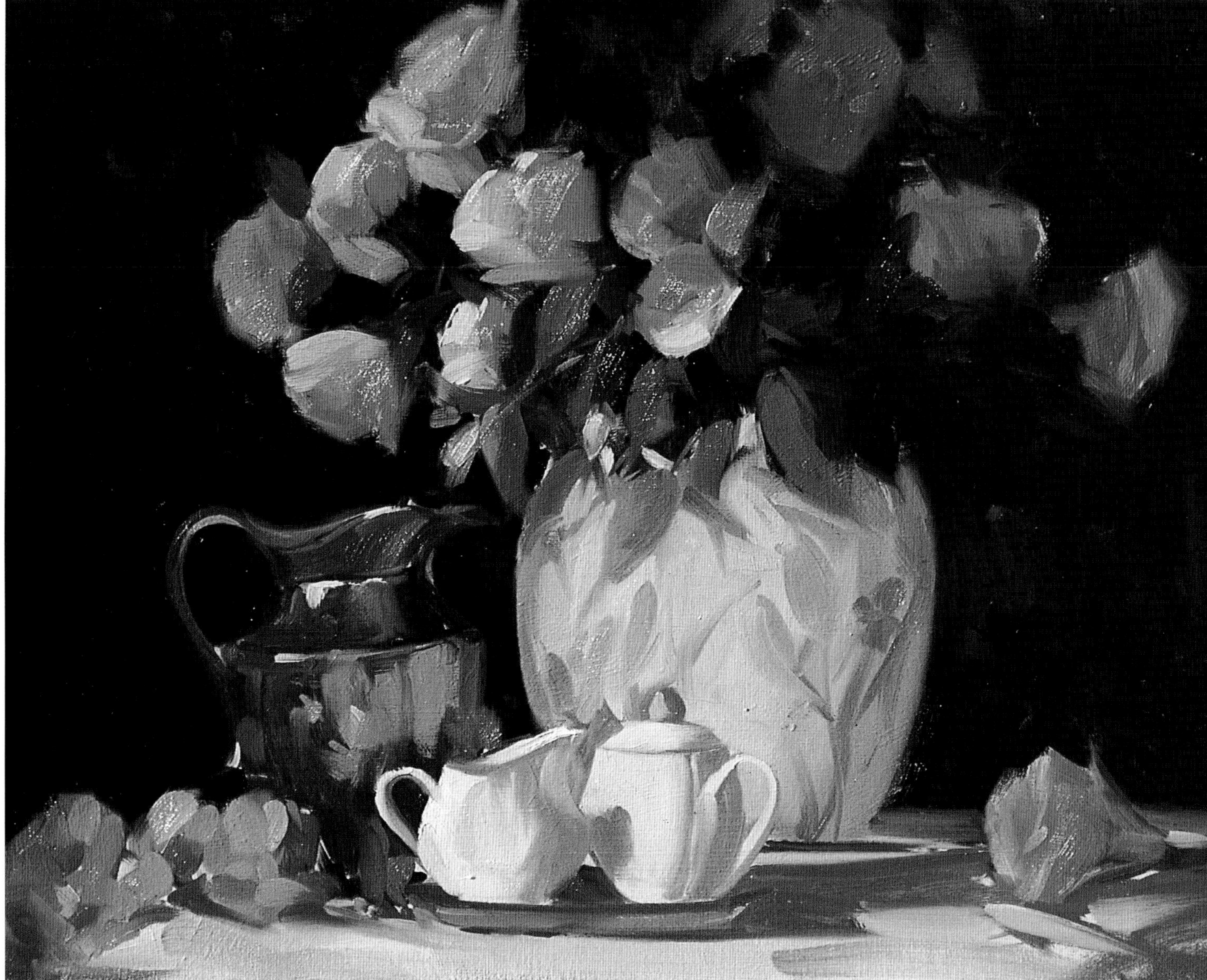

GRANDMA'S ANTIQUES
Howard Carr, oil, 30" × 24" (76.2cm × 61cm)

A Tranquil Still Life

This flower still life is softer and more formal feeling, perhaps even a bit more delicate, than *Floral and Pot*. This, in part, is due to the use of more muted tones in the foreground balancing the richer colors elsewhere. Lots of warm neutrals lend an overall harmony to enhance the tranquil mood of the scene. **Hint:** Stay away from white to lighten bright colors such as the flower colors in the pitcher. Use lighter colors of the same family to lighten and you'll get richer results.

GALLERY

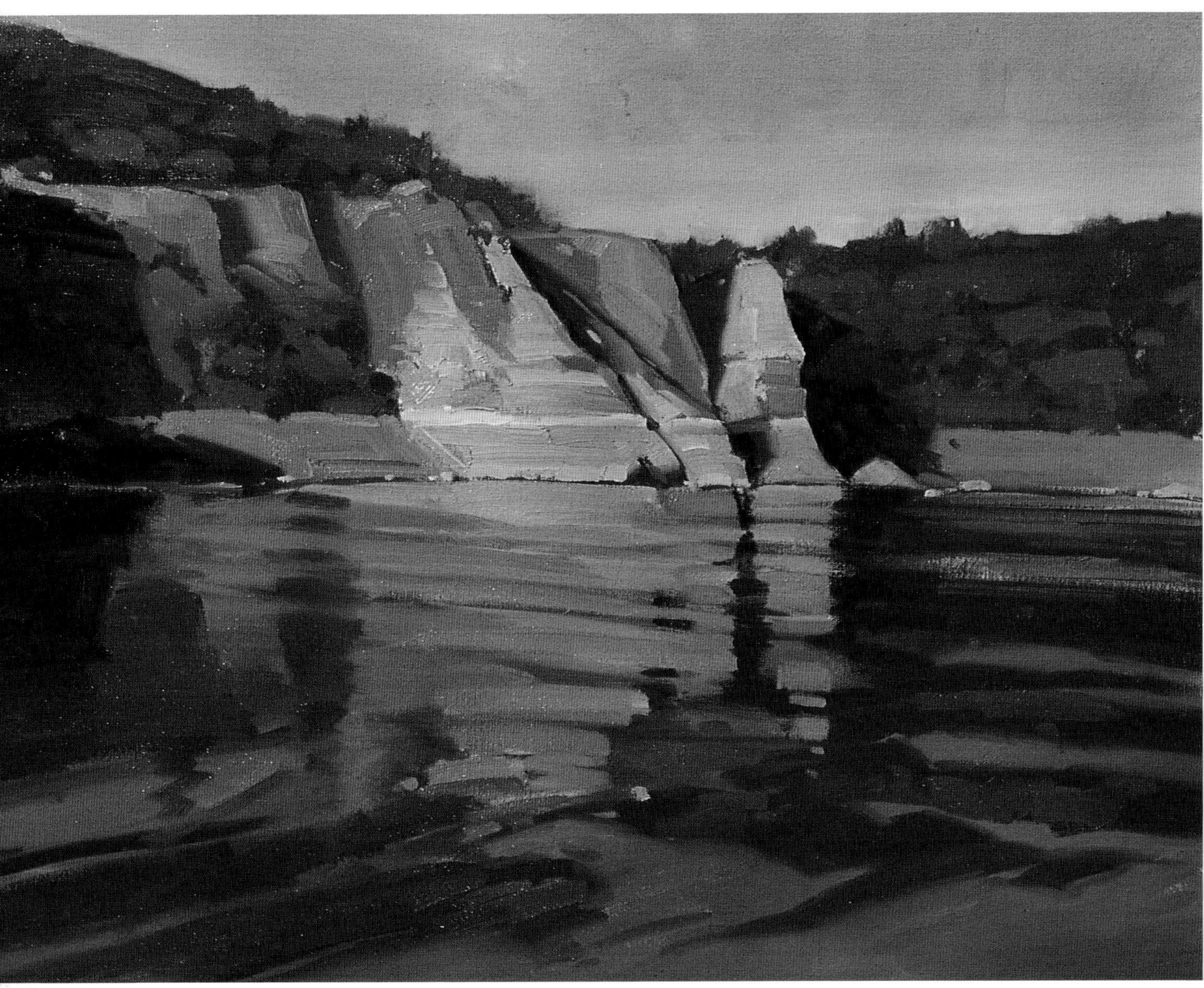

As in *Violet Shadows* (opposite), I piled on rich contrasting colors to help the painting come to life. Cadmium Red, Orange and Yellow dominate the cliff and reflections. Let the color blend freely as you brush these separate colors onto the canvas. Avoid overmixing on the palette; this could make for a dull, lifeless attempt. The reflections in *Desert Waters* help lead the viewer into the scene.

DESERT WATERS
Howard Carr, oil, 24" × 18" (61cm × 45.7cm)

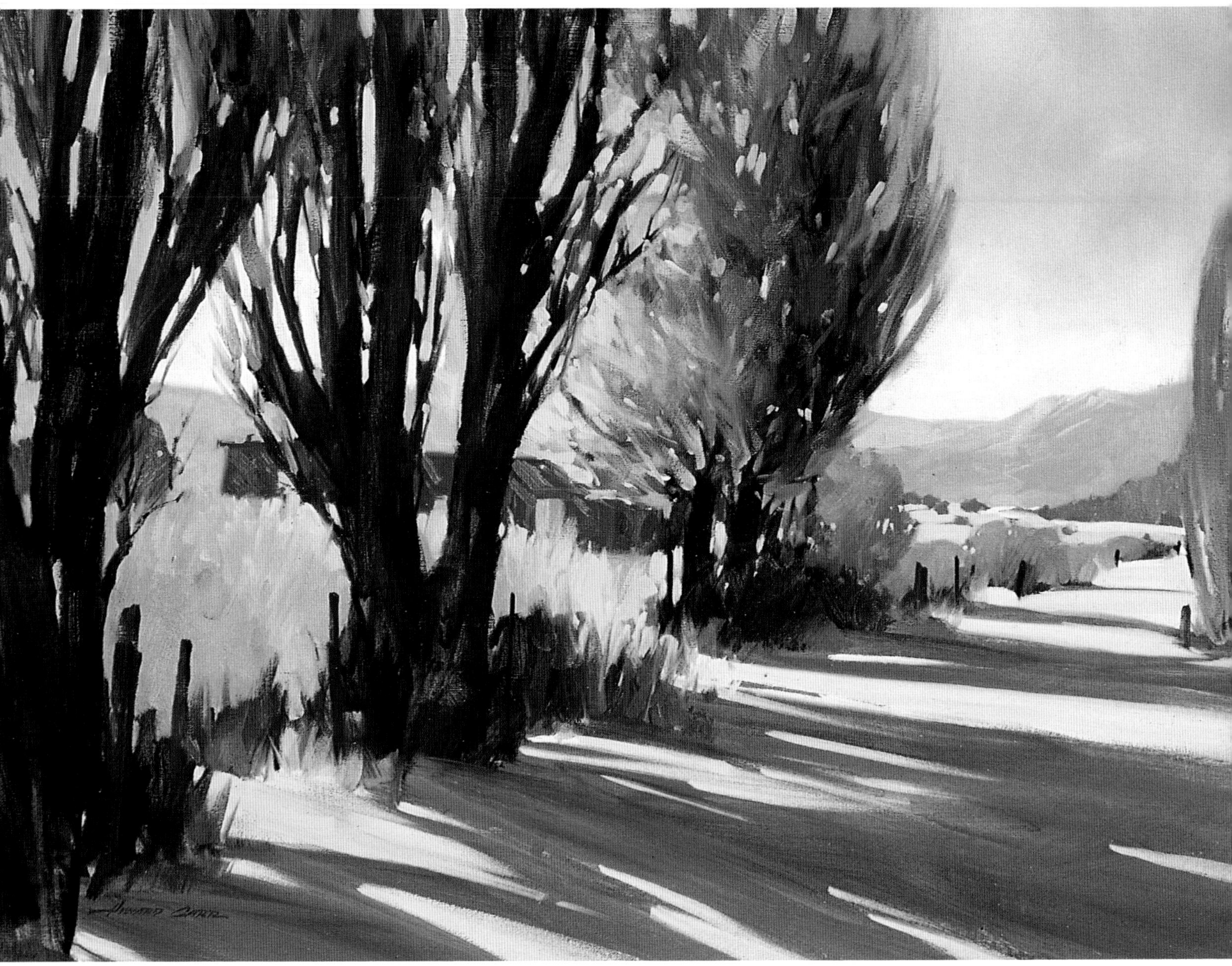

The strong value, color and directional contrasts of the vertical trees and the horizontal shadows in the foreground give a quick and gutsy mood. It's also the balance of these light and dark areas that pulls the viewer into the scene. I used Alizarin Crimson and Ultramarine Blue for darker violet areas, and Light Blue with Rose for the lighter violets.

VIOLET SHADOWS
Howard Carr, oil, 30″ × 24″ (76.2cm × 61cm)

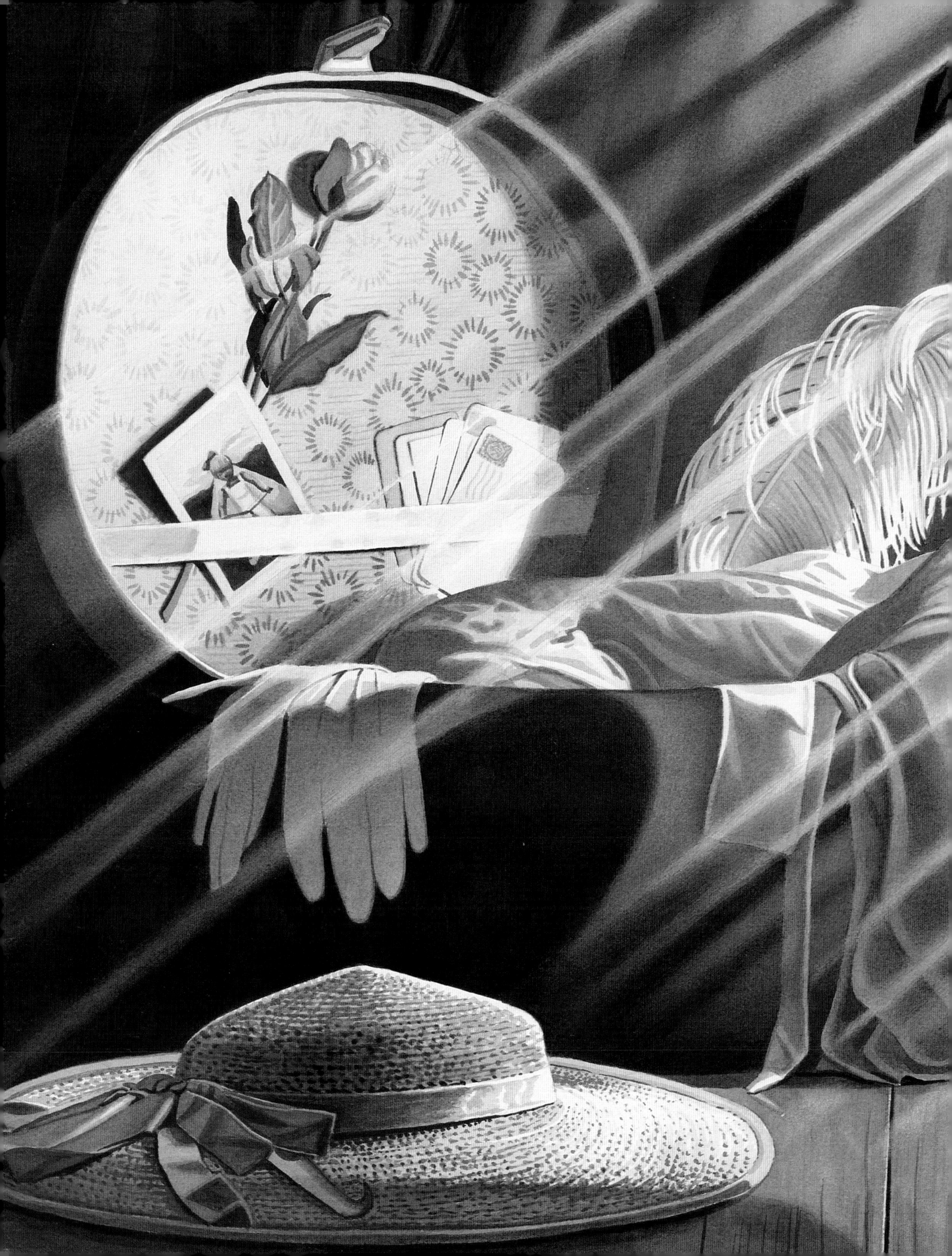

DESIGN A SHOWSTOPPER WITH STAGE LIGHTING IN WATERCOLOR

SHARON MACZKO

CHAPTER 5

In her darkened studio Sharon Maczko creates and witnesses an almost ethereal transformation: An ordinary assemblage of precisely placed objects becomes a captivating still life or interior setting by the careful addition of arresting, often dramatic lighting. For her painting technique, intentional artificial lighting plays an integral role in the compositions she creates; in most cases it is the primary element of focus. Whether a subdued glow or a brilliant flash, creative lighting serves as the catalyst for her, and for the viewer's, imagination.

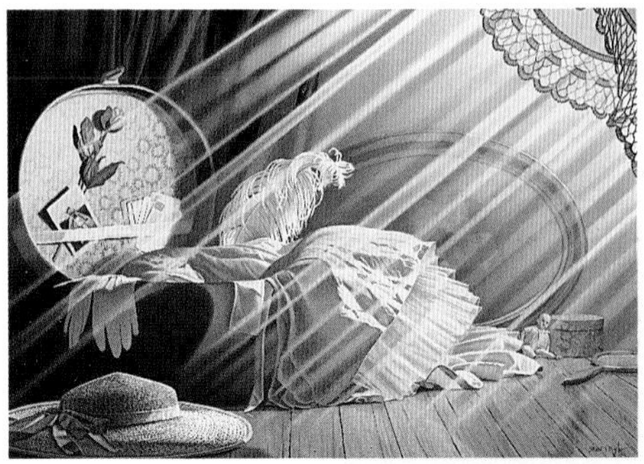

ATTIC FLOOR #3
Sharon Maczko, transparent watercolor, 22" × 30" (55.9cm × 76.2cm)

This is an example of a painting where a fabric called *tulle* simulates sunlight (as explained on page 72).

Since Maczko's paintings are rendered from life, from movielike sets she constructs in her studio, she has enjoyed inventing new and unique ways to generate light in her work. She's amassed a few tricks along the way and shares them in the demonstrations on the following pages.

CREATE ARTIFICIAL SUN RAYS Watercolor

I use a netted fabric called *tulle*, stretched from one point to another within the still life, to simulate the sun's rays, such as the light falling on dust particles floating in an attic. Tulle, however, merely equivocates sunlight; it lacks the actual luminescence that sun rays emit onto surrounding objects. Therefore, if you compare the still life to my finished painting, you will note the improvised differences I found necessary to make.

Try a White Reflector

Another trick incorporated into this still life is the use of a large sheet of white posterboard to reflect and radiate light onto objects I felt were not illuminated to my liking.

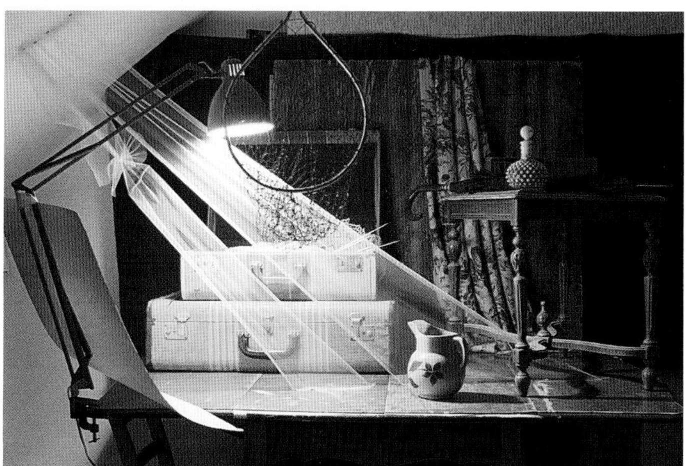

Photo Reference
A netted fabric, tulle, simulates sun rays. As you can see, each object is carefully placed, and the lighting on each is carefully checked.

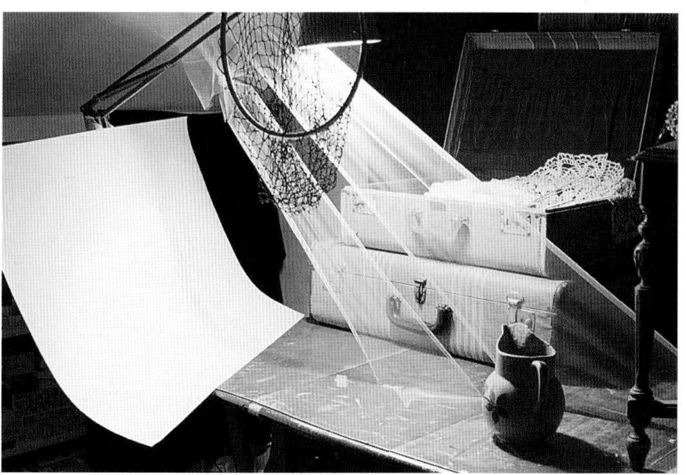

Here's a better view of the white posterboard I use as a reflector in the setup for *Attic Floor #7*.

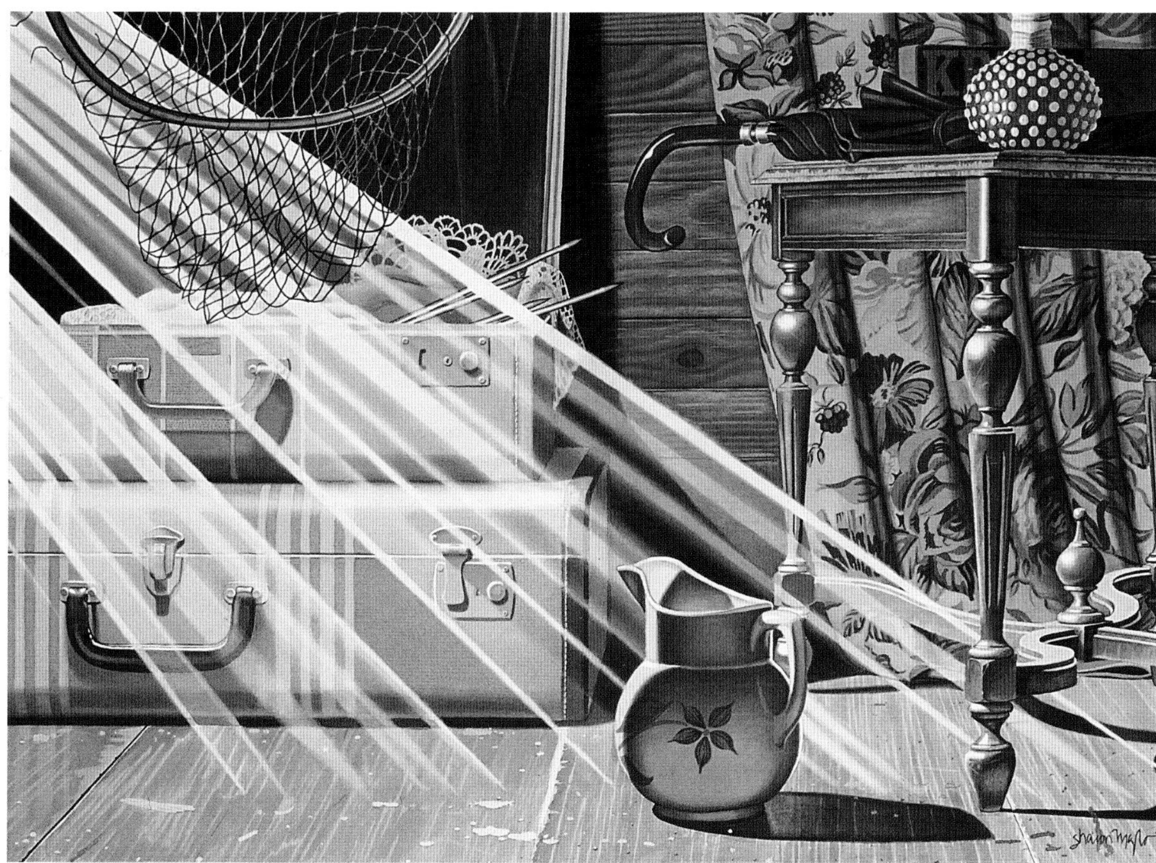

ATTIC FLOOR #7
Sharon Maczko,
transparent watercolor,
22" × 30"
(55.9cm × 76.2cm)

ONE LIGHT SOURCE Watercolor

I nearly always use a solitary light source in my work. I feel the intense shadows created by this procedure introduce an effective sense of drama.

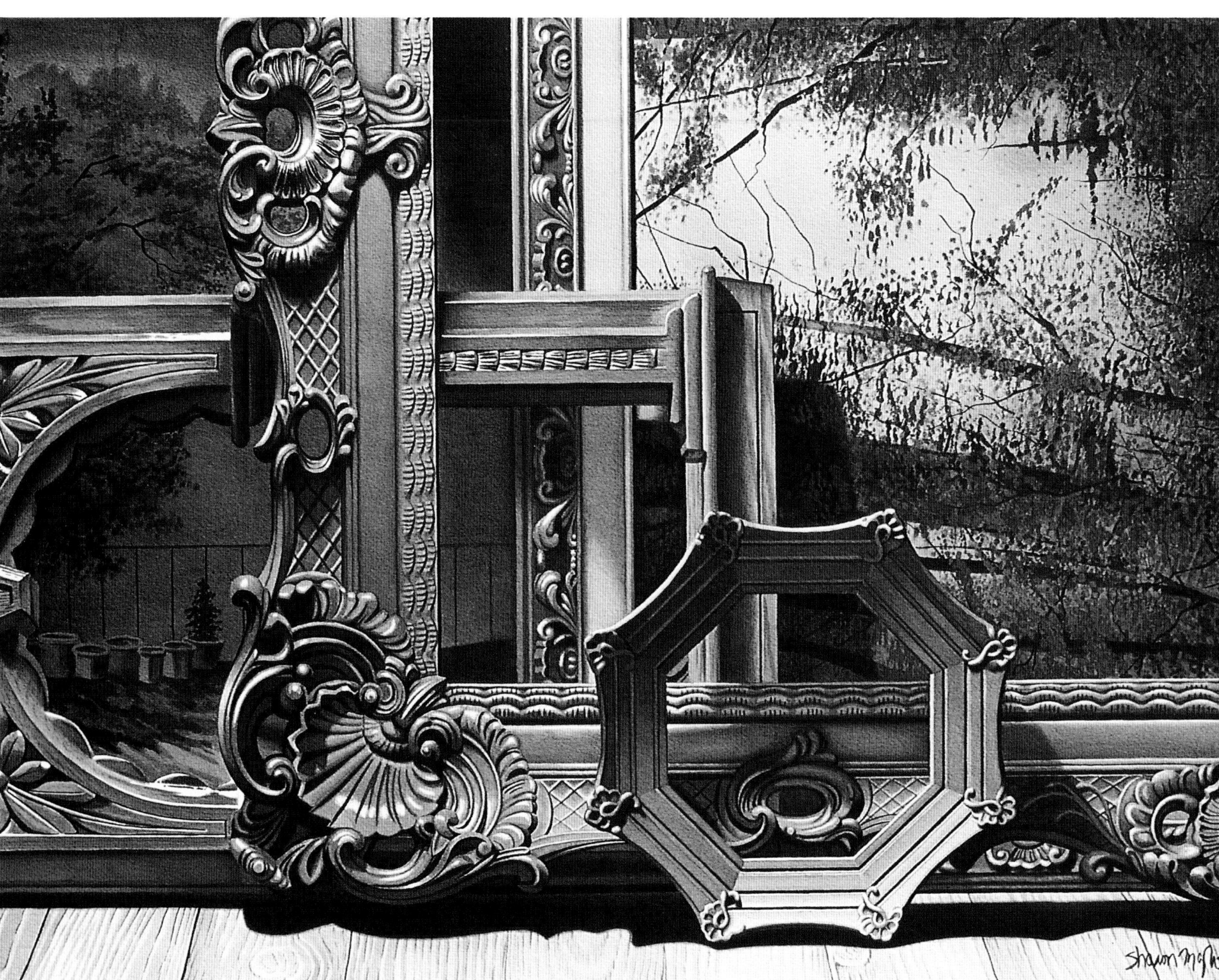

One Light Source Creates Intense Shadows
Here you can see the effects of a single light source, located above and just to the left of the objects.

ATTIC FLOOR #6
Sharon Maczko, transparent watercolor, 22″ × 30″ (55.9cm × 76.2cm)

THE LAMP AS PART OF THE COMPOSITION Watercolor

I sometimes place a lighted lamp directly into the still life as one of the props; the surrounding objects are then bathed in an intimate, subdued glow.

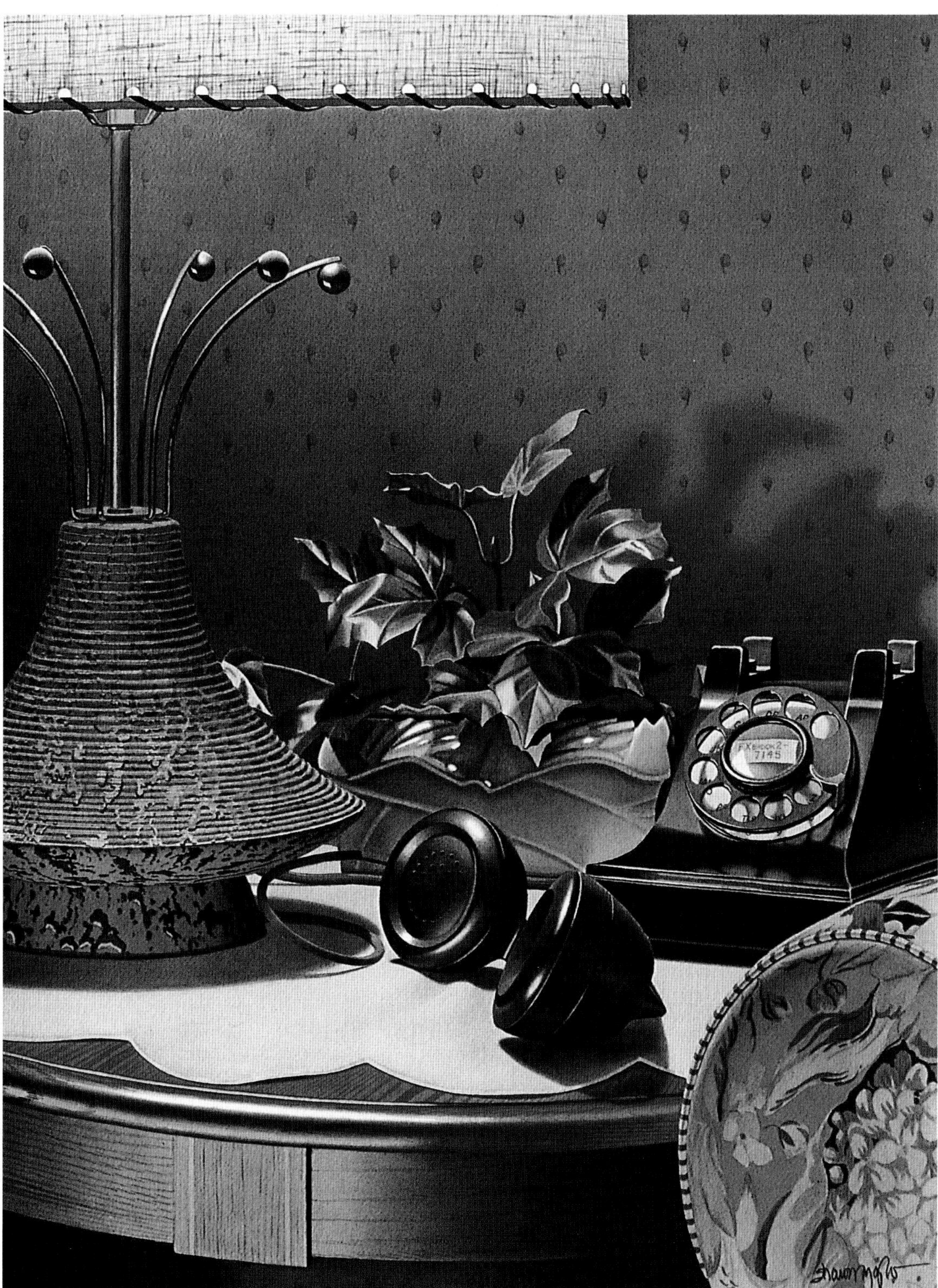

Painting In a Light Source Creates Intimacy

This painting shows the technique of placing a soft light source in the painting, as well as the use of blue bulbs directed from outside the painting onto the objects to simulate light from a television.

EXBROOK 2
Sharon Maczko, transparent watercolor, 30″ × 22″ (76.2cm × 55.9cm)

EFFECTS WITH COLORED BULBS Watercolor

I use colored lightbulbs in my light sources to hint at unseen factors outside the focus of the painting. In my "Long Hot Summer" painting series I paired blue lightbulbs with white ones to simulate a flash of lightning outside the window. In the case of *Exbrook 2* (opposite), blue lightbulbs were utilized to represent the glow emitting from a television located ostensibly within the room.

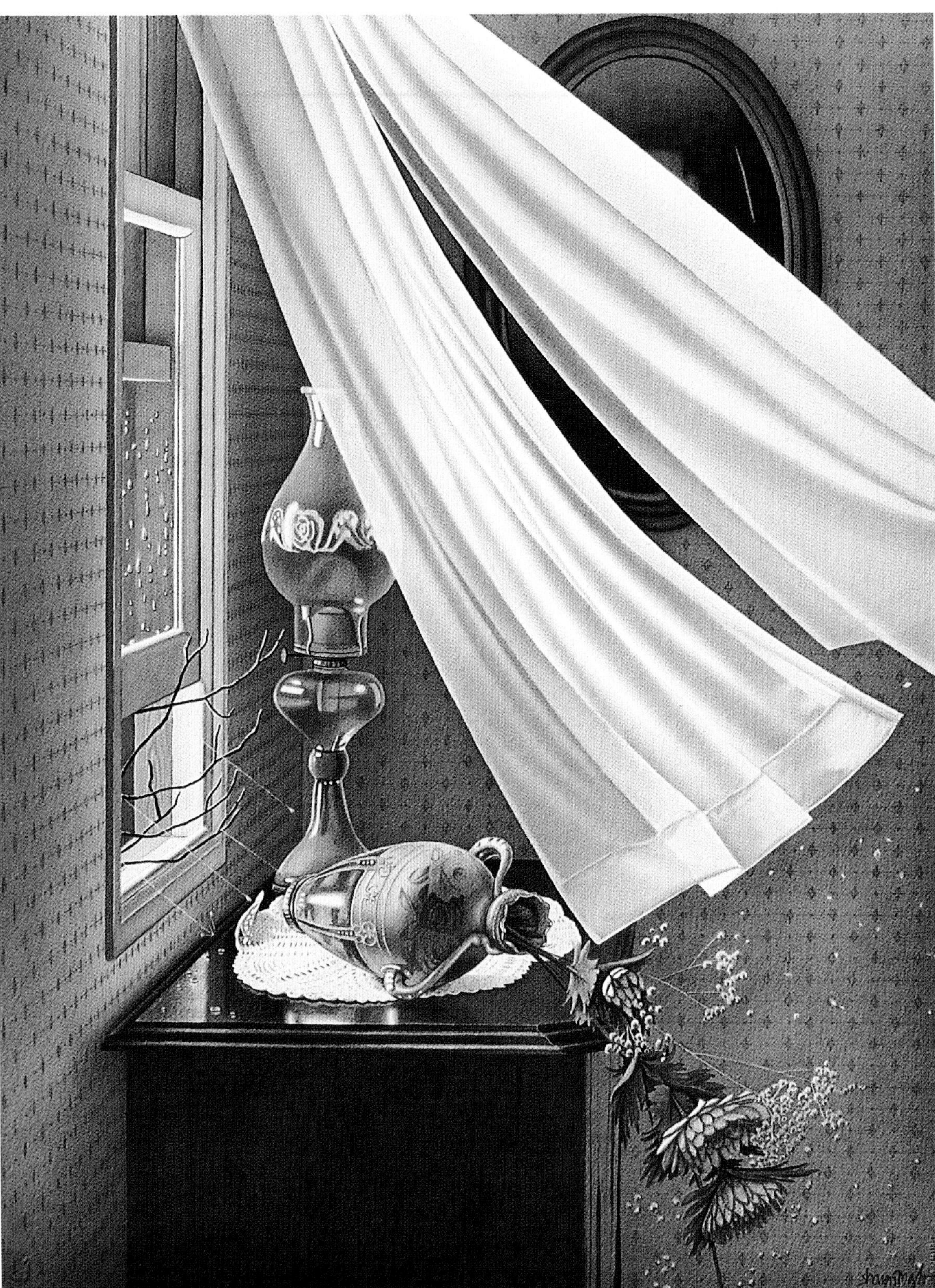

Colored Bulbs Hint at Unseen Factors
The cool, almost eerie light in this painting comes from combining white and blue light.

UNTITLED (LONG HOT SUMMER SERIES)
Sharon Maczko, transparent watercolor, 30″ × 22″ (76.2cm × 55.9cm)

GALLERY

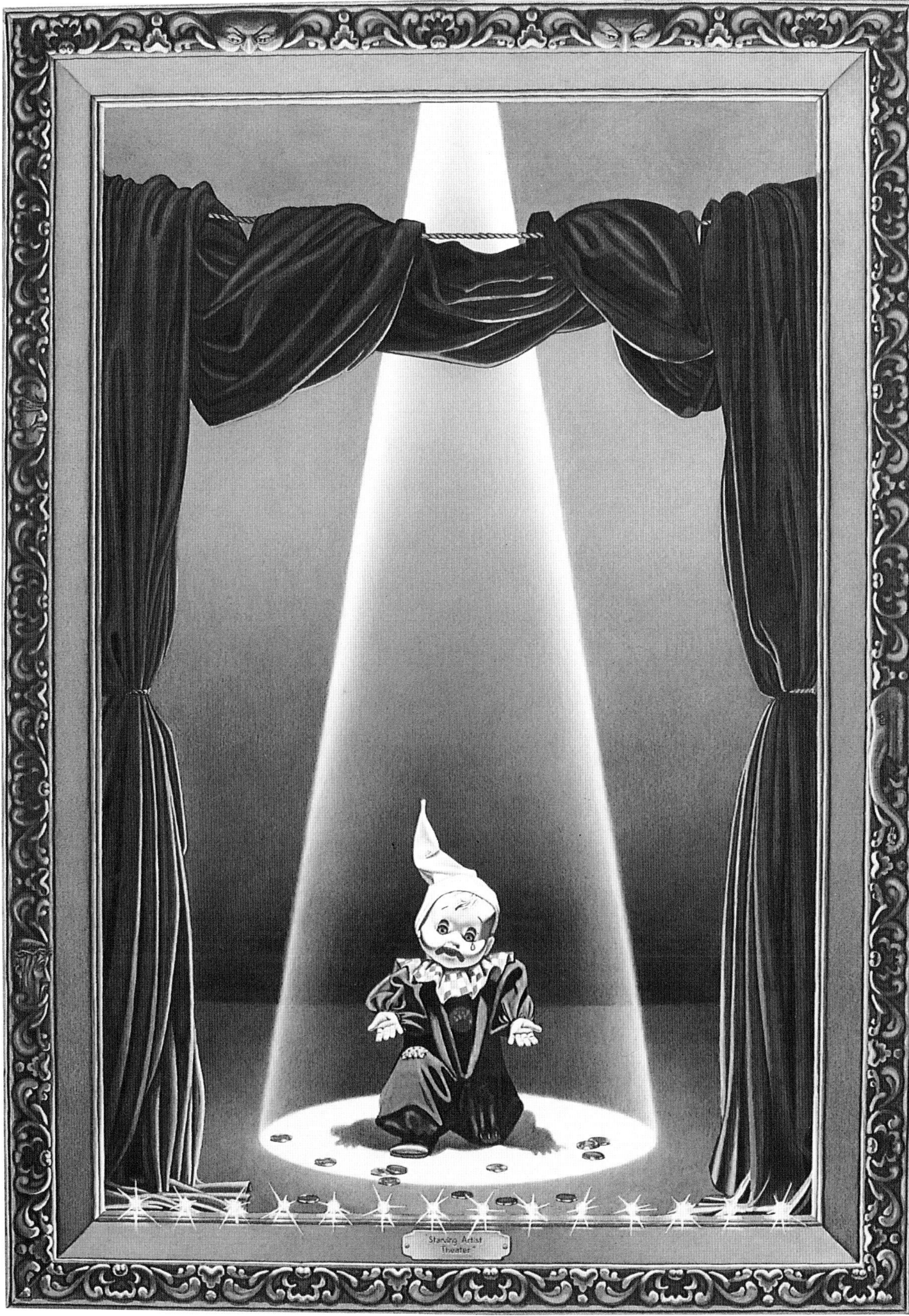

This is a rebellious piece! There is quite a bit of symbolism, much of it worked into the trompe l'oeil frame, including the two faces at the top that look disapprovingly at the little clown. I set up this scene in my studio, as I usually do, with a single strong overhead light source. In this case I had to improvise a few things, such as some of the details on the frame. I set up some small Christmas lights across the bottom of one of my frames to simulate footlights. Although there was light coming from the top, I had to improvise the spotlight beam, which I did by fuzzing out the edges and building the image slowly, layer by layer.

STARVING ARTIST THEATER
Sharon Maczko, transparent watercolor, 30" × 21" (76.2cm × 53.3cm)

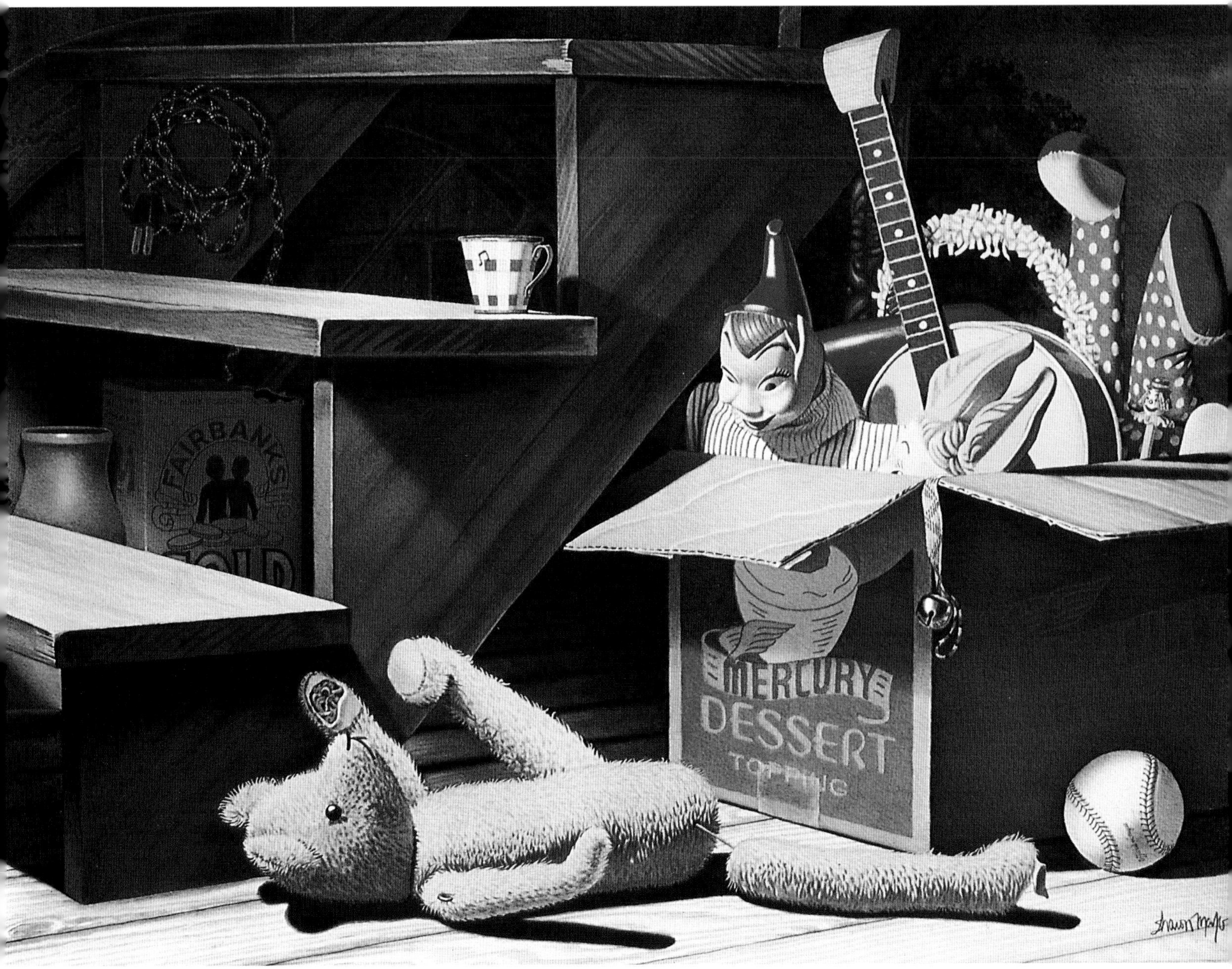

This strong single light source was meant to represent the shock and revelation of turning on a bright light in a usually dark environment.

BASEMENT #1
Sharon Maczko, transparent watercolor, 22″ × 30″ (55.9cm × 76.2cm)

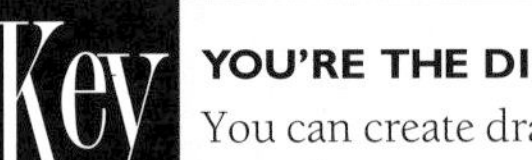

YOU'RE THE DIRECTOR

You can create drama worthy of Broadway or Hollywood right in your studio. Explore how lighting creates an important part of the story you are telling—just as in a movie. Good artificial lighting is not very expensive and is a wonderful creative tool that can be used in the comfort of your own home or studio.

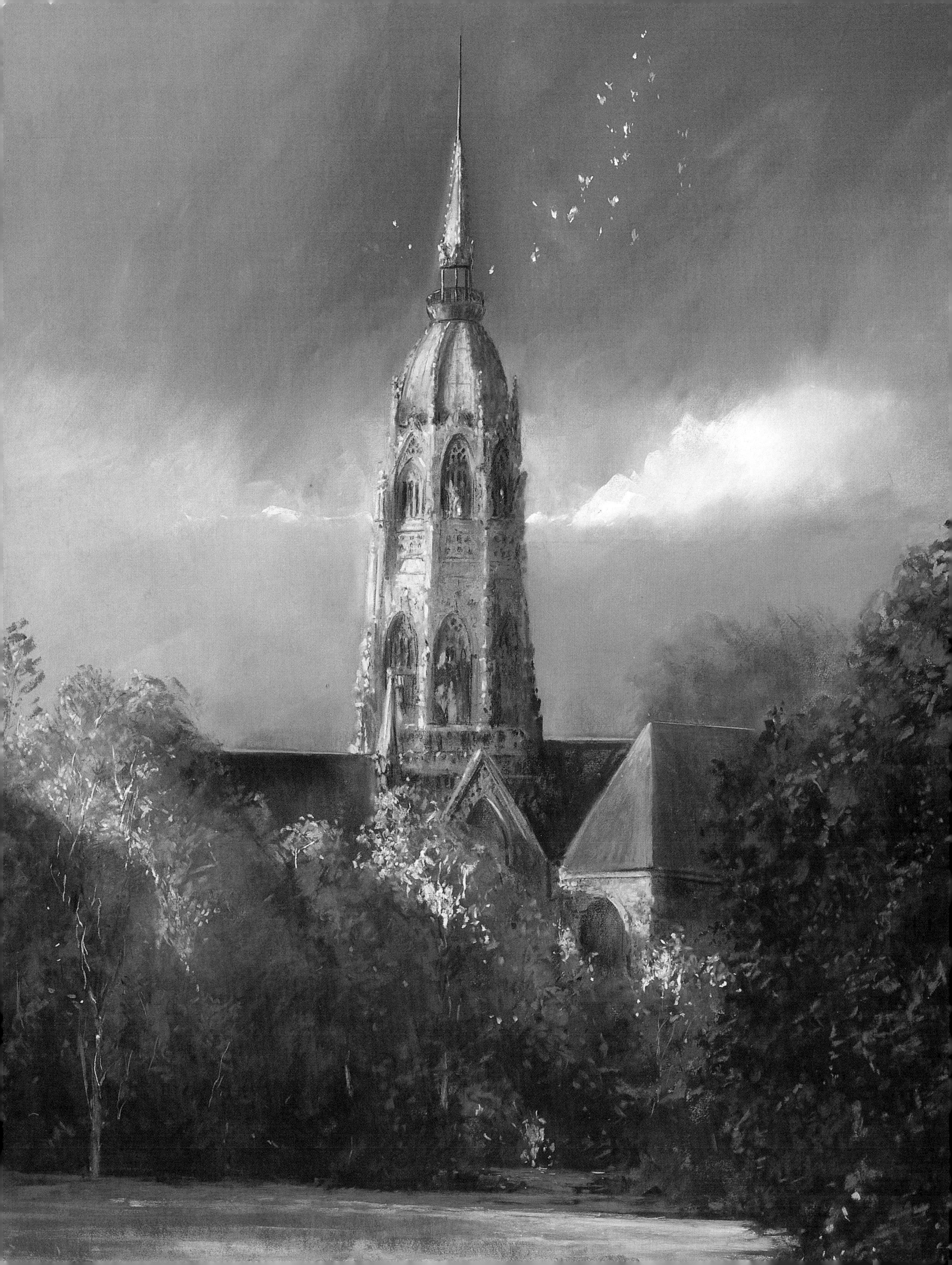

AWAKE TO THE WONDER OF NATURE WITH

PASTEL

GIL DELLINGER

CHAPTER

6

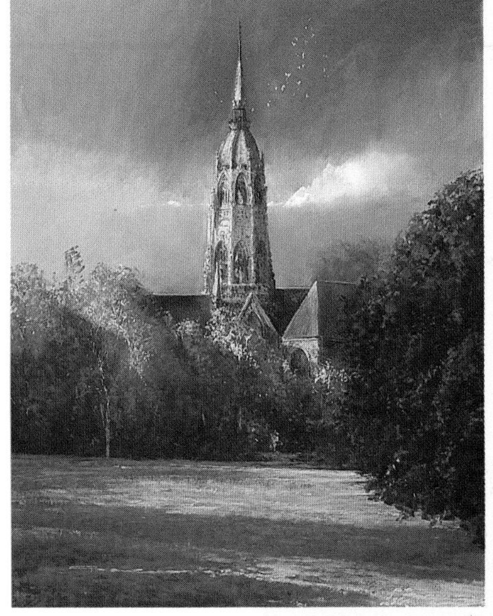

EXULTATION
Gil Dellinger, pastel,
39″ × 29″
(99.1cm × 73.7cm)

In this painting of the cathedral at Bayeux in Normandy, light enhances the cathedral, giving it a spiritual quality. The birds help bring about a feeling of upliftment as they rise up from the cathedral, their highlights portraying a sense of motion.

Gil Dellinger likes his light-filled pastel paintings to look fresh. This means keeping the same spontaneous feeling he acutely observes in nature in the painting. But light is more than a force that allows you to see. Dellinger sees light as the outer manifestation of the deeper mysteries of life, and he seeks to express some of that wonder in his art. Although he often blends his pastels at the early stages of the painting to design large areas of color and value, he finds that overblending pastels kills the light. Dellinger generally saves the lightest colors for last, gently laying them opaquely on top of existing colors. To blend and make those lighter hues transparent would destroy their sparkle. Most of Dellinger's work is done *en plein aire* early in the morning or late in the afternoon. These times of day are more colorful, with longer, more interesting shadows. Even the light has a hue of its own, affecting the mood and tone of the whole painting. To Dellinger, early morning is lemony and acidy. Late afternoon is gold and red. Toning everything in the painting with those colors creates the look of a particular time of day. Surface strokes help enhance mood. Light is the unifying factor in all of Dellinger's work, whether landscape, still life or portrait; the techniques he uses to achieve this harmony and create mood are demonstrated on the following pages.

SUNLIGHT PENETRATING A MORNING FOG Pastel

I awoke in the French countryside to find a morning fog. In a few minutes the light was penetrating through the fog, hitting the village buildings and some old abandoned orchard trees.

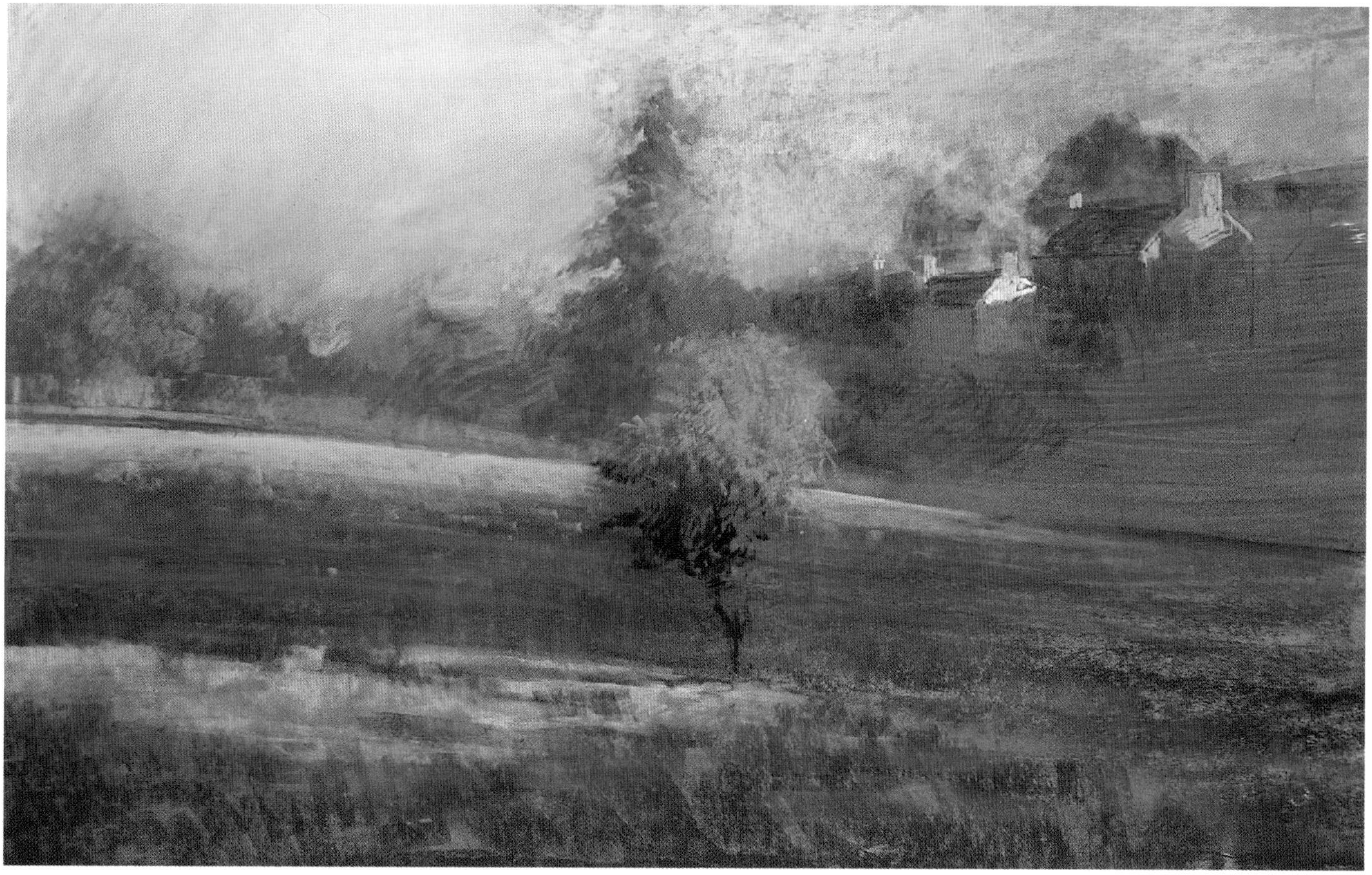

above

STEP 1

Light and Shadow Shapes

Rough in the general shapes of light and shadow on a Wallis pastel paper primed with Dark Gray acrylic. I use a heavy concentration of Golden airbrush acrylic and a wide brush to prime the paper. You can see the color of the acrylic primer on the center right. Let some paper show through to help maintain unity.

left

Detail of Step 1

The first color laid down in a rough-in is not always the finished color. An undertone of bright orange or yellow can create the look of sunlight. Lay down Naples Yellow Nupastel in the sky. As you approach the finished colors it will be covered and will underlay the gray fog to create an illusion of sunlight seen through the mist.

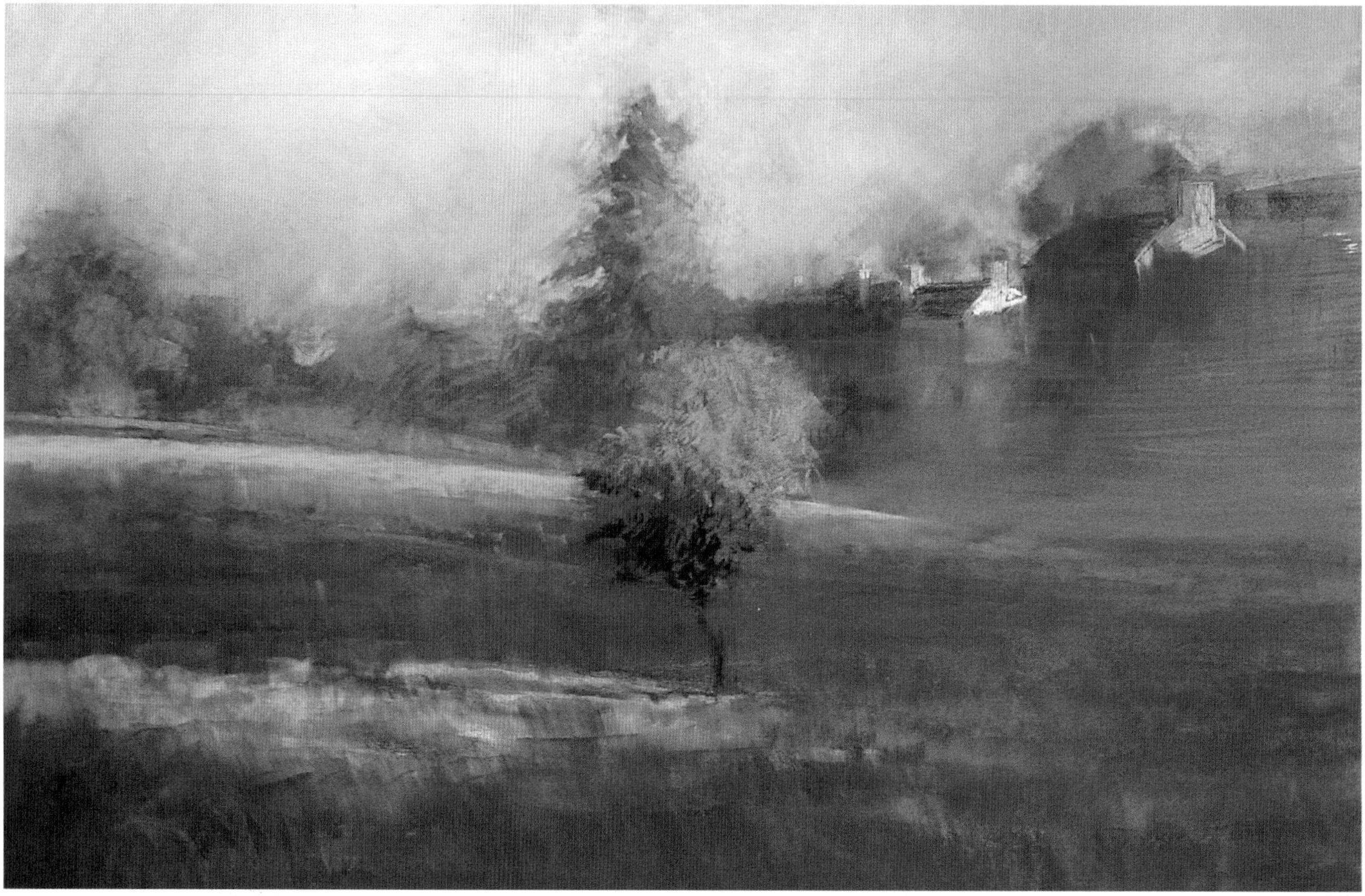

STEP 2

Create Depth

Creating space is the number one concern here. Blend all the initial colors from step one using a piece of packing foam. Add pastel to the foreground so the values are stronger. Add more high-key background values to soften the buildings in the mist.

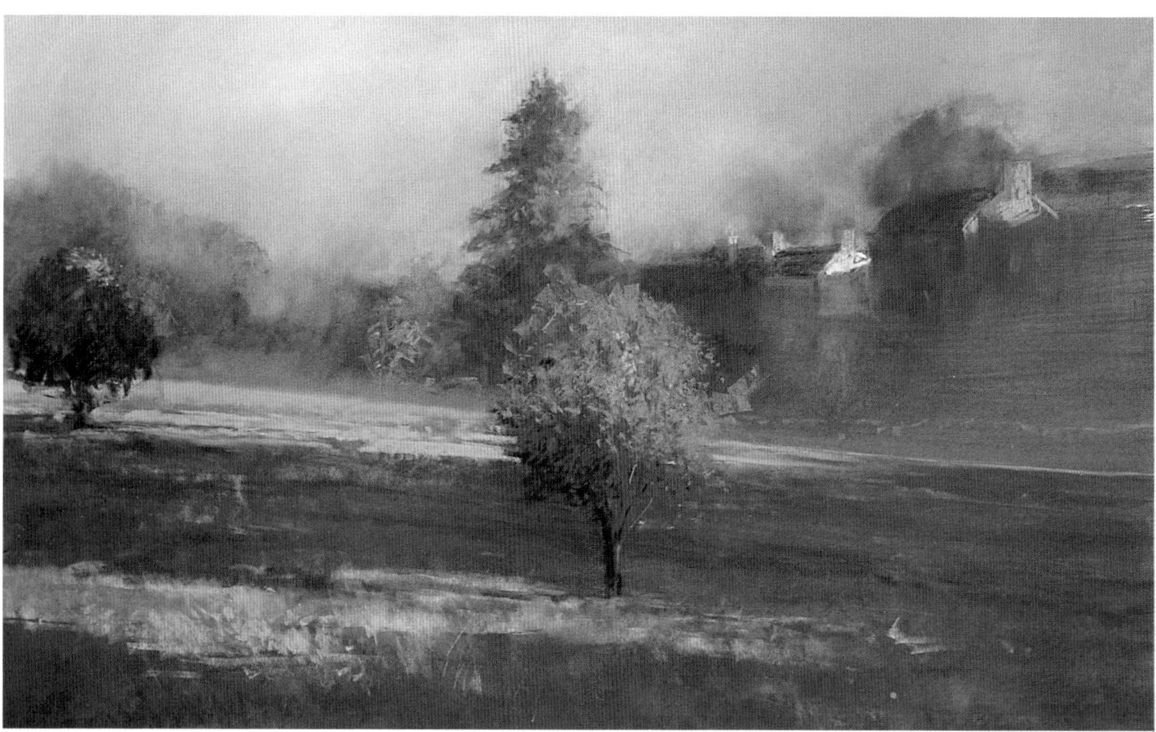

STEP 3

Balance the Composition

I add a tree on the left to balance the composition and help define the space. Blend colors as needed, but the remainder of the picture will be strokes only.

STEP 4

Dark Undercolor

Lay down some dark color as an underlayer for the lighter strokes of grass to come.

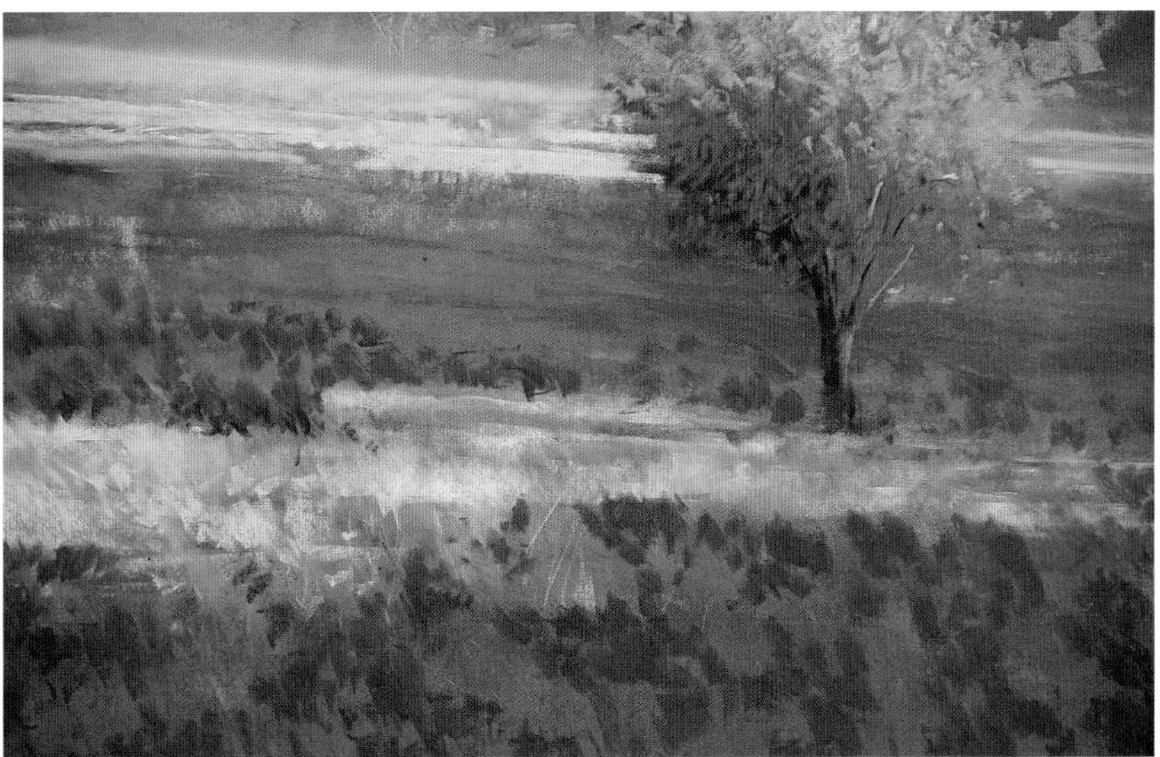

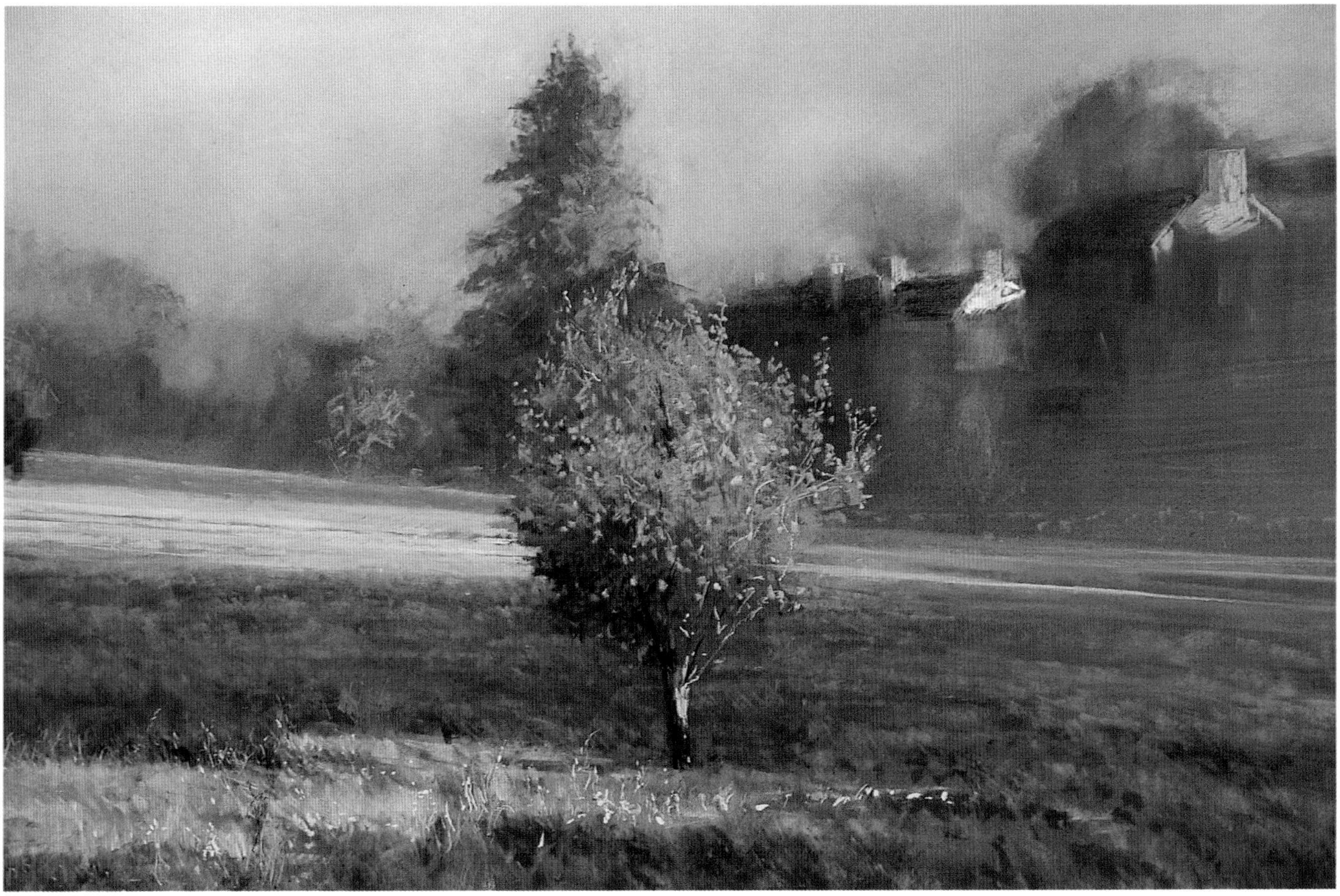

STEP 5

Strokes of Brilliant Light

Add bright, clear strokes to indicate light hitting the tree and grass. Don't do any blending here: These strokes of light set the mood and become the focus of the painting.

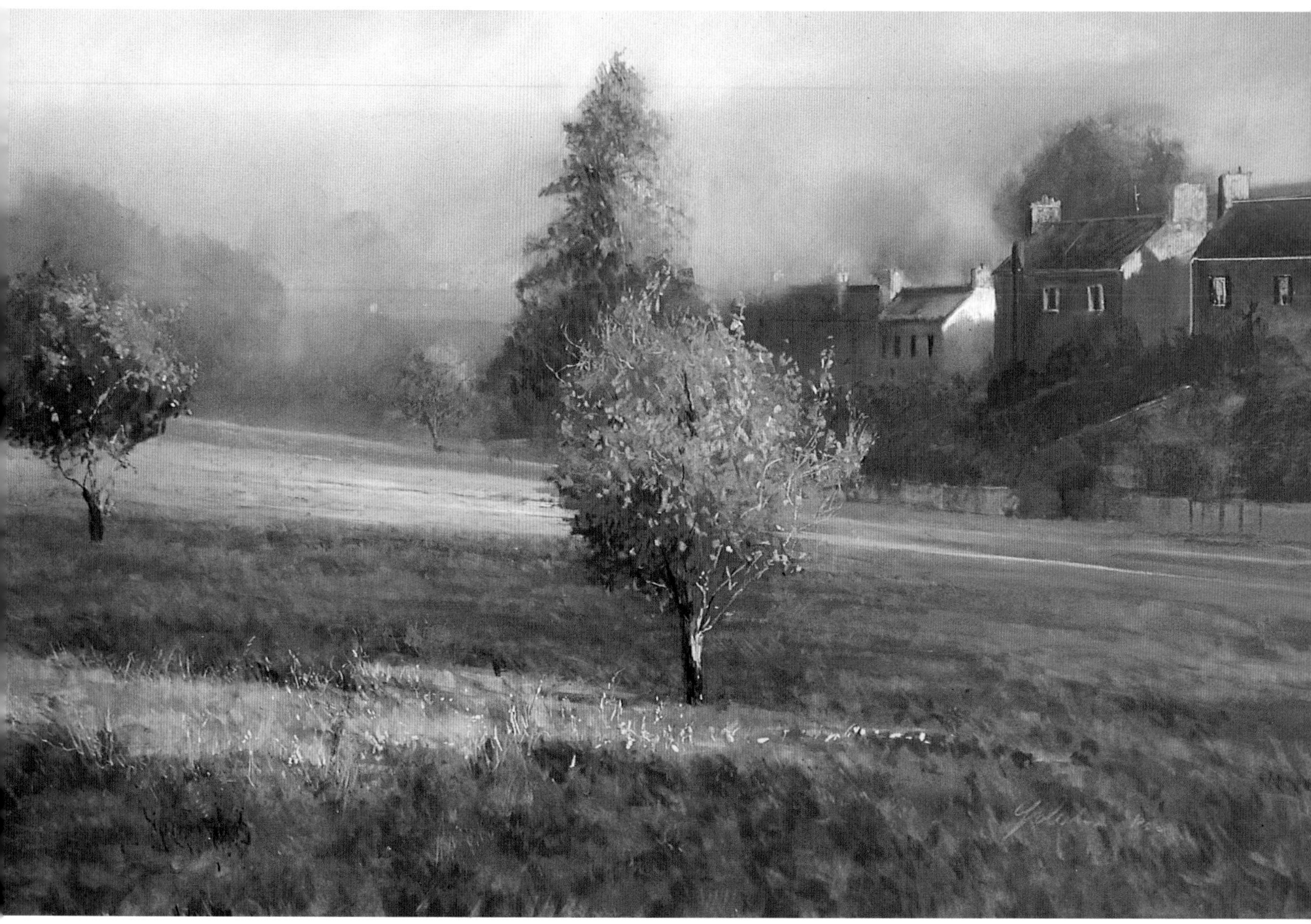

MORNING FOG AT BALLEROY
Gil Dellinger, pastel, 24″ × 36″ (61cm × 91.4cm)

STEP 6

Final Touches

The last act is to add background detail on the right. Add detail to the houses hit by light and soften some trees back in the mist. Notice that I changed the mist by lightening a section at the top to indicate a hillside shrouded in fog.

Key

KEEP PASTELS OPAQUE TO MAINTAIN THEIR SPARKLE

Quite the opposite to watercolor, which is at its most luminous when it is transparent, pastels glow only when kept cleanly opaque. For that reason, save the most sparkling lights for last, so the pure pastel pigment sits undisturbed and opaque on top of previous layers.

ENTICE THE VIEWER WITH A SHADOWED FOREGROUND Pastel

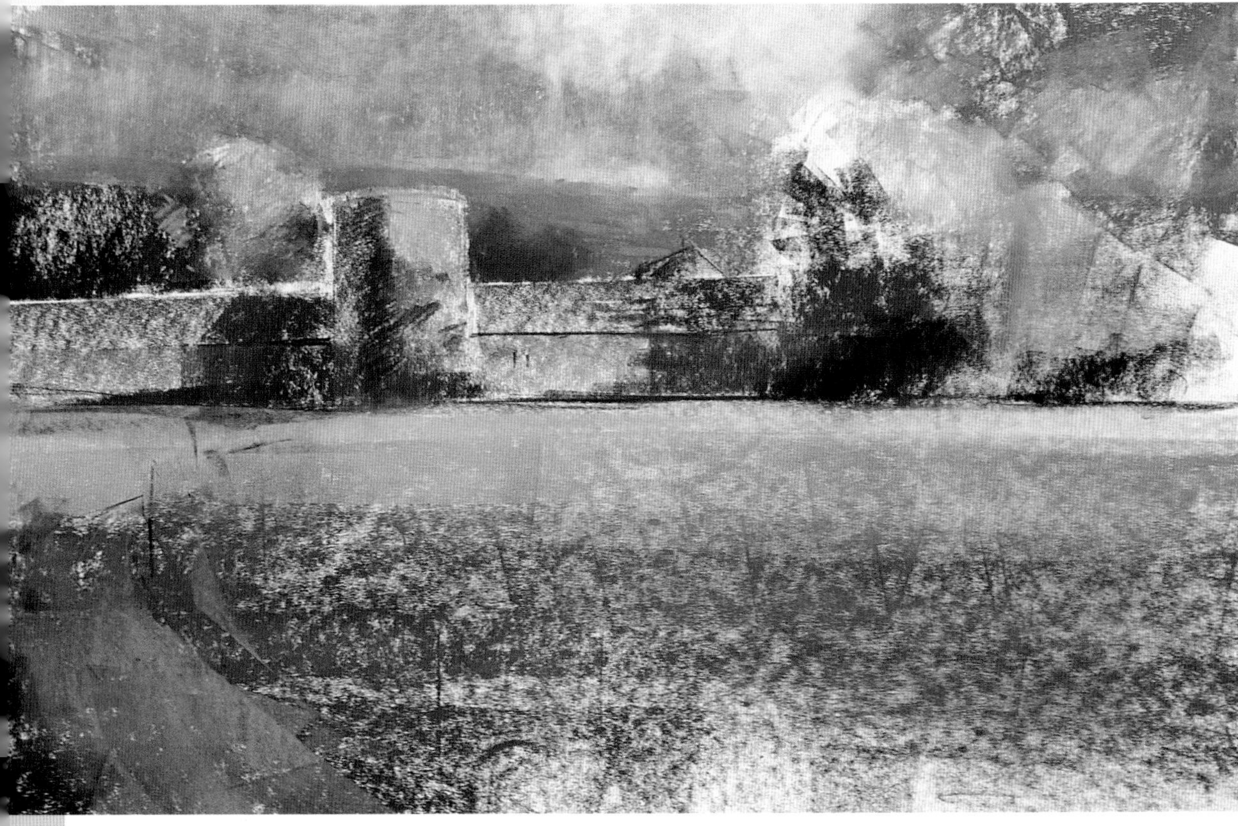

STEP 1

Block In Shapes

On a white background of Wallis pastel paper, block in major shapes with a dark sky behind them to accentuate the foreground lights. When using pastel, block in with hard pastels first to avoid filling the tooth of the paper. You can finish with soft pastels. Use the foreground shadow to pull the viewer in: The coldness of the foreground makes the viewer want to get into the light in the middle ground. The initial block-in takes a long time. I put layer over layer before I achieve the proper color.

STEP 2

Blend the Colors

Blend all the color using a foam block, which saves the fingers but doesn't remove a lot of pastel. This changes the color slightly, so you may have to adjust it by adding more color until the mood is just what you want. Use reds for late afternoon scenes. This sky has some red in the clouds, but not enough to be noticeable, and the buildings and trees have lots of touches of reds.

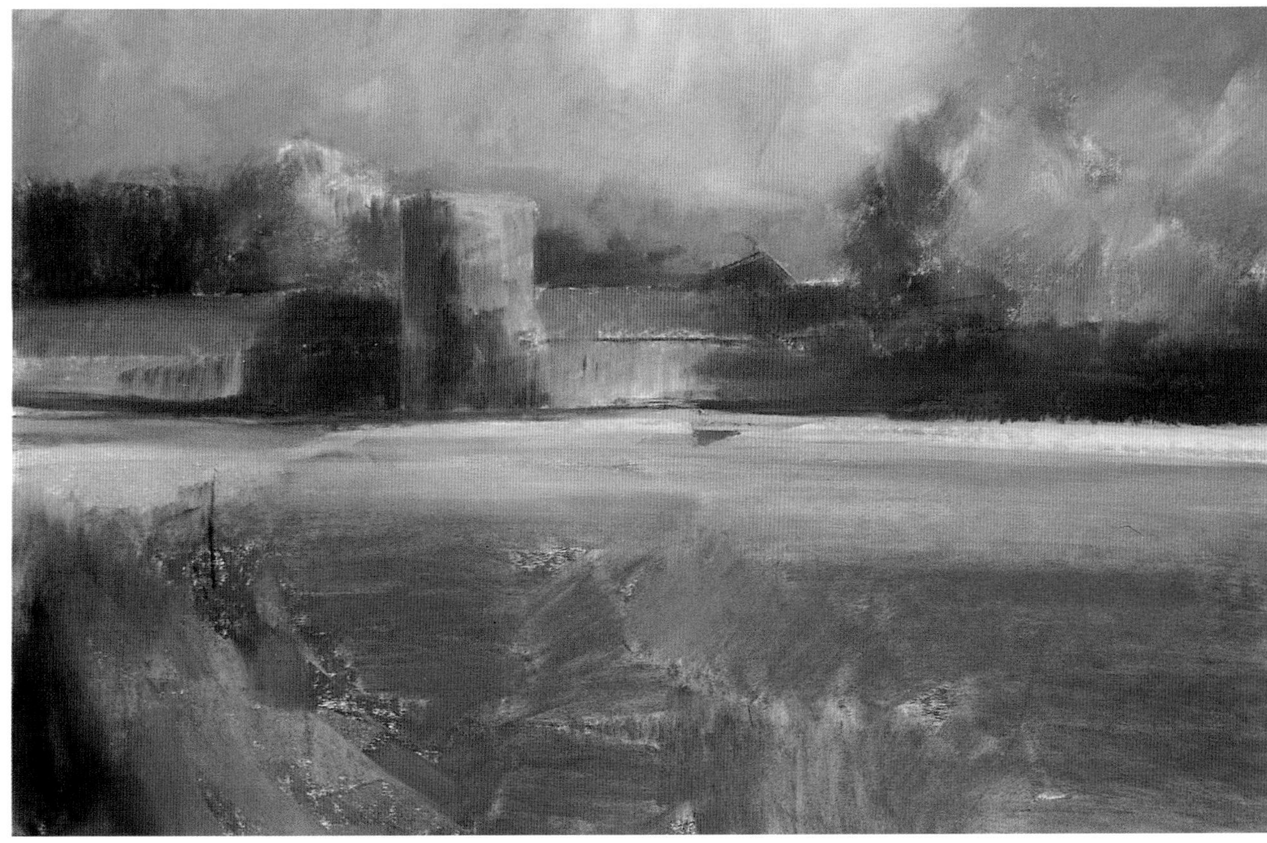

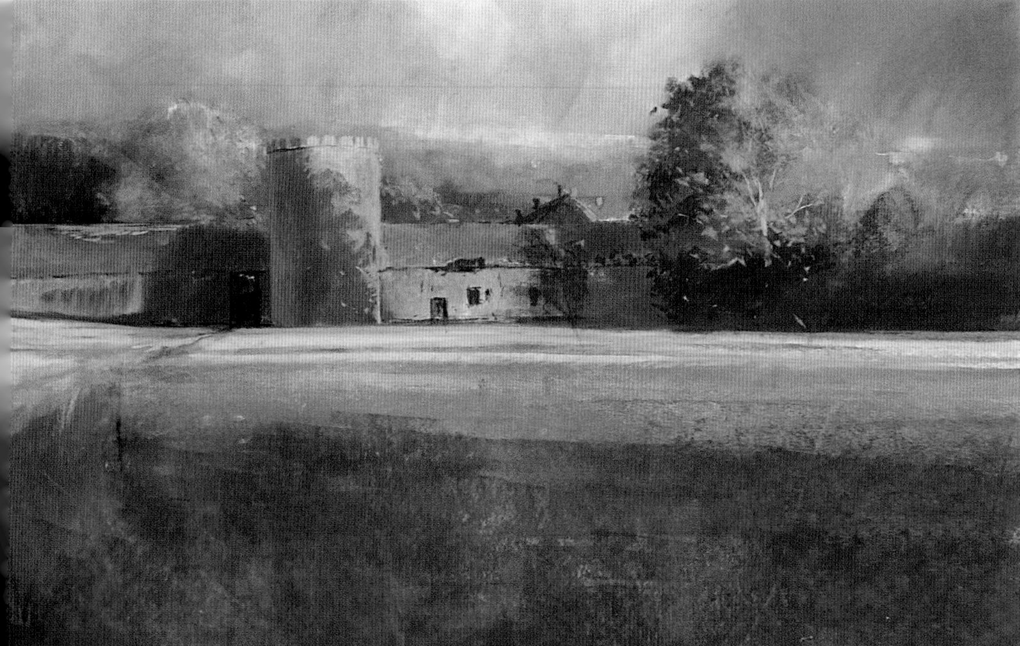

STEP 3

Begin Detailing

When I add detail, I move my eye and hand from the background to the foreground and back many times. I am most concerned with three elements: space, mood and light. Add small touches of background detail, keeping the background very subdued. Notice how the bend of the tree expresses the wind.

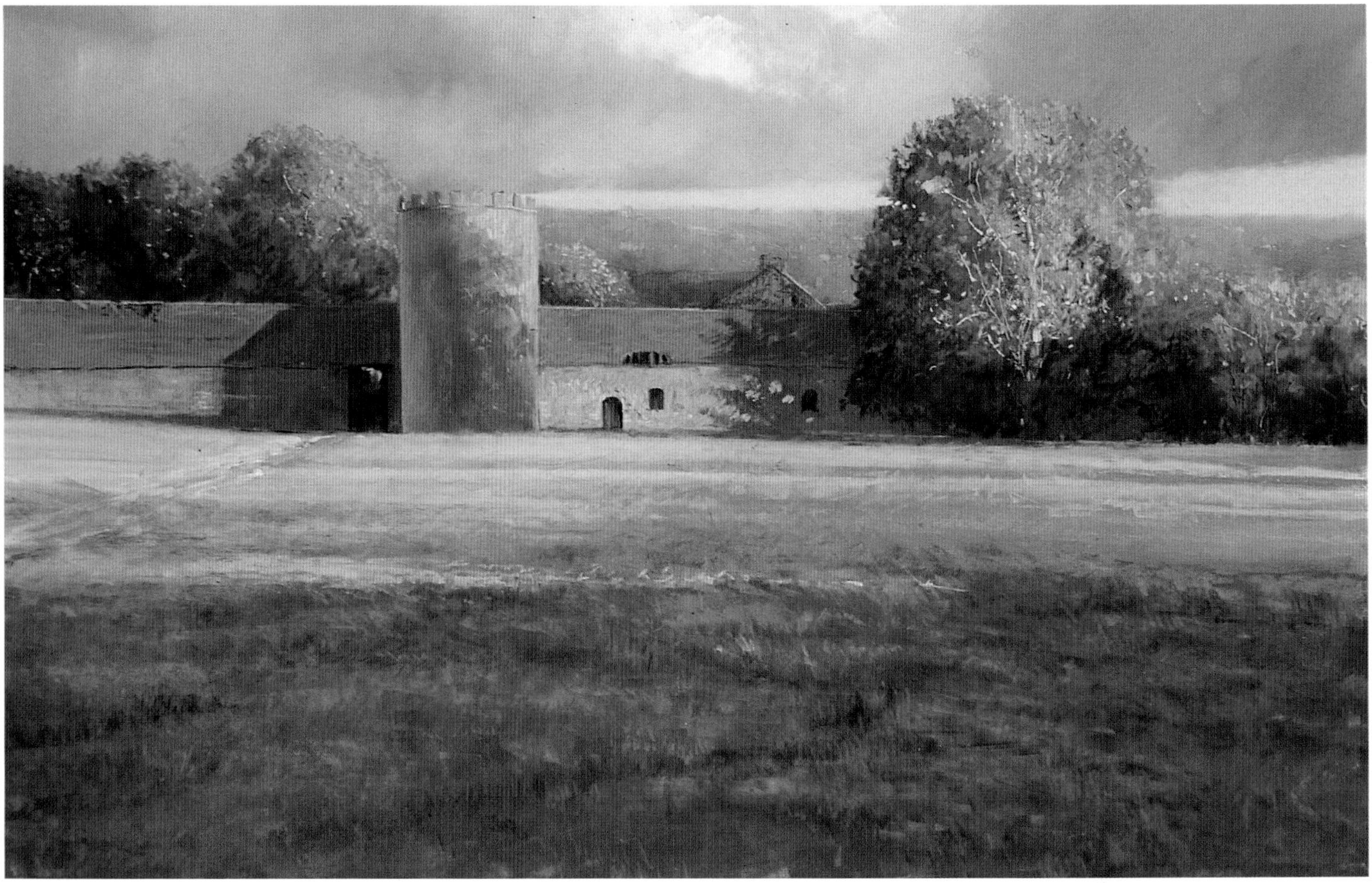

STEP 4

Final Touches

I eliminate most of the road in the lower left-hand corner, blending it in and covering it up with the foreground grass; I didn't like the perspective. Add more detail in the foreground grass, using many vertical strokes. This helps lead the viewer to the almost spotlighted middle distance where the warm light, the greatest contrast and the most detail make it the center of interest. The subtle details in the misty distance and the opening in the sky add to the mood of beautiful possibility.

A 16TH-CENTURY FARM
Gil Dellinger, pastel, 24" × 36" (30.5cm × 91.4cm)

START WITH SUNLIGHT Pastel

Here are three pastel painting "starts." In each one, the use of light is the main theme, and is already evident at this early stage. In most painting, but especially in pastel, it is important to know what mood you want to create from the beginning—and to start expressing it right away.

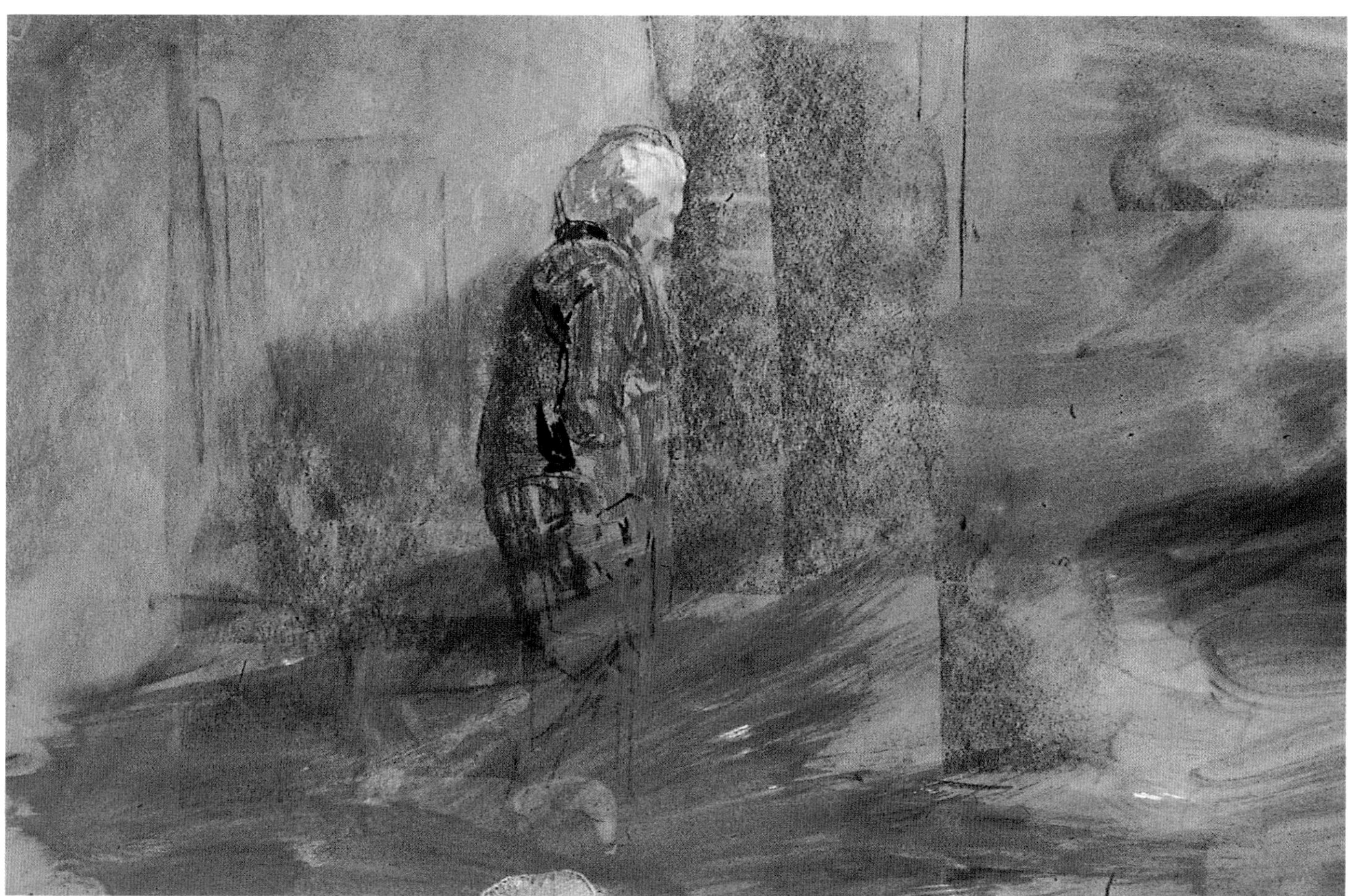

Late Afternoon Light

In this "start" I worked on a gray-toned Wallis sand paper. I was trying to capture late afternoon light as it passed through the buildings in Honfluer, France. I laid down a wide, flat stroke of Orange Nupastel against the blue-gray ground to signify late afternoon light. I highlighted it brighter in the woman's face and made the focal point harmonize by using a yellowy red.

Be Safe

Always wear a respirator and thin plastic/rubber gloves when working with pastel. It's full of poisons and is readily absorbed through skin and lungs! Blending with a small block of foam rather than your fingers helps protect you and helps prevent too much pastel from rubbing off your painting.

opposite, top and bottom

Unify Your Painting With Sunlight

In both of these "starts" shapes are laid in with darks and lights, leaving the background neutral. After the initial drawings I blocked in strong lights to capture the illusion of sunlight, leaving neutral grays as mid-tones. In each case the sunlight is the unifying factor that brings the whole painting together. Because the sunlight colors everything, the light, color and mood are the same throughout each painting, thus imparting unity.

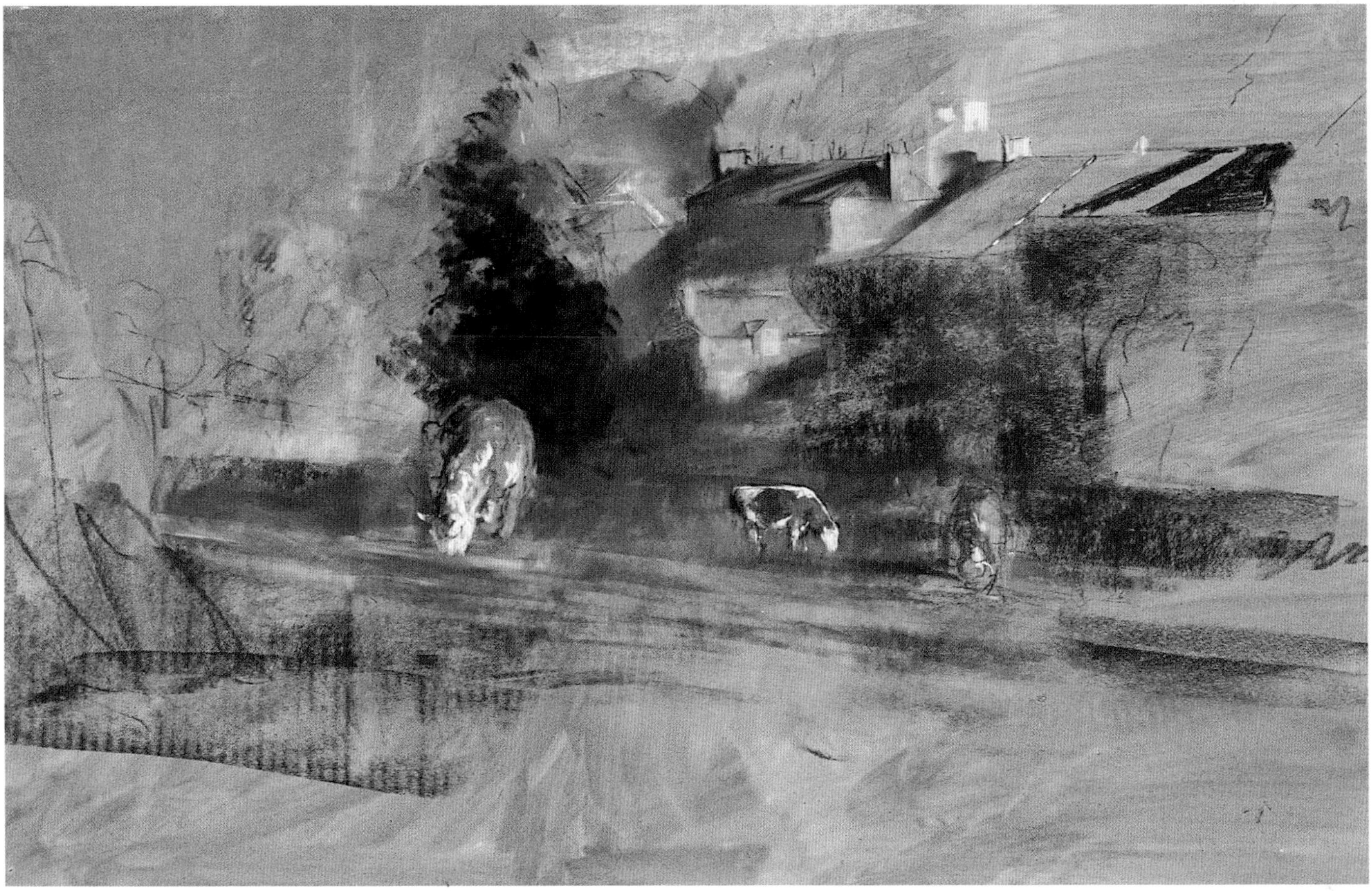

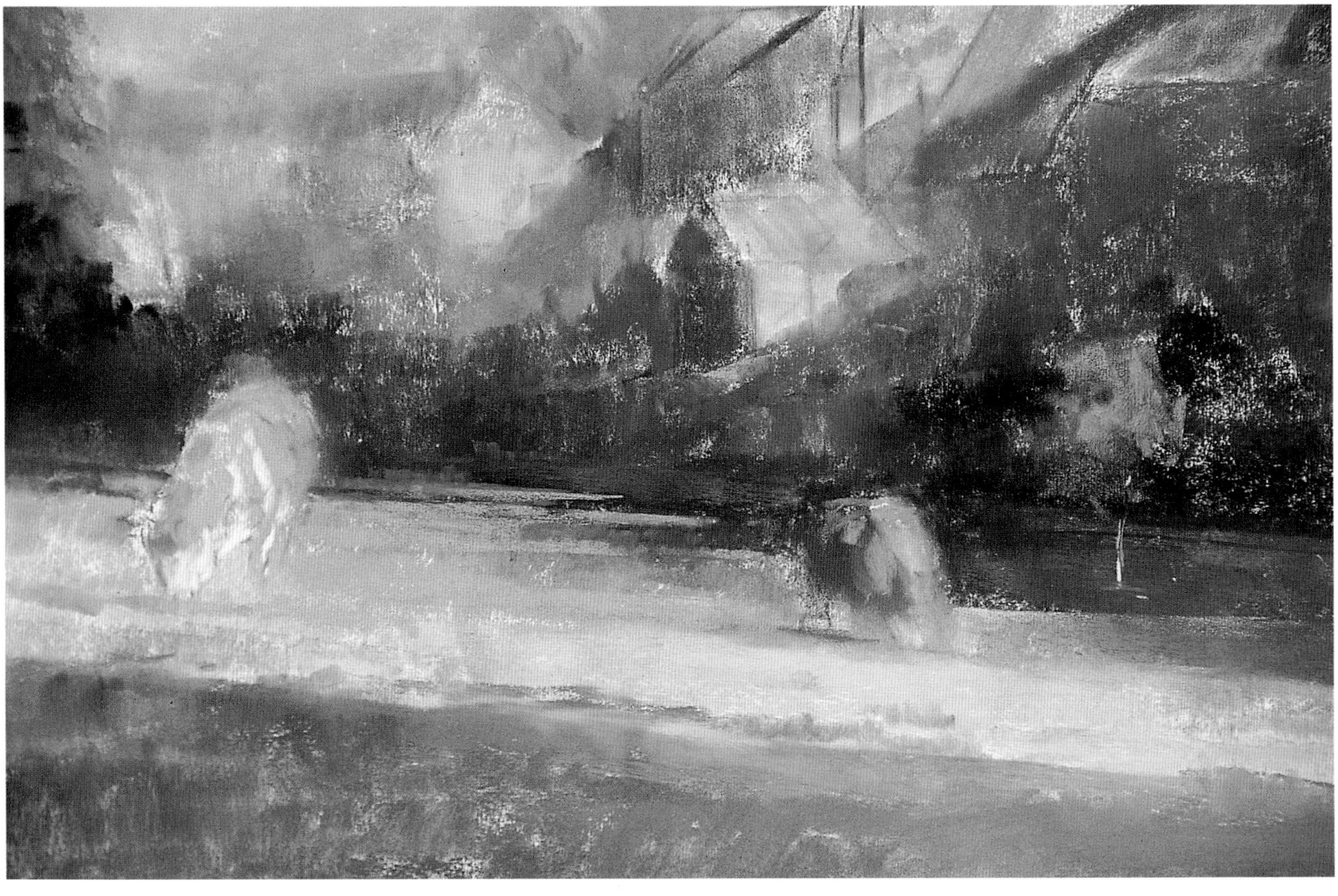

TRY CROSS-HATCHING TO CATCH LIGHT Pastel

Use heavier toothed Canson paper when doing a pastel painting that requires a heavier cross-hatched technique. This paper holds more pigment, allowing for more strokes. The more individualized strokes there are, the more the painting gives a sense of light moving across the surface.

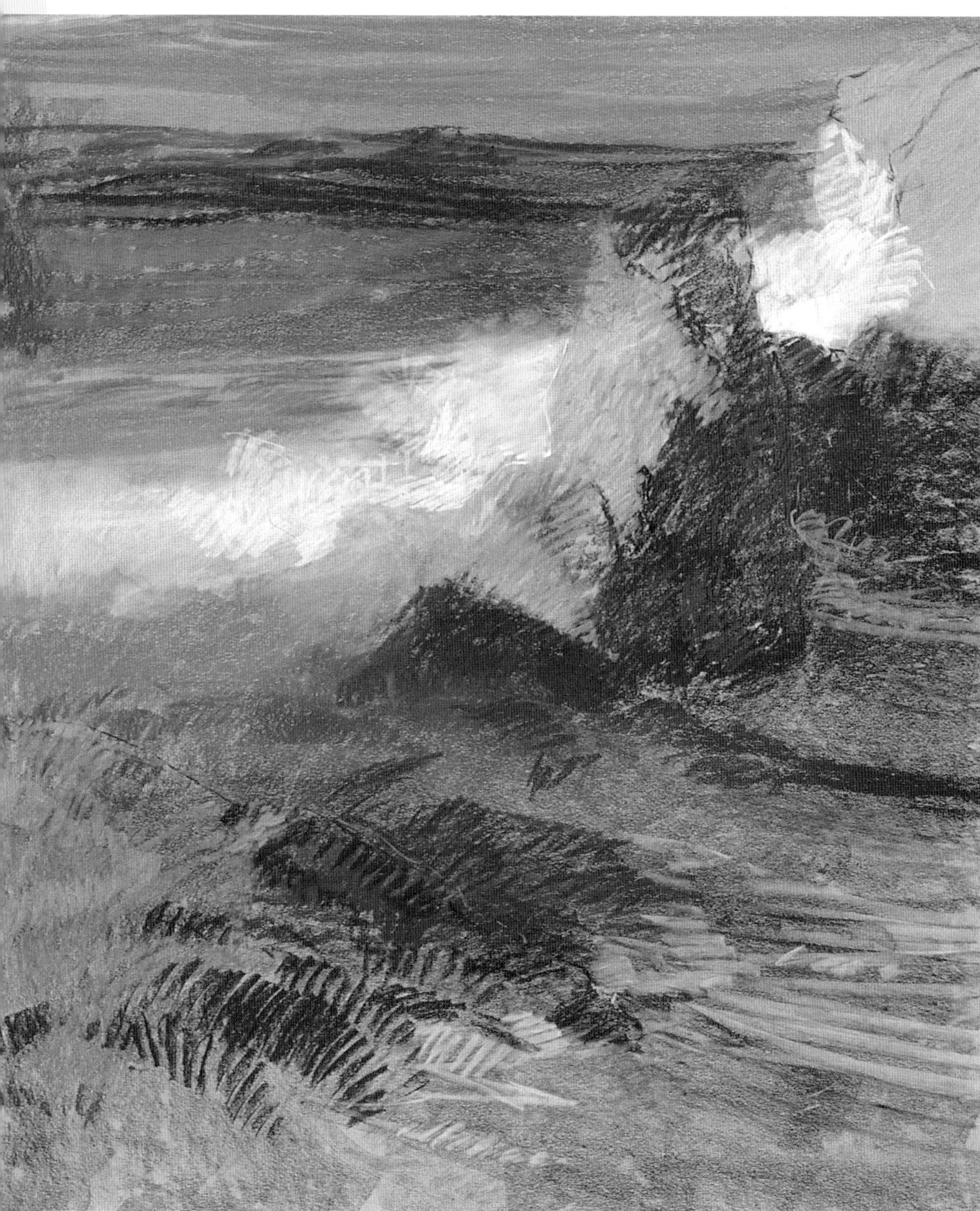

STEP 1

Block In the Shapes

I start this large picture on a 60″ × 40″ Canson steel-gray paper, spray-mounted on foamcore. Block in the shapes using a mixture of hard and soft pastels by cross-hatching color. This covers the paper but prevents filling in the tooth. Keep background details to a minimum. Lay down blue in the area to be filled with background rocks; this will make them appear more three-dimensional.

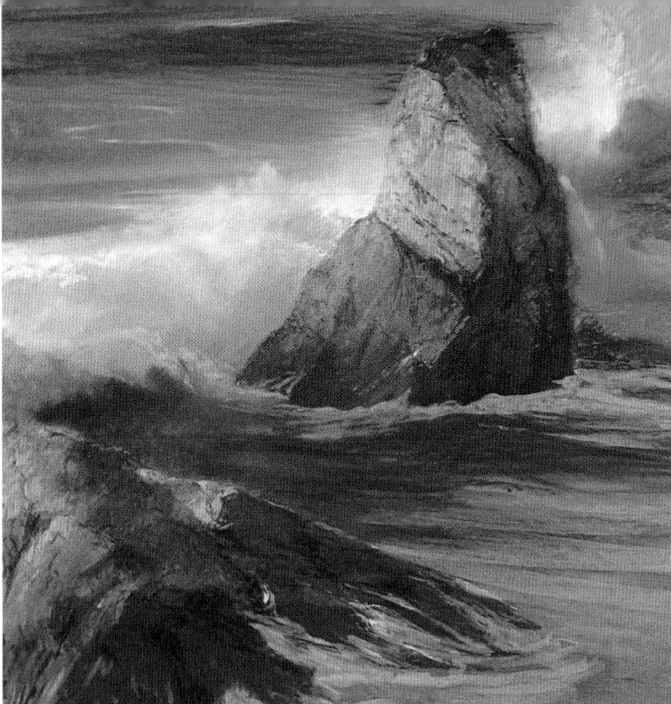

STEP 2

Blend and Detail

Add additional layers of color and blend them with a foam block. From this point on don't touch the surface again with your fingers or a blender. As I add details I realize that the main focal point (the rocks in the middle) looks too small. The scale is uncomfortable, so I decide to trim 10″ (25.4cm) off the bottom as seen in the final painting (below).

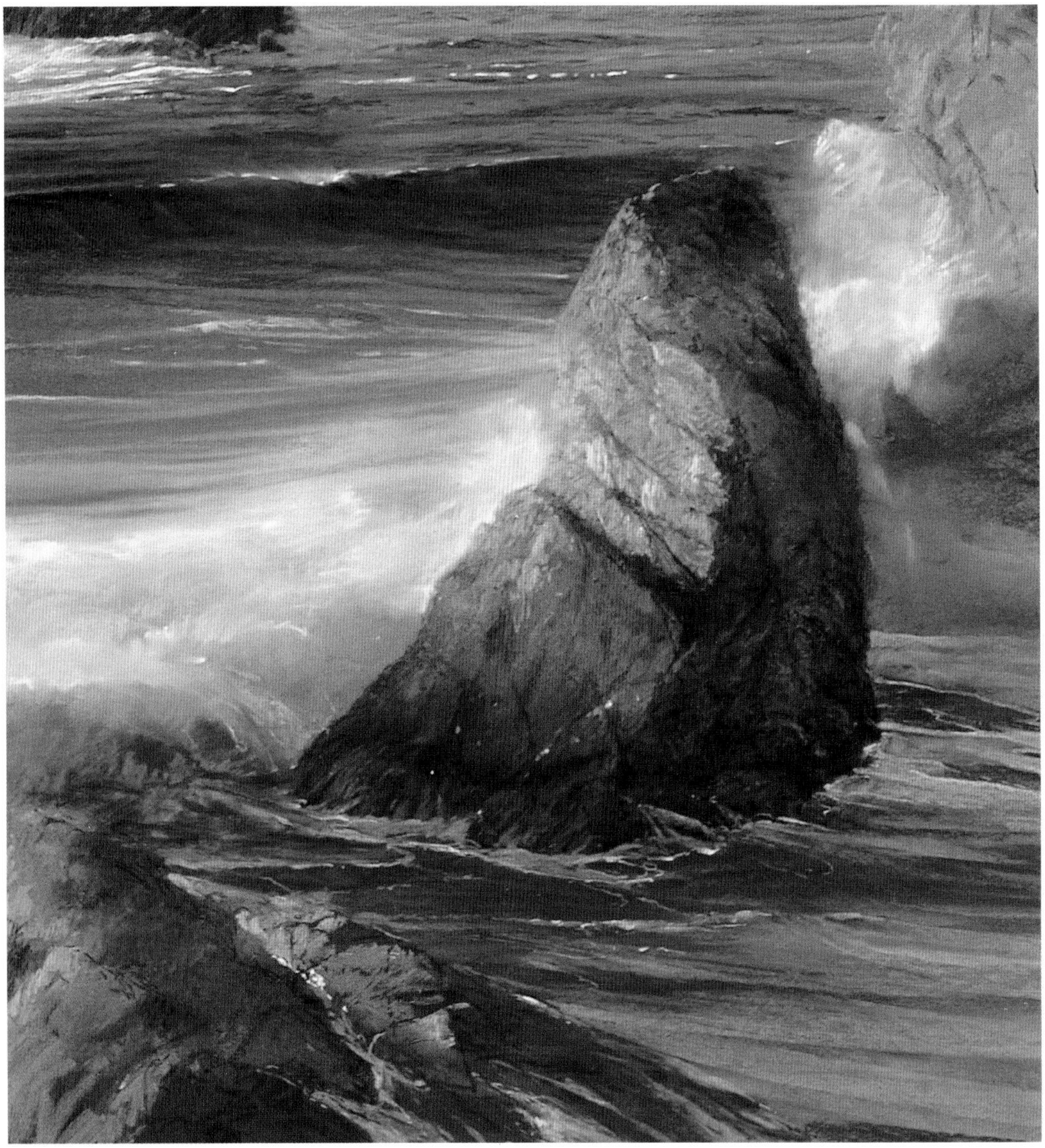

STEP 3

Final Touches

After cropping 10″ (25.4cm) off of the bottom, I do the final detailing, adding wavelets and foam and increasing light and detail in the foreground.

ROCKS NEAR LITTLE SUR
Gil Dellinger, pastel, 50″ × 40″ (127cm × 101.6cm)

FOLLOW THE LIGHT PASTEL

The following is a journal excerpt from the day Dellinger painted *Day Break—North Rim*:

"I am standing at the end of the world. I am in a 50 mph wind with 1,000 feet of cliff below me, and the edge of the cliff is a mere 2 feet away! I am hanging on to the guardrail so that I may see my children grow to adulthood. I am at Point Imperial on the North Rim of the Grand Canyon. It is 6 A.M. and bitterly cold for June. The snow is barely gone from the heavy winter, and I am among the first to visit here since the road opened from the spring thaw. I hate heights but I wouldn't leave this spot for anything because the view is so stunning! No one else is here yet, and the sky grows faintly lighter. I hunker down with a blanket around me, in my thermal underwear, and I watch! It will be an hour until the sun comes up, and two hours until the carloads of tourists speaking every language imaginable come to invade. But for now, all I am seeing is mine, and I watch every nuance of light change. I won't paint today because of the wind, but I will photograph and observe. I am interested in light and how it changes the forms; how they emerge and disappear as the light shifts and the atmosphere becomes more dense. I will be so familiar with this spot when I am done observing that, unless I have amnesia, this day will be mine forever. And it will eventually be part of my paintings."

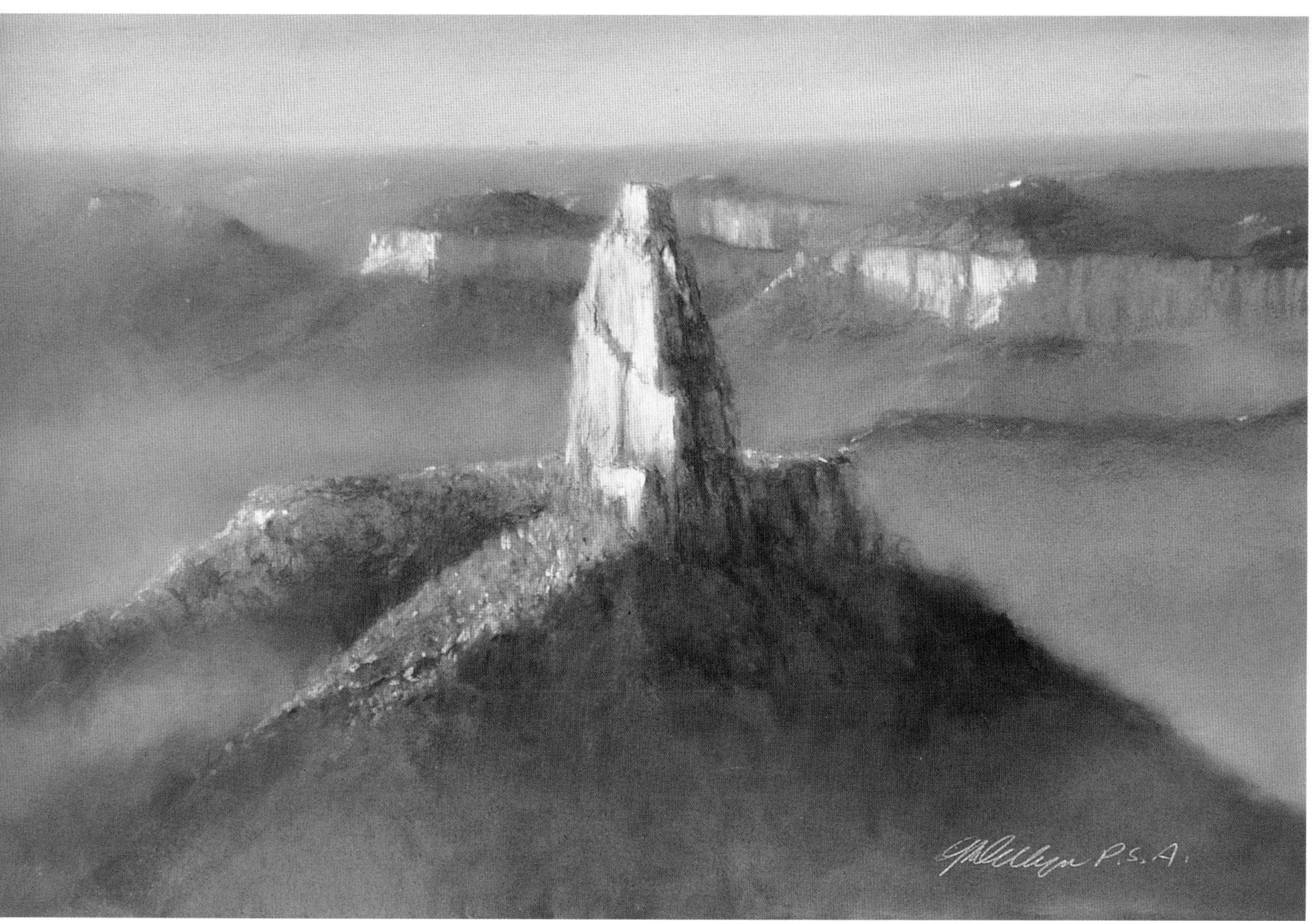

Create Depth

The day I worked at this spot, the wind was so strong that my easel nearly blew to Mexico. So I gave up and photographed it instead. This painting was done in my studio from a slide and my vivid memories. I recreated the space I observed by toning down the background: Reds became mauves; pinks, ochres and yellows were modulated with grays and soft greens. The foreground is much more saturated than the background.

DAYBREAK—NORTH RIM
Gil Dellinger, pastel, 30" × 44" (76.2cm × 111.8cm)

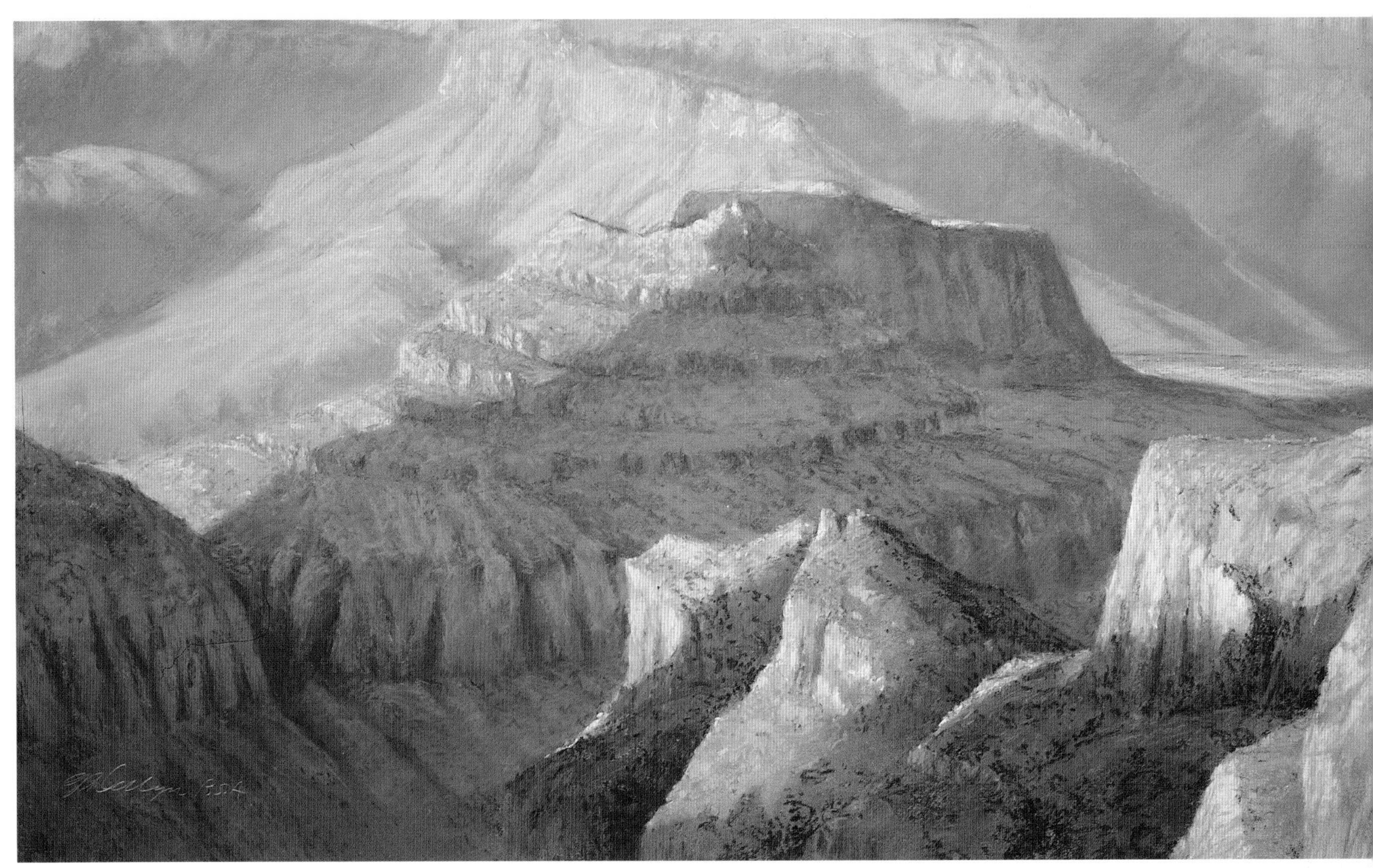

Another Example of Created Depth

This is another Grand Canyon piece using depth-creating techniques similar to those used in *Daybreak—North Rim*.

DAWN AT CAPE ROYAL
Gil Dellinger, pastel, 27" × 40" (68.6cm × 101.6cm)

GALLERY

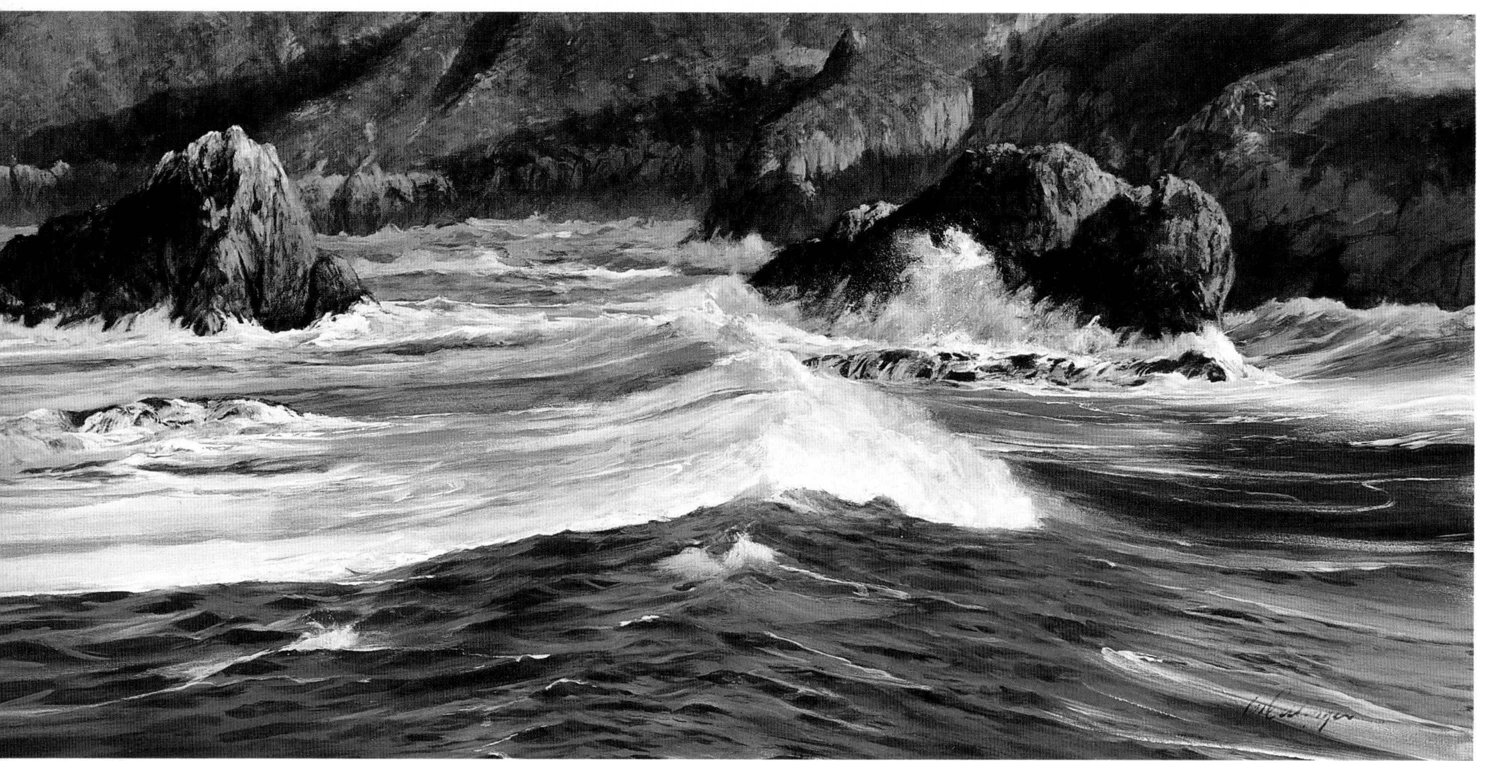

FIRST LIGHT AT GARRAPATA
Gil Dellinger, acrylic, 36″ × 72″ (91.4cm × 182.9cm)

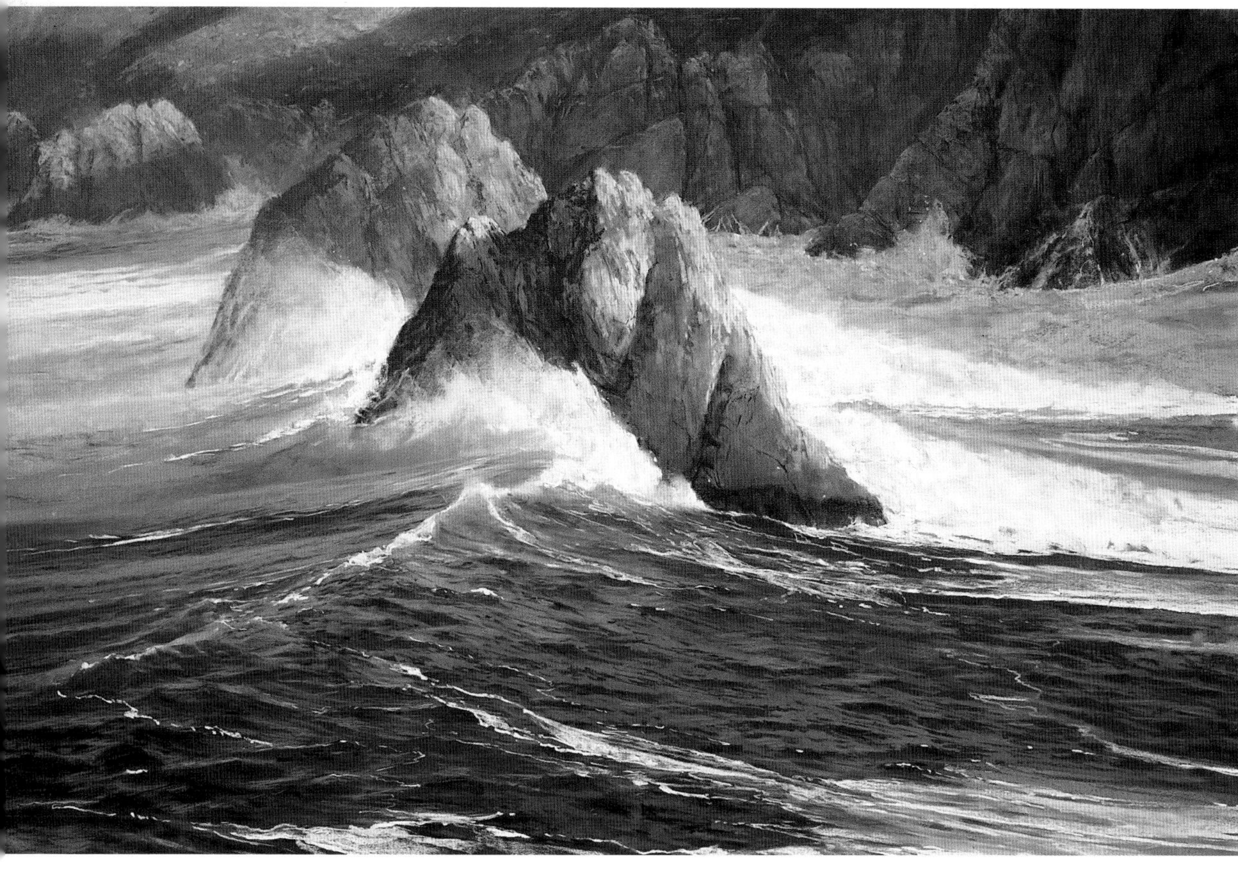

DAWN AT GARRAPATA
Gil Dellinger, pastel, 33″ × 53″ (83.8cm × 134.6cm)

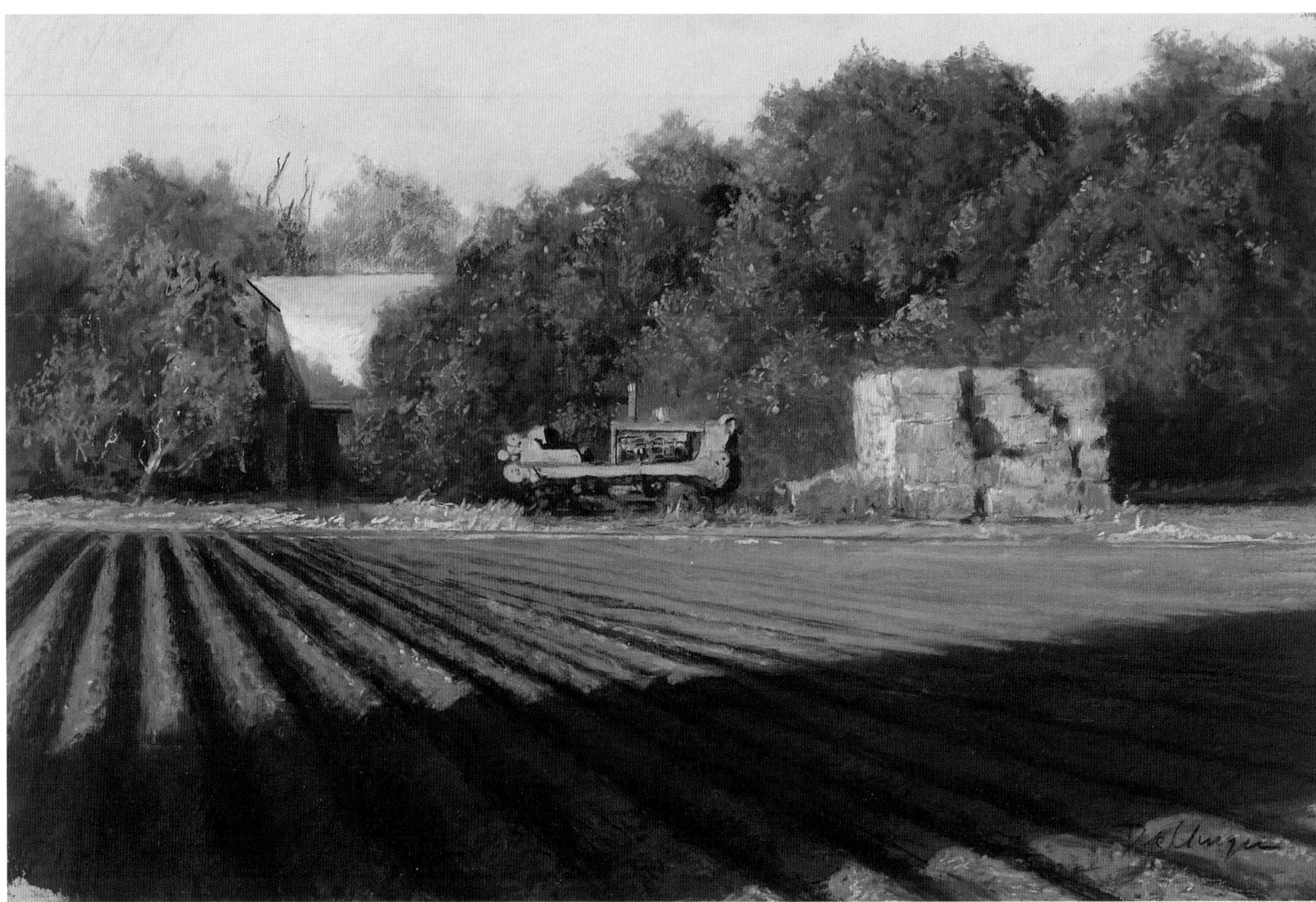

opposite, top and bottom

Same Subject, Different Mediums

These pieces are of the same subject, done at the same time of day but in different mediums. The beauty of the pastel (bottom) is its sparkling quality. Each stroke brings to the surface radiant light captured by the opacity of the medium. Nothing quite matches pastel in the quality of sunlight expressed by a Naples or Cadmium Yellow set down undisturbed. By slightly modulating the color and deepening it, I am able to move the light across the rocks, from the initial point where it strikes the rock until the edge softens at the transition to the shadow.

With acrylic (top), the lights are not quite as brilliant because the paint dries slightly darker than it goes on and does not exhibit the same opacity. But acrylic can establish deep and absorbing shadows, and bounced lights in the shadows that are rich and penetrating. By keeping shadows somewhat transparent, a magical space is created. And by keeping lights opaque, you can create stunning contrast. It is important, therefore, to know the properties of each tube of paint and work toward its strength; I could not create sunlight in acrylic without the opaque cadmiums, ochres and Naples Yellow.

This painting was done in the farmlands of the San Joaquin Valley. The idea of sunlight is enhanced by focus on the yellow tractor. Yellows and oranges help communicate mood in sunlight. The warm brown earth in the foreground has the same effect. In addition I use warmer undertones for the trees, underlaying ochres and siennas. I do this by "glazing" the surface with Yellow Ocher Nupastel and then overlaying my greens. The yellow sunlight colors peek through the greens and suggest the warmth of sunlight hitting the trees.

CAT IN THE SUN

Gil Dellinger, pastel, 20" × 30" (50.8cm × 76.2cm)

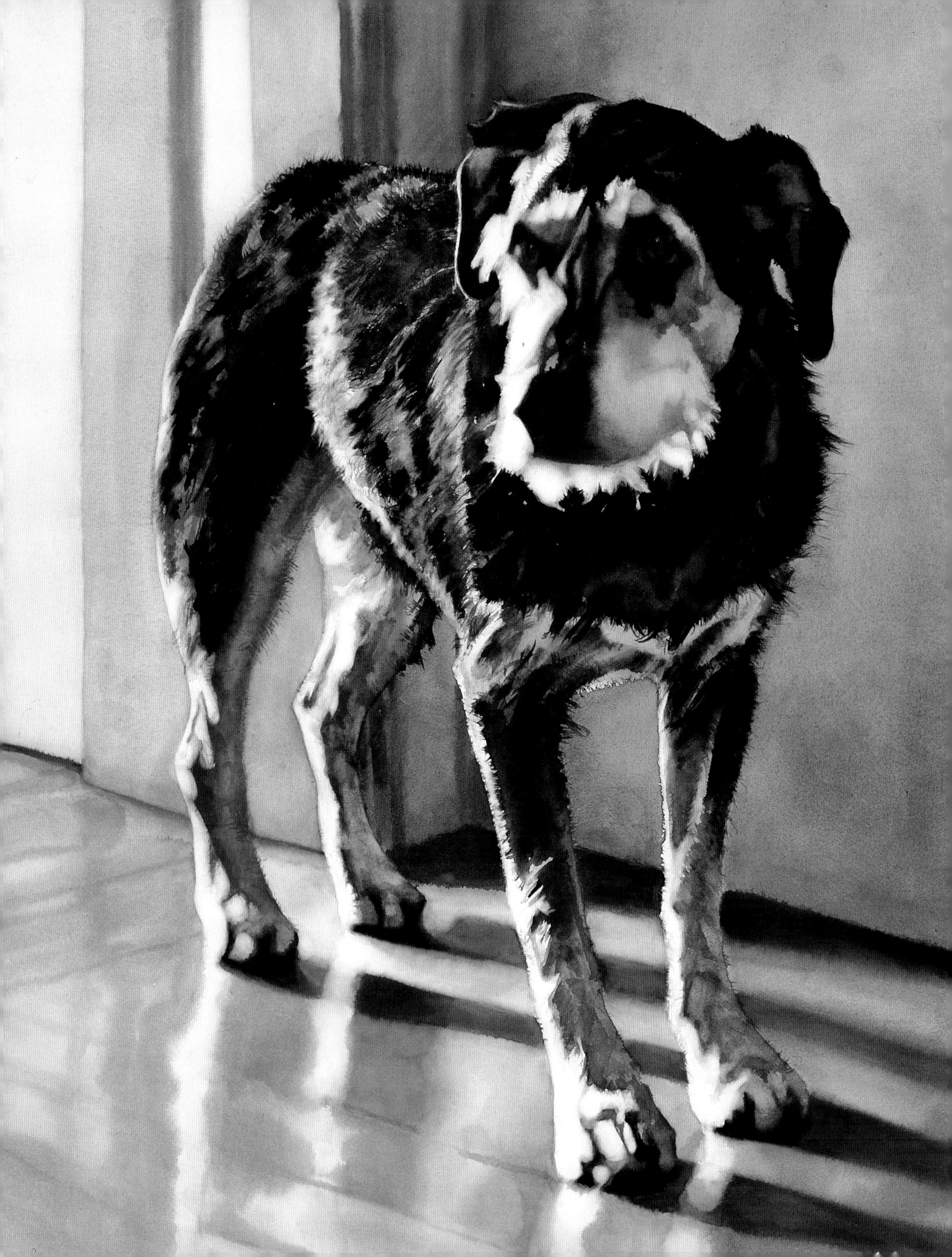

DARE TO DRAMATIZE DOMESTIC SCENES IN WATERCOLOR

CHAPTER 7

KAREN FREY

Light is the essence of most of Karen Frey's paintings. For Frey, light reveals form, relates time and suggests mood. Most of the time she looks for big shapes of light and dark in her subject and then exaggerates the values to achieve a more interesting or dramatic effect. There are three main ways that Frey finds inspiration for the lighting that she wants for her paintings. First, she often works from photos. She keeps her camera loaded and accessible, ready to capture those moments when the lighting is just perfect. Second, interpreting the ever-changing natural light while working on location is an exercise she finds both stimulating and challenging. Third, artificial lighting conditions offer her the opportunity to create and manipulate unique dramatic effects. In translating this inspiration to her watercolor paper, Frey uses an interesting technique, shown in the following demonstrations, that combines a more closely rendered underpainting in staining colors with a loose, bold final layer done completely with a wet-into-wet technique. Regardless of the source, her sensitive observation of light transforms an ordinary image into a magical one.

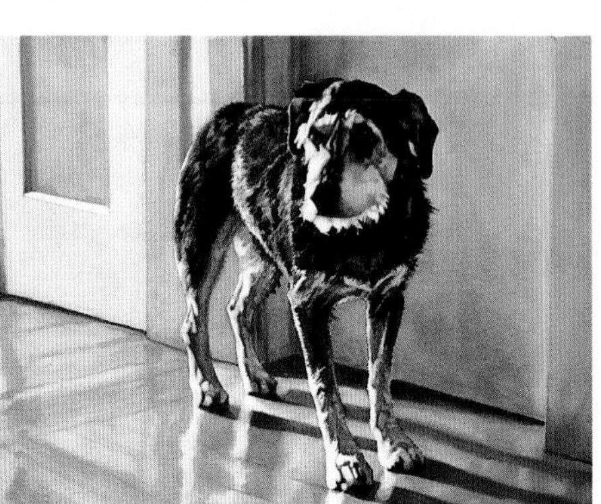

ROSE—IN THE HALLWAY
Karen Frey, watercolor, 36″ × 48″ (91.4cm × 121.9cm)

I wanted the soft, delicate pastel lighting to describe the tentative nature of Rose. Due to the large format, the true challenge of this painting was in the execution. I broke down the background and foreground into workable sections and mixed four or five varied colors in large plastic containers, making sure the pigment-to-water ratio was consistent.

PAINT DAPPLED SUNLIGHT ON FOLIAGE Watercolor

Foliage in dappled or spotty sunlight appears to be a complex, difficult subject. What attracts the eye are the delightful fluttering contrasts and shadows alive with movement. The key to catching that mood is to keep the eye moving by including a variety of contrasts in shape, value, color and texture.

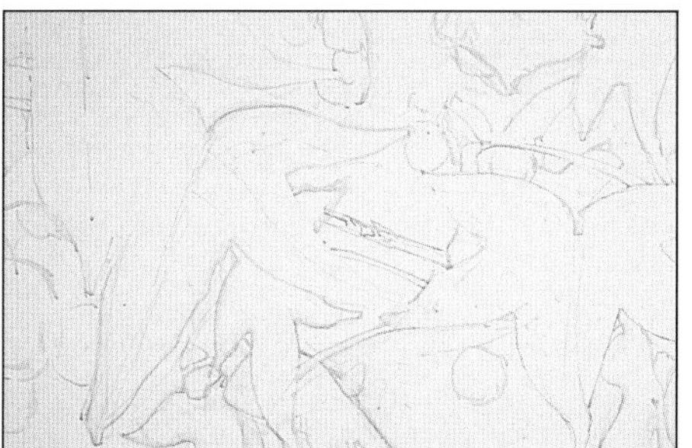

STEP 1

Establish Major Shapes and Divisions of Space

Block in the essence of the composition, using Manganese or Cerulean Blue. These colors have a high degree of opacity but are not staining. If you need to correct a line, they lift with clear water and gentle scrubbing with a soft brush. Include only as much information in the drawing as you personally need to continue painting in comfort. Too much drawing can limit your willingness to adjust as you develop the painting. Be particularly sensitive to the flow of line and the rhythm of shapes.

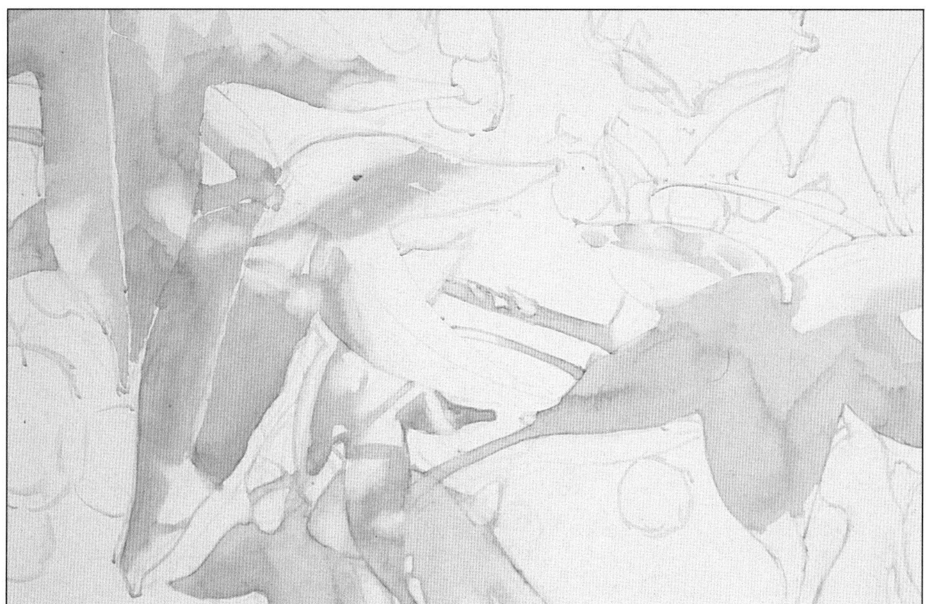

STEP 2

Block In the Underpainting

This is not the time to be primarily concerned with technique. Your focus should be on establishing color, or potential color, and value mass. Develop the point of interest first. Then support and flatter that with the background. Keep color mixtures well diluted to prevent surface congestion.

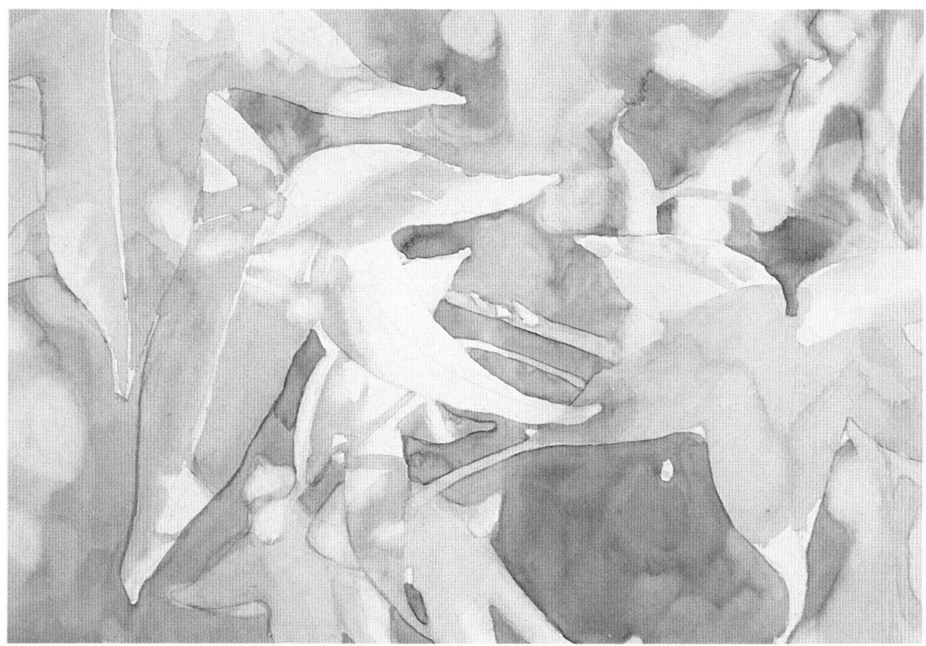

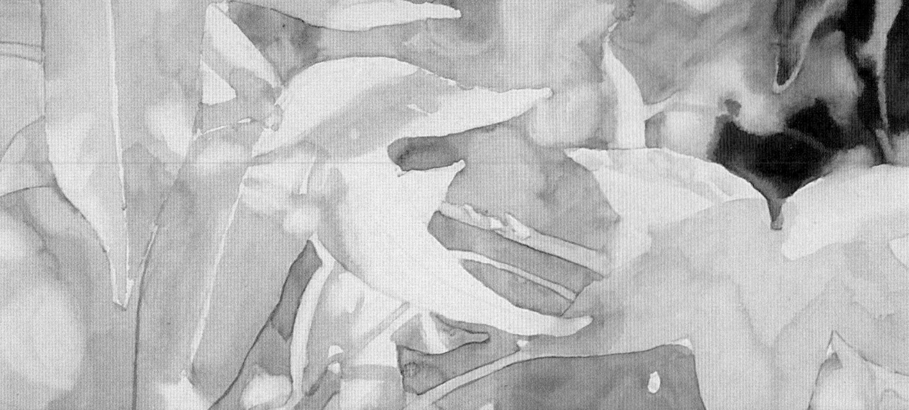

STEP 3

Break the Ice

It is time to start painting the final colors. Use a wet-into-wet technique, dropping clean pigment into a dampened area. Start with smaller areas you can control comfortably.

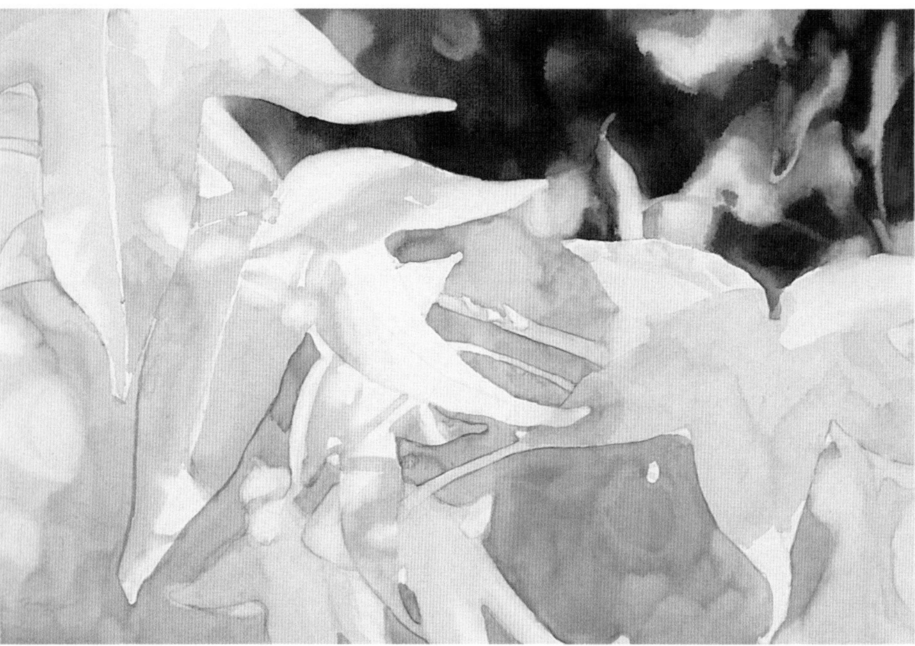

STEP 4

Proceed With the Background

The initial layer of color is highly diluted, but as you develop the final wash, increase the pigment strength and decrease the water. Colors will be layered, so don't dirty the wash with extreme contrasting color (complements). For convenience I flip the painting upside down as I work. It helps me see shapes instead of objects.

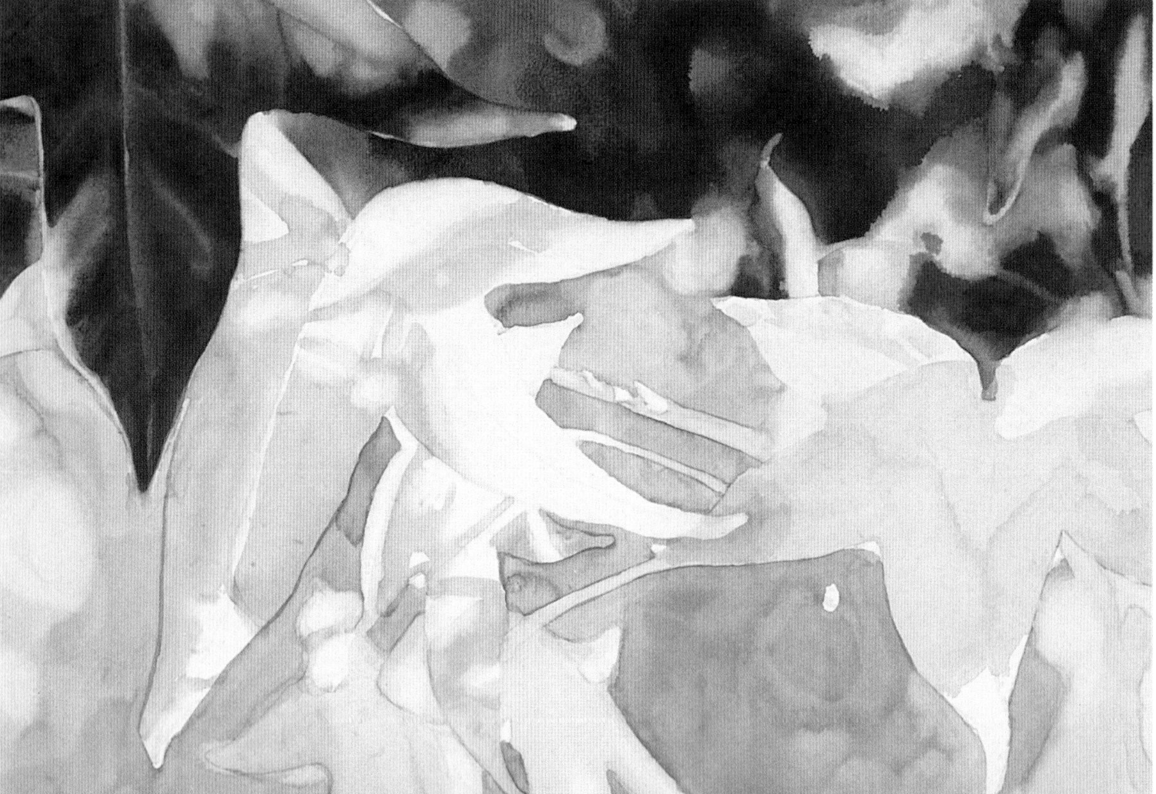

STEP 5

A Balancing Act

Having established the upper background, this is a good time to begin a leaf. It should be different in tone from the background, yet harmonious. Crisp edges stand out from the soft edges of the background. Mix greens with Cadmium Yellow Lemon, Quinacridone Gold, Quinacridone Burnt Orange, Peacock, Cobalt and Prussian Blue.

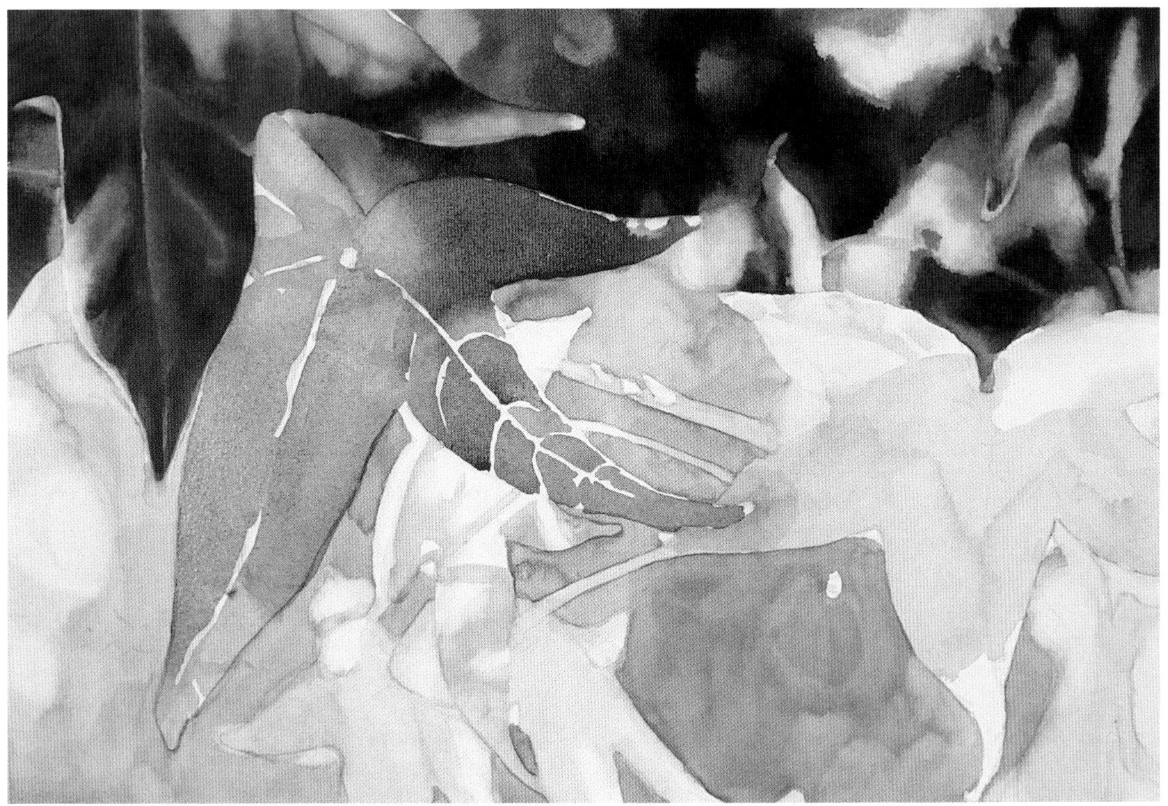

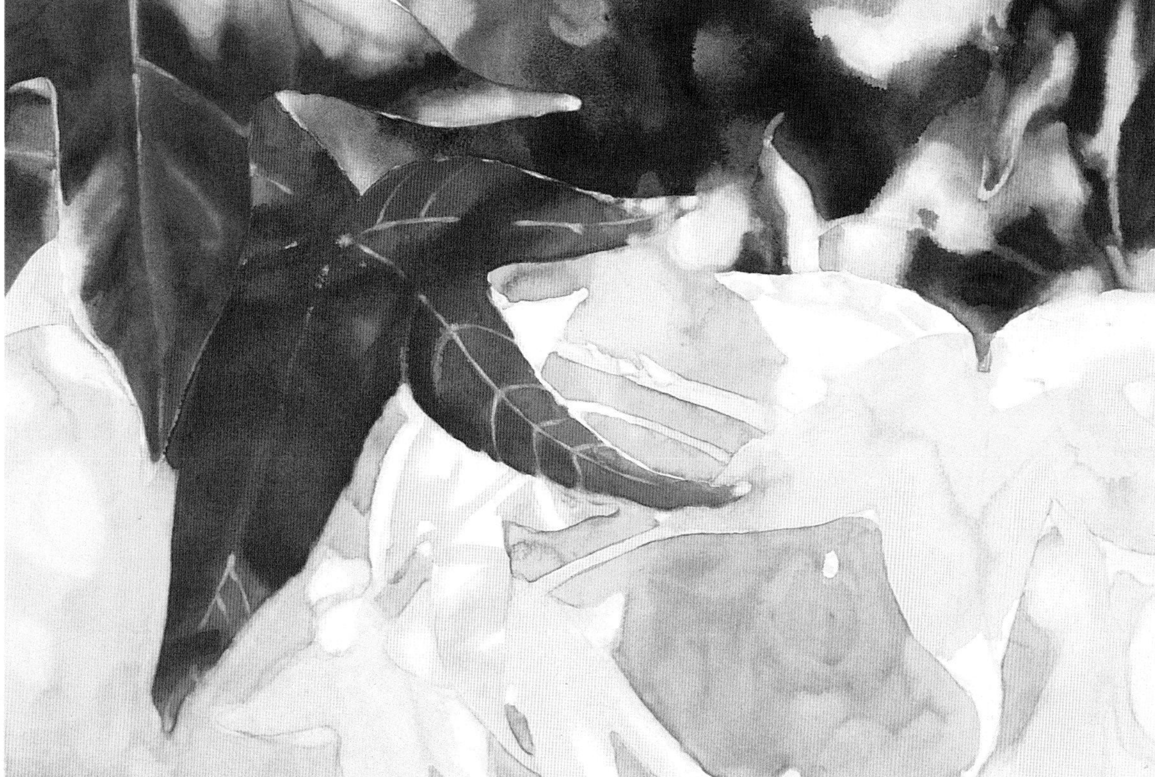

STEP 6

Red Leaf

The basic contrast between warm and cool dictates that the red leaf is a major point of interest. Use Opera, Cadmium Red, Quinacridone Rose and Cadmium Yellow Deep for the illuminated area of the leaf; use Quinacridone Rose, Carmine, Cadmium Red, Cobalt and Ultramarine Blue for the shadows. Work around the veins to keep the edges sharp.

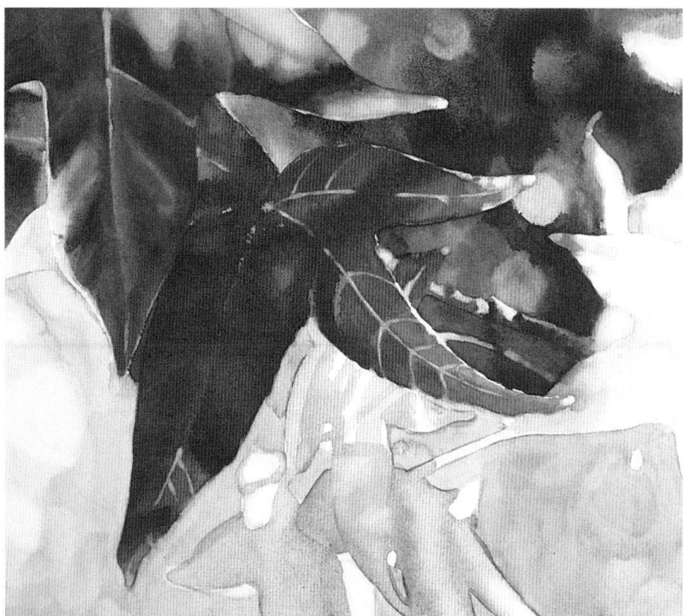

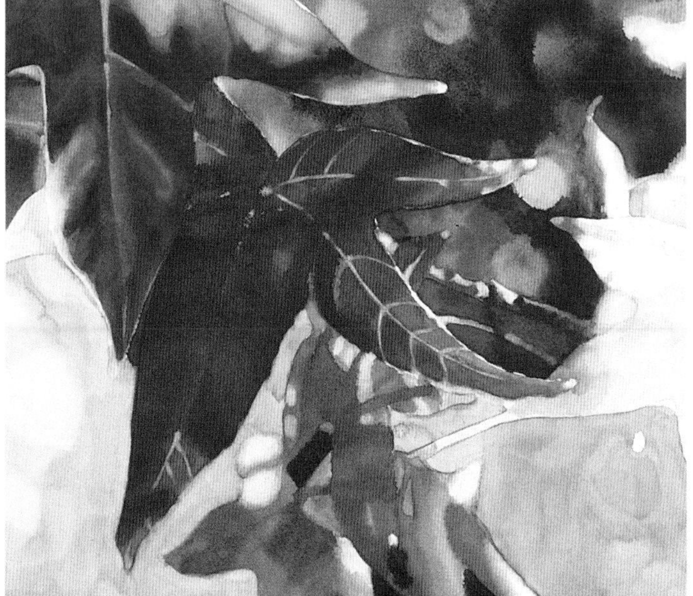

STEP 7

Midspace Leaves

Use background color to the right of the leaf to contrast with and enhance the red. The middle-ground leaves are similar in character to the leaf in the upper right corner (see step six). They are less intense in color and contrast than the primary leaves. Also, they are smaller to indicate spatial depth. To achieve the appropriate soft edge, paint the dark background revealed between the leaves along with the leaves, allowing edges to be soft.

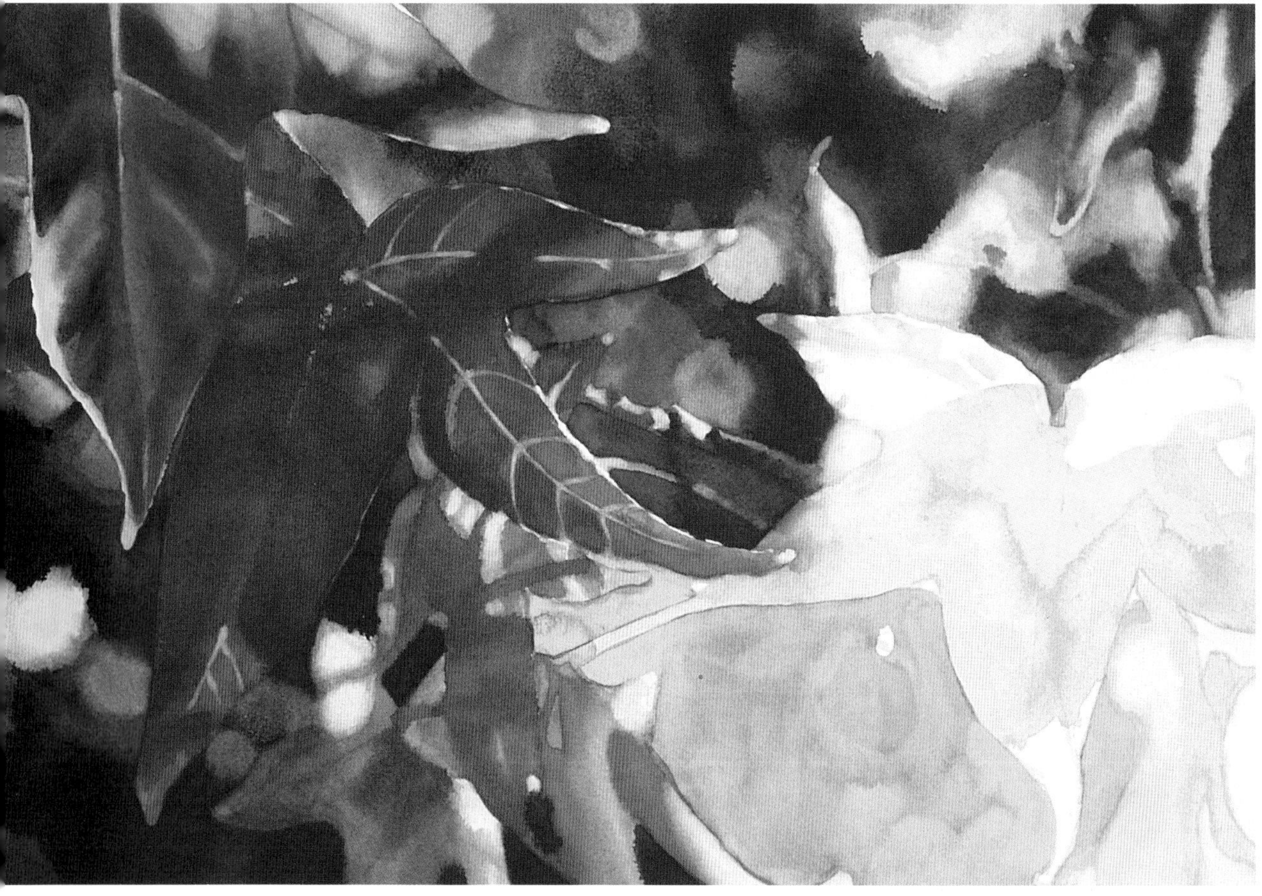

STEP 8

Continue to Develop the Background

The most diluted washes here are the mixtures of Cobalt, Peacock and Quinacridone Rose. Drop a dark mixture of Carmine, Prussian, Thalo Green and Burnt Sienna into this wash. Keep it cool, dark and soft to exaggerate the leaf shapes.

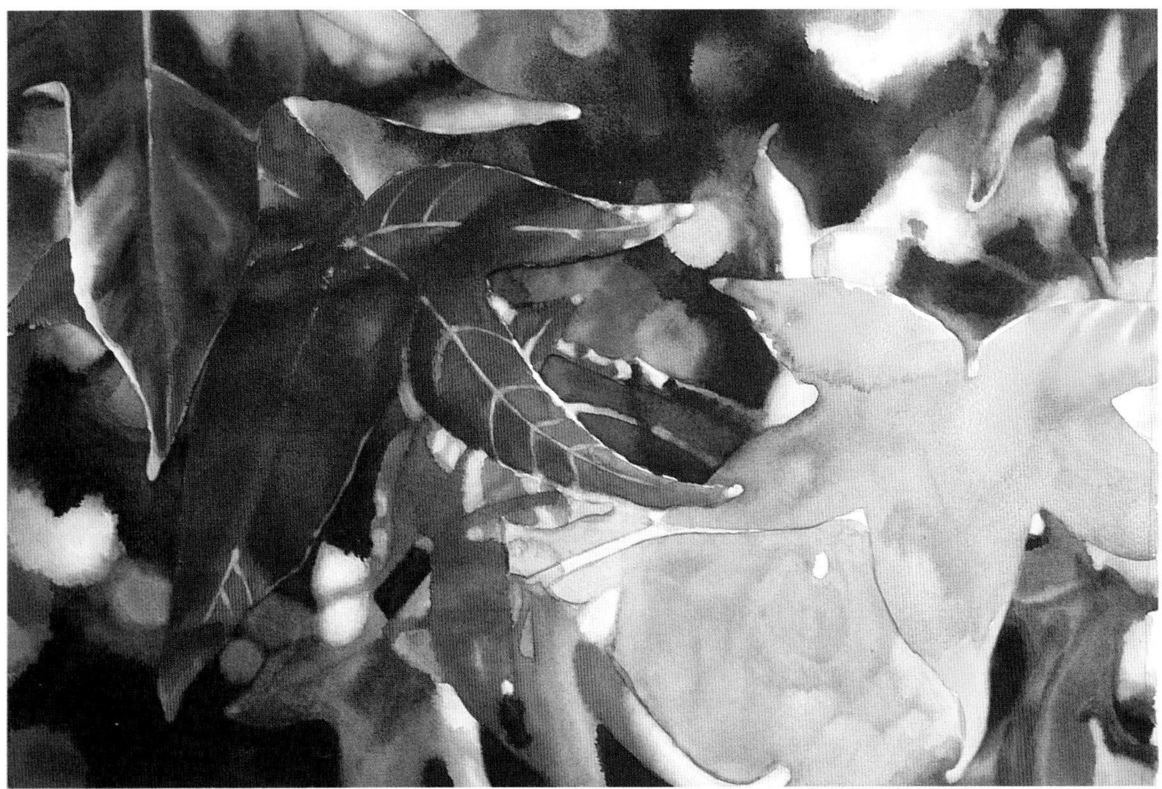

STEP 9

The "Third Wheel" Leaf

This leaf needs to stand on its own and balance the other two primary leaves. To add variety, put down an initial varied yellow wash. Glaze a green shadow over this, along with touches of Cadmium Red and Quinacridone Burnt Orange. Drop the warm colors next to, not on top of, the green area, to avoid creating a dirty color. For harmony, use mostly the same colors in both green leaf mixes.

STEP 10

A Necessary Correction

The lower right-hand corner of the painting has been nagging me like a toothache: The leaf shape is too similar to the upper right-hand corner leaf in color, size and gesture. Usually the painting surface should be covered before making adjustments. But, as in this case, if you are repeatedly bothered by a specific area, go ahead and make the change so you can continue developing the finished painting. My use of Lanaquarelle paper and lighter, nonstaining colors allows me to scrub paint away with a wet brush and add subtle changes as necessary.

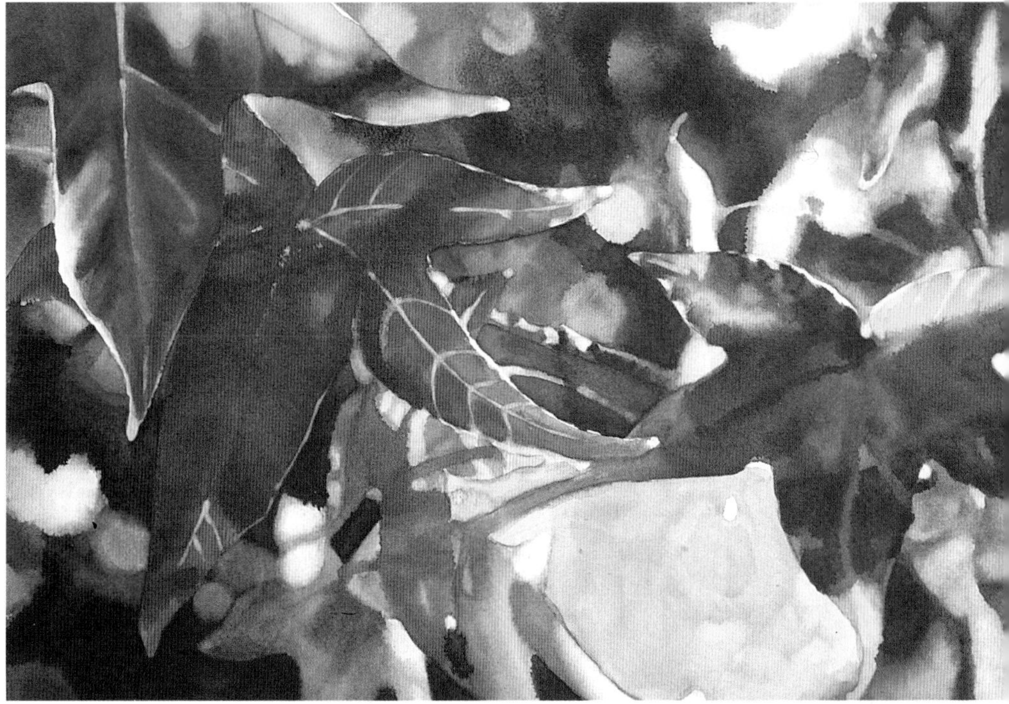

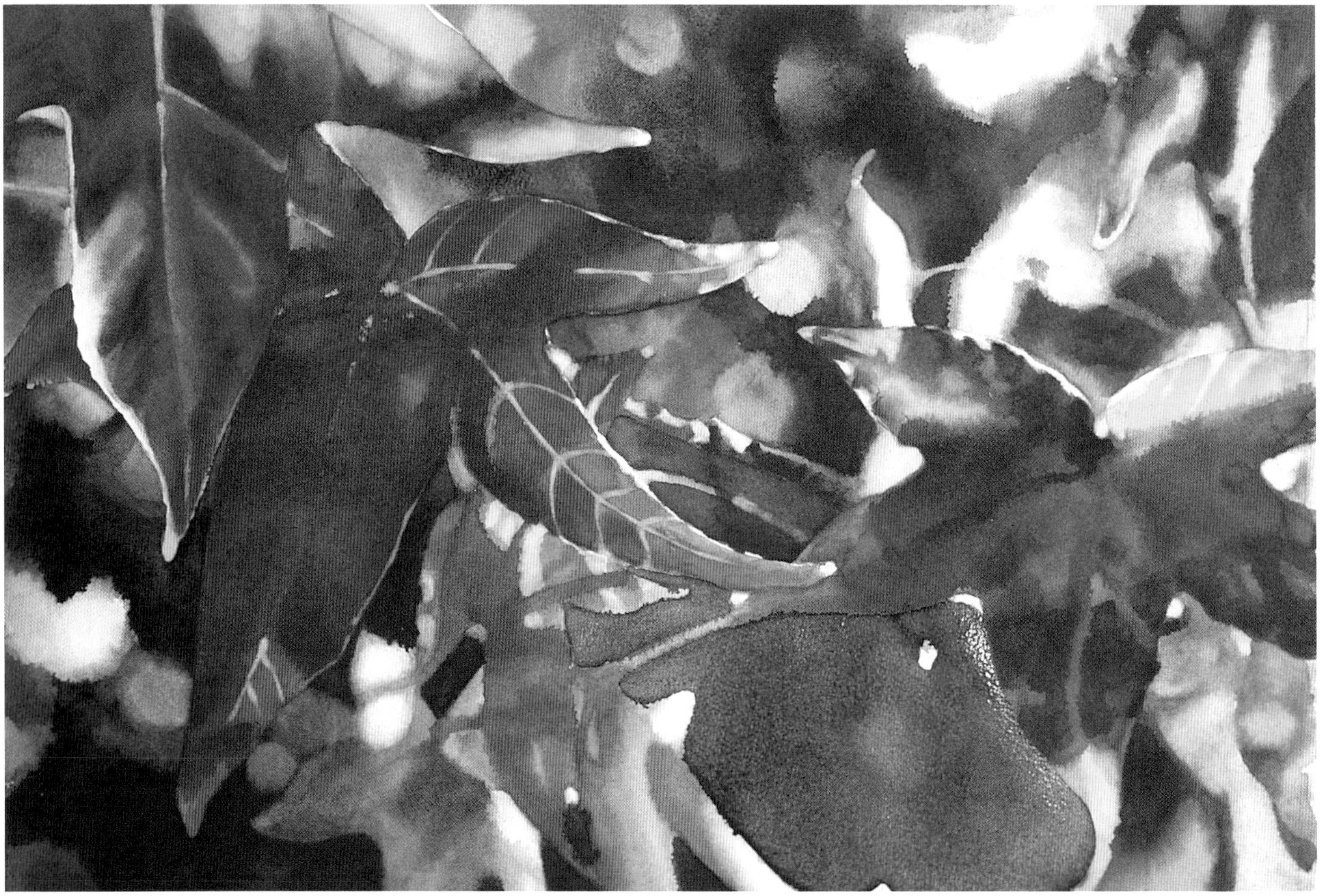

STEP 11

Wrap It Up

This last section at the bottom is something like placing the last piece of a puzzle. Because it is background, keep it soft, cool and dark. To maintain harmony, repeat the colors used previously in the background areas.

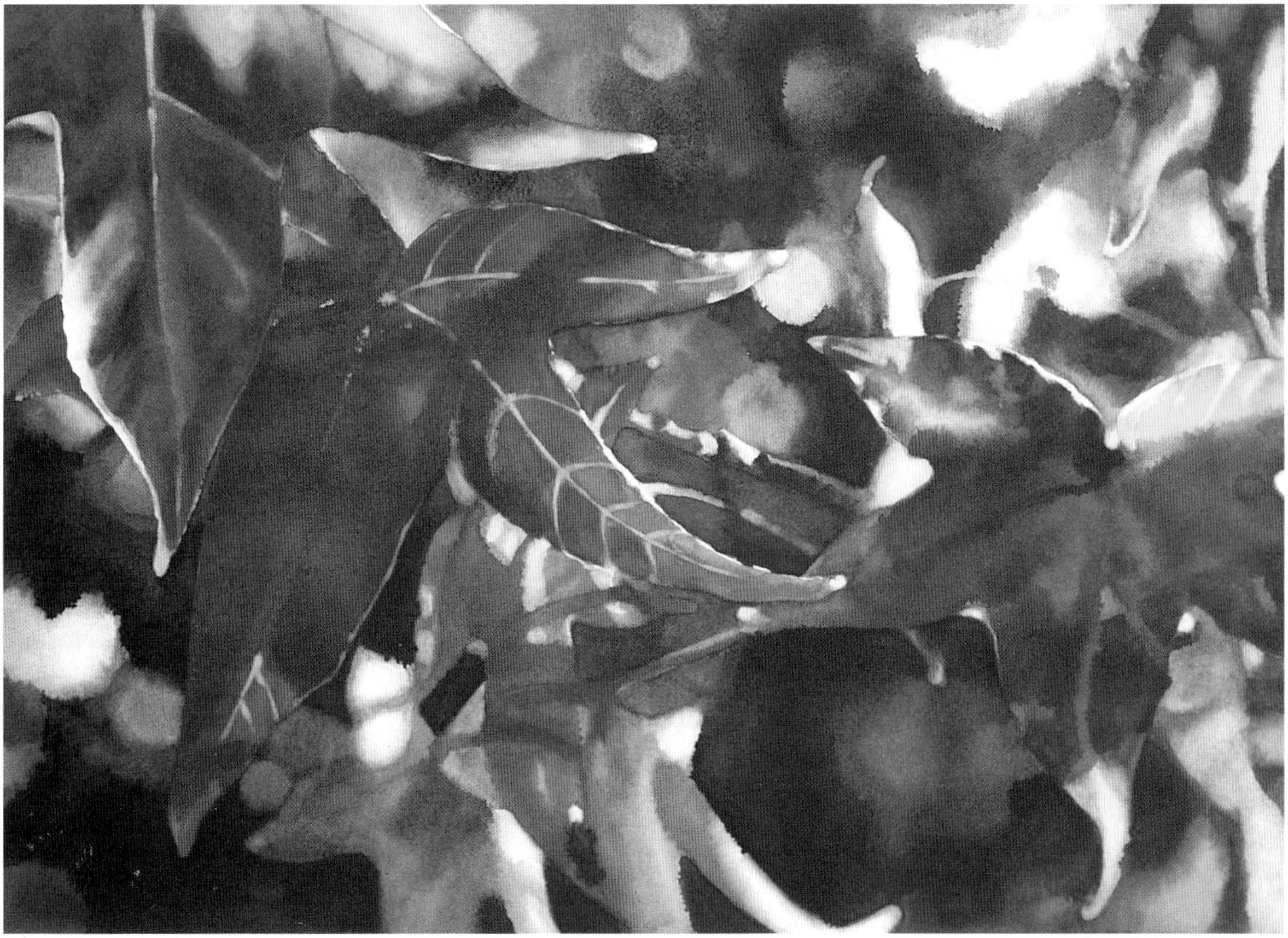

STEP 12

Final Touches

Before making any final alterations, study the painting. Minor adjustments in color can improve the visual flow of the painting.

LIQUID AMBER
Karen Frey, watercolor, 14" × 20" (35.6cm × 50.8cm)

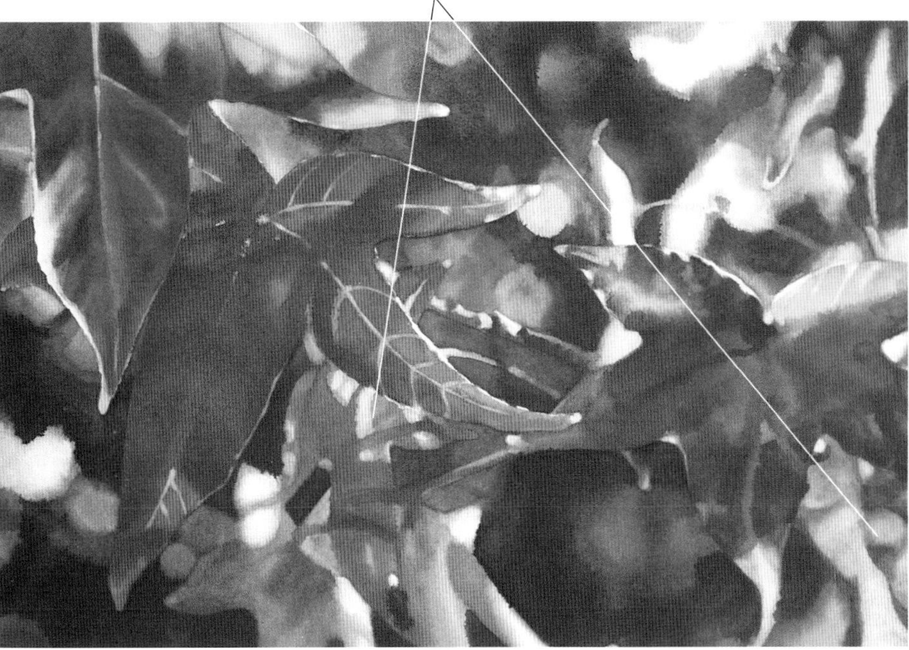

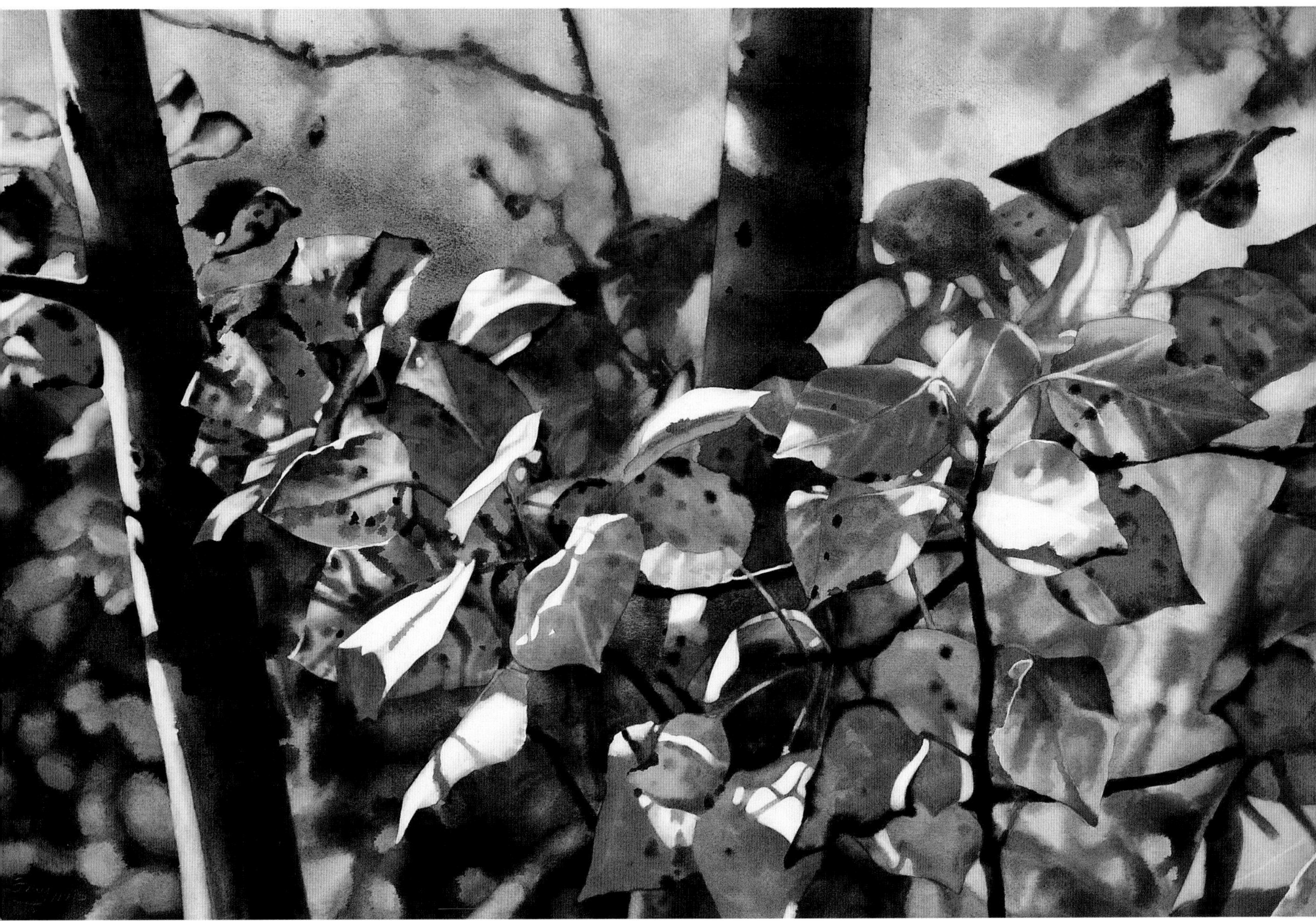

BLUE ASPEN
Karen Frey, watercolor, 25″ × 36″ (63.5cm × 91.4cm)
Collection of David and Robin Sweet

Another Example of Backlit Leaves

In both *Blue Aspen* and *Liquid Amber* I used backlighting to portray the intense color and translucency of fall leaves. The light shining through the leaves reminds me of stained glass and suggests subtle space with the shadow of underlying leaves. Both paintings are very active, and color is used to dictate mood. In *Blue Aspen* the color is subdued to enhance the intensity of the leaves and the trunk; white shapes are distinct and simple. In fact, the painting is comprised primarily of small, rhythmic shapes to suggest the fluttering of leaves. *Liquid Amber* is a much simpler painting. The background is as vivid as the leaves, but done in contrasting colors to suggest a brilliant autumn afternoon.

PAINT DRAMATIC BACKLIGHTING WET-INTO-WET Watercolor

In this painting of my cat in front of a window, I kept both the darkest and lightest values on the cat to provide drama and to direct the viewer's eye. The cat is mainly in shadow, with some bright rim lighting skimming over its form. The colors are built up with wet-into-wet washes of increasing intensity.

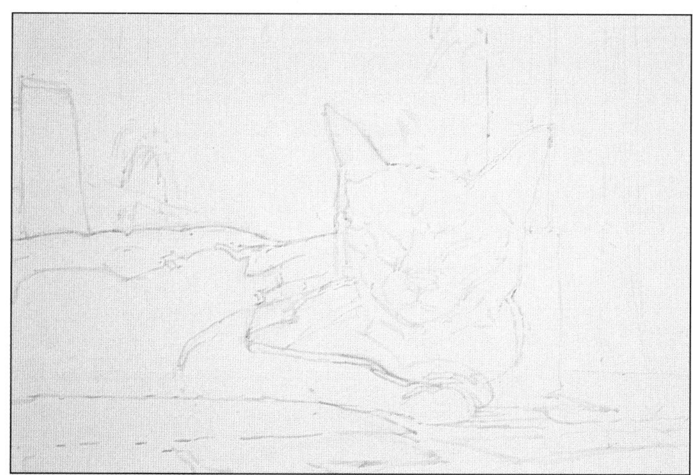

STEP 1

Draw Shapes Loosely

Use Manganese Blue to draw broad, simple shapes. Focus primarily on the delicate shapes of light that subtly reveal the silhouetted form of the cat.

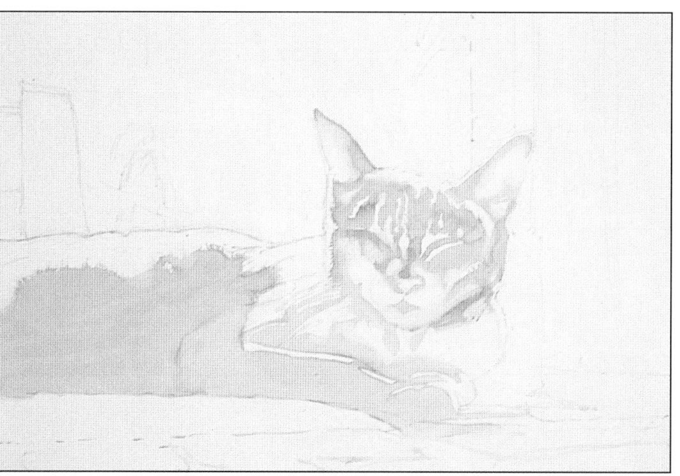

STEP 2

Develop Detail in the Underpainting

Developing detail at this stage is beneficial for three reasons. First, it establishes information essential to reveal likeness and character. Second, it helps you understand and translate what you are painting. Finally, this stained underpainting boosts your confidence to simplify the finished painting. Use highly diluted staining colors, in this case Carmine, Quinacridone Burnt Orange and Peacock Blue. Use staining colors in order to achieve a bond with the paper so that consecutive washes will not remove the underpainting.

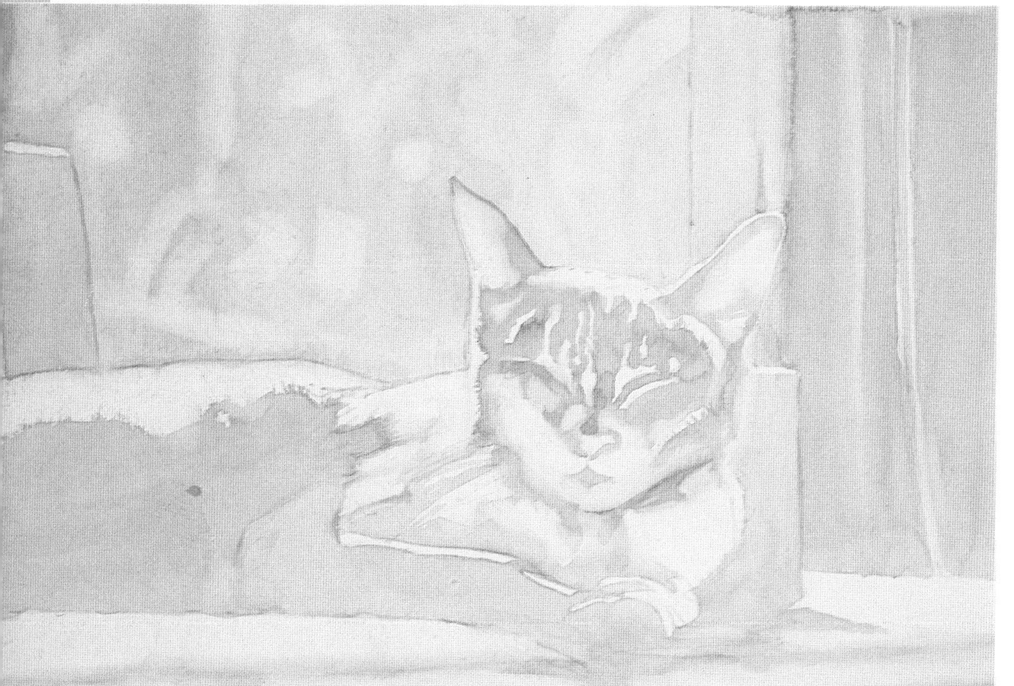

STEP 3

Compose Light and Color

Having established the cat as warm, continue covering the surface, balancing areas of warm and cool. Repeat the use of Quinacridone Burnt Orange, Carmine and Peacock Blue in the warm areas; drop Cobalt, Ultramarine and Peacock Blue into the cool areas. Leave white space: It is important. As the majority of the painting is covered, those white shapes will pop out. Eventually this will become a middle and dark value painting. The contrast with the sharp, small white shapes will create and increase drama.

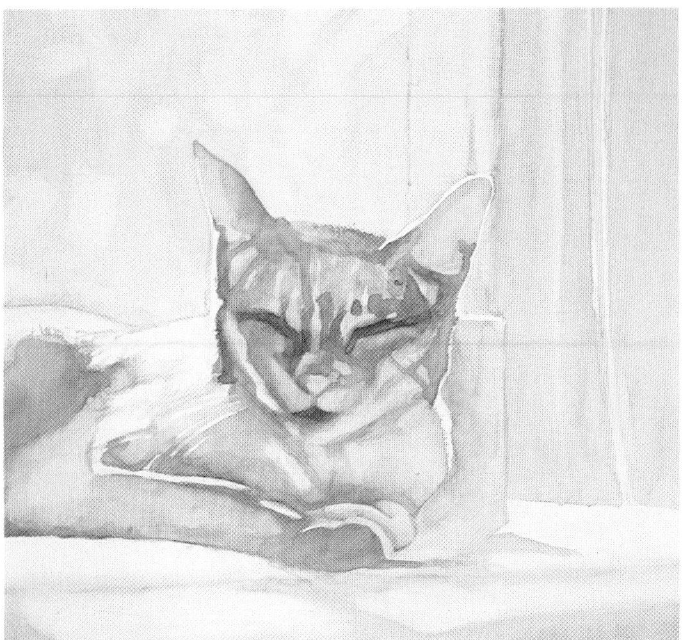

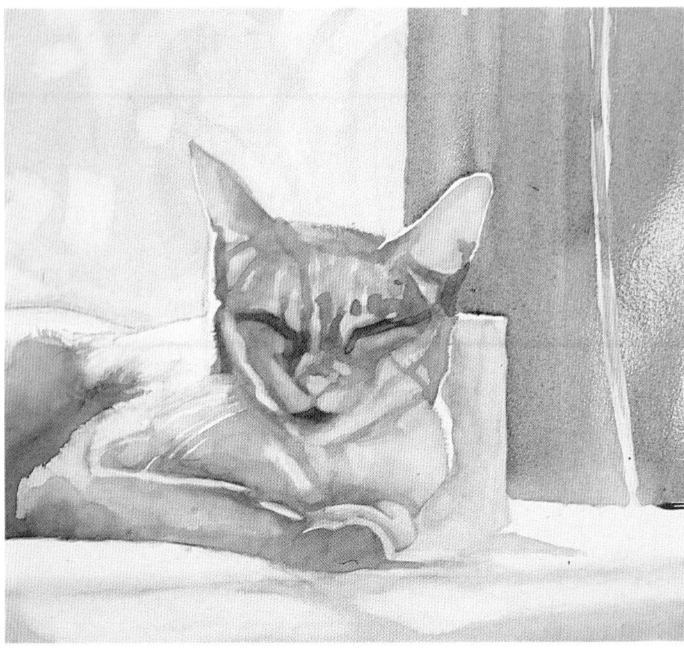

STEP 4

Develop Your Confidence

Continue developing the cat during this underpainting stage until you are satisfied that you can overpaint the final broad washes with confidence. Use mixes of Quinacridone Gold, Quinacridone Burnt Orange and Carmine to reveal form. Beef up facial definition and markings, and define the leg. The plan is to keep the most intense color and value on the cat.

STEP 5

Add Washes

Begin the process of applying finished washes. Once the foundation is well established, technique becomes the primary focus. Start with a section of background that you can comfortably paint to completion: the drape. Apply a wash of Yellow Ochre, Quinacridone Burnt Orange and Quinacridone Rose. When you reach the window jamb, work directly into a mixture of Cobalt, Peacock Blue, Yellow Ochre and Cadmium Orange. When changing color within a wash, it is important to maintain a constant water-to-pigment ratio.

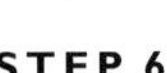

STEP 6

Add Into the Wash

While the wash is wet, continue to darken the drape. Make sure any paint dropped into a dampened surface has more pigment and less water than what has already been applied. To keep the window jamb in the correct value, leave it as is. It will appear lighter after the window is darkened. To maintain soft edges, work directly into the dark blue shape behind the cat while the background is still damp, using Cobalt Blue and Ultramarine Blue. Define the dark within this shape with Carmine, Prussian Blue, Thalo Green and Quinacridone Burnt Orange.

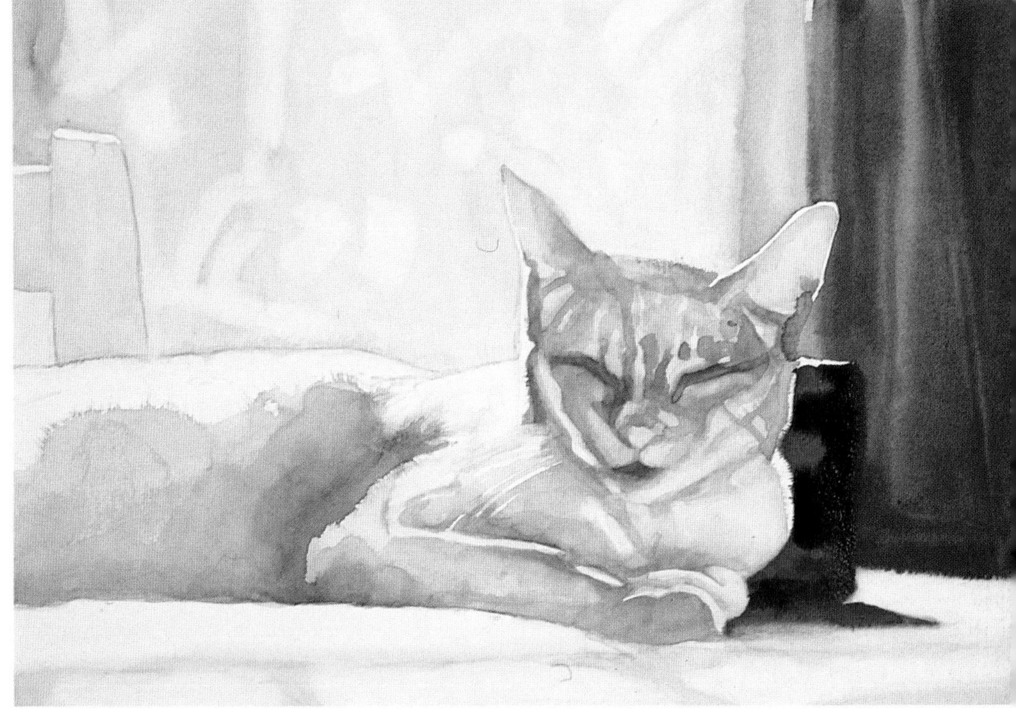

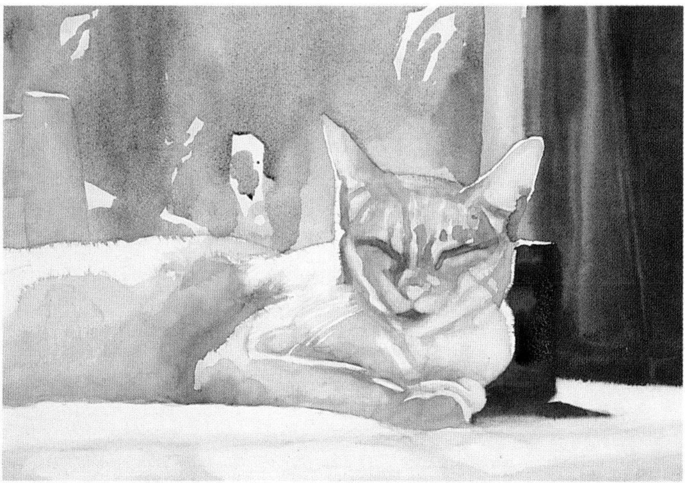

STEP 7

Lay In the Background

Even if the wash is still damp, go ahead and continue with the background. The resulting soft edges will suggest that the background is vaguely out of focus. Lay on a diluted wash for the window consisting primarily of Cobalt Blue, Peacock Blue and Ultramarine Blue. Leave small bits of room to drop in some Cadmium Yellow Lemon, Quinacridone Rose/Opera and Quinacridone Burnt Orange.

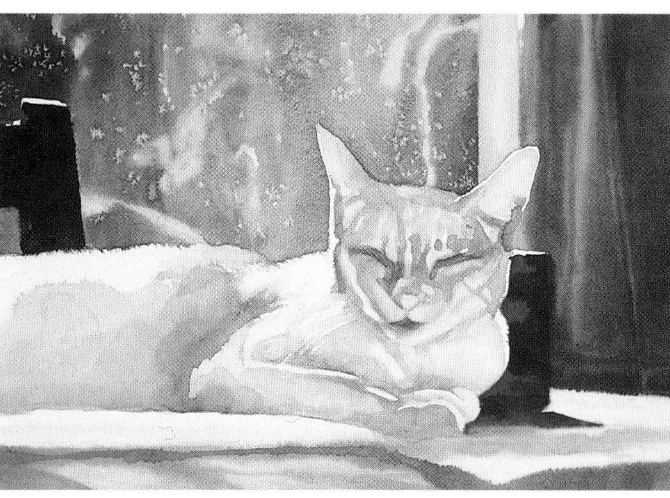

STEP 8

Background and Foreground

Continue dropping in and mingling colors in the background until you achieve the appropriate value range. Use the same color mixtures, but delicately neutralize the blues with some Cadmium Red to cut the intensity. Soften the light shapes with a sponge, and drop a few grains of salt onto the surface for a "frosty window" look. When the wash loses its sheen but is still damp, define the corner of the chair. Using colors already in the background, lay cast shadow in the foreground. Start with cooler colors on the left, adding more reds just right of center and then cooling down (bluer) again on the right. Remember to maintain a constant water-to-pigment ratio.

STEP 9

Attack the Cat

Take a moment to plan your attack. The original plan to keep the darkest darks, lightest lights and most saturated color within the cat seems right on track. In order to complete the cat in one shot, the initial wash should be very wet: A large amount of water should allow you the time you need to continue adding pigment wet-into-wet. But make sure not to wet the areas you want to save as white. These areas will reveal the light coming from behind. Paint a continuous wash of Cadmium Yellow Lemon, Cadmium Orange, Quinacridone Rose/Opera and Cobalt Blue, changing color as you go.

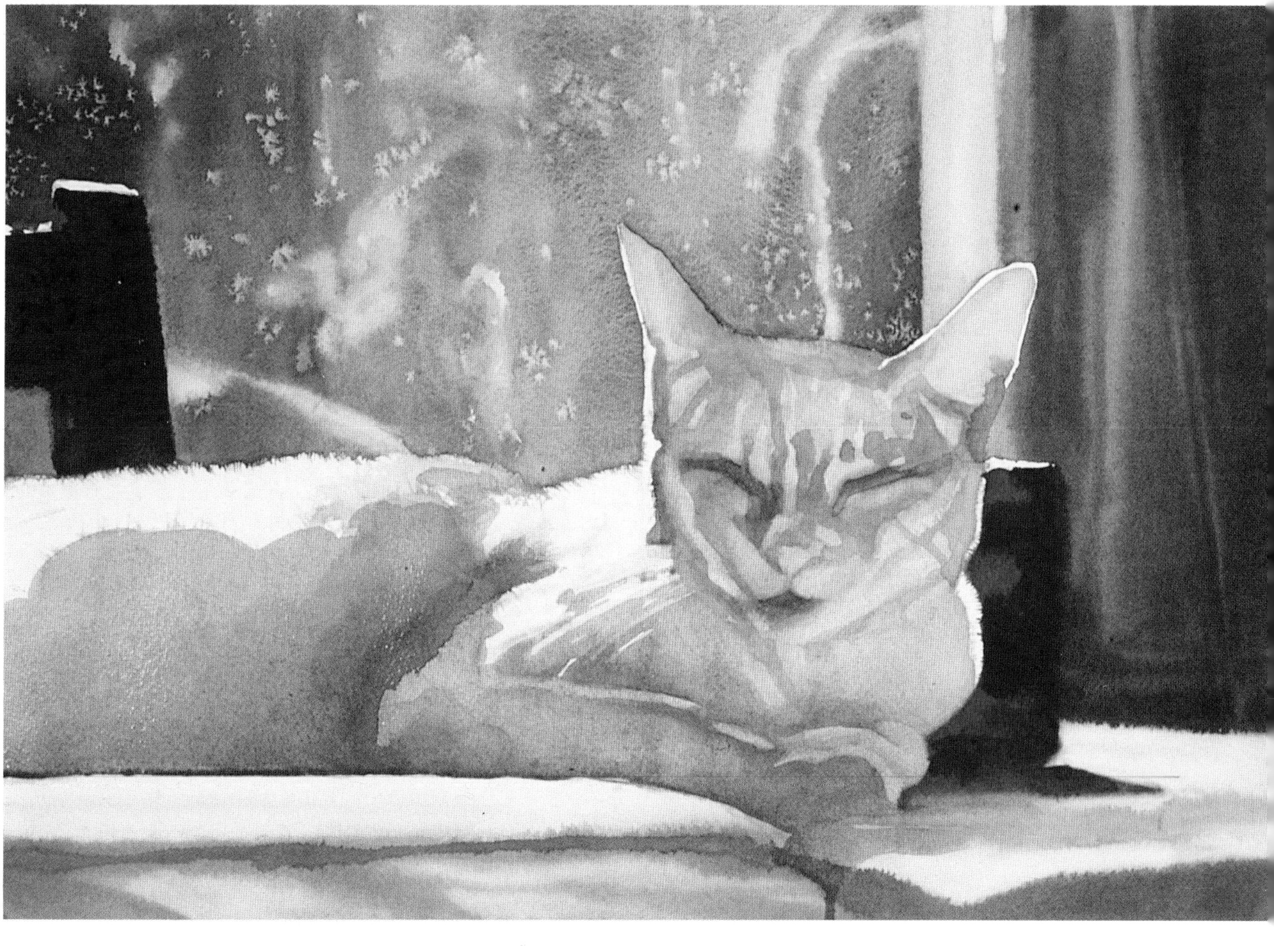

STEP 10

Adding On

The surface should still be wet enough to continue adding more saturated color. This color should not be neutralized, because the saturated intensity attracts attention. Starting with the ears, drop in a mixture of Opera and Cadmium Yellow Deep. Moving into the face and chest, drop in a mixture of Yellow Ochre, Cadmium Orange and Cadmium Red. To render the form, drift the wash into a purple mixed with Cobalt and Opera on the right-hand chest area. Finish with a Yellow Ochre and Quinacridone Gold mixture over the foreleg and body. Notice how the stained underpainting maintains its integrity.

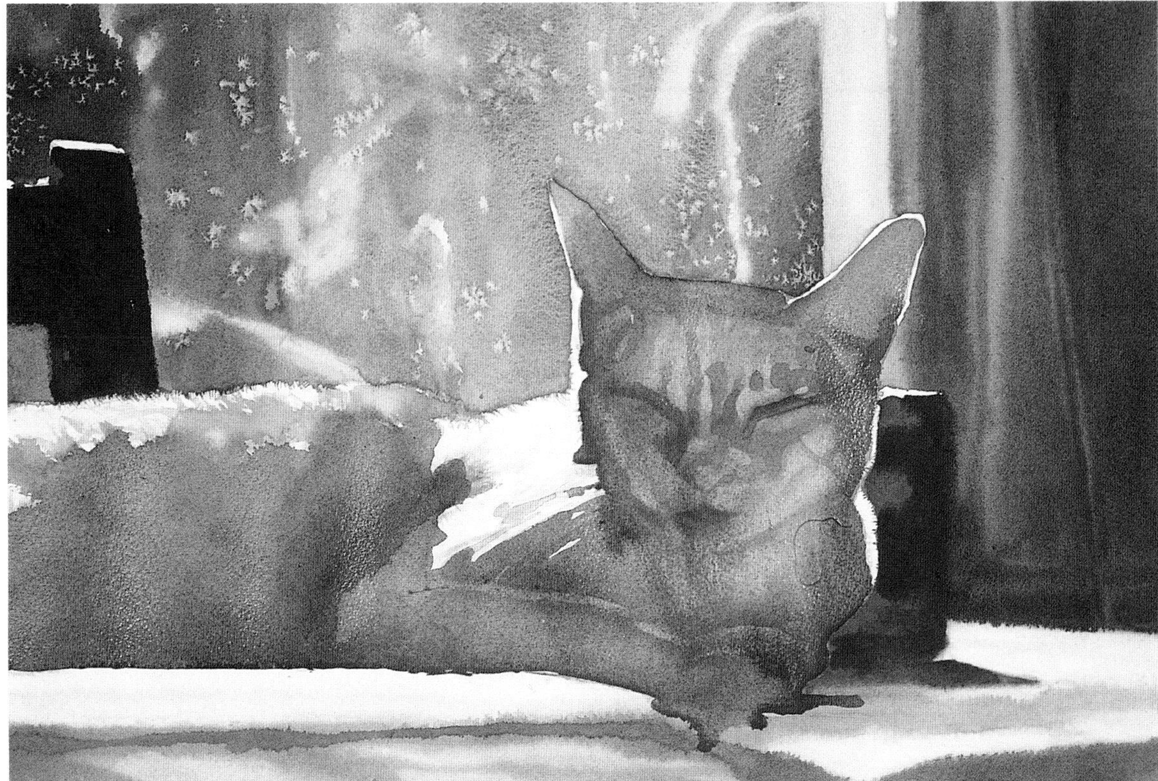

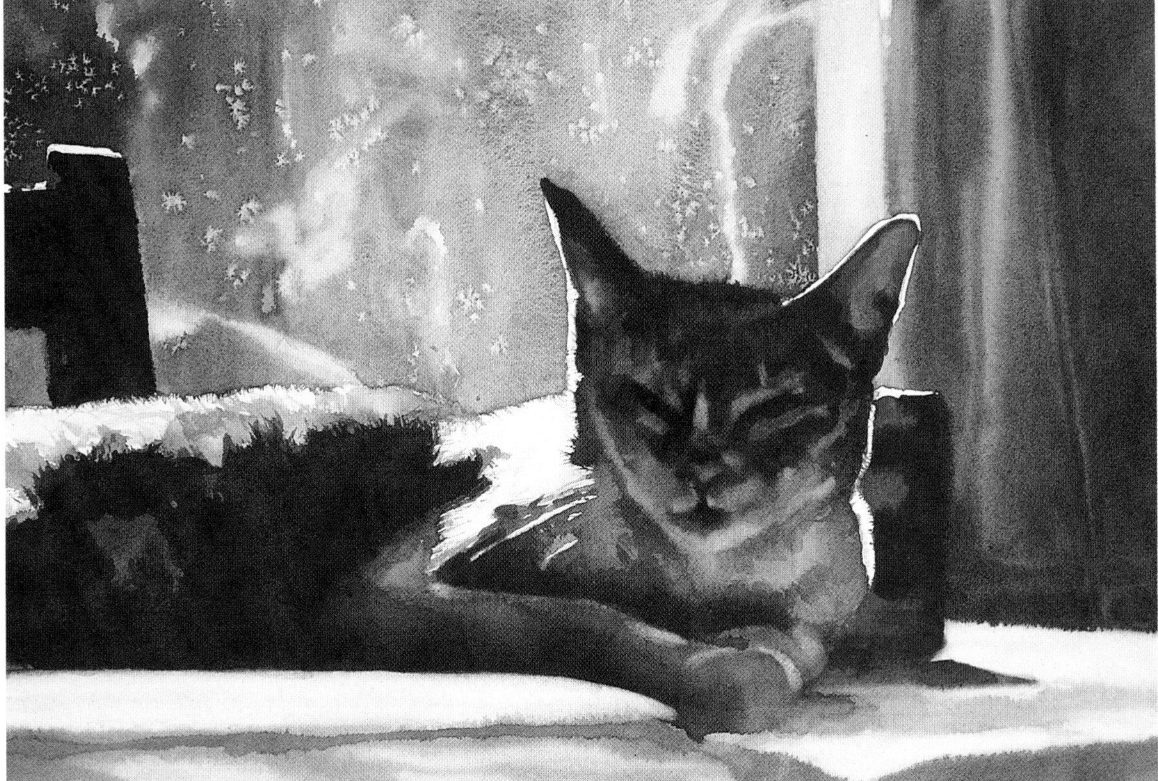

STEP 11

Continue Defining the Cat

Go darker over almost all of the cat with mixtures of Cobalt Blue, Peacock Blue, Quinacridone Burnt Orange and Cadmium Red. These mixtures should be denser than the prior mixtures. Finish with your darkest, thickest combinations of Ultramarine Blue, Prussian Blue, Quinacridone Burnt Orange and Carmine Red. The cat should be defined, but should read as a silhouette due to the narrow value range and the soft edges.

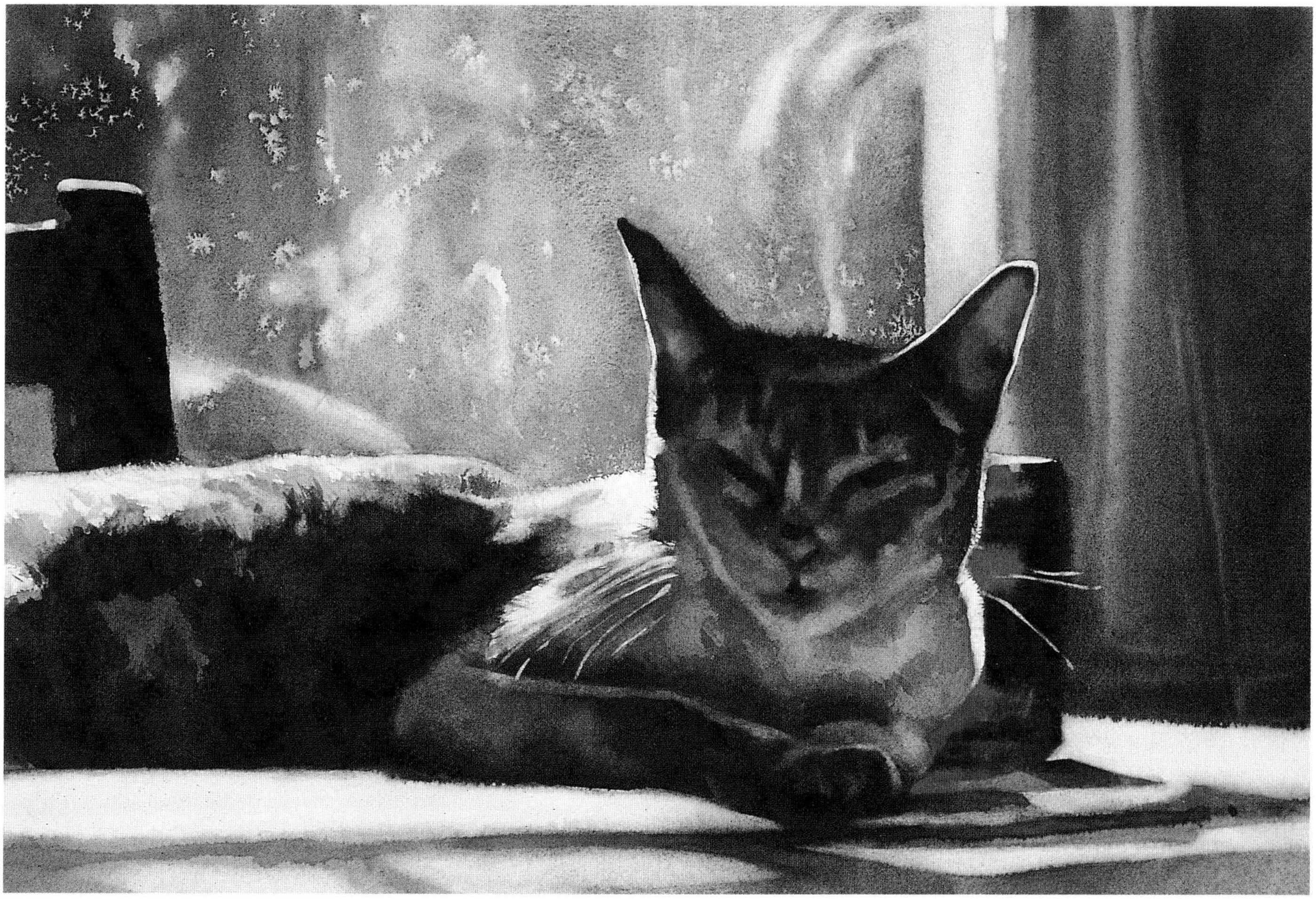

TINY E—AFTERNOON NAP
Karen Frey, watercolor, 14" × 20" (35.6cm × 50.8cm)

STEP 12

Final Touches

The portion of the foreleg unresolved in the previous step leaves an opportunity to link the cat to the foreground. With a midvalue wash, redampen the leg of the already-dry cat. Continue this wash into the cast shadow, defining form and linking the dark, denser mixtures. With a soft oil brush, soften the edge defining the highlight on the cat; with the same brush lift out some whiskers and clean up any crude edges defining white shapes.

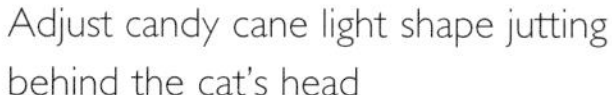

Adjust candy cane light shape jutting behind the cat's head

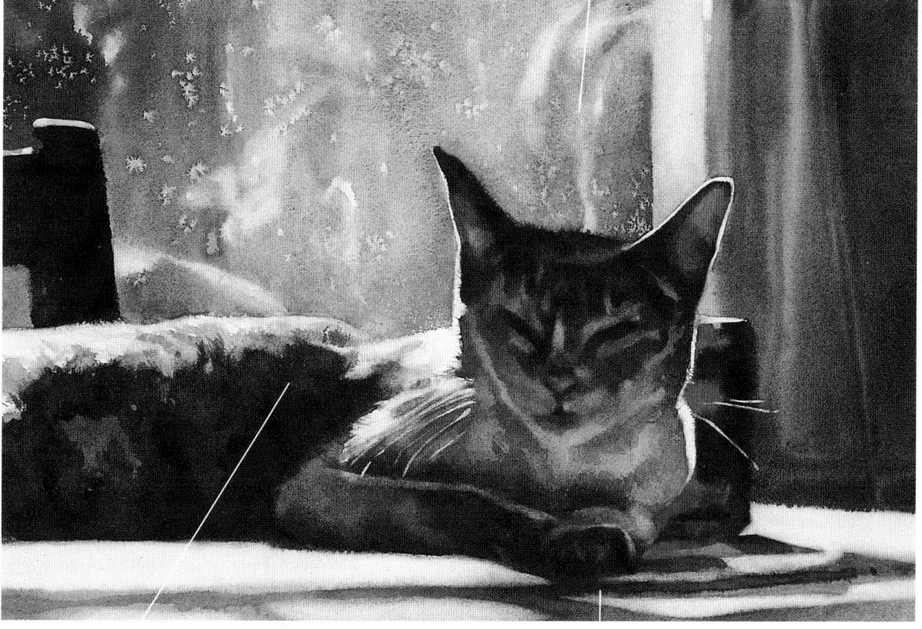

Correction in anatomy (softening white area)

Adjust color of cast shadow and redefine the white shape it forms

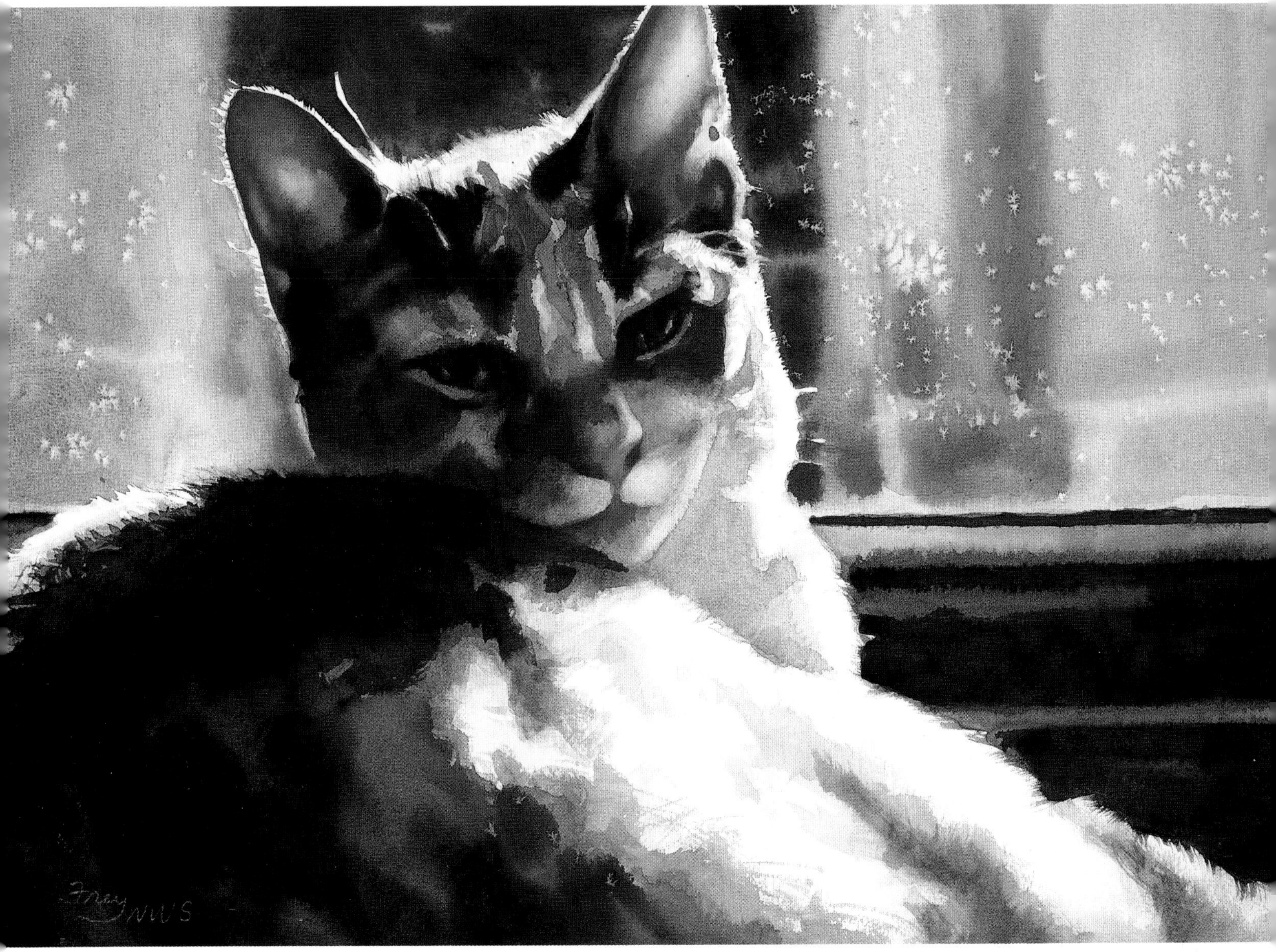

Another Example of Revealing Light

The primary similarity between *Cleo* and *Tiny E* is the use of light to reveal form. Although I developed detail in the underpainting in both, I chose to simplify that information in the final washes, which allows the essence of the cat to be revealed through simple shapes and brushmarks instead of rendered features. Despite these similarities, the mood suggested in the two paintings is quite different. In *Cleo* the light is directly from the side, the value range is very middle of the road and the color is saturated to suggest a sunny morning. In *Tiny E* the light source is from behind, the value range is darker and the contrast is higher. Colors are more neutralized to suggest a colder, possibly rainy or snowy, afternoon.

CLEO—SUNNING HERSELF IN THE KITCHEN WINDOW
Karen Frey, watercolor, 14″ × 20″ (35.6cm × 50.8cm)

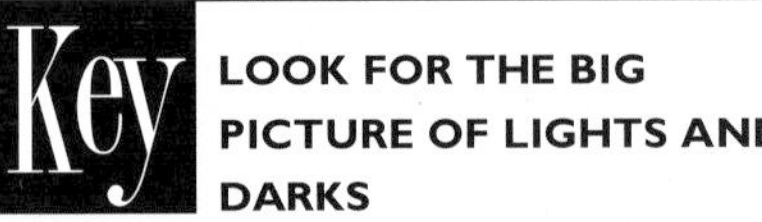

LOOK FOR THE BIG PICTURE OF LIGHTS AND DARKS

Don't be afraid to use a lot of pigment and go really dark in broad areas of shadow. This makes your lights really shine.

GALLERY

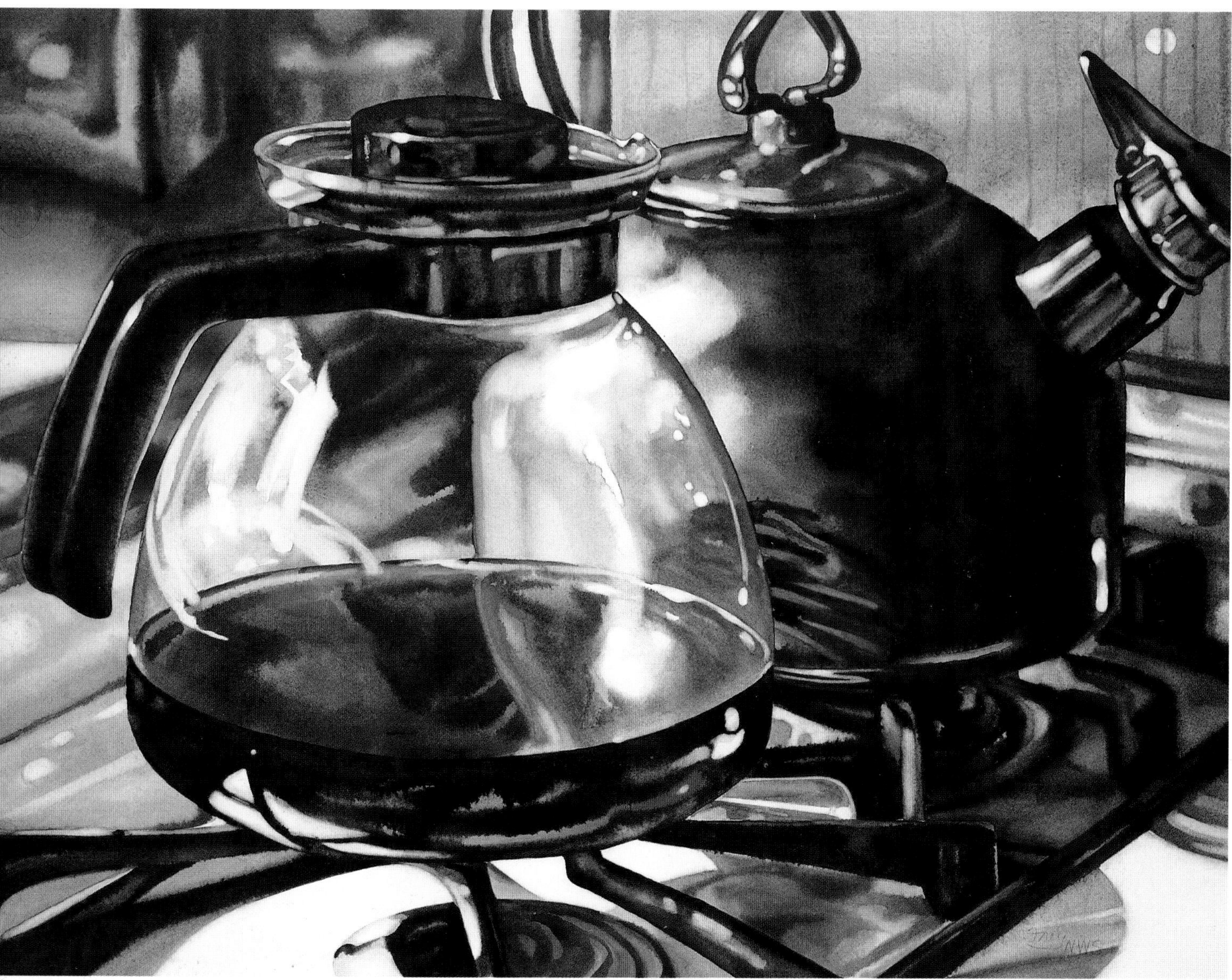

On sunny mornings the light hits our stove for a few glorious minutes. This painting captures that moment when the light sparkles on and through the coffee carafe, accentuating the play between the deep reds of the coffee and the greens of the teakettle. This was painted shortly after my big shift from doing a preliminary drawing with a pencil to drawing directly with pigment. I still remember the excitement and adventure of it. Technically, it was executed in a straightforward wet-into-wet application.

STILL LIFE WITH COFFEE AND TEAPOT
Karen Frey, watercolor, 19″ × 26″ (48.3cm × 66cm)
Collection of Niles Bybel

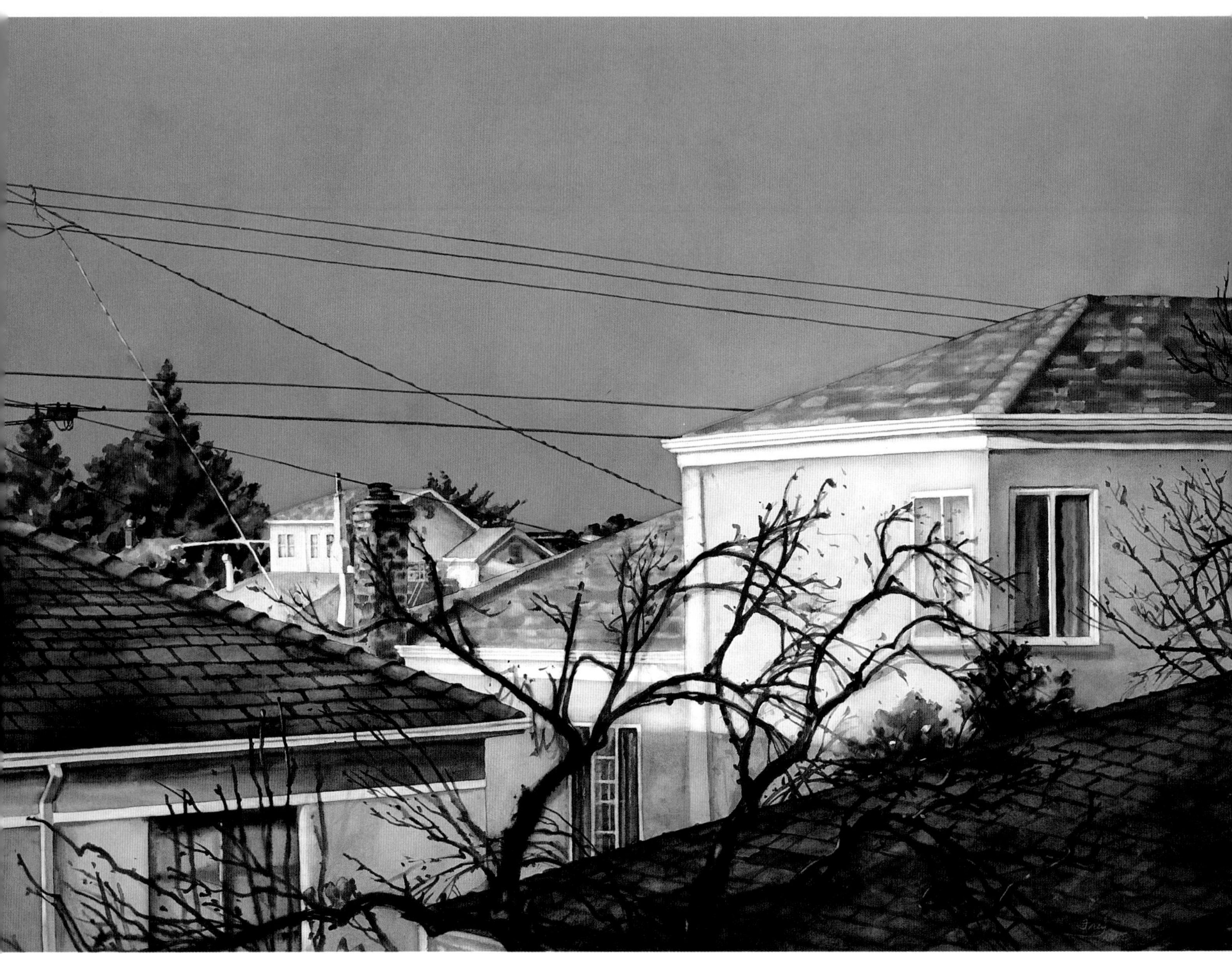

VIEW FROM THE BACK PORCH
Karen Frey, watercolor, 36" × 48" (91.4cm × 121.9cm)

Sometimes on a gray day, late in the afternoon, the sun breaks through, creating a golden glow while the sky remains massive and heavy. This was the quality of light that I was trying to convey here. How to paint it was the real challenge because the painting is so large. Premixing buckets of color is not my usual approach, but it was necessary in order to achieve the flat, even surface I was looking for in the sky. I painted it upside down with several layers of color before I was satisfied. The remaining surface was painted in my usual wet-into-wet approach, using bigger puddles and brushes than usual.

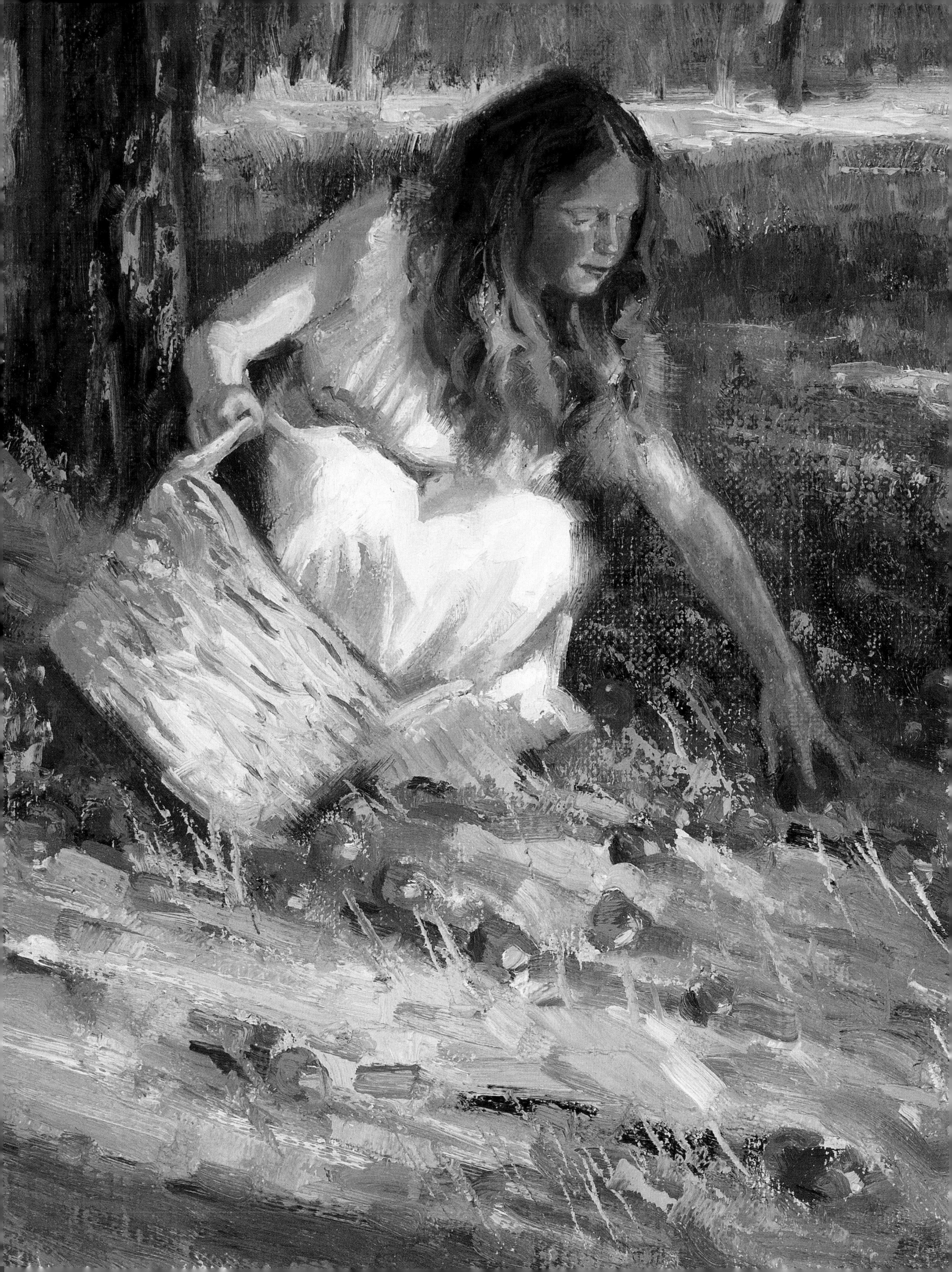

EXPLORE THE ENERGY OF NATURAL LIGHT IN

OILS

RANDAL M. DUTRA

CHAPTER

8

Randal Dutra believes in going to the source: nature. He says, "I believe an artist's work reflects his particular commitment to life. The fuller the life, the richer the art produced. One must gain as great a variety of knowledge as possible, knowing one's subjects in both character and form. The one essential that allows us to paint is light. No light, no vision, no painting. This sounds obvious, but I am amazed at how little time is really spent by painters and sculptors divining this simple truth."

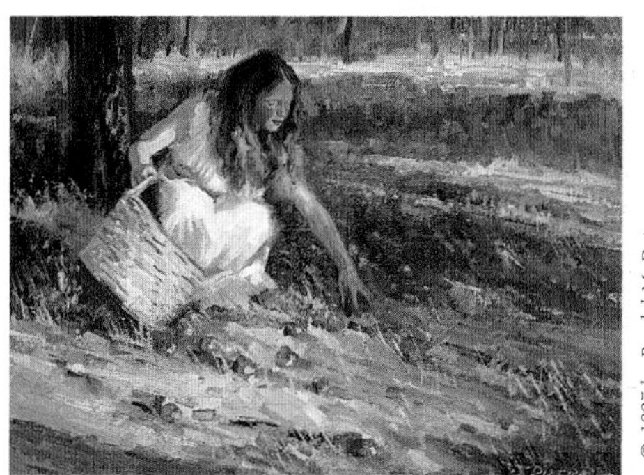

SMALL HARVEST
Randal Dutra,
oil on Belgian linen,
9″ × 12″
(22.9cm × 30.5cm)

The figure and basket dominate the composition, so all other areas were kept simple. The low sun produced long bands of shadow that lead the eye to the figure; the white dress picks up the warm and cool colors in the surroundings and gives the painting luminosity.

Dutra literally imagines himself as the light source flowing over the subject—speeding across flat smooth surfaces, or slowing up on rougher, complicated forms. To him, light is energy; it is active and mutable. Painters create the illusion of light by manipulating both value and color: Of the two, Dutra finds value the most important. It is the structure on which you hang your painting. Value can either fuse or separate masses of color. Because the eye reacts to light, the center of interest in Dutra's paintings usually contains the lightest light and the darkest dark. Where contrast is the highest and color is the most intense—that is where the eye naturally wants to go. The demonstrations on the following pages illustrate Dutra's use of light's energy. As he says, "Light is our greatest tool and, make no mistake, our greatest challenge."

INDIRECT LIGHTING CREATES SUBTLE MYSTERY Oil

This painting of a "snowball" shrub could have been a slavishly rendered subject with myriad small flower and leaf shapes. But the power of suggestion is more interesting to look at—and to participate in. The colors were kept from being too contrived and "pretty." The subject is attractive enough without hitting the viewer over the head with it. Part of the charm is the inherent airiness of the shrub coupled with the solid structure of the fence. The use of indirect lighting adds to the interest. The open background is the lightest area: The foreground is mainly in shadow, with only teasing specks of light hitting some of the blossoms and leaves. It is a study in contrasts, of light and shadow and of nature and man.

Palette
White
Cadmium Yellow Pale
Cadmium Yellow Deep
Cadmium Orange
Alizarin Crimson
Cadmium Red Deep
Terra Rosa
Cadmium Red Light
Yellow Ochre
Raw Sienna
Viridian
Cobalt Blue
Ultramarine Blue
Ivory Black
Raw Umber

Brushes
Bristle flats: no. 2, no. 3, no. 4, no. 10
Bristle rounds: no. 4, no. 5
Sable brights: no. 2, no. 4

Medium
Turpentine should be used sparingly, mostly for the lay-in stage. I prefer using oil paints without diluting or adulterating their content.

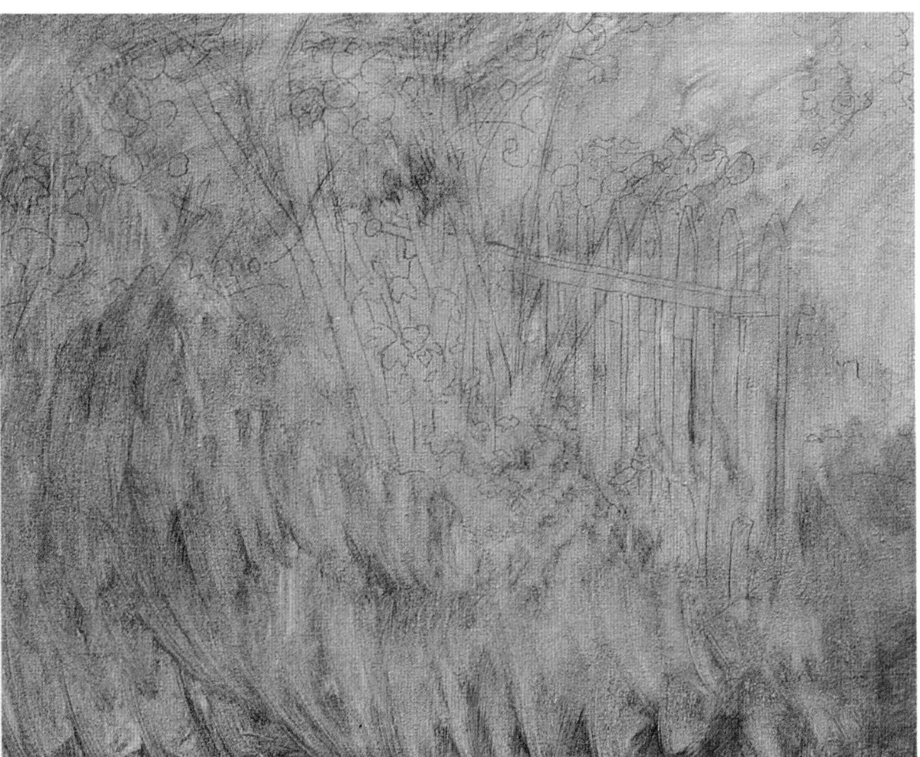

STEP 1

Cover the White of the Canvas

- Make some drawing indications on the white canvas with a hard pencil. This allows you to apply a brief wash of turpentine and paint without losing your rough drawing.
- Apply a turpentine wash of Cobalt Blue and Cadmium Yellow Deep with a no. 10 flat bristle brush. Use a rag to spread the wash around on the canvas. This establishes the foreground grass area and the shrub greens at the top of the canvas.
- Apply a lighter turpentine wash to the upper right quadrant using Cobalt Blue and Cadmium Yellow Pale. This area will appear more distant.
- In the lower right quadrant, add a warmer suggestion of vegetation using Yellow Ochre, Cobalt Blue and Cadmium Orange.

STEP 2

Establish Values and Accents

• For the foreground grass, use Cobalt Blue and Cadmium Yellow Deep applied in short vertical strokes. This produces a pleasing pattern and mimics the growth of the grass. Vary the application of the two colors to give the illusion of light and dark patches, keeping the overall value of the grass area dark.

• On the upper right quadrant, use a no. 5 round bristle brush to apply a thicker mixture of Cadmium Yellow Deep, Viridian, White and Cobalt Blue.

• Establish the lightest light by using a no. 5 round bristle brush to create a few white flowers. For the areas that are catching light, use a mixture of White and Cadmium Yellow Light with a touch of Yellow Ochre.

• Establish the darkest dark by using a no. 5 round bristle brush to add the deep shadow at the base of the shrub. Work Ultramarine Blue straight into the already-wet paint: This darkens the previous green while keeping the shadow edges alive. Be sure to work the paint through the indicated drawing lines to keep the edges varied and interesting, which will be important when you work back into them later.

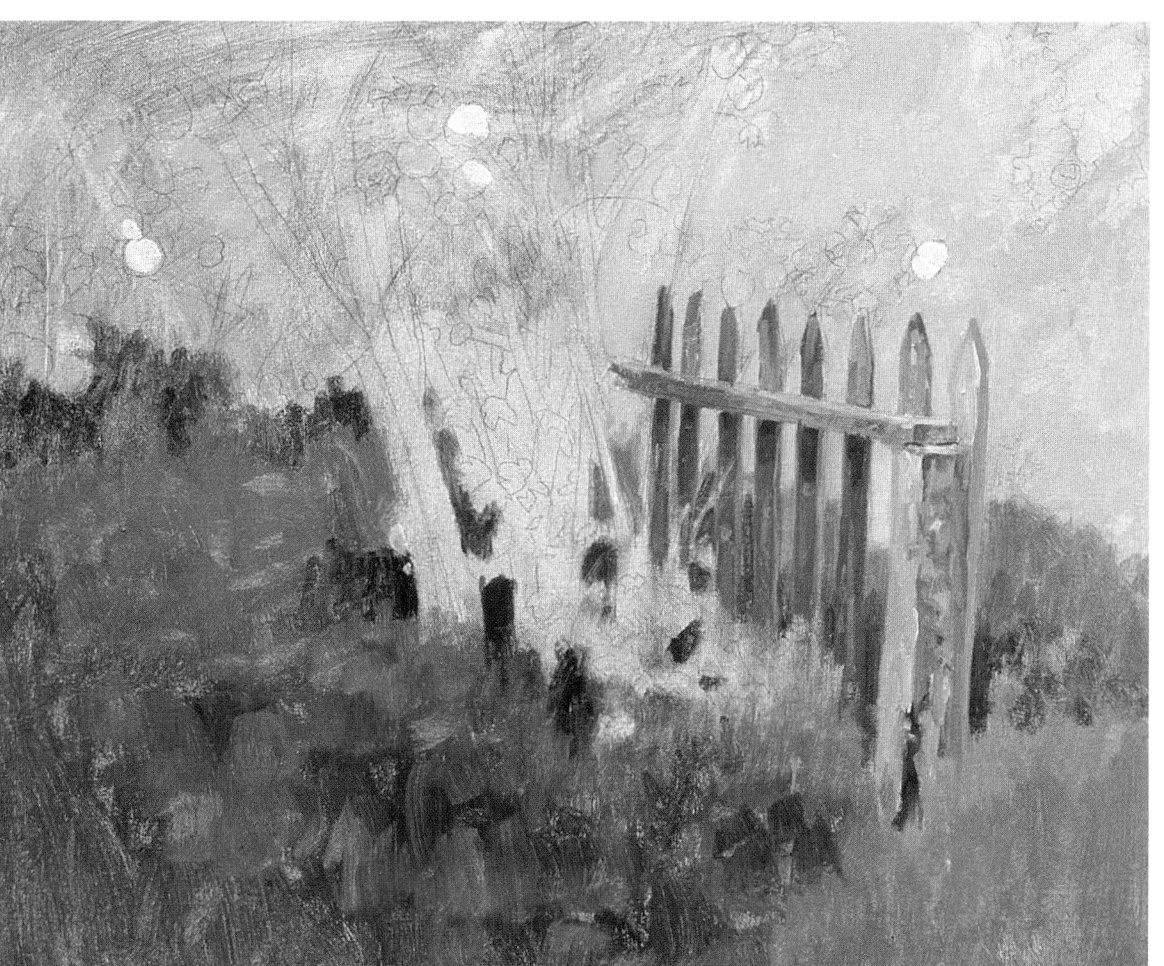

STEP 3

Add the Fence

Paint in the fence using a mixture of Raw Umber, Cadmium Red Deep and White and no. 3 and no. 4 flat bristle brushes. Touches of Cobalt Blue and Yellow Ochre can be used alternately for warming and cooling, and also gives the pickets interest and variation. With the fence in, there are both vertical and horizontal/diagonal references in the painting. Remember that the fence is a hard architectural element, so the light falling on it must be clearly defined, unlike softer edged materials.

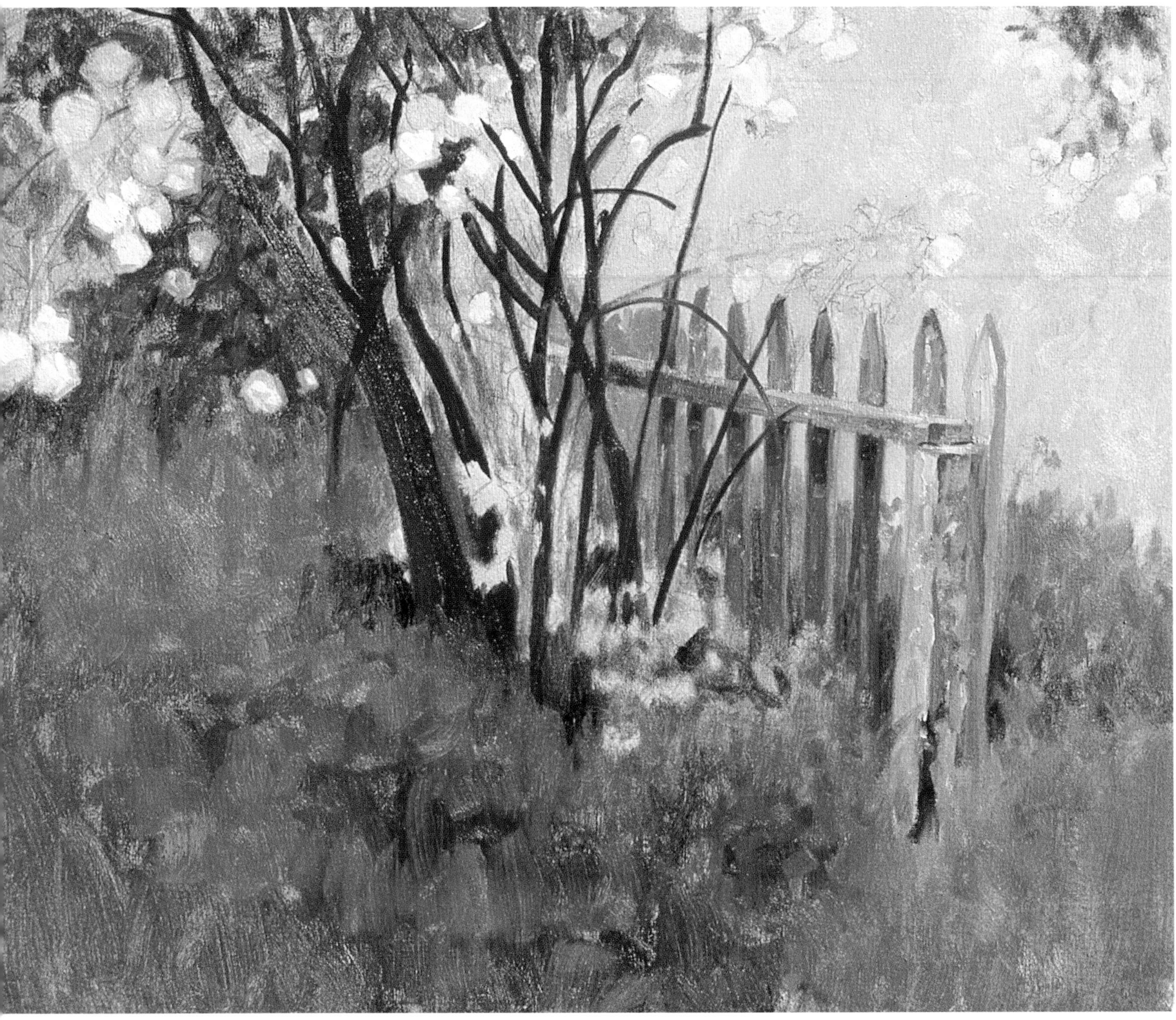

STEP 4

Add Shrubs, Leaves and Flowers

• Paint the shrub trunks and limbs using a no. 2 flat bristle brush and the color mixture used for the fence with red added (you can use some Terra Rosa as well) and deeper in value. Draw the trunks and limbs with paint mixed with a little turpentine to get a flowing application of paint for the important growth patterns and angles. This part of the painting must be organic in nature, not mechanical—be sure to add subtle jogs and crooks in these structures. Although the edges appear hard at this point, they will be painted into and modified later as modeling and paint texture are added.

• In the top left quadrant, use a no. 4 flat bristle brush with a dry mixture of Cobalt Blue, Cadmium Yellow Deep and touches of Ivory Black to portray the dark leaf groups. Vary these mixtures to achieve a natural variety, and let the edges have a dragged or soft look at this point. Defining certain leaves comes later.

• Fill in and establish flowers with a no. 4 round bristle brush. Light parts are the same mixture as before (step two); for the shadow, use White, Cobalt Blue and a touch of Yellow Ochre (to gray the mixture slightly).

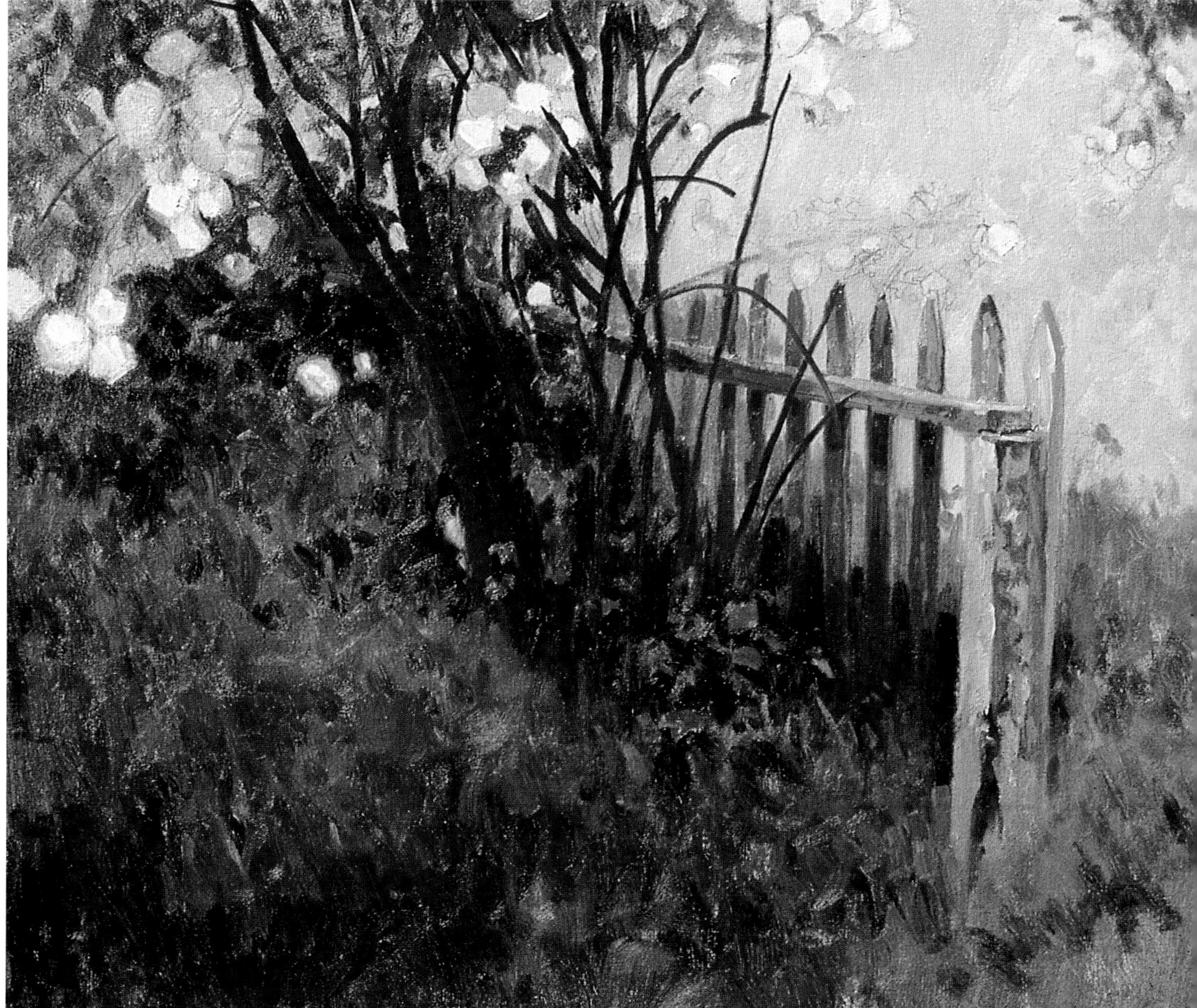

STEP 5

Tighten and Adjust

• Make sure the painting has definite areas of light and dark. The large areas should be well established and designed. These steps must be completed before adding the details outlined in later steps. This is the foundation for the details.

• Add leaves at base of shrub using no. 2 and no. 4 bright sable brushes with mixtures of Viridian, Cobalt Blue, Cadmium Yellow Deep, Cadmium Yellow Pale, Yellow Ochre and White. Keep these edges crisp, reflecting the thinness and sharpness of the leaves. The top plane of the leaves will catch blue from the sky; the bottoms will be deeper in shadow and more green. Remember that these leaves are twisting and turning, so vary their shape and color. If you do not observe and recreate this natural event carefully, your leaves will look pasted on and unbelievable.

• Darken the shadows at the base of the shrub using Ultramarine Blue with a touch of Viridian. This is the darkest dark of the painting.

• Develop the foreground grass by using a no. 4 flat bristle brush to subtly break up the grass area with Ultramarine Blue and Cadmium Yellow. The paint should be dry enough (if left for a day or so) to allow for scrubbing and broad dry-brushed effects that imply detail. Let the texture of the canvas ridges and previously applied paint "pick up" your dry-brush colors.

• Extend the base of the gate down vertically for a stronger composition. This breaks up the straight line of the diagonal fence line. Keep edges loose and overlapping.

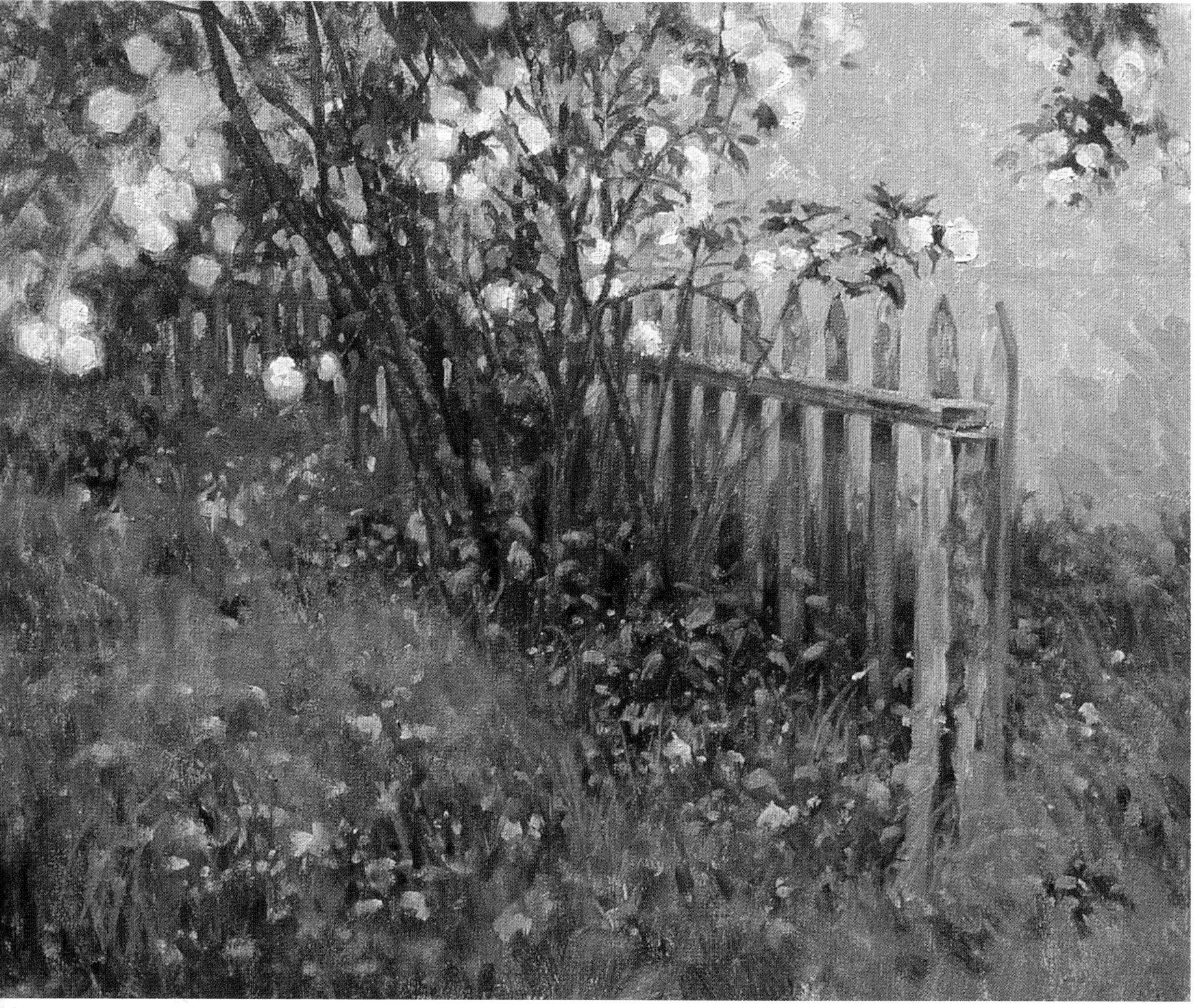

STEP 6

Strengthen the Center of Interest

• In the upper right quadrant, edges and details catch the eye because of the strong contrast. Keep the light background flat and simple. It gives the eye a place to rest amid the details of flowers, leaves, branches and the fence line. Use no. 2 and no. 4 bright sable brushes for the careful detailing of the flowers, leaves, branches and twigs. Capture the delicate character and lacelike quality of this natural beauty.

• The upper right quadrant had an anemic quality, so I warmed it up with a thicker mixture of Cadmium Yellow Deep, Cadmium Yellow Pale, a touch of Viridian and White. Remember, this area must still be kept light in value.

• I broke into the upper left quadrant with suggestions of the continuing fence line silhouetted against the lighter background. This was done by adding lighter flecks of background color to paint the fence's negative shapes.

• Add foreground flowers as spots of color to imply detail and break up the large, flat areas. It does not take much, just well-placed accents. Keep these additions irregular.

• Add "sky holes" in the shrub. Remember that these sky holes are darker and softer around the edges, due to seeing the background light through a "screen" of networking leaves and branches. Lighten the holes slightly in the middle if they are large.

• Add the final flower colors with tints and/or mixtures of Cobalt Blue, Alizarin Crimson, Yellow Ochre, Cadmium Yellow Pale and White.

• Add the final leaf colors with tints and/or mixtures of Viridian, Cobalt Blue, Ultramarine Blue, Cadmium Yellow Pale, Cadmium Yellow Deep and White where necessary.

• Define the fence by adjusting and tightening up edges and values.

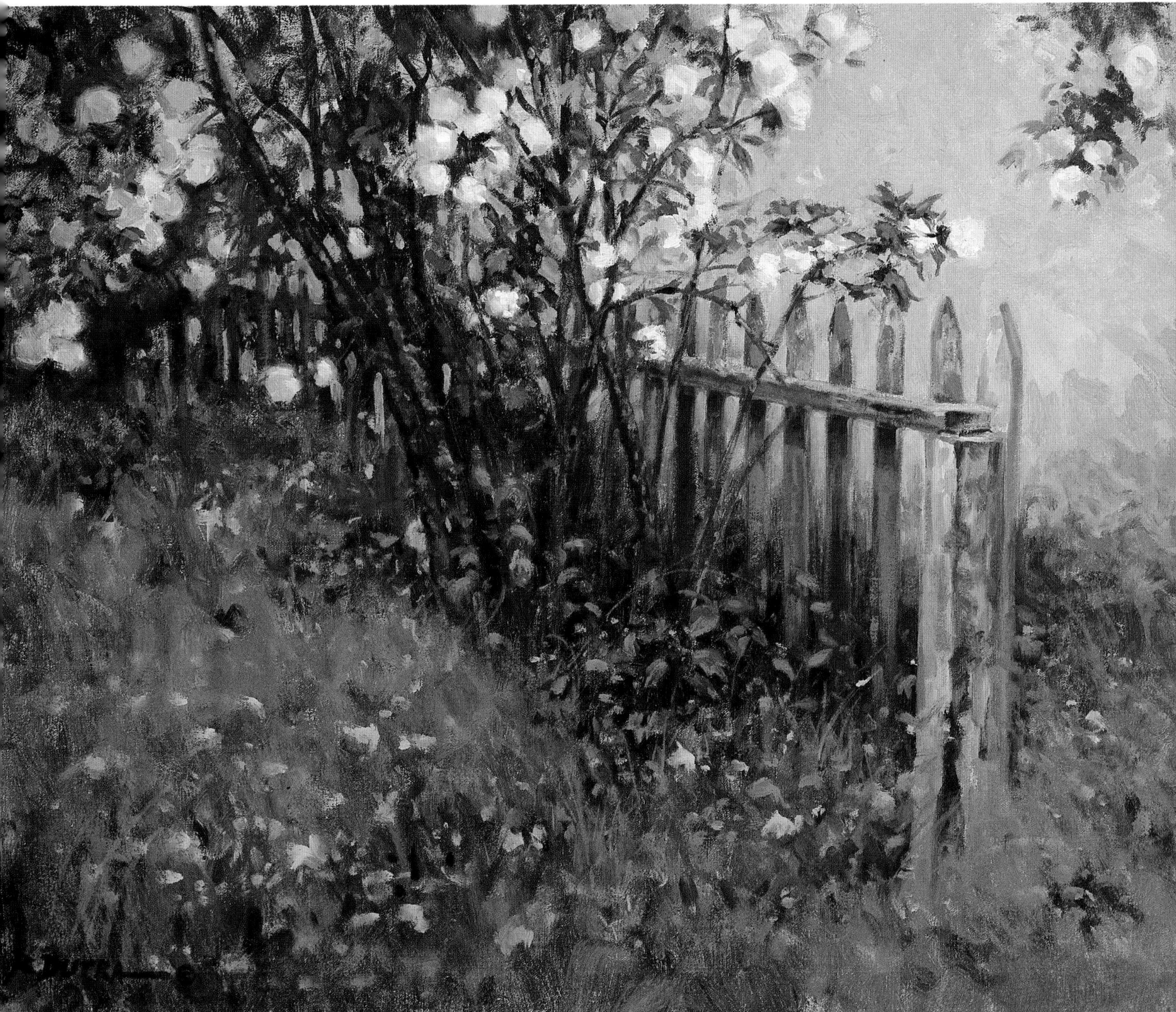

HOMESTEAD MEMORIES
Randal Dutra, oil on Belgian linen, 20″ × 24″ (50.8cm × 61cm)

STEP 7

Final Adjustments

- The upper left quadrant needed more resolution. The light value of the flowers on the left detracted from the more important flowers in the upper right quadrant. I put the left flowers in shadow and tightened up the illusion of the leaves by adding judicious flecks of paint with more definite edges.
- Square off some of the round flower forms. This gives them a more solid and pleasing geometry.

Key

FOCUS YOUR VIEWER'S ATTENTION

Where do you want people to look first? What is delightfully stumbled upon a moment later? The eye is drawn first to the place of most intense contrast in both color and value. Various elements of composition, including the path of the light, then lead the viewer on your planned pathway.

GALLERY

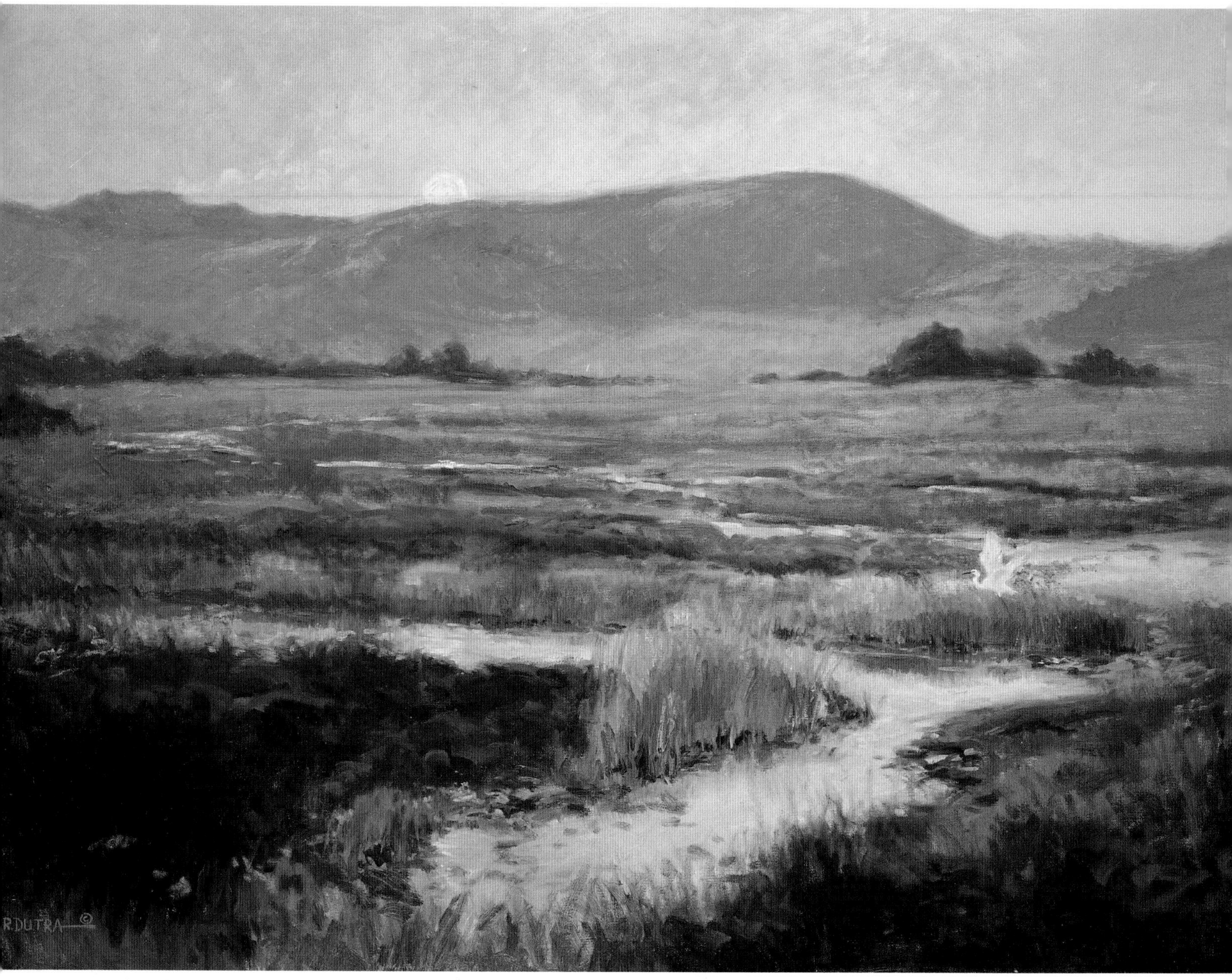

Use Soft Diffused Lighting to Create a Quiet Mood

This has the elements of a true tonal/mood piece—close values, muted color and calming horizontals. To me, this is Nature at her healing best. All is still except for the egret in flight. The bird is also the only white note on the canvas.

The water channels snake back and forth, inviting the viewer into the painting. The lighting is diffused, with no harsh shadows. The soft evening glow brings a pinkish purple veil of harmony to the palette. The moon and its accompanying reflection adds subtle detail to this work, and it is the only major vertical to be found, other than the lesser one of the central reed grouping. To introduce strong areas of pure reds, blues or yellows into this particular painting would have been fighting the intent.

MOONRISE OVER EGRET MARSH
Randal M. Dutra, oil on Belgian linen, 30″ × 40″ (76.2cm × 101.6cm)

opposite

A Spotlight Effect Enhances Natural Camouflage

The hard light striking the doe makes her the obvious center of interest, but as the viewers' eyes travel through the environment they notice the two young deer in the upper right. Of those two deer, only one has a small defining patch of light hitting its rump; natural camouflage is in play. To give this painting snap, I worked the complements: combinations of blue against orange and green against red-orange. This is also a good example of keeping a painting weighted either to the light or to the dark. Two-thirds is a good ratio to keep in mind. This painting is two-thirds dark. Avoid half light, half dark because it tends to be indecisive; the values cancel each other out.

SUNLIGHT AND SHADOW
Randal M. Dutra, oil on Belgian linen, 30″ × 40″ (76.2cm × 101.6cm)

Low Evening Light Offers Unique Color

I enjoy coastal motifs because they are so elemental. They afford the painter great freedom in design and color, while still allowing recognizable shapes and hues to emerge. Also, the stunning effects one sees in marine scenes are unique and often call for inventive applications of paint. In *Day's End*, where passages of absolute purity of color were desired, the palette knife proved to be a useful tool for creating the glassy sheen of wet sand in the center and the sparkle of water near the top of the canvas.

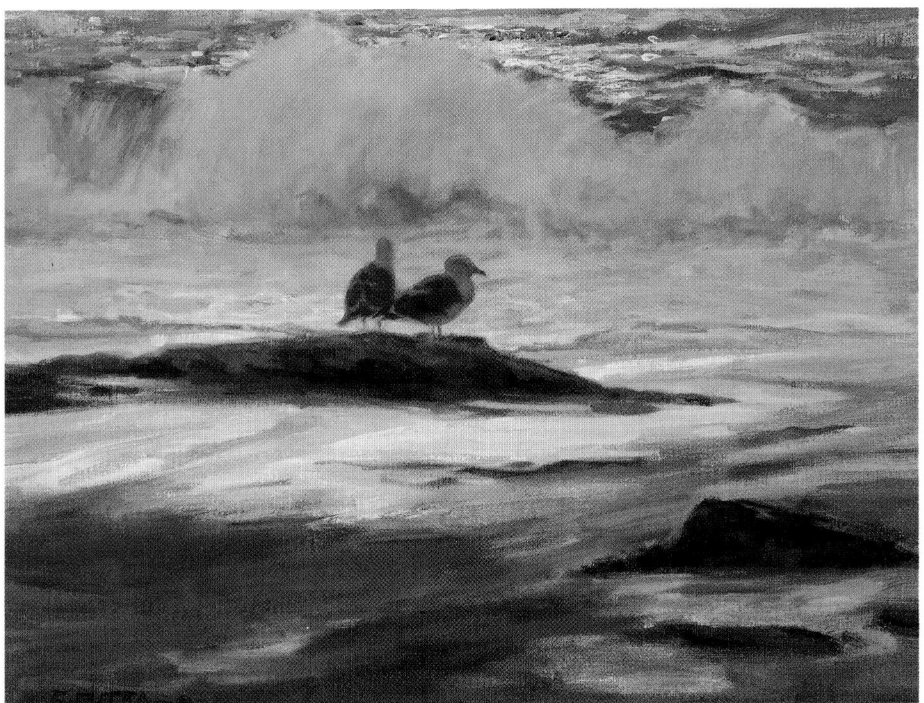

DAY'S END
Randal M. Dutra, oil on Belgian linen, 14" × 18" (35.6cm × 45.7cm)

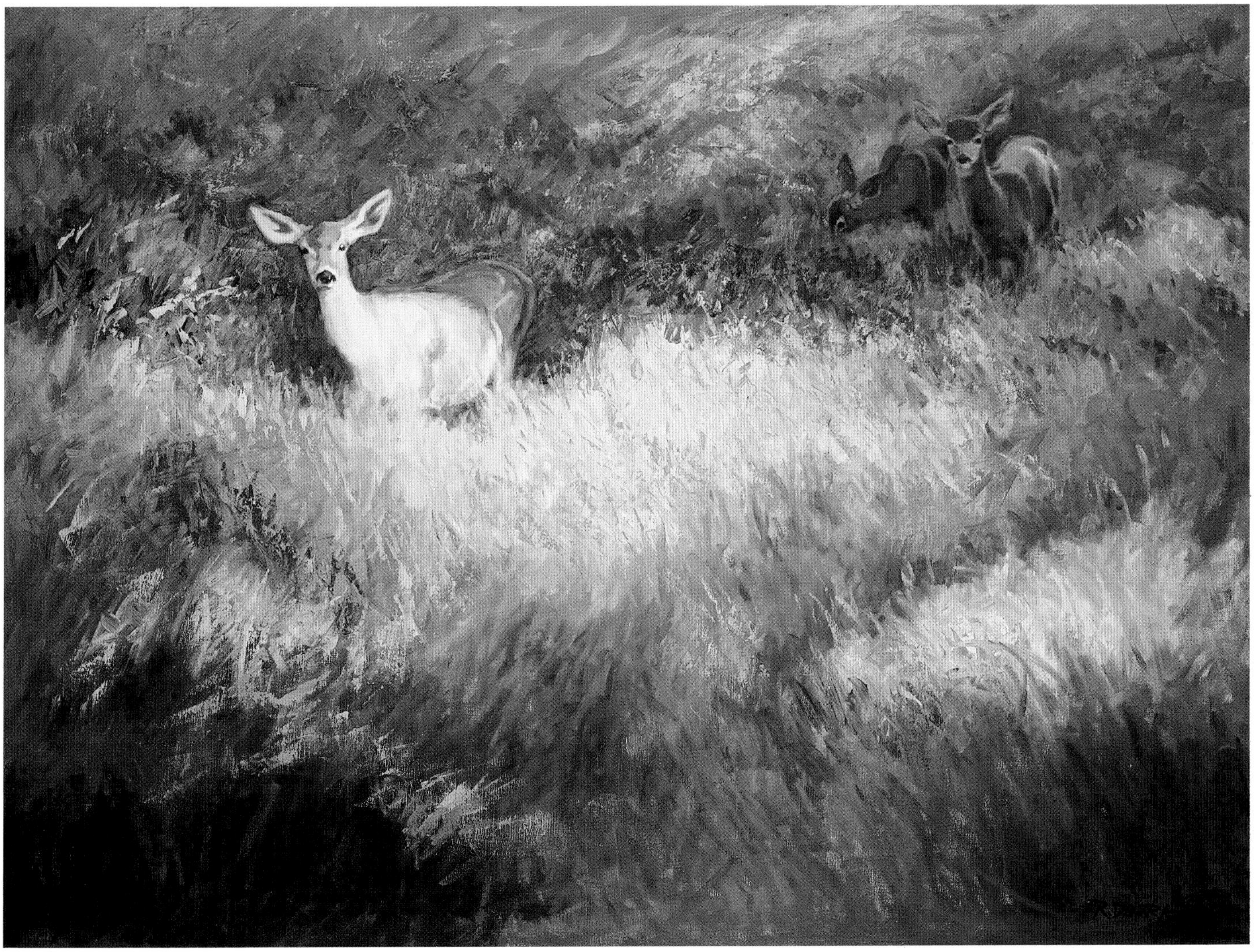

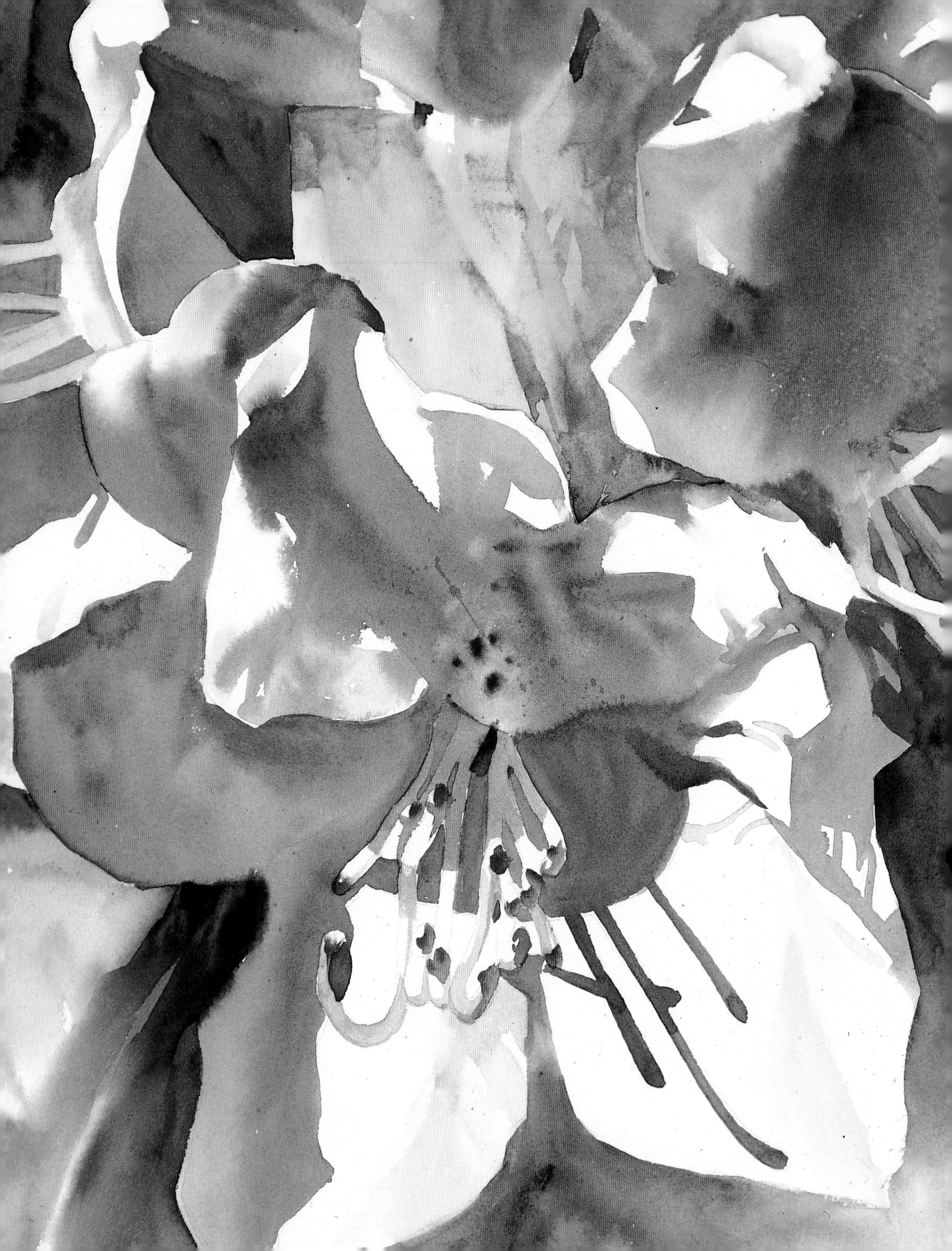

FLOWER POWER WITH DRAMATIC LIGHT IN WATERCOLOR

ANN PEMBER

CHAPTER 9

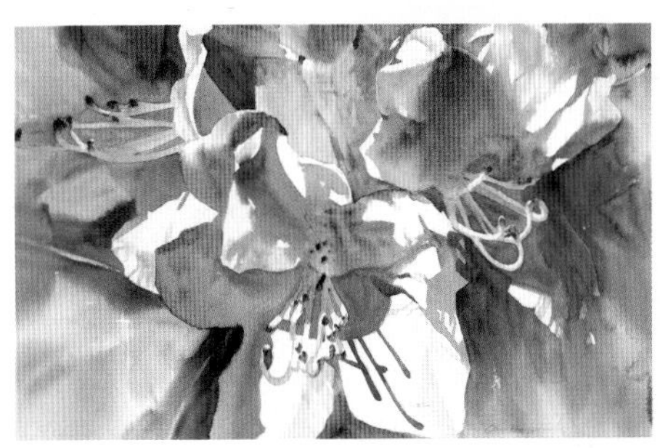

RHODODENDRON RADIANCE
Ann Pember, watercolor, 14" × 21" (35.6cm × 53.3cm)

This brightly lit group of flowers was painted very quickly over just a suggestion of a drawing. The light formed well-defined shadows. I simplified shapes, wetted general areas and charged in transparent colors (sometimes tilting the paper), mingling the colors. The edges were softened by letting the paint flow into and through the background.

To Ann Pember, light is the fundamental element of painting because no matter what the subject is, light affects everything from pattern and values to mood and emotion. In the following demonstrations, Pember shows how light's endless variations can be used to create many effects. Pember is best known for painting dramatic flower subjects up close. To create these striking subjects she usually uses one of three main categories of light: spotlight, floodlight or backlight. A spotlight effect gives dramatic value changes. This can create a powerful image, but you must be careful not to overuse hard edges when using this effect. With a floodlight effect, the lighting is more even and produces softer edges and contrasts. It can produce a feeling of tranquillity, subtle movement or color changes. But perhaps the most evocative lighting effect in Pember's repertoire is backlighting. Because most flower petals are translucent, flowers make fascinating and beautiful subjects to paint in backlighting. When backlit, most of the flower is in shadow. Sunlight glows through the outer petals, illuminating the edges of the others.

EXERCISE: PRACTICE MINGLING COLORS ON WET PAPER Watercolor

Color-mingling is a key ingredient in the following demonstrations. Take time to practice this technique so you will know how much water and paint to use, and what the colors do when they combine. Draw several squares at least 3″ to 4″ (7.62cm–10.2cm) in size. With a flat brush, apply clear water to cover a square and then float two or more colors in it. Keep the colors changing back and forth as you paint. Work with your board and paper tilted at a slight angle to get the best results: Gravity will help you make lovely mixtures. Try painting with brushes of different shapes and sizes to see which ones work best for you. The examples shown here mingle the different blues with Aureolin and New Gamboge.

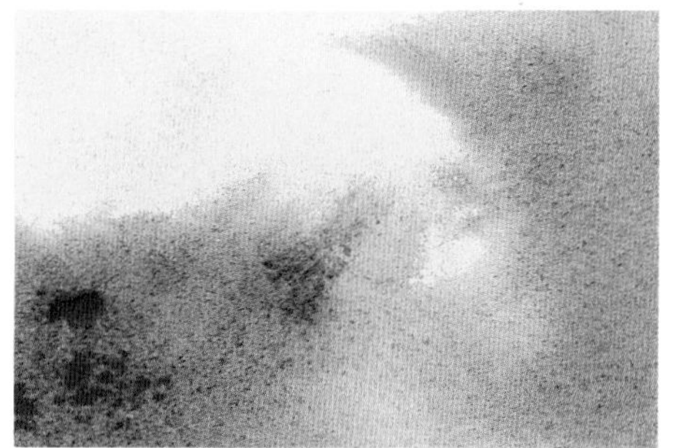

Aureolin and Cobalt Blue

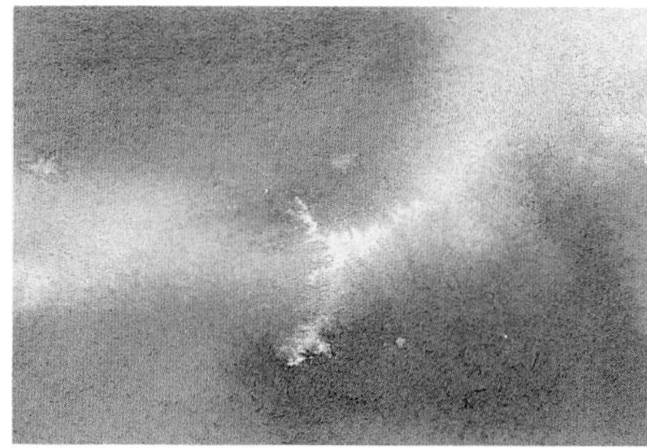

Aureolin and Antwerp Blue

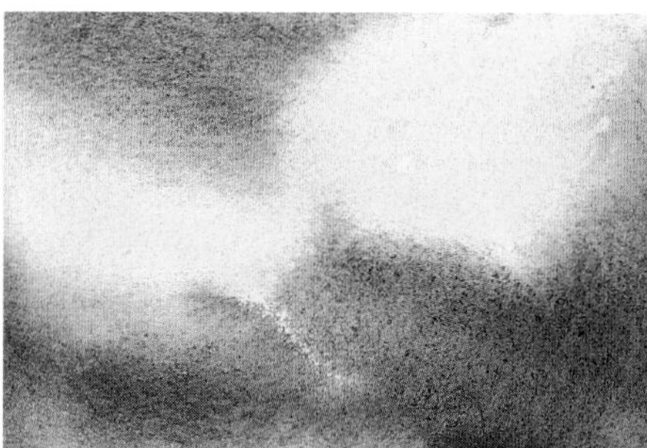

Aureolin and French Ultramarine Blue

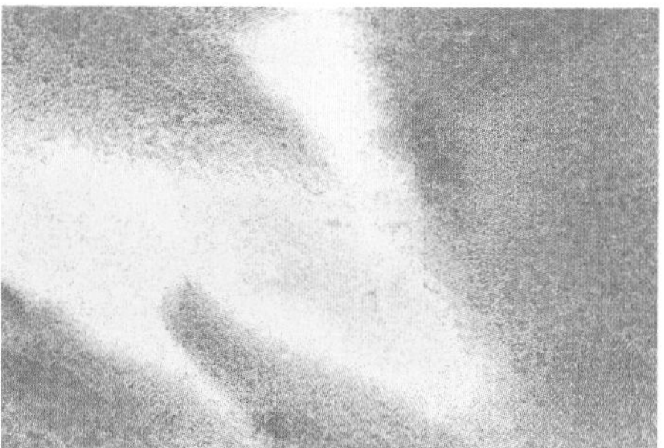

Aureolin and Cerulean Blue

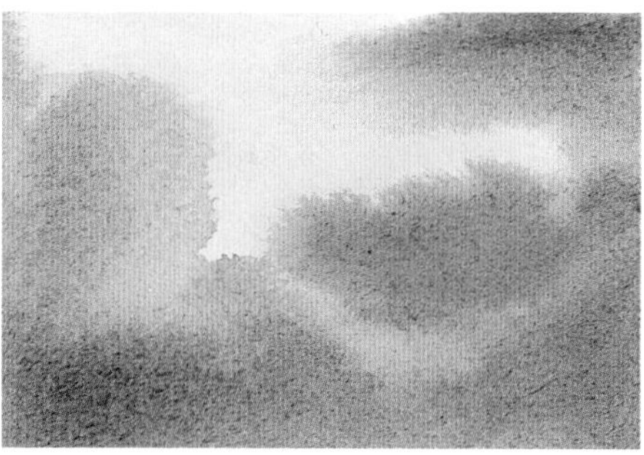

New Gamboge and Cobalt Blue

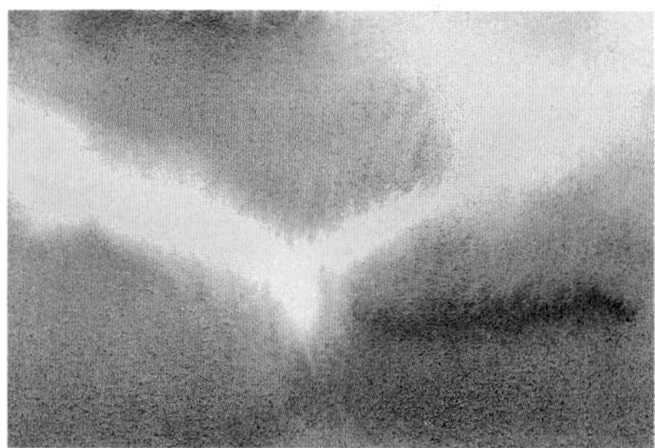

New Gamboge and Antwerp Blue

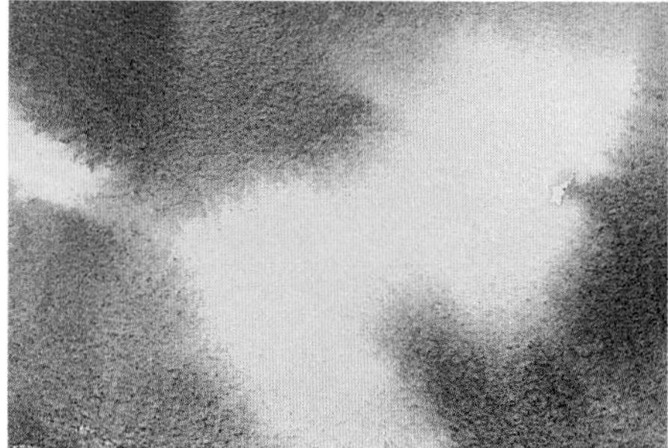

New Gamboge and French Ultramarine Blue

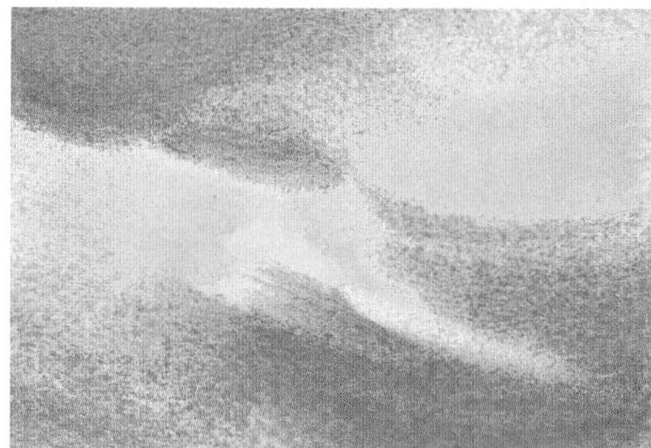

New Gamboge and Cerulean Blue

CREATE DELICATE, TRANSPARENT PETALS WITH BACKLIGHTING Watercolor

Backlighting can create very powerful paintings because of the intensified contrasts between lights and darks. Flowers with thin petals, such as roses, petunias and peonies, make good subjects because they allow maximum light to pass through them. They also tend to have many overlapping petals that can be linked together and treated as one shape, giving many design options.

The outer petals and edges of leaves that become translucent when light shines through them will be the lightest areas of the painting. Paint these first, prewetting each area and then adding colors and letting them mingle together. Vary color often for interest as you move around the flower. Soften some edges as you work, using a wet, clean brush. As the paint dries, but while it is still damp, charge in darks. This is tricky. If the area is too dry you may get a hard edge or a bloom; if it is too wet the paint will diffuse and dry too light. It helps to practice with different degrees of wetness on extra paper to learn what to look for.

Depending on the flower, backlighting may cause the center to have a glow of light. Overlapping petals keep some light out and may appear dark. The petals nearest the center will be quite dark. Try to paint these petals simply, combining some shapes. Add darks and details at the end. If you need to lift color or clean up some edges, do this with a small, fairly stiff flat bristle brush. "Tickle" the spot with a damp brush and blot it with a tissue, gently removing the paint from the surface.

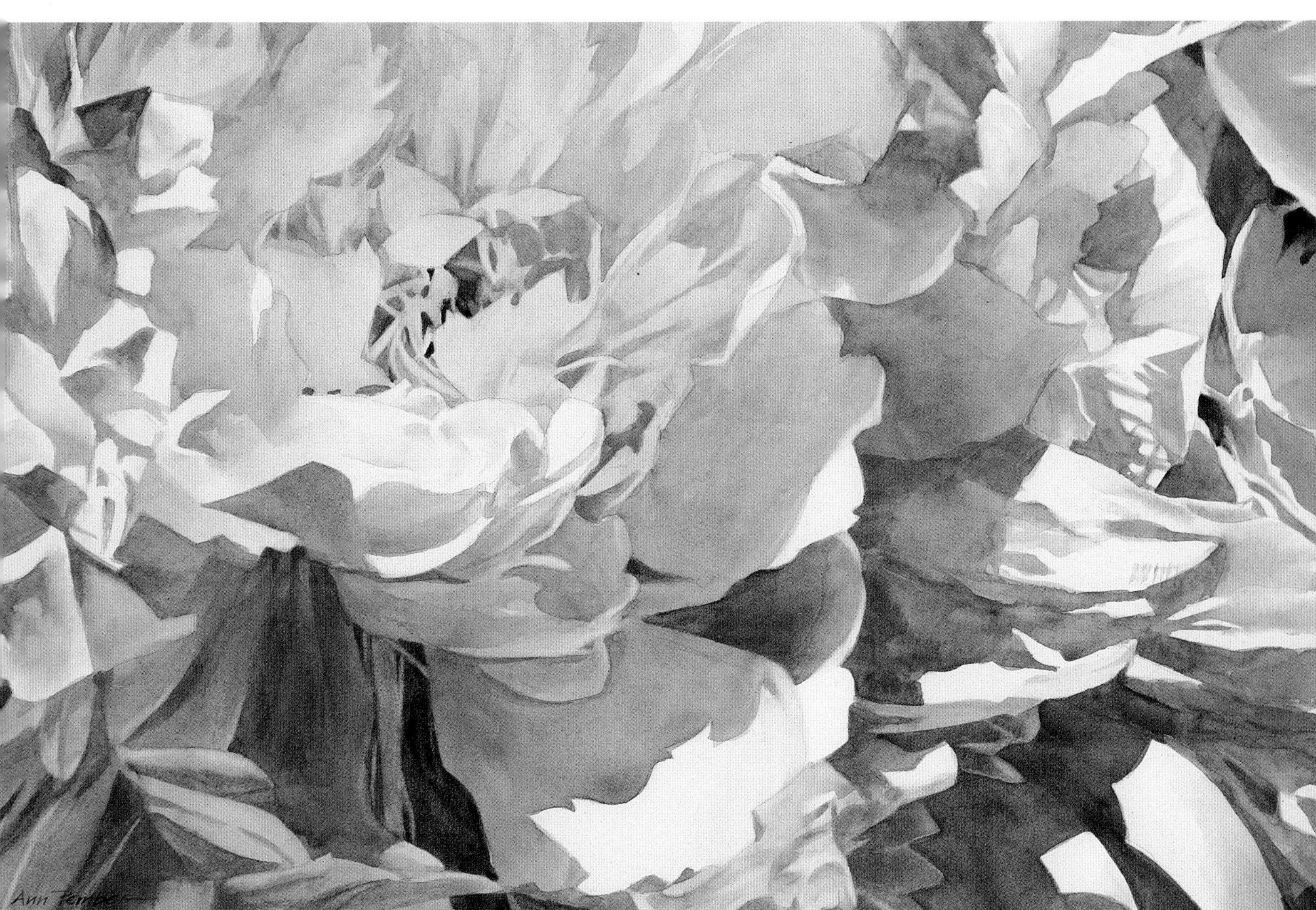

This backlit flower is painted from a very close point of view. Only the edges of some of the petals receive full light. The large middle value shadow over the center was poured into the prewetted area so the colors would mingle together. The palette is quite limited: Aureolin Yellow, New Gamboge, Cobalt Blue, Raw Umber and Raw Sienna. The painting is very high key (light in value), producing a feeling of warmth and light.

PEONY BLOOM
Ann Pember, watercolor, 14" × 21" (35.6cm × 53.3cm)

PAINTING BACKLIGHT ON A WHITE PEONY Watercolor

This demonstration gives you a close-up point of view with a feeling of sunshine. When a flower is backlit, a majority of its petals are in shadow. That is true here as well; however, because the peony is so translucent and its hue is bright white, even the shadow areas are a relatively light value. The backlit petals are stark white and so bright that they lose some of their definition, as if the light is blinding the viewer.

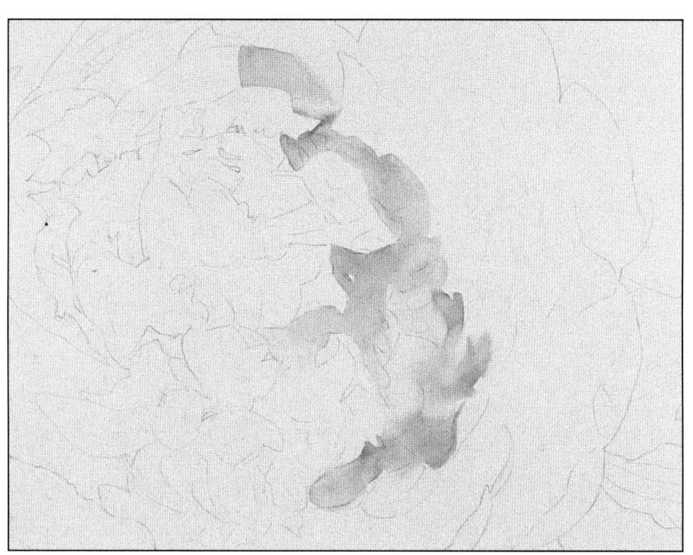

A

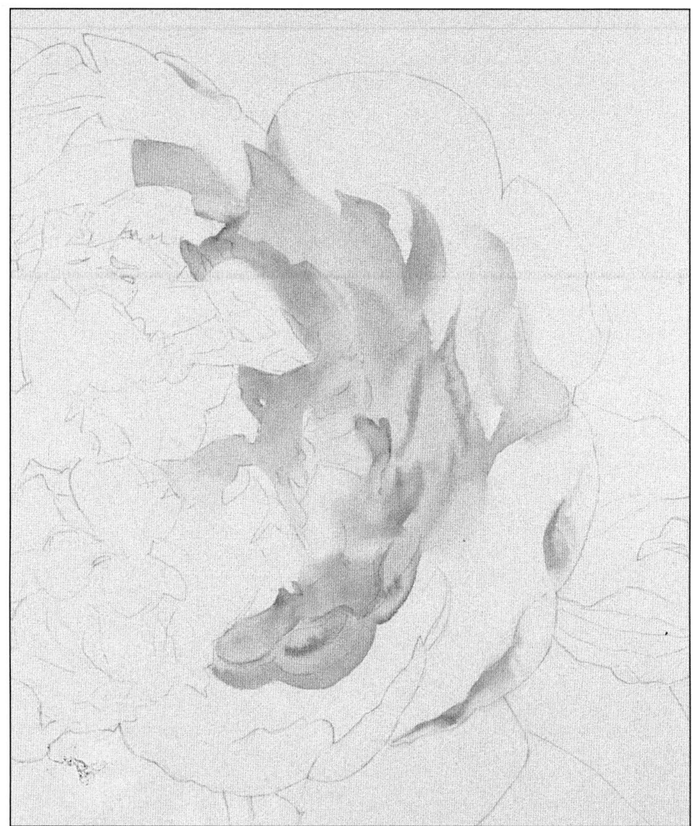

B

STEP 1

Begin the Painting

A. After drawing your flower close-up (see "Starting Right" on page 130), begin painting to the right of center. Wet the connecting petals with water using a medium brush. Add New Gamboge at the top, and then Permanent Rose and Antwerp Blue toward the bottom. Let these colors mingle. Soften any edges you do not want to dry hard.

B. Move on to the petals to the right using the same technique and colors.

C. For the dark lavender shadow in the large petal near the bottom, add Antwerp Blue and Permanent Rose when the area is dry. Soften the edges with a clean wet brush.

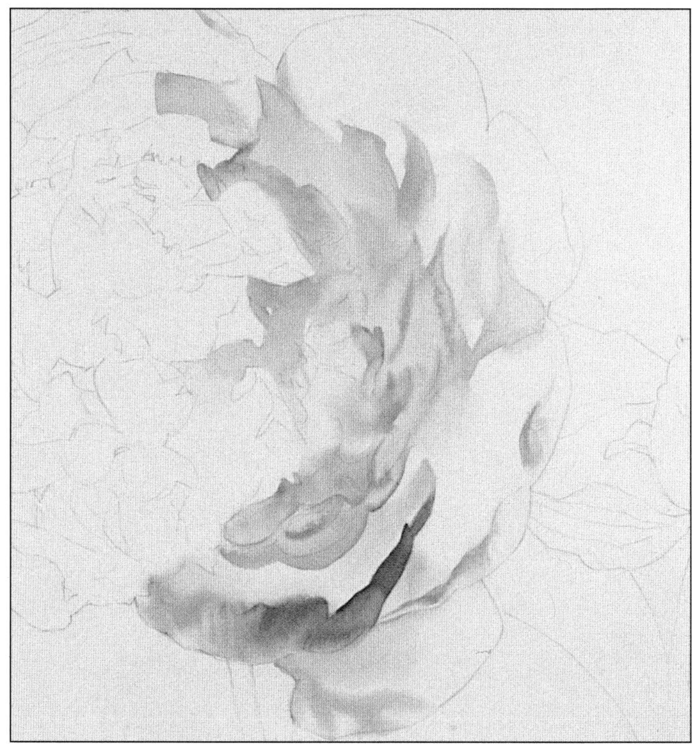

C

STEP 2

Develop the Petals

A. Wet the shapes of the pale petals on the upper left. Drop in Permanent Rose, Antwerp Blue and New Gamboge and allow the colors to mingle.

B. Wet the whole shape of the left side outer petals and float in Antwerp Blue, Permanent Rose and New Gamboge. Make the values a bit darker on this side of the flower. Lift out a few lights with a damp brush and add darks as the area dries to just damp.

C. These inner petals of the upper left have light shining through them and will be warm and light in value. Wet the inner part of the upper petal and float in Aureolin Yellow, New Gamboge and Permanent Rose. For the lower petal, wet and paint with Permanent Rose, Antwerp Blue and Aureolin Yellow. Clean up any edges or highlights with a clean damp brush. Soften edges where necessary.

Palette

Permanent Rose
Permanent Alizarin Crimson
New Gamboge
Aureolin Yellow
Raw Umber
Burnt Sienna
Burnt Umber
Antwerp Blue
Winsor Green
Cadmium Red Purple

Brushes

Winsor Newton Sceptre Gold
Rounds: no. 12, no. 10
Flats: 1″ (25mm), ¾″ (19mm), ½″ (12mm)

Brushes should hold plenty of paint and keep a good point or edge: Manmade/natural blends work well.

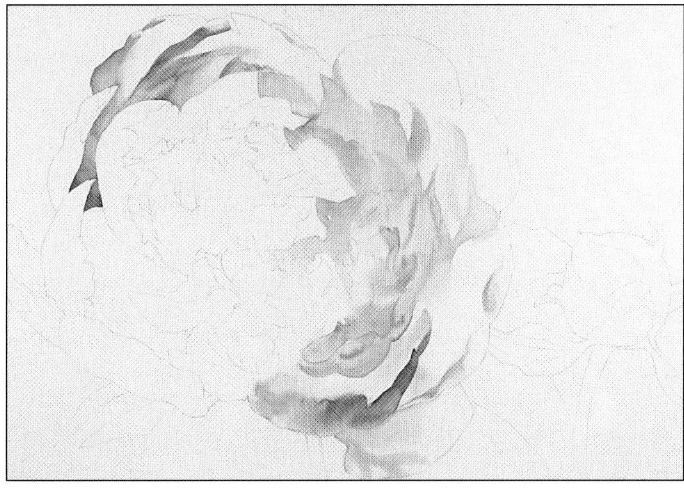

A

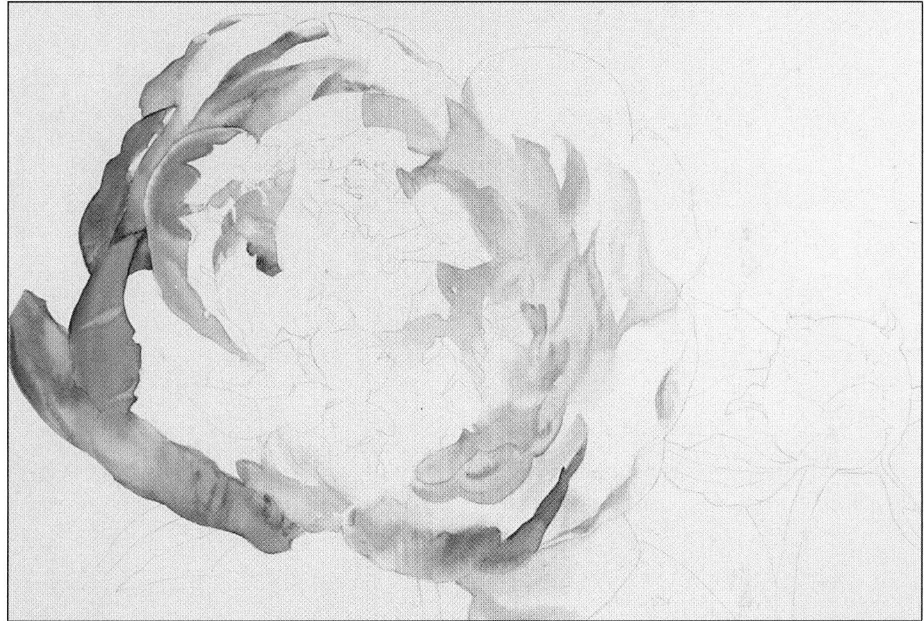

B

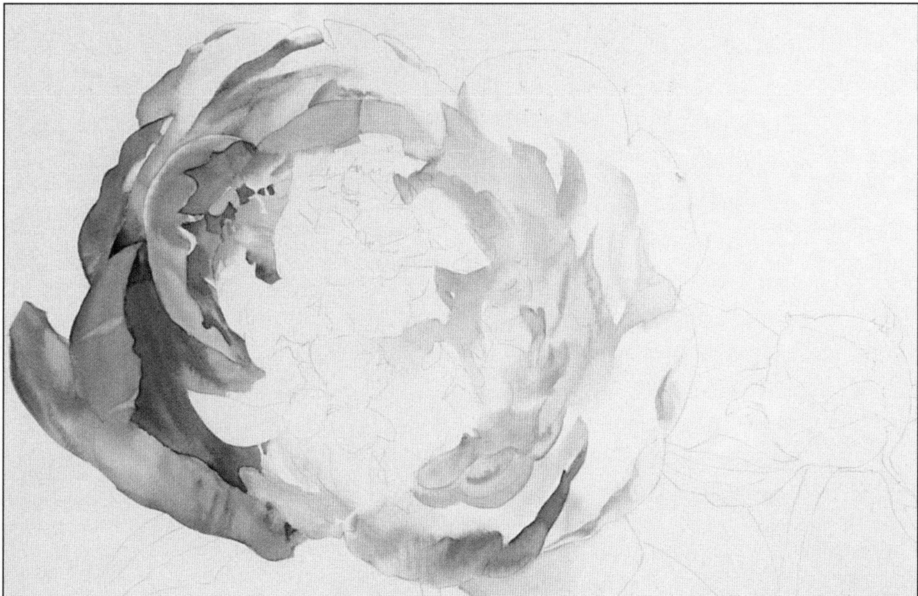

C

STEP 3

Paint the Flower's Center

A. Wet and paint the many connecting petals that form the large center shadow. It is quite cool, since the light does not shine through it. So even though it is a white flower, use Antwerp Blue and Permanent Rose, letting them mingle throughout the whole shape. Let this layer dry.

B and **C.** Define the center shapes with darks by wetting each small area and painting with New Gamboge, Permanent Rose and Antwerp Blue. Use Permanent Alizarin Crimson for the darkest reds. Keep thinking of the negative and positive shapes and work around the "puzzle" of shapes and values.

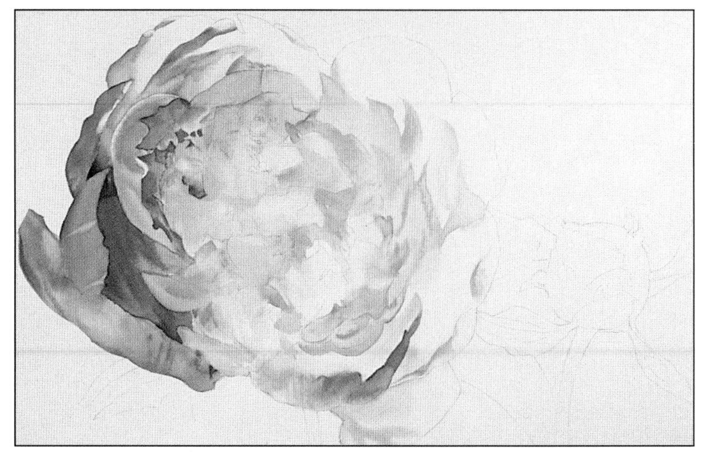

A

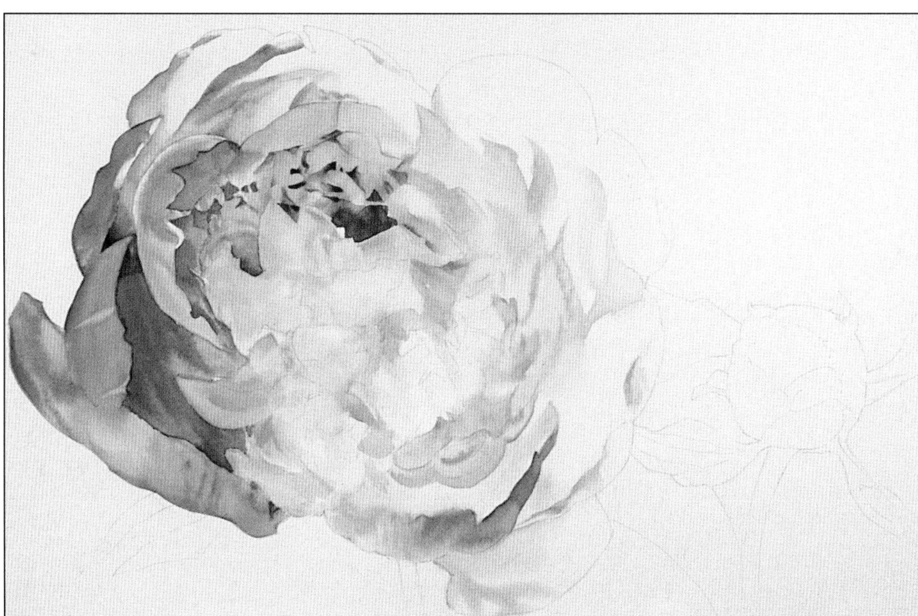

B

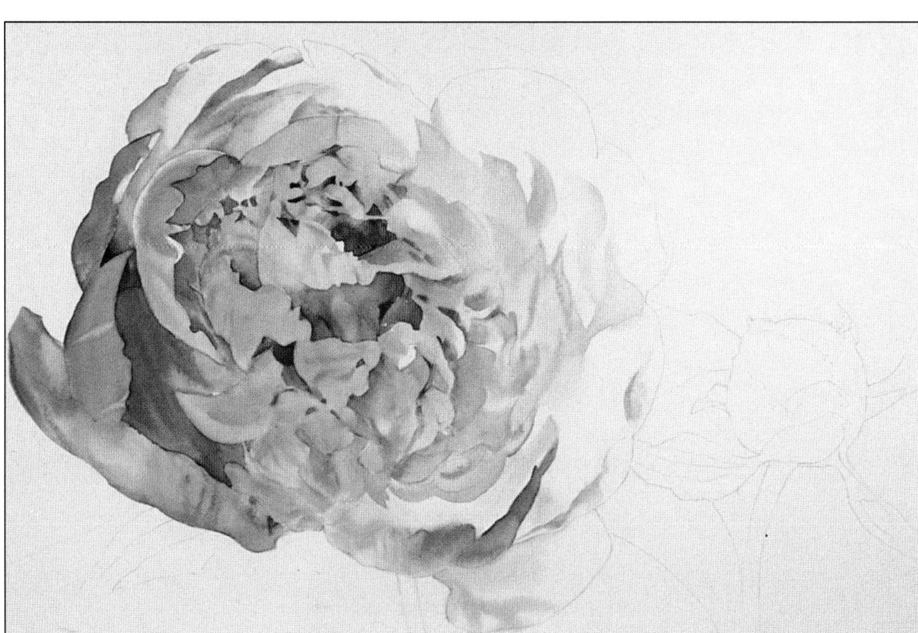

C

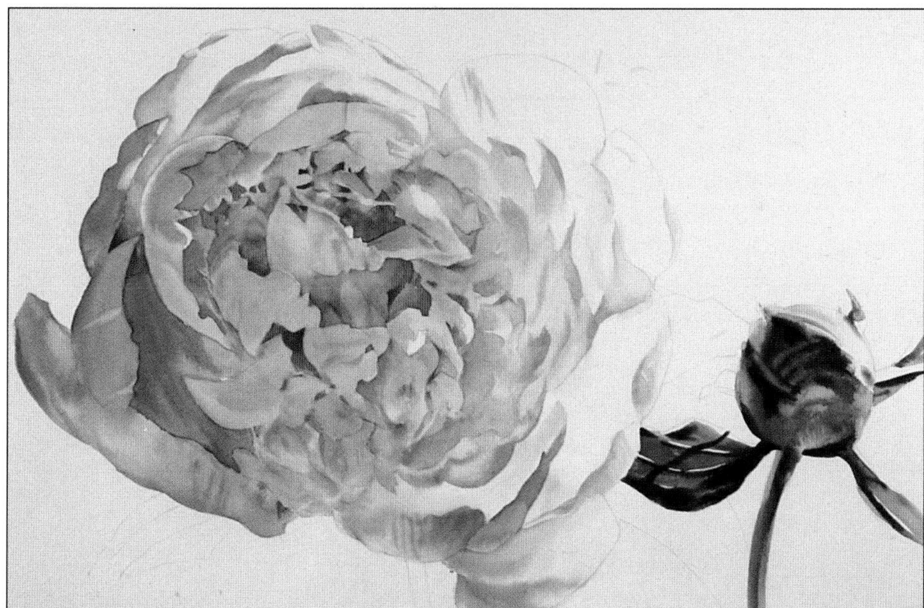

STEP 4

Paint the Bud

Wet the area of the bud and its leaves. Float in Aureolin Yellow and New Gamboge, and then Permanent Rose and Raw Umber. As the paint reaches the damp stage, add the dark greens using Antwerp Blue, Burnt Umber, Winsor Green and Permanent Alizarin Crimson. Soften the edges where there are highlights. You can also lift highlights with a thirsty brush.

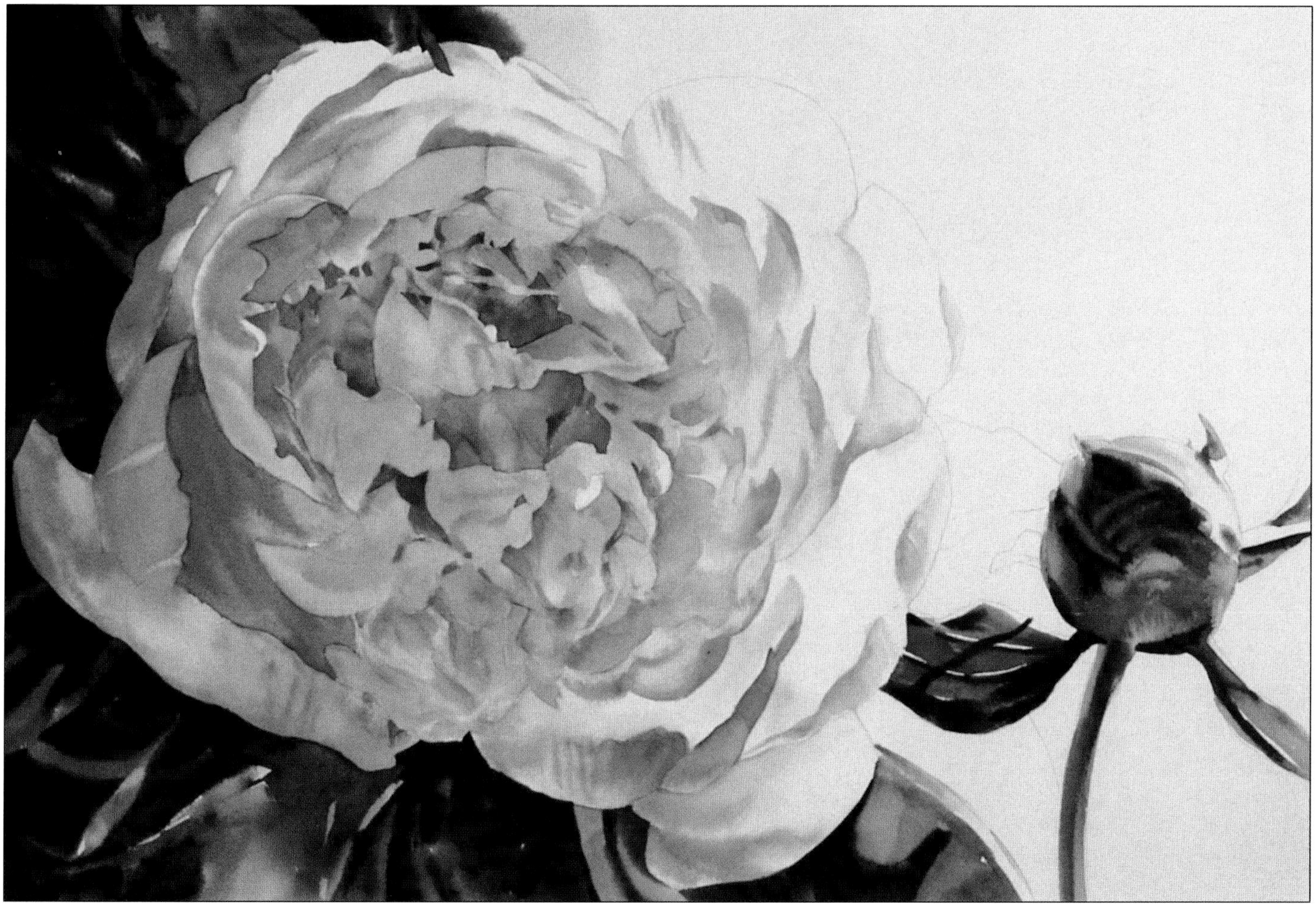

STEP 5

Background

Turn the paper on its side so that gravity will work for you. (The top of the painting should be on your left.) Wet around the flower at its upper left corner. Drop in rich amounts of Antwerp Blue, New Gamboge, Raw Umber, Winsor Green, Burnt Sienna and Alizarin. For darks, add more paint as the area reaches the damp stage. Soften the outer edges to blend them; keep the edges next to the flower clean and sharp. Turn the paper back to a normal position. Wet the left side, going over a bit of the last wash (only after it is dry) and including the bottom, under the flower up to and including the leaf at the lower right. Paint this by mingling the same colors as above. Keep the strokes next to the flower sure and clean.

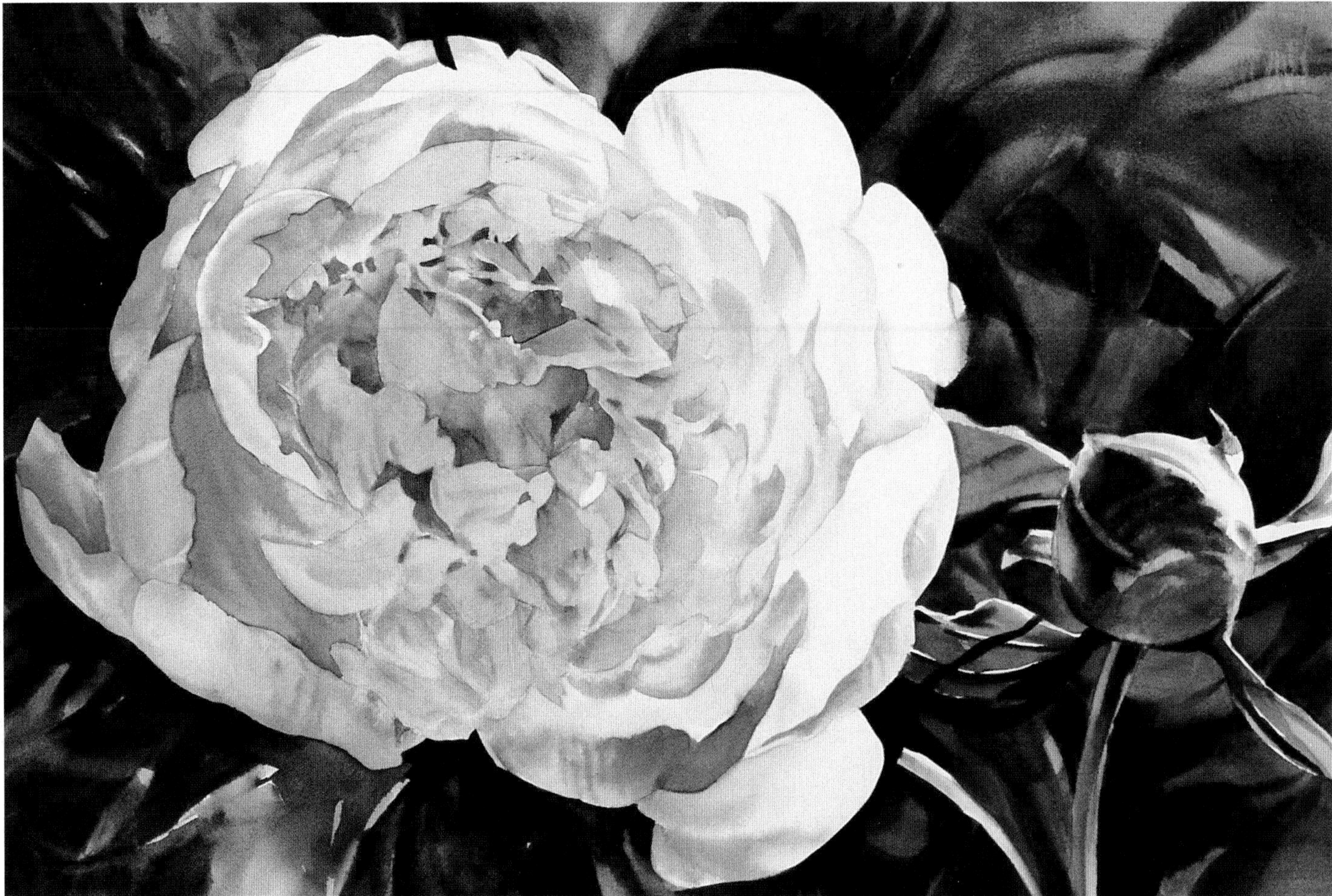

PROVOCATIVE PEONY
Ann Pember, watercolor, 15″ × 22″ (38.1cm × 55.9cm)

STEP 6

Refine and Finish

With the paper on its right side, wet the rest of the background area and paint with the colors used in step five, suggesting leaf shapes and working in darks toward the end. Paint down to the bud and leaf shapes at the bottom right and stop. Let this layer dry. Turn the paper back upright. Wet around the bud and its stem and leaves. Leave a narrow dry highlight area on the upper left leaf. Refine the left outside petal by carefully deepening the inner part of it with a glaze. Adjust any other areas, including the background, that need to be deeper by glazing and softening the edges.

Starting Right

When you do your preliminary drawing, think about values and shadow patterns and how they could be simplified. When possible, link shapes together, making the pieces fit like a puzzle. Simplify! Change or eliminate elements for better design. With backlighting, the outer petals will be light and have less detail. Don't make the drawing too dark: The marks should just be guidelines. (The drawings for the demonstrations in this chapter are darker than I would normally make them so that they are visible to the reader.)

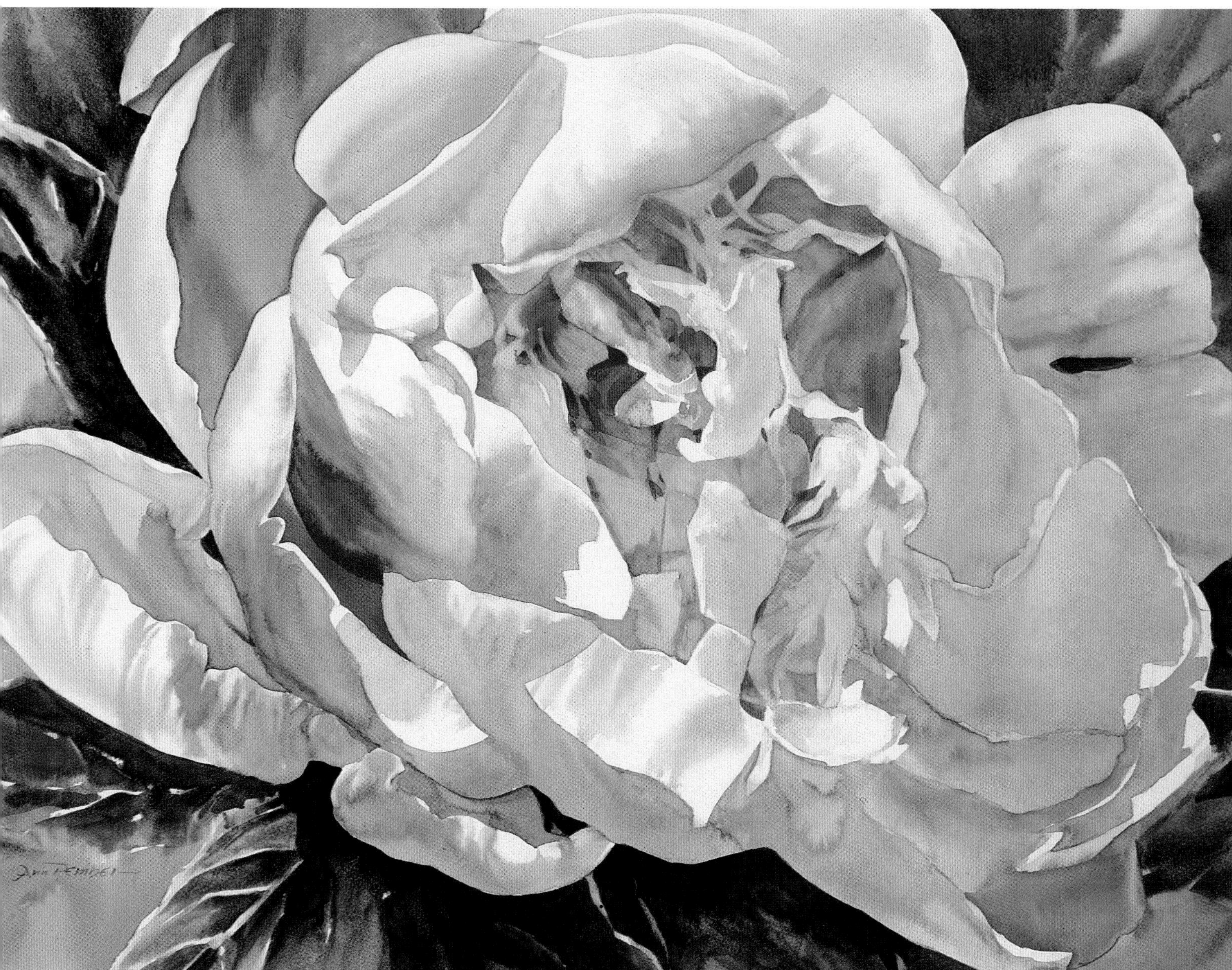

POETIC PEONY
Ann Pember, watercolor, 21" × 29" (53.3cm × 73.7cm)

Another Backlit Flower

This painting is quite similar to *Provocative Peony* (opposite). The flower is backlit, creating a shadow over most of it. I took advantage of this large shadow area to combine many petal shapes and paint them as larger shapes. These areas, painted wet-into-wet, were completed cleanly and directly. I really pushed color changes wherever I could for sparkle.

DRAMATIC FLORAL WITH SPOTLIGHT EFFECT Watercolor

This lighting is different from the previous demo. In a spotlight effect, the bright light comes from one direction, usually from the front, off to one side. This creates a strong interplay of light and dark values throughout the composition, not just at the edges of a flower. It gives an opportunity to use the colors from their lightest to their most intense forms.

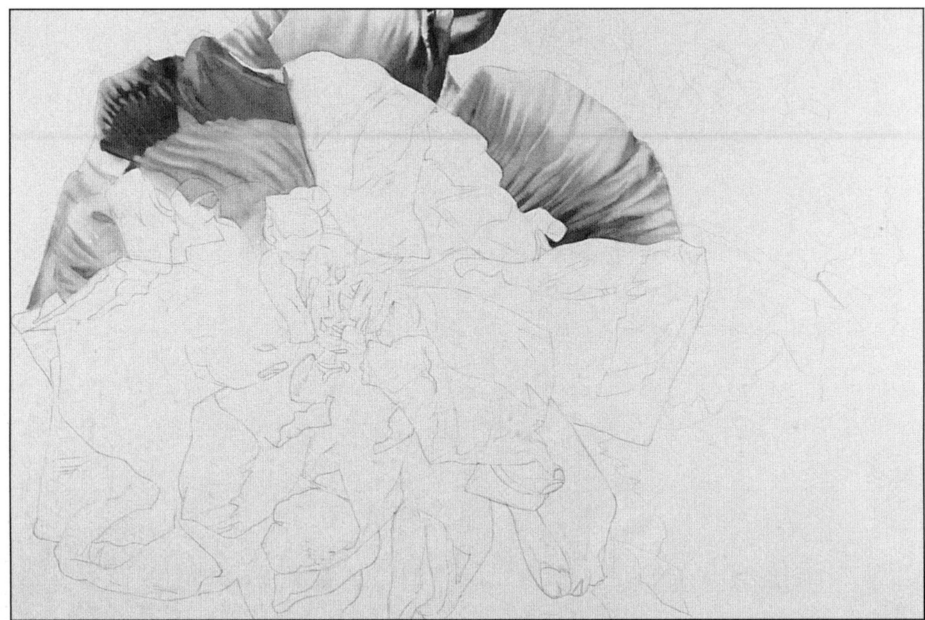

STEP 1

Drawing and Painting the First Petals

Sketch just enough to guide you through the shapes: Don't get bogged down with too much detail. On the upper part of the flower, wet the top petals and float in Permanent Rose, Permanent Alizarin Crimson and Antwerp Blue, letting them mingle. Change color often, softening and blending the edges. As the paint begins to dry, add darks to form the ridges on the petals. Lift lights with a thirsty clean brush before the paint is fully dry.

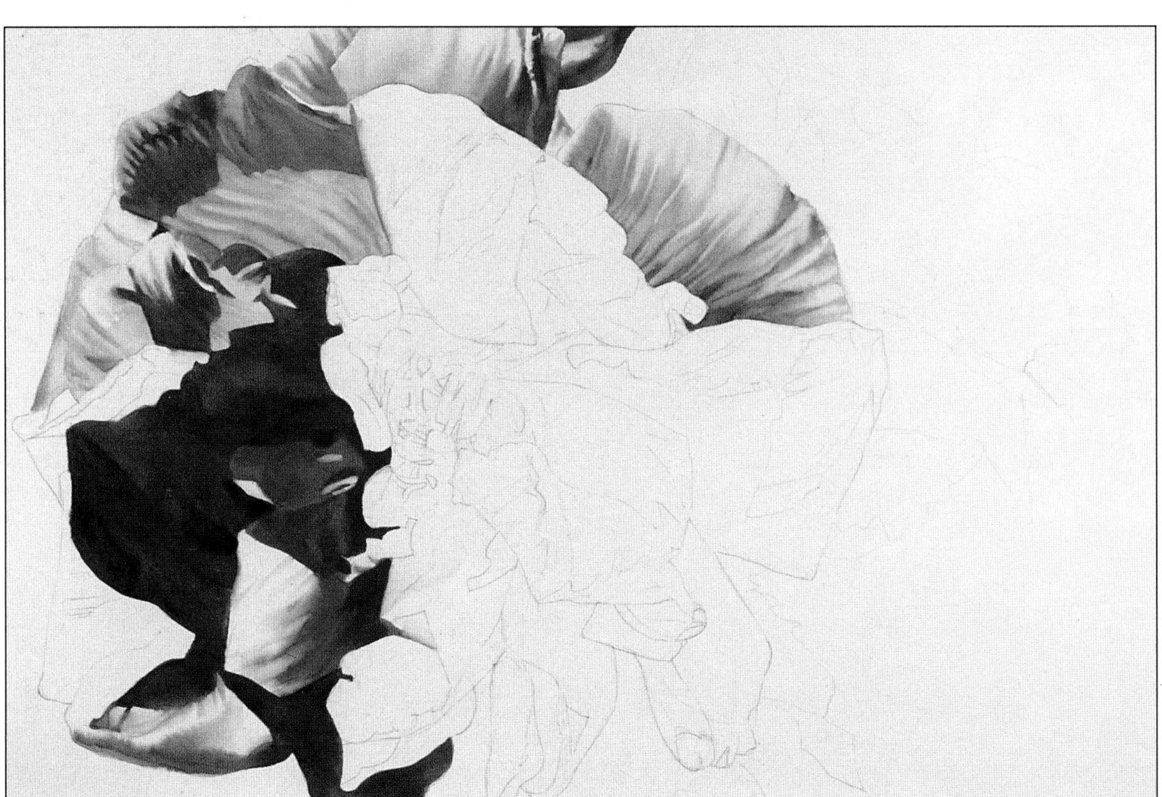

STEP 2

Add Shadow

Wet the whole left side, carefully connecting shapes, and charge this area with rich amounts of Permanent Rose, Permanent Alizarin Crimson and Antwerp Blue. Make it dark, but keep the edges soft. Be sure to change colors, letting them mingle. Work quickly; keep it liquid.

STEP 3

Areas Around Shadow

Wet and float in light strokes of Permanent Rose and Antwerp Blue to fill in petal areas to the left of and above the shadow you just painted. Wet the petal shape in the center top and float in Permanent Rose, Antwerp Blue and Permanent Alizarin Crimson. Add darks to give form and shadow when the paint reaches the damp stage and pick out highlights with a clean, thirsty brush. Soften some edges, including the bottom.

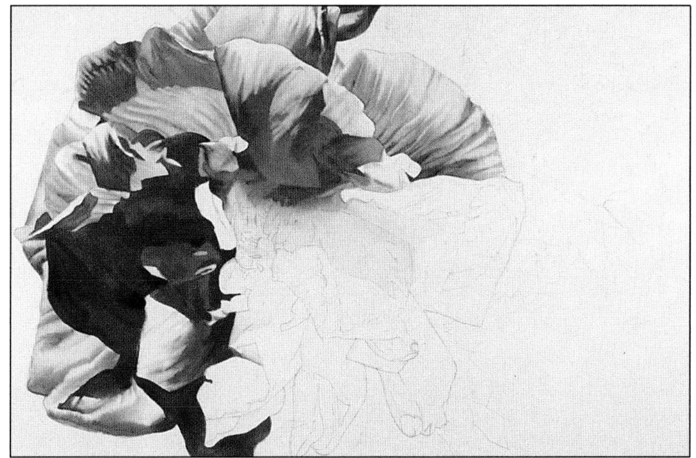

STEP 4

Petal on the Right Side

Wet the shape and float in the light tones using Permanent Rose, Antwerp Blue and Permanent Alizarin Crimson. When just damp, add more intense colors of the same hues to give form and show ridges, and also add Cadmium Red Purple. Soften the edges where desirable.

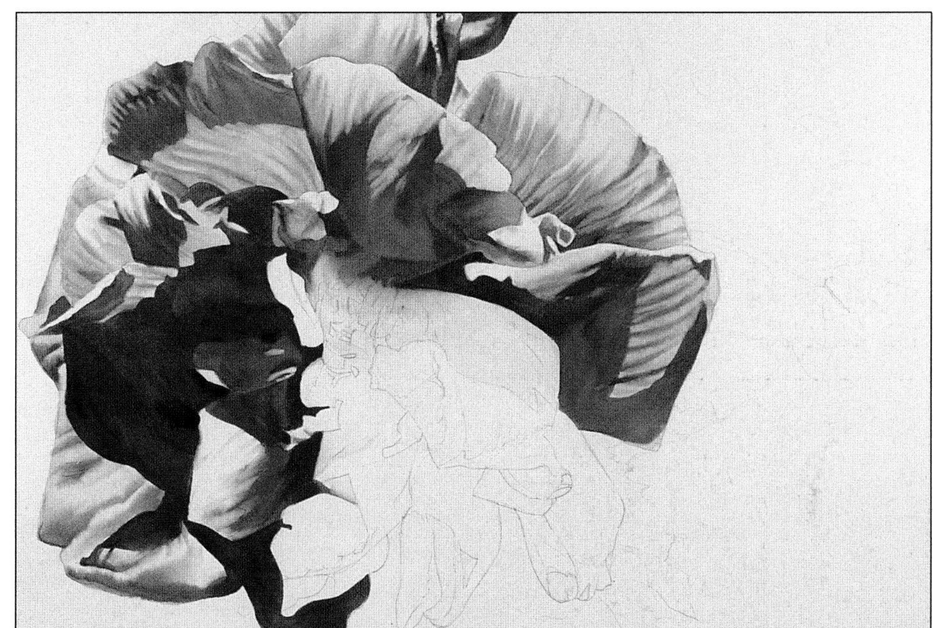

STEP 5

Dark Center

Carefully glaze over adjacent shapes and blend the edges, using Permanent Alizarin Crimson, New Gamboge, Cadmium Red Purple and Antwerp Blue in darker ranges. As the area dries, add the darkest darks. Blend the edges.

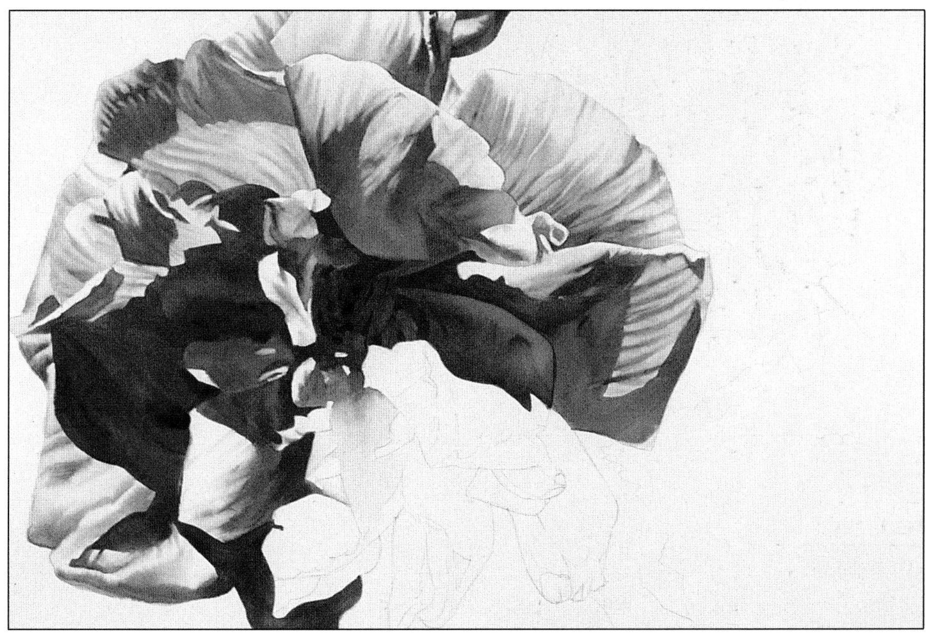

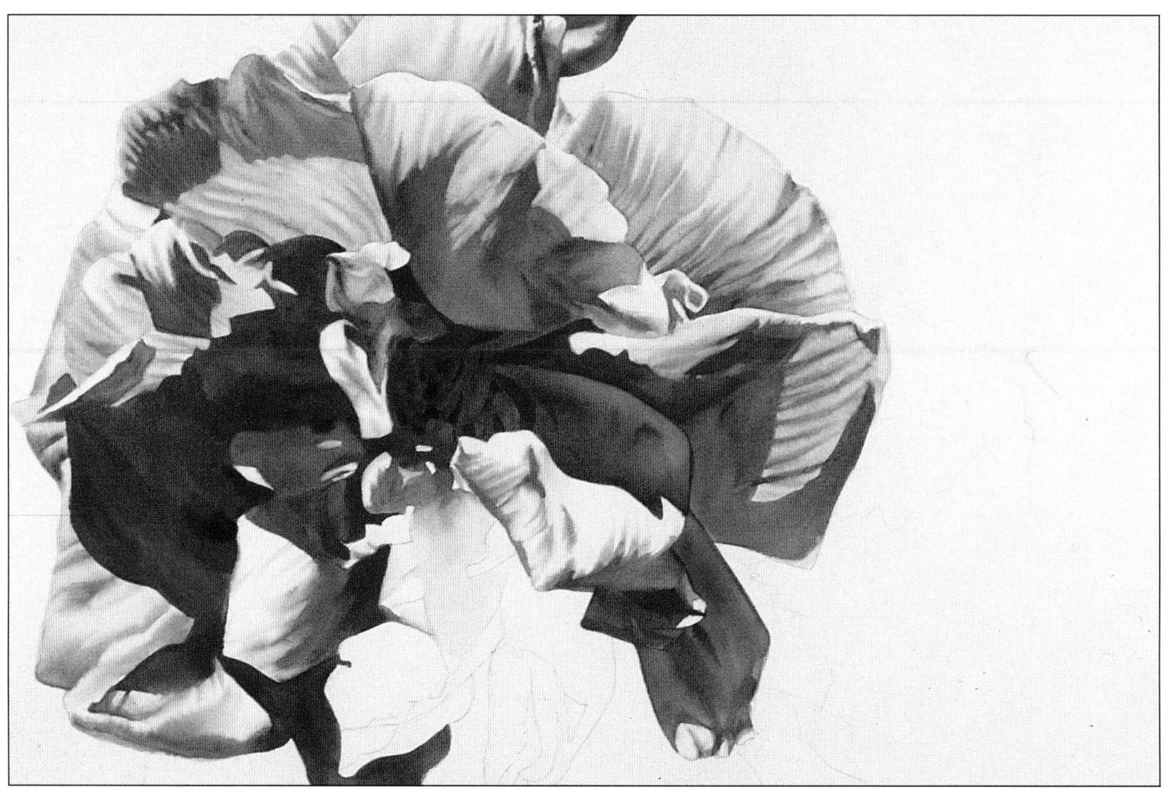

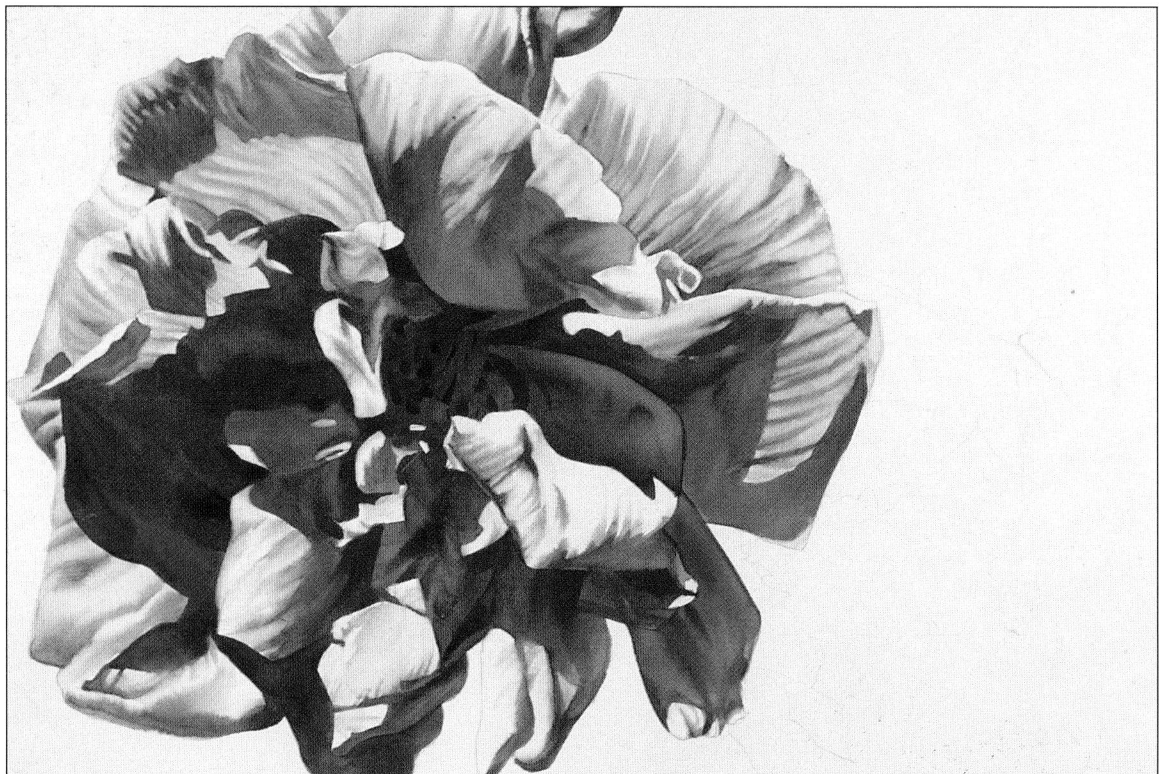

STEP 6

Lower Petals

Wet the shapes on the bottom right as one and charge with Permanent Alizarin Crimson, Permanent Rose, Cadmium Red Purple and Antwerp Blue. Clean up the edges; soften and pick out highlights. Add darks toward the end of the drying time for shadow, form and ridges. Handle the bottom petals the same way.

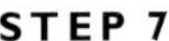

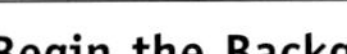

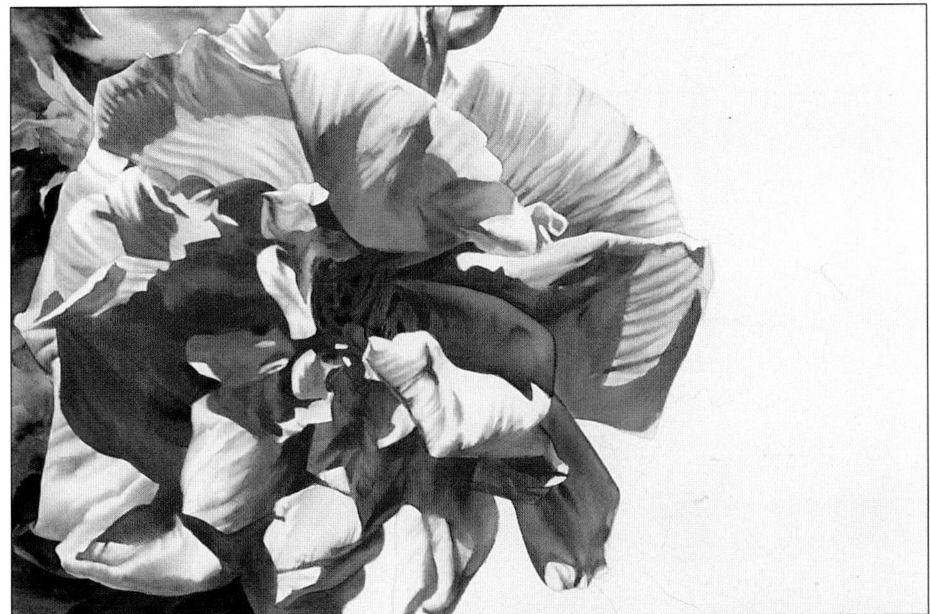

STEP 7

Begin the Background

Wet the upper left background area and charge with Permanent Rose, New Gamboge, Permanent Alizarin Crimson, Antwerp Blue, Winsor Green and Raw Umber. Paint around the bud. For the bud, wet and then mingle New Gamboge and Raw Umber on the leaves and Permanent Rose and Permanent Alizarin Crimson on the bud. Continue painting the background down the side to the bottom. Add the darks last, and use some Permanent Rose in the bottom areas.

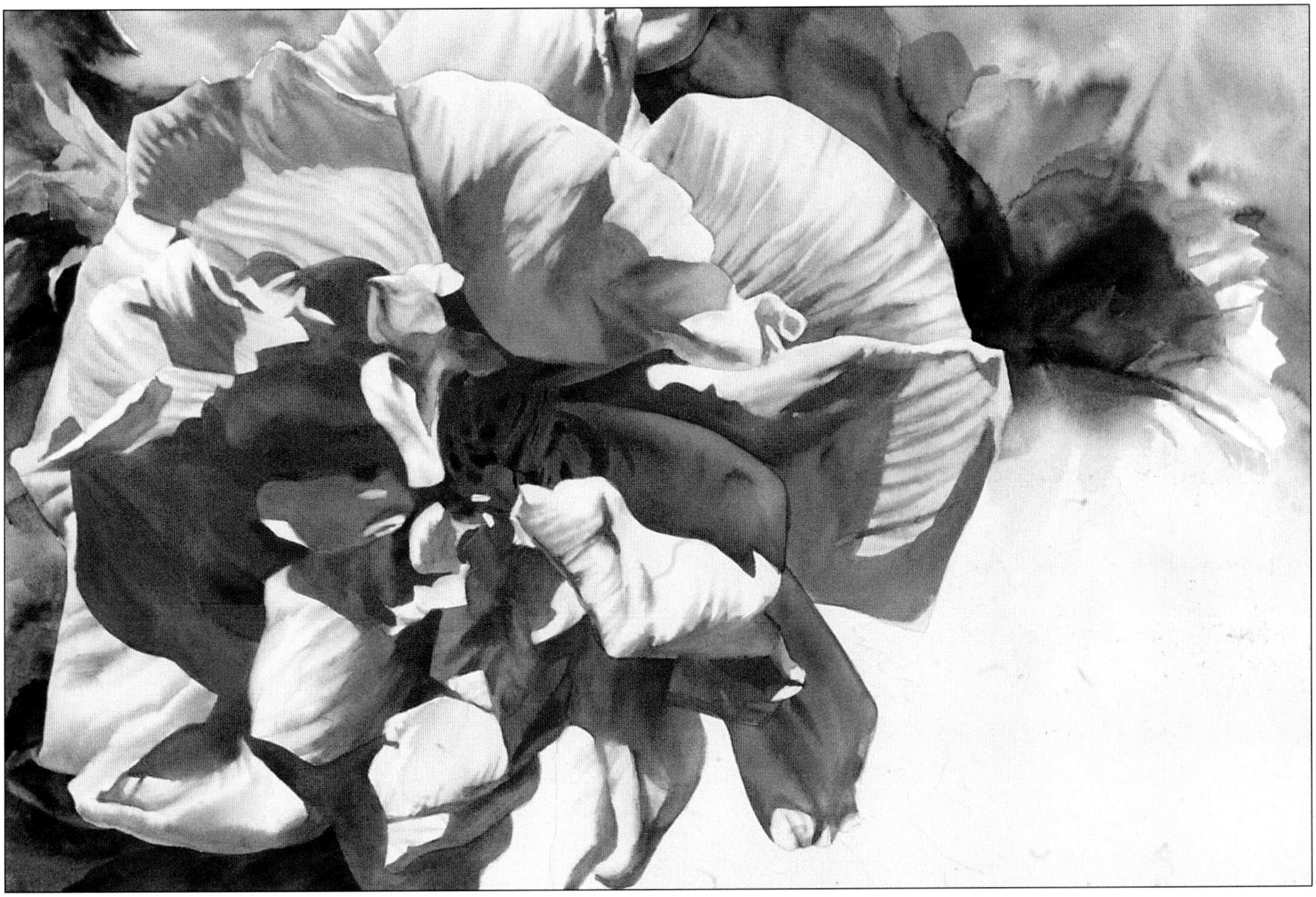

STEP 8

Develop the Background

Wet the upper right background area and charge with rich amounts of Permanent Alizarin Crimson, Antwerp Blue, New Gamboge and Permanent Rose to suggest flowers behind the rose. Next to that, float in New Gamboge, Antwerp Blue, Permanent Rose and Winsor Green. Change colors often, soften the edges and keep things wet. As the area dries, add darks and pull out highlights.

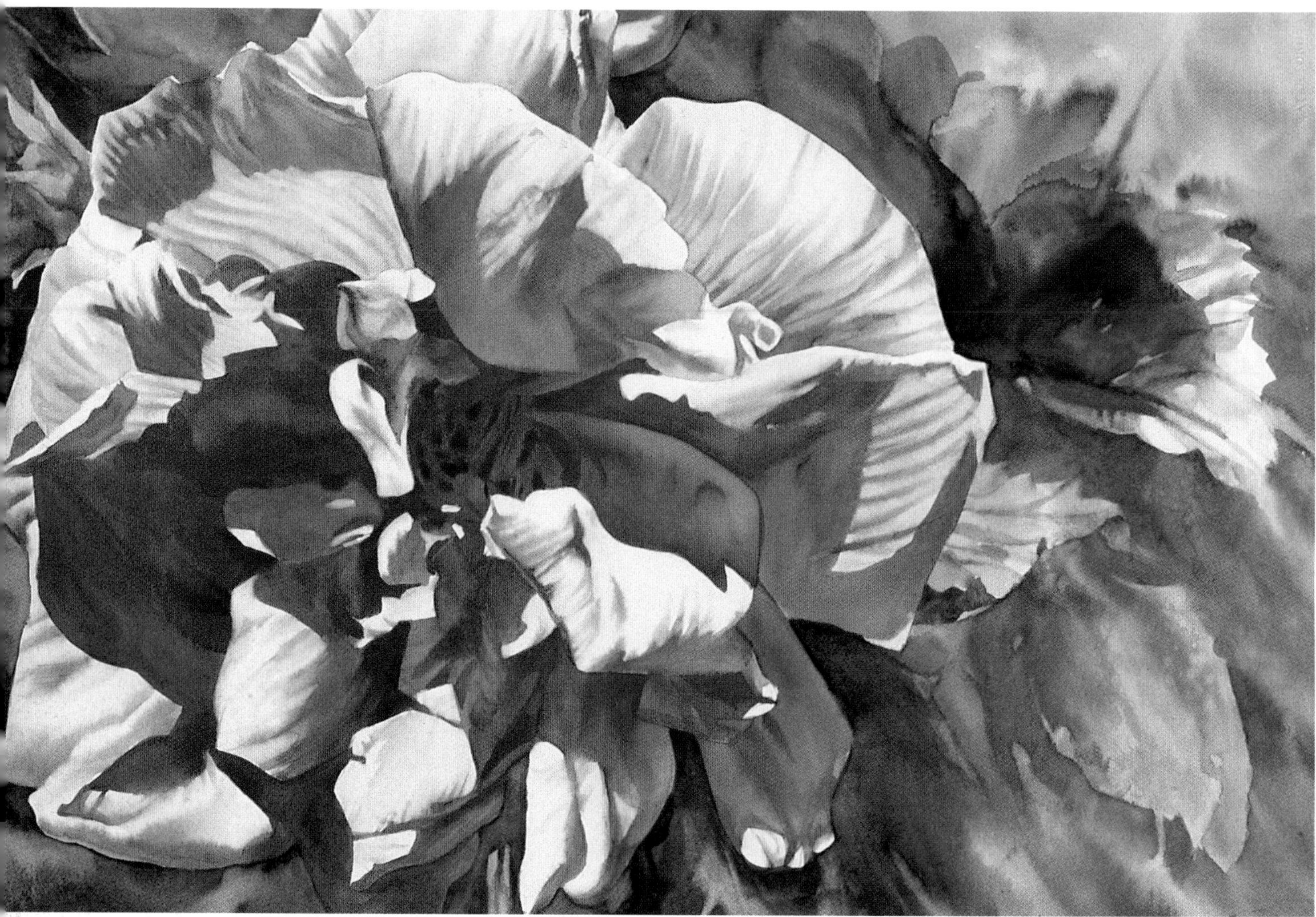

ROSE GLOW

Ann Pember, watercolor, 15″ × 22″ (38.1cm × 55.9cm)

STEP 9

Refinements and Finish

Wet the lower right background and float many color changes into the whole area. Use New Gamboge, Antwerp Blue, Permanent Rose, Raw Umber and Permanent Alizarin Crimson. Toward the end of the drying time, spritz with a spray bottle just a little to add texture. Let this dry. Add some darks under the flower. Add darks and some lavender in the upper left. Below the rose, remove some darks with a clean brush, and then float in Antwerp Blue, Permanent Rose and New Gamboge. This area was too dense. Form another leaf at the right by glazing with the colors used in step seven, deepening the tone around the leaf to give it an interesting shape. Clean up the edges and lift, or lightly tone, a few lights. Add another glaze of purple under the new leaf and soften the edges. Know when to stop.

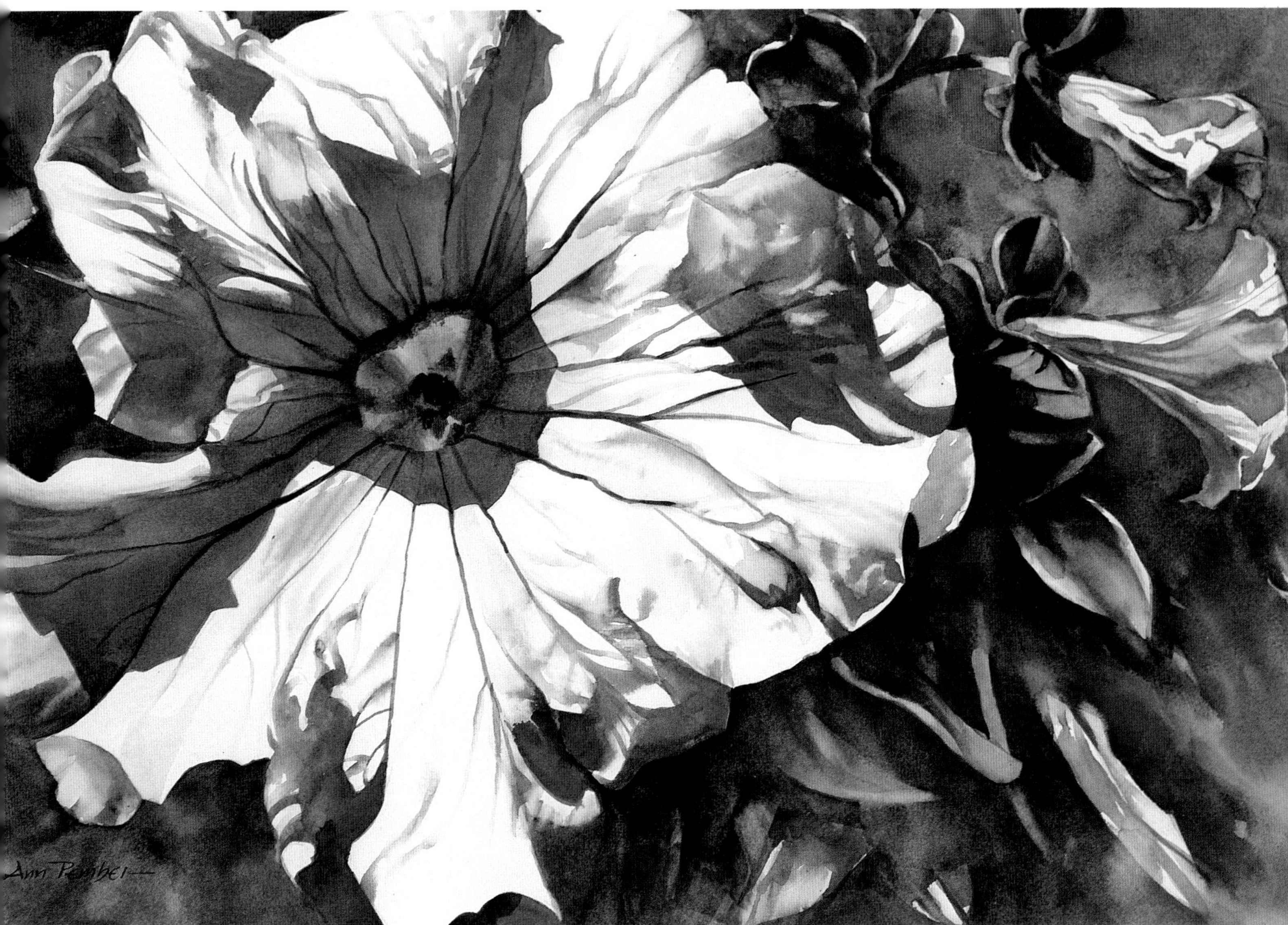

WHITE PETUNIA
Ann Pember, watercolor, 14" × 21" (35.6cm × 53.3cm)

Another Flower in the Spotlight

This painting shows the same type of dramatic lighting as *Rose Glow*: a spotlight effect. To be sure to keep the dramatic contrast of this effect, it helps, again, to simplify the complexity of your flower, connecting shapes where possible. With my usual technique, colors were floated into wet areas of the paper and allowed to mingle. The loose, out-of-focus background is quite dark in value, making the flower shapes stand out. Most details were added as the painting dried. In this case I also added some calligraphy in the veins of the flower. Calligraphic touches such as these can give a loose painting welcome focus, if not overdone. Finely painted features must always be done on dry paper.

Key VARY COLORS WITHIN A STRONG DESIGN

First, bathe your flower subject in marvelous extremes of sunlight. Then, once you have lights and darks worked out on paper, link similar value shapes together, dropping in new colors with a wet-into-wet technique. This forms interesting colors and patterns through the painting and strengthens the painting's design.

GALLERY

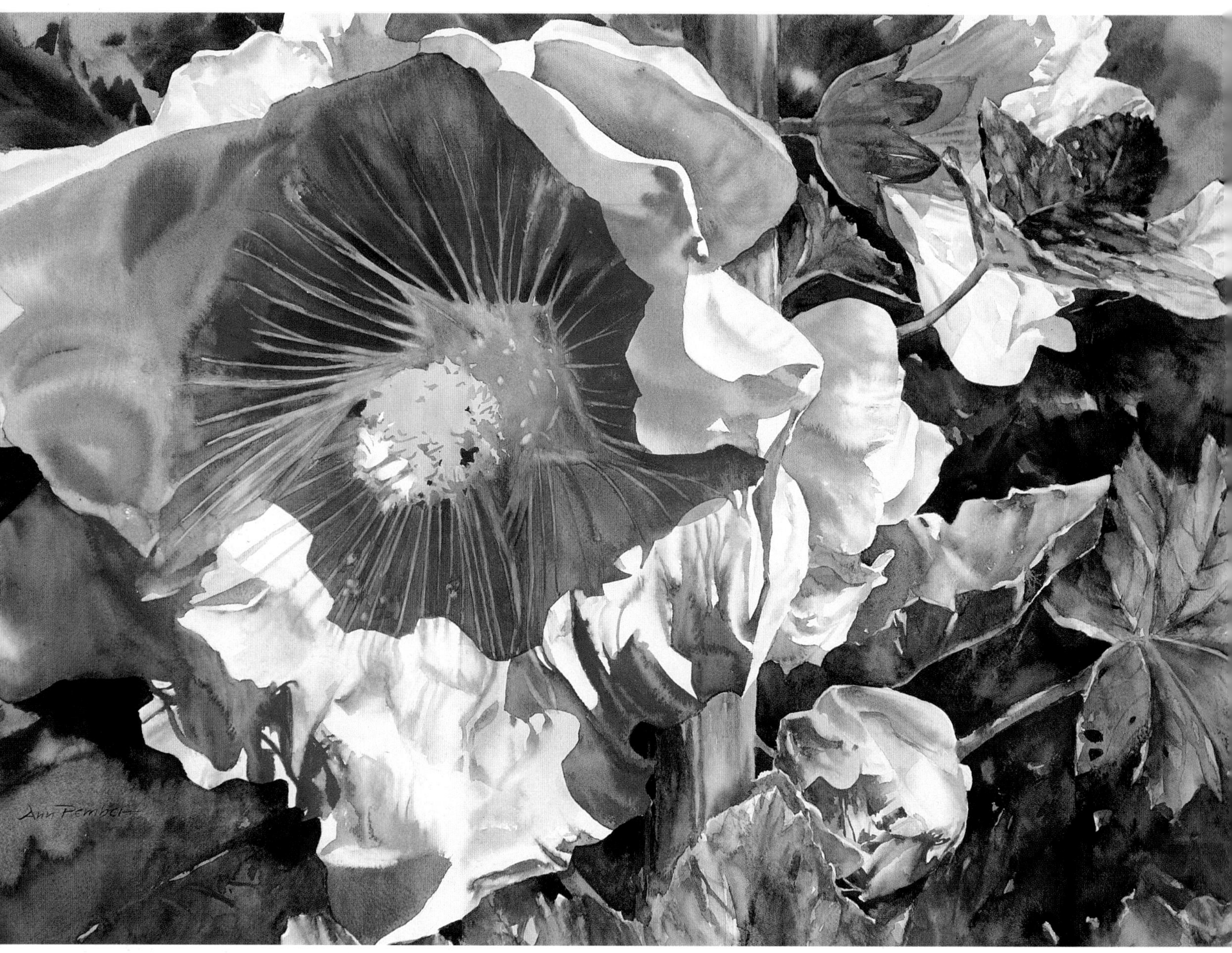

The hollyhock is a flower I look forward to painting each year because of its ruffled edges and unique shapes and colors. For this painting I worked from several photos, composing a simple design accenting one flower. The buds and leaves in the background are supportive material and should not compete with the main subject. The image is flooded with light, creating a large dark shadow over the flower's center. This large center shadow was treated as a big juicy wash, with darks added as the area dried. It was given a small amount of careful glazing when dry.

SUN-KISSED HOLLYHOCK
Ann Pember, watercolor, 21"×29" (53.3cm×73.7cm)

opposite
Every year when my gloxinia plant blooms it becomes a painting subject. Here, it was lit with bright sunlight streaming over the whole plant. After making a careful drawing, I painted the flower shapes first, keeping them bright and colorful. Then I painted the foliage and the pot, simplifying the shadows. For the deep reds I used Permanent Alizarin Crimson, Permanent Rose and Cadmium Red Purple. The darks in the foliage were painted using Winsor Green and these reds.

RED GLOXINIA
Ann Pember, watercolor, 14"×21" (35.6cm×53.3cm)

This was one of a series of peony paintings. The mood is high key, with light flooding over the flower and shining through some of the petals. I wanted to emphasize the fragile nature of the petals and their luminosity. The background was downplayed, with dark values and very little detail, allowing the flower to be the star. Within the flower, I pushed the color and "found" subtle color variations throughout.

PEONY UNFOLDING
Ann Pember, watercolor, 21" × 29" (53.3cm × 73.7cm)

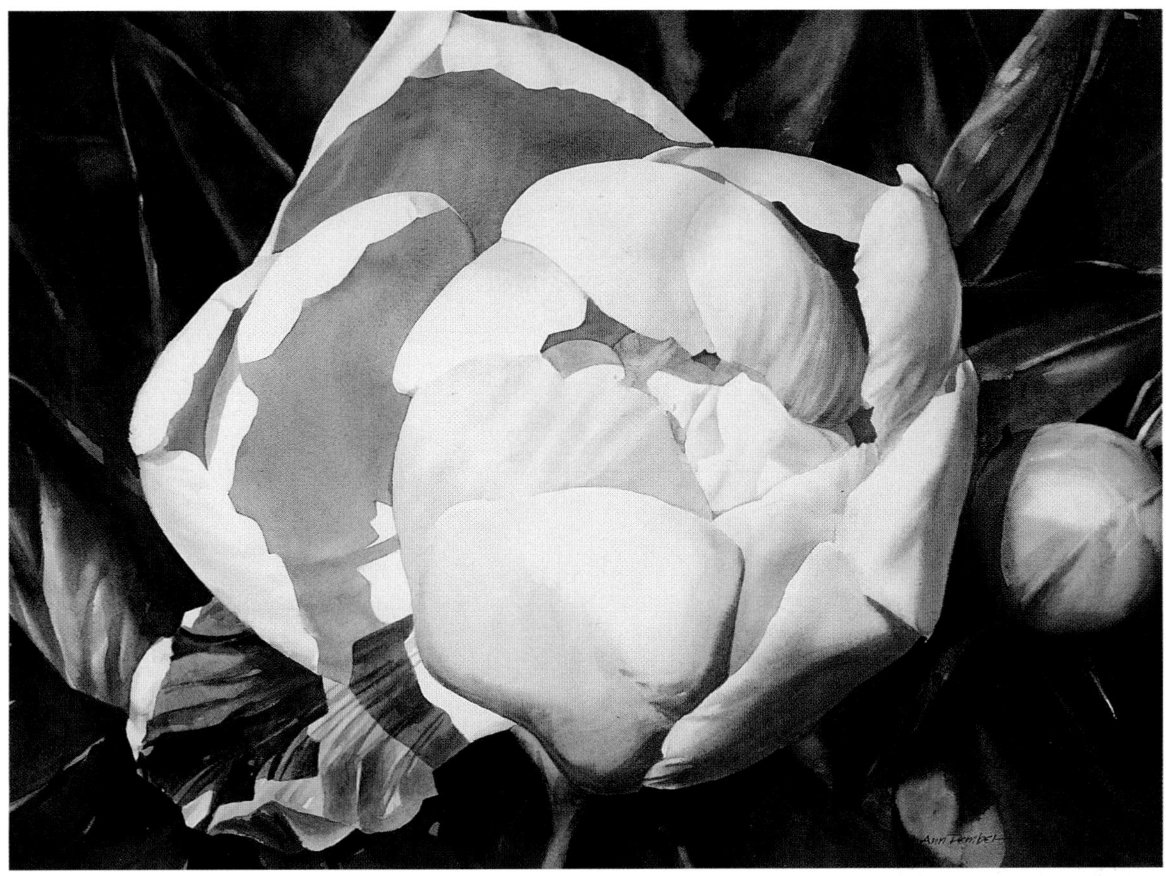

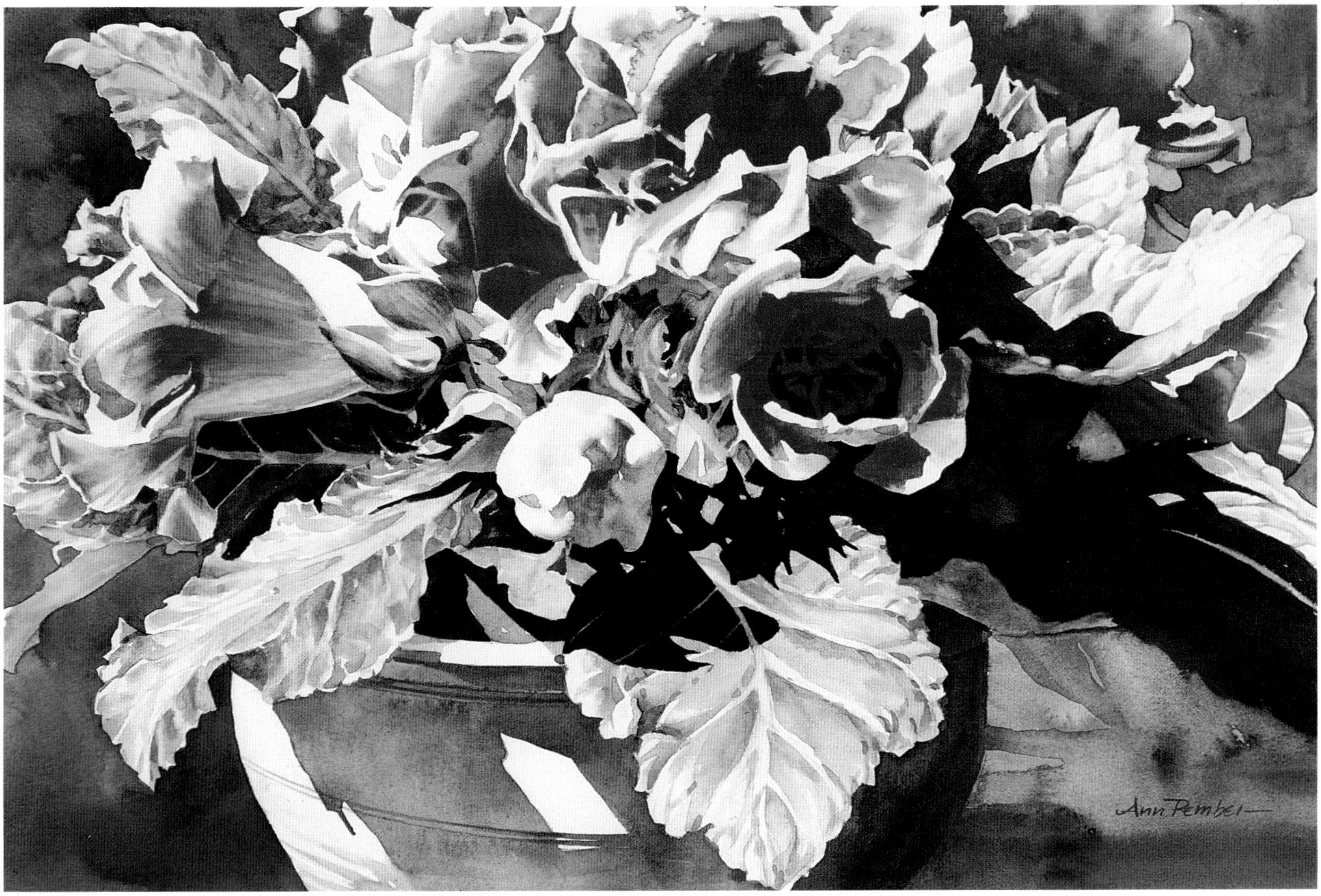

ABOUT THE ARTISTS

HOWARD CARR

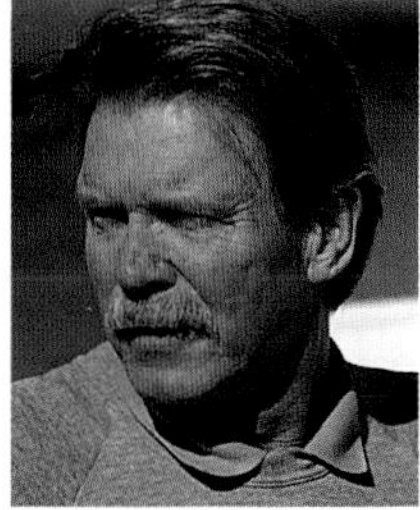

Carr was educated as an artist in California, and for almost twenty years was a successful graphic designer, illustrator and sign painter. In the late 1980s he moved into full-time painting, along with his artist-wife Betty, a watercolorist. They each teach several painting workshops a year in various locations around the country. Carr enjoys painting a variety of subjects in oil, but is particularly enamored of the open landscapes of the West and Southwest, where the Carrs now make their home. Carr is represented by Breckenridge Gallery, Breckenridge, Colorado; May Gallery, Scottsdale, Arizona; Mountain Trails Gallery, Sedona, Arizona; and Michael Atkinson, Santa Fe, New Mexico.

GIL DELLINGER

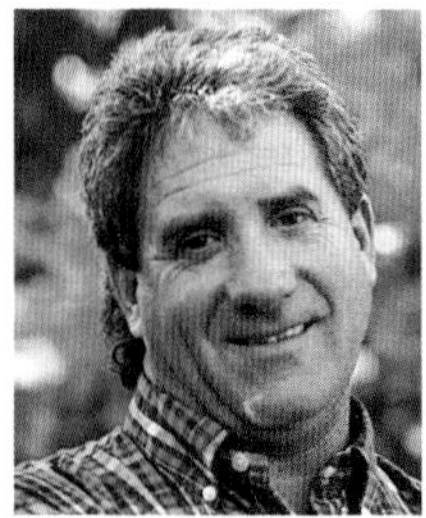

An elected Signature Member and "Master Pastelist" of the Pastel Society of America, Dellinger has achieved many honors for his work, including Landscape Awards from *Art of California* magazine and Pastel Society of America Exhibitions, as well as a Salmagundi Award. He has received recognition and awards for his teaching excellence and professional contribution to the University of the Pacific. Dellinger's work appears in many exhibitions and galleries and is represented in collections at the Nestle Corporation and *Forbes* magazine among others. His art has been featured in articles by *The Artist's Magazine*, *Art of California*, *American Artist* and *Southwest Art*, and has appeared in books including *The Watson-Guptill Handbook of Landscape Painting* by M. Stephen Doherty and *Painting With Passion* by Carole Katchen (North Light Books).

RANDAL M. DUTRA

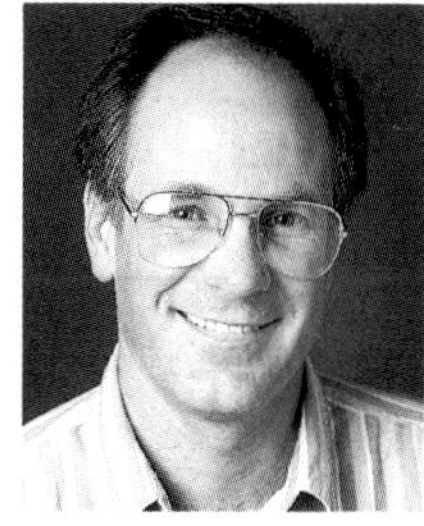

A native Californian painter and sculptor, Dutra studied drawing at the Art Students League, New York; studied painting with Robert Lougheed, NAWA; studied sculpture with George Carlson, NAWA; and studied with a number of other fine artists. From 1981 to 1993, Dutra was special visual effects artist for George Lucas, Steven Spielberg and Disney for cinema (*Star Wars*, *Gremlins*, *Robocop*, *Willow*, *The Nightmare Before Christmas*, *Jurassic Park* and *101 Dalmatians*). In 1997 he was an Academy Award nominee for Best Visual Effects for his work as director of animation on *The Lost World: Jurassic Park* (1996–1997). Dutra paints and sculpts in the school of impressionism/realism. His subject matter includes the figure, animals, landscape and seascape. He is a member of the Society of Animal Artists (SAA) based in New York. He has been published in *The Best of Wildlife Art* (North Light Books, 1997), *Making of the Lost World: Jurassic Park* (Ballantine Books, 1997), *Industrial Light and Magic: Into the Digital Realm* (Ballantine Books, 1996), *Wildlife Art* (Nov./Dec., 1996), *Wildlife Art—1996 Art Collector's Yearbook*, *Cinefex* (no. 59, September 1994), *Wildlife Art News* (Jan./Feb., 1994) and *The Making of Jurassic Park* (Ballantine Books, 1993). Dutra has had numerous exhibitions, including "American Art in Miniature" at the Gilcrease Museum, Tulsa, Oklahoma, and "Birds in Art" and "Wildlife—The Artist's View" at Leigh Yawkey Woodson Art Museum, Wausau, Wisconsin. He is represented by Settlers West Gallery, Tucson, Arizona, and Stephanie Roberts, Greeves, Wyoming, and Scottsdale, Arizona.

BRAD FAEGRE

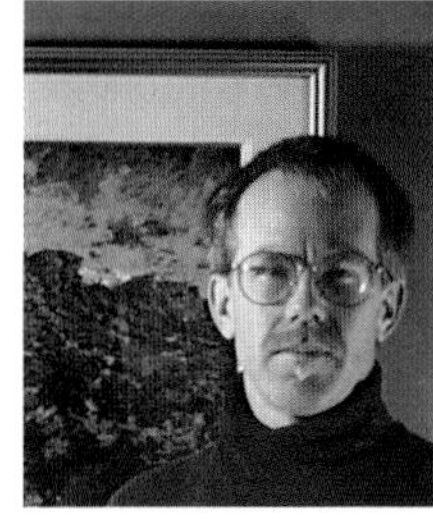

Brad began his art career as an illustrator, graphic designer, cartoonist and portrait painter. He has an extensive list of awards from regional and national exhibitions. Designated "Master Pastelist" by the Pastel Society of America, his painting in soft pastel has been featured in *American Artist* magazine, and his work in acrylics is featured in *The North Light Book of Acrylic Painting Techniques*. Faegre's railroad subjects have been featured in *Railfan & Railroad* magazine and sponsored in exhibition by the Caltrans Division of Rail/Amtrak; his landscapes have earned him exhibitions in Yosemite National Park (as Artist-in-Residence) and Grand Canyon National Park. His painting *Storm Over the South Rim* was one of twenty works chosen for an exhibition at the Grand Canyon National Park's 75th Anniversary Celebration. His painting *On the Tee with Jack Nicklaus at Bel-Air C.C.* appears in the book *Bel-Air Country Club: A Living Legend*. Brad is represented by Stary Sheets Fine Art Gallery, Laguna Beach, California, and Poulsen Gallery, Pasadena, California. He teaches private workshops in drawing and painting and is in much demand as a lecturer and demonstrator.

KAREN FREY

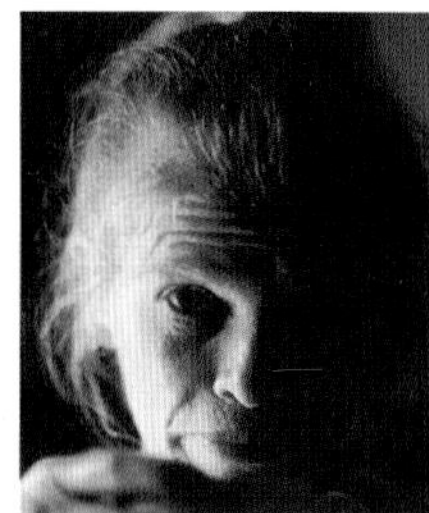

Karen Frey received her B.A. degree from the California College of Arts and Crafts in Oakland, California. She is a signature member of the National Watercolor Society, a member of the Watercolor USA Honor Society, and a teacher of private classes from her studio in Oakland and in workshops nationally. Her paintings have been exhibited in national competitions and have appeared in numerous publications such as *Splash 3*, *Splash 4* and *Splash 5* (North Light Books), the *Best of Watercolor* series (Rockport Publishers), *Understanding Transparent Watercolor* by Gerald Brommer, *The Artistic Touch 2* by Chris Unwin, and the magazines *Watercolor Magic* and *American Artist*. She has also supervised and participated in the painting of several murals in Northern California.

SHARON MACZKO

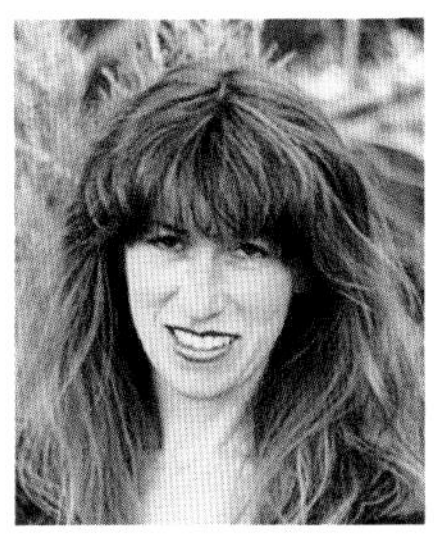

Sharon Maczko, a self-taught artist, currently resides in Nevada. She has exhibited her work widely in numerous solo and group exhibitions, and counts the San Diego Museum of Art among her many collectors. A frequent contributor to the *Splash* series (North Light Books) and other books on watercolor, she has won several awards, including an Artist Grant from the Sierra Art Foundation, and she was a finalist in the 1997 Artist's Fellowship from the Nevada State Council on the Arts.

DONALD W. PATTERSON, AWS, KA, NWS, PWCC, PWS

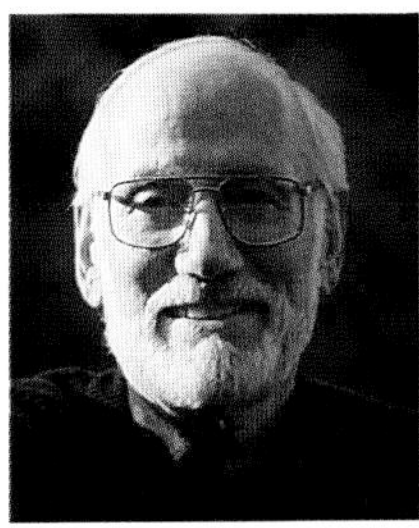

Don Patterson is an internationally recognized watercolorist. He has exhibited in museums and galleries from coast to coast, as well as in Japan and Canada. He is the recipient of numerous awards from national competitions and juried exhibitions. He has been elected to membership in the American Watercolor Society, the National Watercolor Society, Allied Artists of America, Audubon Artists, Inc., Knickerbocker Artists, USA and the Pennsylvania Watercolor Society, and has been a Board Member of the Philadelphia Water Color Club since 1982. Patterson has been featured in several magazine articles and PBS Television's *Outdoor Pennsylvania*. His work appears in *Splash 2*, *Splash 4* and *Splash 5* (North Light Books). He is represented by the following galleries: Bianco Gallery, Buckingham, Pennsylvania; Virginia Lippincott Gallery, Phoenixville, Pennsylvania; Snow Goose Gallery, Bethlehem, Pennsylvania; and Wild Goose Gallery, Intercourse, Pennsylvania.

ANN PEMBER

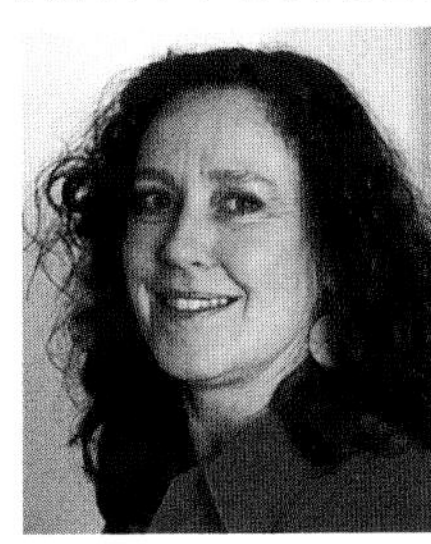

Ann Pember received a B.F.A. degree from the Massachusetts College of Art in Boston in 1968. She has studied watercolor with many respected instructors and spent twelve years working as a freelance commercial artist. In 1976 she relocated to the Adirondack region of New York. The artist and her husband reside on the shore of Lake Champlain; they built Pember's dream studio there in 1993. She has been painting full time in watercolor since 1980. Pember's light-filled paintings have been selected for inclusion in more than eighty-five national juried exhibitions and have won numerous awards. Her work has been featured in over a dozen books and publications, is widely exhibited and is held in many public, corporate and private collections. The artist is a signature member of Knickerbocker Artists, USA, American Artists Professional League (fellow), Catharine Lorillard Wolfe Art Club, National Association of Women Artists, Audubon Artists, Watercolor West and many other regional societies. She has been teaching painting workshops since 1988.

TERI STARKWEATHER

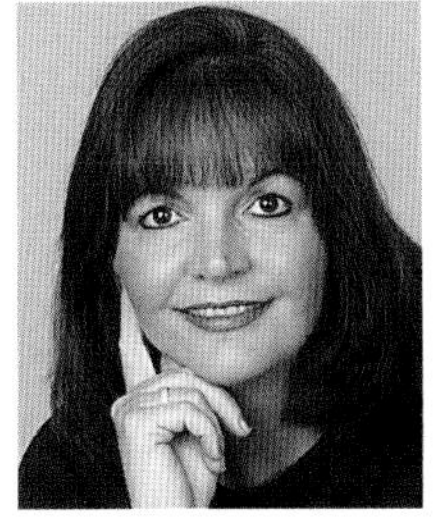

Teri Starkweather has been painting watercolors for the past eleven years. She received her art education at Art Center College of Design in Pasadena, California, and Atlanta College of Art, Georgia. Her work has been in many publications, such as *Splash 4* and *Splash 5* (North Light Books), *Best of Watercolor* (Rockport Publishers), and *American Artist* magazine. Her paintings have been published as posters by Prestige Graphics, printed on notecards and printed on designer mugs for Chaleur. She is also in *Who's Who of American Women*. She has won many awards for her watercolors in national watercolor competitions and has exhibited in many national-level watercolor shows. She is a signature member of Watercolor West, California. She is represented by Orlando Gallery, Sherman Oaks, California. She resides in West Hills, California.

INDEX